CW01614872

NEW INTER
BIBLICAL CO

Old Testament Editors,
Robert L. Hubbard Jr.
Robert K. Johnston

JEREMIAH, LAMENTATIONS

Rab Craig
rab.craig@tiscali.co.uk
07968 283095

Old Testament Series

NEW INTERNATIONAL BIBLICAL COMMENTARY

JEREMIAH, LAMENTATIONS

TREMPER LONGMAN III

Based on the New International Version

HENDRICKSON PUBLISHERS

Paternoster: thinking faith

Jeremiah, Lamentations
New International Biblical Commentary
© 2008 by Hendrickson Publishers, Inc.
P. O. Box 3473
Peabody, Massachusetts 01961-3473

First published jointly, 2008, in the United States by Hendrickson Publishers and in the United Kingdom by the Paternoster Press.

Paternoster is an imprint of Authentic Media,
9 Holdom Avenue, Bletchley, Milton Keynes, MK1 1QR, UK
1820 Jet Stream Drive, Colorado Springs, CO 80921, USA
OM Authentic Media, Medchal Road, Jeedimetla Village,
Secunderabad 500 055, A.P., India
www.authenticmedia.co.uk
Authentic Media is a division of IBS-STL UK, a company limited by guarantee (registered charity no. 270162).

All rights reserved.

Printed in the United States of America

First printing — April 2008

Library of Congress Cataloging-in-Publication Data

Longman, Tremper.
Jeremiah, Lamentations / Tremper Longman III.
p. cm. — (New international biblical commentary.
Old Testament series)
Includes bibliographical references (p.) and indexes.
ISBN-13: 978-1-56563-224-0 (alk. paper)
1. Bible. O.T. Jeremiah—Commentaries. 2. Bible. O.T.
Lamentations—Commentaries. I. Title.
BS1525.53.L66 2008
224′.207—dc22
2007037715

ISBN 978-1-56563-224-0 (U.S. softcover)

British Library Cataloguing in Publication Data
A catalogue record for this book is available from the British Library.

ISBN 978-1-85364-735-2 (U.K. softcover)

Scripture taken from the HOLY BIBLE, NEW INTERNATIONAL VERSION. Copyright © 1973, 1978, 1984 by International Bible Society. Used by permission of Zondervan Bible Publishers. All rights reserved.

to Alan Groves (1952–2007)

Table of Contents

Lamentations

Foreword
New International Biblical Commentary

As an ancient document, the Old Testament often seems something quite foreign to modern men and women. Opening its pages may feel, to the modern reader, like traversing a kind of literary time warp into a whole other world. In that world sisters and brothers marry, long hair mysteriously makes men superhuman, and temple altars daily smell of savory burning flesh and sweet incense. There, desert bushes burn but leave no ashes, water gushes from rocks, and cities fall because people march around them. A different world, indeed!

Even God, the Old Testament's main character, seems a stranger compared to his more familiar New Testament counterpart. Sometimes the divine is portrayed as a loving father and faithful friend, someone who rescues people from their greatest dangers or generously rewards them for heroic deeds. At other times, however, God resembles more a cruel despot, one furious at human failures, raving against enemies, and bloodthirsty for revenge. Thus, skittish about the Old Testament's diverse portrayal of God, some readers carefully select which portions of the text to study, or they avoid the Old Testament altogether.

The purpose of this commentary series is to help readers navigate this strange and sometimes forbidding literary and spiritual terrain. Its goal is to break down the barriers between the ancient and modern worlds so that the power and meaning of these biblical texts become transparent to contemporary readers. How is this to be done? And what sets this series apart from others currently on the market?

This commentary series will bypass several popular approaches to biblical interpretation. It will not follow a *precritical* approach that interprets the text without reference to recent scholarly conversations. Such a commentary contents itself with offering little more than a paraphrase of the text with occasional supplements from archaeology, word studies, and classical theology. It mistakenly believes that there have been few insights into the Bible since Calvin or Luther. Nor will this series pursue an *anticritical* approach whose preoccupation is to defend the Bible against its detractors, especially scholarly ones. Such a commentary has little space left to move beyond showing why the Bible's critics are wrong to explaining what the biblical text means. The result is a paucity of vibrant biblical theology. Again, this series finds inadequate a *critical* approach that seeks to understand the text apart from belief in the meaning it conveys. Though modern readers have been taught to be discerning, they do not want to live in the "desert of criticism" either.

Instead, as its editors, we have sought to align this series with what has been labeled *believing criticism.* This approach marries probing, reflective interpretation of the text to loyal biblical devotion and warm Christian affection. Our contributors tackle the task of interpretation using the full range of critical methodologies and practices. Yet they do so as people of faith who hold the text in the highest regard. The commentators in this series use criticism to bring the message of the biblical texts vividly to life so the minds of modern readers may be illumined and their faith deepened.

The authors in this series combine a firm commitment to modern scholarship with a similar commitment to the Bible's full authority for Christians. They bring to the task the highest technical skills, warm theological commitment, and rich insight from their various communities. In so doing, they hope to enrich the life of the academy as well as the life of the church.

Part of the richness of this commentary series derives from its authors' breadth of experience and ecclesial background. As editors, we have consciously brought together a diverse group of scholars in terms of age, gender, denominational affiliation, and race. We make no claim that they represent the full expression of the people of God, but they do bring fresh, broad perspectives to the interpretive task. But though this series has sought out diversity among its contributors, they also reflect a commitment to a common center. These commentators write as "believing critics"—scholars who desire to speak for church and academy, for academy and church. As editors, we offer this series in devotion to God and for the enrichment of God's people.

Robert L. Hubbard Jr.
Robert K. Johnston
Editors

Preface

To be honest, I don't know what I was thinking when I accepted the kind invitation of the editors of the series to contribute a commentary on Jeremiah. I was already working on more projects than I should have accepted, and when I finally began the work in earnest, I was reminded of just how complex—and long!—a book it is. Not only that, but apparently Jeremiah wasn't long enough, the editors threw in Lamentations as well. What's another five chapters?

Those thoughts did cross my mind at the beginning and from time to time as I was writing this book. However, especially now that I am finished, I am deeply grateful to have spent the past number of years reflecting on these two books. Jeremiah is a vivid, profound, exciting book; Lamentations is moving in its grief, guilt, and anger. Both books are deeply emotional as well as intellectually stimulating. It is my hope that my commentary encourages the reader to interact with them with both mind and heart.

I want to thank the editors, Rob Johnston and Bob Hubbard, for the invitation to participate in this series. Bob also provided helpful feedback on the original manuscript and I want to offer him my thanks. This book is the third of my commentaries that he has edited and each time he has improved the original effort. I also benefitted greatly from the editorial comments of Allan Emery at Hendrickson Publishers. How wonderful to have an in-house editor who is an expert in the ancient Near East and biblical studies. While thanking them, I also want to take sole responsibility for any errors and the final decisions on exegetical matters.

Finally, I dedicate this book to the memory to my dear friend and former colleague of eighteen years at Westminster Theological Seminary, Alan Groves. Many in the field know Al not only for his important and pioneering work on the Hebrew Bible and the computer, but also for his wonderful caring personality. Al knew he was dying for a little over a year, and he was a model to many of dignity and deep faith during that time. I talked to Al for the last time just two days before his death, when the cancer was effecting his speech. I had to force him to talk about himself; he was more concerned with how I was doing. . . . That was Al not only at the end of his life, but through our whole long friendship. He is deeply missed by his lovely wife Libbie, his children, and his many friends.

Tremper Longman III
Robert H. Gundry Professor of Biblical Studies
Westmont College
Santa Barbara, California

Abbreviations

4QJer[a]	= 4Q70; E. Tov, "Jeremiah," in *Qumran Cave 4*. X: the Prophets. Edited by E. Ulrich, et. al.; DJD 15; Oxford: Clarendon Press, 1997, 145–207, plates XXIV–XXIX.
4QJer[b]	= 4Q71; E. Tov, "Jeremiah," in *Qumran Cave 4*. X: the Prophets. Edited by E. Ulrich, et. al.; DJD 15; Oxford: Clarendon Press, 1997, 145–207, plate XXX.
4QJer[c]	= 4Q72; E. Tov, "Jeremiah," in *Qumran Cave 4*. X: the Prophets. Edited by E. Ulrich, et. al.; DJD 15; Oxford: Clarendon Press, 1997, 145–207, plates XXXI–XXXVII.
AB	Anchor Bible
ANET	*Ancient Near Eastern Texts Relating to the Old Testament*. Edited by J. B. Pritchard. 3d ed. Princeton, 1969.
b.	Babylonian Talmud
B. Bat.	*Baba Batra*
B.C.	before Christ
BJRL	*Bulletin of the John Rylands University Library of Manchester*
BM	tablets in the collections of the British Museum
ca.	circa
ch(s).	chapter(s)
CBQ	*Catholic Biblical Quarterly*
COS	*Context of Scripture*. Edited by W. H. Hallo. 3 vols. Leiden, 1997–2003.
DBI	*Dictionary of Biblical Imagery*
ed(s).	editor(s), edited by
e.g.	*exempli gratia*, for example
FOTL	Forms of Old Testament Literature
Int.	Interpretation

IVPBBCOT	*The IVP Bible Background Commentary: Old Testament,* edited by J. Walton, V. H. Matthews, and M. V. Chavalas (Downers Grove, Ill.: InterVarsity, 2000).
JBL	*Journal of Biblical Literature*
JSOT	*Journal for the Study of the Old Testament*
MT	Masoretic Text
NCB	New Century Bible
NICOT	New International Commentary on the Old Testament
NIDOTTE	*New International Dictionary of the Old Testament Theology and Exegesis.* Edited by W. A. VanGemeren. 5 vols. Grand Rapids, 1997
NLT	New Living Translation
NT	New Testament
NRSV	New Revised Standard Version
OT	Old Testament
TNIV	Today's New International Version
v(v).	verse(s)
VT	*Vetus Testamentum*
WBC	Word Biblical Commentary
ZAW	*Zeitschrift für die alttestamentliche Wissenschaft*

Jeremiah

Introduction: Jeremiah

Title and Place in Canon

The book is known by the name of the prophet whose words and actions provide its content (see commentary on 1:1–3). In both the English (based on the Greek Septuagint) and the Hebrew order of books, it occurs with the other prophetic books, after Isaiah and before Ezekiel and the Twelve. The order of the three major prophets is according to their putative historical settings. Isaiah son of Amoz was a figure of the eighth century B.C., whereas Jeremiah and Ezekiel reside closer to the events of 586 B.C. Jeremiah's life and work begins before that of Ezekiel, though the latter is contemporary with the last part of Jeremiah's prophetic work. The Twelve are grouped together because of their length and have a rough chronological order between them.

In terms of length, Jeremiah is notable for being the second longest biblical book, preceded only by the massive book of Psalms. According to Lundbom, Jeremiah has 21,835 words, followed in length by Ezekiel with 18,730 words and then Isaiah with 16,932 words.[1]

The appeal of the book of Jeremiah not only has to do with the content of his prophecies or the intriguing nature of his life, but also with his personality as it shines through the book.[2] Jeremiah broods, worries, mourns, lashes out. It is no wonder that he is often considered the "weeping prophet" (2 Chr. 35:25).

Author and Date: History of Composition

The superscription to the book ascribes its contents to "Jeremiah son of Hilkiah, one of the priests at Anathoth in the territory of Benjamin" (Jer. 1:1). It further dates his prophetic activity[3] to the period between "the thirteenth year of the reign of Josiah son of Amon king of Judah, and through the reign of Jehoiakim son of Josiah king of Judah, down to the fifth month of the eleventh year of Zedekiah son of Josiah king of Judah, when the people of Jerusalem went into exile" (1:2–3). These dates translate to 626–586 B.C. in a modern calendar. Later prose chapters narrate even later events in Jeremiah's life, extending into the exilic period (post-586 B.C.), for which see chapters 40–44.

The testimony of the superscription, however, should not blind the reader to evidence that the book of Jeremiah represents the conclusion of a long oral and written tradition. The connection with Jeremiah it asserts also does not require the reader to believe that every word of the book must come from the mouth or pen of the prophet, though it likely intends to closely associate him with the prophetic oracles of the book. For instance, it is possible, perhaps even likely, though not provable, that stories about Jeremiah emanate from his close circle of disciples and followers.

No doubt attends the understanding that the book is the result of a long process, even though explicit evidence locates the redaction of the book within the lifetime of the prophet (though it does not exclude the idea that the process extended for some time after his death). Jeremiah 36 is intriguing in this regard. The time is the "fourth year of Jehoiakim" (= 605 B.C.), some years after the beginning of Jeremiah's ministry (= 626 B.C.).

At the beginning of the chapter, God tells Jeremiah to get a scroll and write down "all the words I have spoken to you concerning Israel, Judah and all the other nations from the time I began speaking to you in the reign of Josiah till now" (36:2). The verse reveals that these prophetic oracles were not written down for years, even decades, after they were spoken on the streets by the prophet.

Jeremiah did not write these words down himself. He was assisted by Baruch, son of Neriah, who functioned as his scribe, though we must not imagine him to be a mere lackey of the prophet (see commentary at 43:1–3). Once the text was completed it was taken to the temple area and read to the people, but eventually came to the attention of the king. The king reacted strongly against the message of the scroll and burned it. Even so, the concluding verse of the chapter (v. 32) informs us that Jeremiah simply had Baruch rewrite the scroll. Notable for our present subject, however, is the fact that on this new scroll Baruch added "many similar words." Thus, we get a glimpse at the growth of a biblical book. We know that these are only the beginning stages of a long process, because many oracles and stories about Jeremiah are dated well after 605 B.C.

Even without chapter 36 it is fairly obvious that the book is the result of a long and complex history of composition. Yates well summarizes the evidence when he points to the relatively confusing structure, the lack of chronological development in the book,[4] the significant differences between the Masoretic Text and the Septuagint (see below), different genres of literature, as well as the question of the relationship with a Deuteronomic theology.[5]

The modern discussion of this issue starts with the work of Duhm,[6] who differentiated different strands within the book of Jeremiah. Mowinckel[7] adopted this basic approach and described three sources (though in his later writings he thought of them as layers of tradition rather than sources per se) that constituted the book of Jeremiah.

> Source A: Described as dirgelike poetic oracles, found primarily in the first twenty-five chapters of the book, and attributed to Jeremiah. Duhm believed there were about 280 verses in this material.
>
> Source B: Composed of prose stories about Jeremiah. He located about 220 verses that he believed belonged to this source. He believed that this source was a biography of Jeremiah written by Baruch, though later scholars question the label "biography."
>
> Source C: Found throughout the book, these are prose speeches/sermons and narratives that he believed betray a Deuteronomic perspective. This source consists of about 850 verses.

Since Duhm and Mowinckel, scholars have debated the exact shape of the sources and their association with Jeremiah. Mowinckel disagreed with Duhm about the role that Baruch supposedly played in the production of Source B, instead treating the material as produced by an anonymous figure before 480 B.C. in Egypt.[8] Other significant disagreements include the relationship between the prose speeches (Source C) and Deuteronomic theology. McConville casts suspicion on the Deuteronomic character of the material, while Eissfeldt affirms the connection but believes it can be explained by Jeremiah being influenced by Deuteronomic theology.[9]

The view of the present commentary is that, while the history of composition of the book is complex, it is virtually impossible to gain any certainty about the specifics of its growth. Attempts like that of Holladay[10] to recover the pre-605 scroll from later developments are precarious and distracting from the message of the final form of the book.[11]

The Historical Jeremiah

One practical consequence of the issue of the history of composition is to raise questions about the relationship between the book of Jeremiah and the historical prophet. Does the book give us window to the real Jeremiah and to his words?

Carroll and McKane[12] have argued negatively, but their radical views have been tempered in recent commentaries. No one believes that the words of the poetic oracles are the *ipsissima verba,* as if they were captured by an audio recorder, for all narrative involves some matter of shaping. The stories are not objective reports as if captured on camera. Fretheim well expresses the view accepted by this commentary: "As is true to a greater or lesser degree with the presentation of any historical figure, the portrayal of Jeremiah reflects both the speech and action of an actual individual and a literary construction by editors or authors informed by varying perspectives. The book presents us with both a powerful personality and an interpretation of his role and significance. Because the editors are inevitably selective and have been shaped by their perspective in the past and the present issues they seek to address, Jeremiah emerges as both more than and less than the actual historical prophet."[13]

Historical Context

Jeremiah's prophecies are best read against the backdrop of the historical context of his life and ministry.[14] Neither the prophet nor the editor consistently dated each oracle, nor are they arranged in a chronological order. Nonetheless, Jeremiah's words are deeply enmeshed in the turbulent events of his day. The superscription (see also 25:3) dates his prophetic work from the thirteenth year of the reign of Josiah (626 B.C.) to the eleventh year of Zedekiah (586 B.C.). The historical narrative in Jeremiah 39–44 takes the reader beyond the time of Jeremiah's prophetic activity and follows his story into the early exilic period. This section provides a brief overview of the period.

626 B.C. was a year of great significance. In the first place, it was the beginning of Jeremiah's prophetic ministry.[15] At this time, Josiah was king of Judah. According to 2 Chronicles 34:3a, this king, whose father and grandfather were notorious for their idolatrous practices, began to seek the Lord. Then the year before Jeremiah's ministry started, 2 Chronicles 34:3b–7 says that Josiah began to purify Judah and Jerusalem, destroying pagan shrines. Thus, Jeremiah's ministry began in a context where the king was working to promote the interests of proper worship. Significant events were also unfolding outside of Judah. Nabopolassar, a Chal-

dean tribal chief, began a Babylonian uprising against Assyria. This revolt would have great importance for the history of Judah, at that time a vassal of Assyria. Judah under Josiah would be happy to be rid of Assyria, but as events develop we will see that Judah's freedom from oppression involves more than being rid of Assyria.

Babylon's rebellion did not reach quick resolution. It was not until 612 B.C. that a coaliton of Medes and Babylonians defeated the Assyrian capital of Nineveh. This defeat, anticipated by the prophet Nahum, meant the certain demise of Assyria, but a remnant under a self-proclaimed leader who took on the name Asshur-uballit ("Assyria lives!") reassembled in the vicinity of Carchemish.

In 609 B.C., Neco, pharaoh of Egypt, got involved when he led an army up the Levant to try to bolster Assyrian forces against Babylon. At this time, Josiah showed his interests when he mustered a Judean army to ambush Neco at the pass near Megiddo. He obviously wanted Assyria to disappear and tried to stop this Egyptian attempt to help them. However, Josiah was defeated and killed at Megiddo. The Egyptians continued on the march but were defeated in the battle of Carchemish. The Judeans placed Josiah's son, Jehoahaz on the throne.

The defeated Egyptian army, still under Neco, retreated through Judah and on the way meddled with the succession. They removed Jehoahaz from the throne and replaced him with another son of Josiah, Jehoiakim, whom they identified as more in keeping with their aspirations in the region.

Unfortunately for the Egyptians and for Jehoiakim, Babylon's armies, now led by Nabopolassar's gifted son Nebuchadnezzar, were able to subdue Syria, and from its staging area in Riblah, exerted their power into Judah. This is demonstrated in 605 B.C. in a siege where Jehoiakim is required to turn over to Babylon some of the temple utensils as well as a few of the young noblemen of Judah (see Dan. 1:1–3). This same year, Nabopolassar died and Nebuchadnezzar assumed the throne of Babylon.

Nebuchadnezzar seemed content to have Judah as a vassal rather than move to incorporate it into his empire as a province. His real interests were in subduing Egypt and he needed Judah as a staging area. He also benefited from the annual tribute that Judah as a tribute state would pay. However, Jehoiakim disturbed the relationship by rebelling against Nebuchadnezzar in 597 B.C. Such a rebellion entailed refusal to pay annual tribute and perhaps also the ejection of Babylonian agents from Judah.

In the time it took to mobilize and march the Babylonian army to Jerusalem, Jehoiakim was removed from the throne and replaced by his son Jehoiachin.[16] After a relatively short siege, Nebuchadnezzar prevailed and removed Jehoiachin from the throne, deporting him (and other leading Judean citizens including a priest named Ezekiel) to Babylon. The Babylonian king then chose yet another son of Josiah, Mattaniah, though his name was changed to Zedekiah, to sit on the throne in Jerusalem.

Nebuchadnezzar may have had some reason to think that Zedekiah would be an amenable vassal, but ultimately even this choice proved wrong when in 586 B.C. the Judean king revolted. This time Nebuchadnezzar was in no mood for half measures. He came and decimated Jerusalem. He exiled leading citizens and he killed Zedekiah's sons before blinding him and taking him in chains to Babylon never to be heard from again.

It was during this time period (626–586) that Jeremiah carried on his prophetic ministry, though chapters 39–44 narrate events in the early exilic (post-586) period. Nebuchadnezzar made Judah a province of his empire, complete with native Judean governor, Gedaliah, and a Babylonian garrison. However, there were still insurgents on the loose. One named Ishmael, with Ammonite support, assassinated Gedaliah and attacked the Babylonian garrison. The remnant of Judah chose then to go to Egypt rather than face the wrath of Nebuchadnezzar one more time. They went despite Jeremiah's warnings, dragging him along with them.

Jeremiah's death is not mentioned in the book. The last datable event is the release of Jehoiachin from a Babylonian prison. This event can be dated to 562 B.C.

The Text of Jeremiah

Though certainly related to the issue of the history of composition of the book of Jeremiah, we will briefly treat its well-known text critical issue separately. Since this commentary series treats the text of the NIV, which uses the Masoretic Text (MT) as its basis, it is that tradition's text that will be the subject of the commentary to follow.

That there is a textual issue is immediately recognizable since the Septuagint represents a text that is significantly shorter, indeed about one-eighth shorter since it lacks about 2,700 words represented in the MT. Further, the order is not the same between the two. For instance, the oracles against the foreign nations in chapters 46–51 in the MT are found right after 25:13, and the nations are treated in a different order. With the discovery of the Dead Sea Scrolls, it was determined that the Septuagint text reflects a different Hebrew tradition. Two (4QJer[a] [4Q70], 4QJer[c] [4Q72]) of the three fragmentary texts discovered at Qumran supported the MT tradition, but the third (4QJer[b] [4Q71]) agreed with the Greek tradition in both brevity and arrangement. These texts have recently been published by Tov (1997).

While the shorter text could conceivably represent an abridgment of the longer text,[17] it is more likely that the longer version represents the later stage. As remarked above, the end of Jeremiah indicates that there were multiple editions of the book during the lifetime of the prophet and we have speculated that there may well have been post-Jeremiah editions as well. Tov argues that changes that exist between the longer and the shorter text are the kinds of changes one might expect in the process of expansion (editorial and exegetical) rather than abridgement (for details see Longman and Dillard, *Introduction to the Old Testament,* pp. 328–32). Modern translations (NIV, NRSV, NLT, TNIV) all follow the longer Masoretic Text. While some might think that the earlier, shorter text should be considered authentic and in some cases canonical, on the basis of what we know about the development of the book, it is better to think that the longer, later text supersedes the earlier in importance. The other major ancient versions (Aquila, Symmachus, Theodotion, Lucian, Syriac, and Vulgate) follow the MT.

The Covenant in Jeremiah

In a book as varied and complex as Jeremiah, no single theological theme can capture its theological scope and depth, but covenant comes very close to doing so. In one sense, that is not surprising since covenant is one of the most productive theological themes in the Bible. But even in comparison to other biblical books and the other prophets, Jeremiah is the one of the most explicitly covenantal in its theology. In this, we find ourselves in agreement with Holladay, who says, "central to Jeremiah's proclamation is the covenant established by Yahweh with Israel," and "the covenantal relation is the constant basis of Yahweh's words to Israel."[18]

"Covenant" (*berit*) is a legal term that describes a relationship between two parties. The word is used to describe agreements between two parties on a human level where there are promises given and obligations imposed (Gen. 31:44).

The word "covenant" is used to describe the relationship between God and his followers beginning with Noah (Gen. 9:9, etc.). It also describes the relationship between Abraham and God (Gen. 15:18; 17:2, etc., but reflecting back on the divine promises and human obligation described in Genesis 12:1–3), Moses and God (Exod. 19:5; 24:7–8, etc.), and David and God (Pss. 89:3, 28, 34, 39; 132:11, reflecting back to 2 Samuel 7).

The scholarship of the past half century has recognized that the covenant idea and even its literary form has a relationship with ancient Near Eastern treaties. Deuteronomy is a case in point. The book may be understood as the libretto of a covenant renewal ceremony and has the rough structure of a Near Eastern treaty,[19] specifically a vassal treaty, as follows:

Introduction: 1:1–5

Historical Review: 1:9–3:27

Law: 4:1–26:19

Rewards and Consequences: 27:1–28:68

Witnesses: 30:19–20

Review and Succession: 31:9–13

After an introduction that names the parties involved in the relationship (in this case God and Israel with Moses serving as mediator between the two), the treaty/covenant rehearses the relationship between the two parties up to the present. The burden of this report, whether in a secular or biblical treaty, is to demonstrate the good services of the sovereign king (God in Deuteronomy) to his vassal people, thus providing a foundation for the next section. Since the sovereign has been so good to the vassal, the latter should follow the instructions (law) that the sovereign commands. In Deuteronomy, this section is the longest and is sanctioned by the next section, the blessings resulting from obedience to the law and the curses that follow upon disobedience. As a legal document, there must be witnesses that monitor the relationship and to whom appeal can be made if there is a breach of the covenant. Finally, many, but not all covenant/treaties stipulate a review and recommitment. In the case of Deuteronomy, this renewal is to happen every seven years.

The prophets in general, and Jeremiah in particular, may be helpfully thought to be the lawyers of the covenant, particularly the Mosaic covenant as established in Exodus 19–24 and exposited and renewed for the first time in Deuteronomy (see also, but not as extensively Josh. 24; 2 Sam. 12; Neh. 8–10). In particular, Jeremiah is a prosecuting attorney for the Lord. The covenant law has been extensively broken for a prolonged time. Jeremiah's ministry is to charge God's people with wrongdoing and call them to repent, otherwise God will effect the covenant curses—curses like those found in Deuteronomy 28:25–26, 64–68, which speak of defeat at the hands of an enemy and a scattering among the nations: Since they have broken the covenant and thus deserve to experience the curses of the covenant, Jeremiah "brings charges" (from the verb *rib*) against them on behalf of God:

> "Therefore I bring charges again you again," declares the LORD, "And I will bring charges against your children's children." (Jer. 2:9; see also 11:1–8; 12:1–6; 30:12–17 and discussion in the commentary below.)

How have the people of God broken the covenant according to Jeremiah? The most egregious charge that the prophet brings against his people is that they have committed idolatry in direct violation of the first two commandments. Such is the charge in the oracle found in Jeremiah 11, which begins with a general statement outlining the theological dynamic we have been discussing:

> "Listen to the terms of this covenant and tell them to the people of Judah and to those who live in Jerusalem. Tell them that this is what the LORD, the God of Israel says: 'Cursed is the man who does not obey the terms of this covenant—the terms I commanded your forefathers when I brought them out of Egypt. . .'" (11:2–4a)

He goes on to charge them with idolatrous worship of Baal:

> "You have as many gods as you have towns, O Judah; and the altars you have set up to burn incense to that shameful god Baal are as many as the streets of Jerusalem." (11:13)

But the people of God break the covenant in other ways as well. The covenant called on them to depend on God alone for their protection, but against God's wishes, they sought military and political shelter against Babylon from other superpowers of the day, leading the prophet to ask: "Now why go to Egypt to drink water from the Shihor? And why go to Assyria to drink water from the River?" (2:18).

Besides a fundamental betrayal of the divine-human relationship by their worship of other gods and their trust in other nations, the Judeans also offend God by desecrating the Sabbath (the fourth commandment). Contrary to God's will, they carry on their commercial work on this holy day of rest and worship (17:19–27).

If these offenses are not bad enough, Jeremiah also cites violations of God's instructions regulating the relationship among human beings. They lie and cheat (9:1–6); they do not release their slaves in accordance with the law (34:8–22). They even sacrifice their children to false gods (32:35). These are just a few of the horrible ways in which they break the covenant.

But it is not just Jeremiah's message of judgment that echoes with the language of covenant. When he looks beyond the judgment that is surely coming because they do not repent, he sees a period of restoration that is also described in covenantal language. The people have broken the old covenant. The old covenant refers to the relationship that God established with his people particularly from Abraham through David, but the explicit reflections about covenant come most pointedly from the Mosaic covenant because of its heavy emphasis on law.

God will punish them for their breech of covenant loyalty, but that is not the end of the story. In the future, God will establish a "new covenant" with them (31:31–34).

In the exposition notes to 31:31–34 we have commented on the fact that the "new covenant" is specifically contrasted to the Mosaic covenant. This accusation makes sense since the Mosaic covenant emphasizes law, and it is that law which is broken and its curses that thus go into effect. Even so, it would be a mistake to treat the Mosaic covenant in isolation from other covenants. With Paul (Gal. 3), it is better to understand the various covenants as building on each other rather than replacing each other. By the time of the covenant at Sinai mediated by Moses, we already have heard of covenants with Noah (Gen. 9) and Abraham (Gen. 12:1–3; 15; 17). After Moses and before Jeremiah, there was one other covenant administration and that was with David (2 Sam. 7). Quite simply stated, it would be difficult to imagine Jeremiah just contrasting the Mosaic covenant with the new covenant. It is better to regard the new covenant over against the entire system of covenants up to that point in redemptive history.

Jesus announces the new covenant on the eve of his death during the celebration of the Last Supper.[20] As he passed the cup to his disciples, Luke 22:20 reports his words as, "this cup is the new covenant in my blood, which is poured out for you" (see also 1 Cor. 11:24–25). Previous covenants were often associated with specific signs that represented the covenant. The Noahic covenant sign was the rainbow (Gen. 9:13), the Abrahamic covenant's was circumcision (Gen. 17:11), the Mosaic covenant's sign was the Sabbath (Exod. 31:13, 17). While the Davidic covenant never speaks of a sign, and the new covenant does not actually use the term sign in reference to the cup, the cup representing Christ's death functions as the sign of the new covenant. The point is that the new covenant is founded on the death and resurrection of Christ.

And this new covenant replaces the old. This is the argument of the book of Hebrews, which twice cites the relevant passage in Jeremiah to make the point (Heb. 8:8–12; 10:15–17; see also 2 Cor. 3). According to the author of Hebrews, the old covenant failed, not because of a defect in God or his instrument, but rather because of the people (8:8). They consistently broke that covenant by disobeying the law explicated in the covenant with Moses. As a result, as Jeremiah himself announced, the people would be expelled from the land (reversing the fulfillment of the Abrahamic covenant),[21] and the monarchy (a provision of the Davidic covenant) would be brought to an end.

But what does it mean that the new covenant replaces the old? It is perhaps better to say that the new covenant fulfills the old. Specifically, Jesus fulfills the old covenant. As O. P. Robertson forcefully puts it: "The heart of this consummative realization consists of a single person. As fulfiller of all the messianic promises, he achieves in himself the essence of the covenantal principle: 'I shall be your God and you shall be my people.' He may therefore be seen as the Christ who consummates the covenant."[22] One can immediately think of Galatians 3:16: "The promises were spoken to Abraham and to his seed. The Scripture does not say 'and to his seeds,' meaning many people, but 'and to your seed,' meaning one person, who is Christ." As lawgiver (Matt. 5–7), perfect lawkeeper, and the one who bears the punishment for breaking the law, Jesus fulfills the Mosaic covenant. And in the extensive teaching about Jesus position as son of David, we see that God indeed did establish the David's throne forever (2 Sam. 7:13).

Literary Components

The book of Jeremiah utilizes a set of literary types as it presents its message to the reader. The following provides a brief description of the most commonly occurring types. They may be divided into poetry and prose genres.

Poetry

Judgment and Salvation Oracles

Jeremiah's oracles are often delivered in a poetic form. Jeremiah announces that he is speaking in the name of the LORD. The prophet is a messenger of Yahweh while he delivers these oracles. Jeremiah 1–25 contains the largest portion of his judgment oracles, while 30–31 is a collection of poetic salvation oracles.

Oracles against the Nations

A special category of judgment oracle may be seen in chapters 46–51. These are oracles directed not toward the people of God, but toward the nations. Theologically, they may be rooted in the Abrahamic covenant, which announced that God would curse those who cursed his people (Gen. 12:1). Even though God used many of these nations to punish Israel, they did it for their own selfish reasons and so they themselves deserved punishment.

Confessions/Laments

Jeremiah's so-called confessions are in the form of laments in which he complains about the burdens that his prophetic task has brought on him. These laments have many similarities with laments in the psalms, including such elements as an invocation, a declaration of innocence, an imprecation against enemies, and divine response. While the lament has a certain ritual form, there is no good reason to deny that they authentically represent the emotions of the prophet. The confessions/laments are found in 11:18–23; 12:1–6; 15:15–21; 17:14–18; 18:19–23, and 20:7–17.

Prose

Prose Oracles

Not all of Jeremiah's oracles came in poetic format. Jeremiah 7, the so-called temple sermon, is a good example of an oracle that was delivered in a prose literary vehicle. A particularly close connection has been drawn between these prose oracles and Deuteronomic theology. However, no good reason may be given for using this connection to draw a division between the prophet and these oracles. Jeremiah could very well be writing from a Deuteronomic perspective.

Biographical Material

A significant part of the prose material may be described biographical in that it tells events in Jeremiah's life (chs. 26–29; 34–45). These descriptions often carry a prophetic oracle. It may be likely that these biographical descriptions were written by someone other than Jeremiah (Baruch?), but there is no necessity to that hypothesis.

Prophetic Sign-Acts

A special category of the above may be the biographical description of Jeremiah's life and acts that carry prophetic significance. Jeremiah 13:1–11 is a good example as it narrates Jeremiah's trip to the Euphrates (?) River to bury his dirty underwear.

Structure

From the description of the history of composition, we might anticipate that the book does not have a crisp structure, and this intuition would be correct. Of course, Jeremiah is not unique among the prophets. It is reported that Martin Luther said: "They [the prophets] have a queer way of talking, like people who, instead of proceeding in an orderly manner, ramble off from one thing to the next, so that you cannot make head or tail of them or see what they are getting at."[23]

While this observation is correct when applied to Jeremiah, we may still make some general observations about the flow of the book and its large sections, even though we cannot always account for why one oracle follows another or why, when they are given chronological indicators, they are not arranged sequentially.

There are reasons to think that chapter 25 plays a pivotal role in the book, though it may be that this was more explicit in an earlier form of the book (when the oracles against the foreign nations followed immediately after it, as in the Septuagint version). Even so, Jeremiah 25:1–14 summarizes the message of chapters 2–24 and then Jer. 25:15–38 announces judgment against the nations. Chapter 1 then is an introduction to the book with its account of the prophet's commissioning and chapter 52 an epilogue describing the fall of Jerusalem.

Within these two large sections we can recognize blocks of material.

Jeremiah 1 introduces the prophet, recounts his call, and presents two undated oracles that serve to introduce important themes of the book.

Jeremiah 2–24 is a collection of sermons, poetic and prose oracles, prophetic sign acts that are undated. Indeed, it is often difficult to tell when one oracle ends and another begins. Some scholars (Craigie, Kelley, Drinkard, *Jeremiah 1–25,* p. xxxii); suspect that these are the oracles that come from the first part of the prophet's ministry, i.e., his first scroll described in chapter 36.

After Jeremiah 25 summarizes the first part of the book and turns attention to the judgment against the nations, we see a block of prose material that consists of stories about Jeremiah as well as reports of oracles (chs. 26–29).

Jeremiah 30–33 is a collection of salvation oracles, a break from the heavy barrage of judgment in the book up to this point. Traditionally, these chapters are known as the Book of Consolation. Chapters 30–31 are poetic oracles, while 32–33 are prose.

Jeremiah 34–38 returns to prose stories about Jeremiah and oracles of judgment. It culminates with the first account of the fall of Jerusalem.

The next section, chapters 39–44, gives the distressing account of the exile and the continuing failures on the part of those who stay in the land with Jeremiah. They end up in Egypt because of their lack of confidence in God's ability to take care of them. Chapter 45 is an oracle directed toward Baruch, Jeremiah's associate.

The book ends with a collection of oracles against foreign nations (chs. 46–51), culminating with a lengthy prophetic statement directed toward Babylon. The book then culminates with a second account of the fall of Jerusalem (ch. 52).

This brief description supports Fretheim's (*Jeremiah,* pp. 19, 22) description of the structure of the book as "a collage, a work of art in which materials of various kinds are thrown onto a screen, then the intended effect is achieved by an imaginative profusion of different genres, images and metaphors, life settings, and personal encounters." The following commentary intends to explore this collage. When connections can be mapped and subunits identified, they will be pointed out.

Notes

1. Together the Twelve contain 14,335 words. See Lundbom, *Jeremiah 1–20*, p. 57.

2. The view that it is not the "historical" Jeremiah who is presented by the text is discussed below.

3. Though some (see footnote 15) believe the first date is the date of his birth, not the beginning of his prophetic activity.

4. Some oracles are dated (e.g., the oracles against Egypt in 46:1–49:33 to the fourth year of Jehoiakim [605 B.C.]; see Longman and Dillard, *An Introduction to the Old Testament*, p. 341, for a list of all dated materials in Jeremiah) and some are undated (particularly in the first twenty chapters of the book). Those that are dated are not in chronological order in the book.

5. Yates, "New Exodus and No Exodus," p. 2.

6. Duhm, *Das Buch Jeremia*.

7. Mowinckel, *Zur Komposition des Buches Jeremia*.

8. J. Lundbom ("Text, Composition, and Historical Reconstruction in Jeremiah," p. 6) reports that Mowinckel came to believe that Baruch was responsible for the Source B prose in his book *Prophecy and Tradition*.

9. J. McConville, *Grace in the End: A Study in Deuteronomic Theology* (Grand Rapids: Zondervan, 1993), 55–57; a longer discussion in idem, *Judgment and Promise: An Interpretation of the Book of Jeremiah* (Winona Lake, Ind.: Eisenbrauns, 1993), 12–13; also O. Eissfeldt, *The Old Testament: An Introduction* (trans. P. R. Ackroyd; Oxford: Blackwell, 1965), 352–54.

10. W. L. Holladay, *Jeremiah*, vol. 2, pp. 10–24. Indeed, Holladay goes so far as to suggest that Jeremiah's preaching can be associated with the public reading of Deuteronomy (see Deut. 31:9–13) every seven years (622, 615, 608, 601, 594, 587 B.C.).

11. In agreement with B. S. Childs, *Introduction to the Old Testament as Scripture*, p. 345.

12. Carroll, *The Book of Jeremiah*, and W. McKane, *A Critical and Exegetical Commentary on Jeremiah*.

13. Fretheim, *Jeremiah*, p. 12. This view is essentially the same as J. Bright, *Jeremiah*, 2 vols., W. Brueggemann, *A Commentary on Jeremiah: Exile and Homecoming*, and J. G. McConville, *Judgment and Promise: An Interpretation of the Book of Jeremiah*. Holladay (*Jeremiah*, 2 vols.) too is optimistic about the relationship between actual prophet and text.

14. See Provan, et al., *A Biblical History*, pp. 274–85.

15. This date is disputed by J. P. Hyatt ("The Beginning of Jeremiah's Prophecy," in Perdue and Kovacs, *A Prophet to the Nations*, pp. 63–72) and

others who believe that the date refers to the prophet's birth year, not the year of his prophetic call.

16. The conditions under which Jehoiakim was removed are not known. Assassination is not out of the realm of possibility.

17. Lundbom ("Text, Composition, and Historical Reconstruction") has made a strong case that indications of shortening by haplography are frequent in the Greek text, citing far more (330 cases) than previous studies (Janzen cites 63 cases). In this way he argues for the superiority of the MT.

18. Holladay, *Jeremiah* 2, p. 78.

19. As may be seen especially in the Hittite treaties of the mid-second millennium, though one may also point to the neo-Assyrian treaties of the seventh century B.C. See most recently, K. A. Kitchen, *The Reliability of the Old Testament*, pp. 242–44, 283–94.

20. That the new covenant comes to full realization in the New Testament does not preclude the fact that there is an anticipatory fulfillment of these promises in the return from exile. As Rata (*The Covenant Motif*, p. 85) states, "the coming days (of Jeremiah 31:31) refer to the immediate postexilic restoration as well as to the future restoration in the eschaton."

21. Even when they returned to the land, it was under foreign domination.

22. Robertson, *The Christ of the Covenants*, p. 273.

23. Cited by L. Allen, *Joel, Obadiah, Jonah, and Micah* (NICOT; Eerdmans, 1976), 257.

§1 The Superscription (Jer. 1:1–3)

1:1–3 / Most prophetic books (Isa. 1:1; Hos. 1:1; Joel 1:1; Nah. 1:1) as well as some wisdom books (Prov. 1:1; Eccl. 1:1; Song Sol. 1:1) begin with a superscription that serves a similar function to a title page on a modern book. The superscription was likely added by an editor or later tradent, and in the case of Jeremiah identifies the genre, author, the author's priestly status, and the time period in which he ministered. The genre assigned by the superscription is quite general. The books contain **words,** and indeed the bulk of the book is a collection of sermons. These words are further specified to be those **of Jeremiah** who is identified as the son of **Hilkiah** from **Anathoth,** a priestly village in **Benjamin.** Anathoth (near modern 'Anata, which preserves the name) is just a few miles northeast of Jerusalem. This village was assigned to the Levites according to Joshua 21:18. It was the village where Solomon sent Abiathar after he was deposed from the priesthood (1 Kgs. 2:26), and there is some speculation that perhaps Jeremiah was a descendent of Abiathar. Hilkiah was the name of the high priest who discovered the lost book of the law in the temple during the reign of Josiah (2 Kgs. 22:4, 8–14). It is not impossible that this high priest was Jeremiah's father, but if this Hilkiah were meant, it is likely that would have been specified. In addition, that Jeremiah was from Anathoth and not Jerusalem also militates against the identification of the Jeremiah's father with the high priest. That Jeremiah was from a priestly family makes his later criticism of the ritual of Judah even more powerful.

The next two verses set the historical context for the oracles of Jeremiah. It begins by mentioning that his prophetic ministry began in the **thirteenth year** of **Josiah.** That Jeremiah's ministry began during Josiah's reign is supported by 3:6; 25:3; 36:3. The superscription thus places the beginning of his work in the fateful year of 627/26. According to the Chronicler, Josiah started ruling when he was eight years old and in his eighth year he turned to the Lord. Then in his twelfth year, he started a religious reform by destroying all the idolatrous sites in Judah (see 2 Chr. 34). It was not until his eighteenth year according to both 2 Kings (22:3–20) and 2 Chronicles (34:8–11) that he discovered the book of the Law and began in earnest to centralize the cult in Jerusalem. It is interesting that the beginning of Jeremiah's prophetic ministry roughly coincides with the beginning of this important religious reform. Nonetheless, some questions have plagued scholars' understanding of the relationship between Jeremiah and Josiah. Our conclusion is that Jeremiah's ministry did coincide with Josiah's reign, and he indeed did support Josiah's reform. Another event of significance in 627/26 was the initiation of Babylonian hostilities toward Assyria. For more about these international events, see Introduction: Historical Context. Indeed, verse three indicates that Jeremiah's oracles continued through the reign of **Jehoiakim** and down to the eleventh year of **Zedekiah,** which was 587/86, the year in which Nabopolassar's son, Nebuchadnezzar defeated the city of Jerusalem, devastated it, and exiled its leading citizens. Interestingly, two short-lived kings of this era are not mentioned, Jehoahaz, who briefly succeeded his father Josiah until a meddling pharaoh Neco replaced him with his pro-Egyptian brother Jehoiakim, and also Jehoiachin, the latter's son who succeeded his father on the throne after Jehoiakim's sudden and unexplained death after he rebelled against Nebuchadnezzar. Jehoiachin was captured and deported to Babylon and replaced by his uncle Zedekiah. Josiah, Jehoiakim, and Zedekiah are mentioned since they are the most significant kings of Judah of the time of Jeremiah's active ministry (627/26–587/86).

Additional Notes §1

1:1 / The most recent suggestion for the location of biblical **Anathoth** is the modern Arabic village of 'Anata (Y. Nadelman, "The Identification of Anathoth and the Soundings at Khirbet Der es-Sidd," *Israel Exploration Journal* 44 [1994]) though other suggestions include nearby Ras el-kharrubeh and Deir es-Sud.

1:2 / Some understand the **thirteenth year** of Josiah to be the date of Jeremiah's birth rather than the beginning of his formal ministry. The conclusion is reached because there are few oracles able to be dated to Josiah's reign and there is no clear affirmation or distancing from Josiah's reforms. An appeal to 1:5 supports the idea that the prophet felt he was called to his prophetic office in the womb. However, in spite of 1:5, which seems to be hyperbole, it is more natural to take the reference in the superscription to his actual call narrated in 1:6–10.

§2 *Jeremiah's Call (Jer. 1:4–19)*

While authorship is not an important issue in much of biblical and ancient Near Eastern literature, it is significant for the genre of prophecy. Prophets must be people who have had an encounter with God and been commissioned by him for their task. Thus, the identity and credentials of prophets are significant and often described in anticipation of their oracles. One can see this concern in the Mari prophecies where a prophetic oracle must be connected to a name and accompanied by some token of the prophet's identify (hem of clothing, finger nail clippings, lock of hair). In the Bible, many prophets report their call, and Jeremiah is no exception, these present verses describing the time God spoke to him to send him to his people with a message of judgment and hope.

The remainder of the first chapter will describe Jeremiah's call to the prophetic ministry. It will also introduce many of the major themes of the rest of the book.

1:4–8 / Jeremiah's call narrative begins with God informing him that he was chosen before he was even born (v. 5). To this, Jeremiah responds by declaring his inadequacies. First, he points to his limited speaking skills, and as he does so, he reminds us of Moses, the paradigmatic prophet (Exod. 4:10). Indeed, in this way the book of Jeremiah may be situating the prophet in the line of prophets that Deuteronomy 18:14–20 announced would follow Moses' pattern. "The book of Jeremiah begins with a public declaration of his authority to follow in the Mosaic lineage of prophets and mediators for Israel" (Lewin, "Arguing for Authority: A Rhetorical Study of Jeremiah 1.14–19 and 20.7–18," *JSOT* 32 [1985], p. 106). He also appeals to his age, calling himself a **child** (*naʿar*). Unfortunately, this reference does not allow us to attribute a precise age to Jeremiah, since it is a general term for youth, but whatever his age, he feels that he is too young for the task that God has given him. After all, ancient biblical society privileged the elder, not youth.

No matter what his age, however, God urges him to act and promises to be with him. In his weakness, God will make him strong. In God's economy, it is not one's inherent strength, abilities, or credentials that count, but rather God's presence. For that reason, Jeremiah is not to **be afraid** to go to the people with God's message. Indeed, in the light of the divine command (**"you must go"** v. 7), he should only be afraid of not acting.

1:9–10 / At this point, God acts to give Jeremiah the confidence that he needs to begin his ministry among the people. He reaches with his **hand** and touches Jeremiah's **mouth.** With this act, we see a connection with the call to Isaiah (Isa. 6:7). In Isaiah's case it was an angel, specifically a seraph, who touched his lips with a burning coal, but the acts are similar enough to associate them with one another. In part, then, this act shows that Jeremiah is a prophet in the line of Isaiah. It also shows the consecration of Jeremiah's mouth, the tool that God is setting apart for the accomplishment of his purpose. Along with the action, God also speaks to Jeremiah with an explanation. He has put his **words** in Jeremiah's mouth. In essence, this unit tells the reader that Jeremiah's words to follow are not to be understood as the opinion or advice of a mere human, but rather as God's very words. Verse 10 then gives the divine motivation for this action, and it is double-edged. There is a positive and a negative purpose. As with Jeremiah's oracles that follow, there is an emphasis on the destructive, judgmental aspect of his ministry (**uproot, tear down, destroy, overthrow**), but also, anticipating in particular the Book of Consolation (chs.. 30–33), there is a positive aspect as well (**build, plant**). Lastly, we should notice that the message he is commissioned to deliver is not just focused on Judah, but over **nations** and **kingdoms.** Most explicitly, we will see this in the oracles against the nations (chs. 46–51).

1:11–16 / After reporting his call to the prophetic ministry, the book continues by giving a preview of oracles to come. Two oracles introduce the prophetic activity of Jeremiah. They illustrate the prophet's technique as well as two major themes that pervade the book. The word of God that comes to Jeremiah creatively articulates past tradition through the use of vivid imagery and other rhetorical devices. As is typical of Jeremiah's prophecies, these are not dated. Are we to assume that they came early in his career and interpret them in the light of that time period? We cannot be certain, since after all, we know that a chronological impulse was not operative in other parts of the book. However, they do occur first, and thus many commentators take for granted that they were early.

Both oracles are introduced by the question **What do you see?** that engages Jeremiah in repartee with God. The first oracle is based on a word play. Jeremiah's vision is of a **branch of an almond tree.** This does not necessarily imply that the almond tree was in blossom or, if so, that it is springtime. After all, this is a vision of a stylized almond rod (see Additional Notes). The point of the oracle is made by virtue of the fact that the Hebrew word for **almond tree** (*saqed*) is similar to the verb **watch** (*saqad*). Indeed, the almond was the first tree to blossom after winter. The point is that God is watching over his word. He will accomplish it. This oracle serves as a warning to God's people who hear of God's coming judgment on their sin, but doubt that he has the will or the ability to affect it.

The second of the two opening oracles is introduced in verse 13 again by the divine question: **What do you see?** Jeremiah responds that he sees **a boiling pot, tilting away from the north.** God then interprets the vision for the prophet by warning him that **disaster** will be **poured out** over the land, presumably like the hot water from the north.

With this oracle, we encounter for the first time the idea of trouble coming from the north. The lack of identification of the enemy from the north and the lack of precise reference have led to all kinds of speculation and discussion. One supposed problem is that if this oracle was given early in Jeremiah's career, and if we suppose, as I believe we should, that Jeremiah's prophetic ministry began in 626 B.C. (see Introduction), then the foe was unlikely to have been thought to be Babylon. This is a problem in part because it is clear that in later oracles Jeremiah finally identified the foe from the north as Babylon.

In answer to this question, we first of all take note of the fact that, with the exception of Egypt to the south of Judah, all other possible foes would attack from the north, even if, like Babylon, they were geographically situated to the east, since armies did not cross the wilderness area to the east. Second, we should realize that we do not know when to date this oracle in Jeremiah's career. We have no indication that there is any kind of chronological arrangement of the oracles. Third, and most importantly, it is quite possible that the oracle was ambiguous at first and only historical circumstances clarified its fulfillment. In addition, the north possesses symbolic/mythological connotations, foreboding evil and enemies.

Historically, though it is possible that those who heard this oracle early on may have thought that the enemy might be a someone like the Scythians, there is no doubt that in the book as it now stands that the danger from the north is to be identified with Babylon.

Verses 15–16 poetically expand on the threat from the north. It will be a political/military intrusion of Judah. The picture of kings setting **their thrones** in Jerusalem's **gates** is a metaphor for a foreign takeover of the city. Finally, the reason for this disaster is given—the people's sin, specifically their worship of false gods. Idolatry is the primary means by which God's chosen people betrayed their covenantal commitments, and it is a topic that we will encounter frequently in the book.

1:17–19 / God now completes his commission of Jeremiah by encouraging him in the face of the opposition he knows the prophet will face. In verse 17, God tells Jeremiah what he should do; in verses 18–19, God tells Jeremiah what he will do for him.

God begins by motivating with fear. If Jeremiah is **terrified** by the people, he should be even more terrified of God. But fear is not the only method of encouragement that God uses at this beginning point of Jeremiah's ministry. He not only insists **Get yourself ready,** he also informs Jeremiah that he has readied him for the task. By using a series of military metaphors—**fortified city, iron pillar, bronze wall,** God describes how he has prepared the prophet to encounter hostility. No one will be able to **overcome** him. Why is the prophet so resilient? God tells him **I am with you and will rescue you.** This is a variation of the covenant theme. God is with his prophet to protect him and to see that his prophetic word will come to realization. Nonetheless, the commission leaves no doubt. Jeremiah is about to enter a war; his opposition will be powerful (**kings of Judah, its officials, its priests and the people of the land**) and determined.

Additional Notes §2

1:11 / There has been much discussion about the significance of the **branch of an almond tree.** The Hebrew word translated branch (*maqqel*), according to Carroll (*Jeremiah*, p. 103), can be used for a diviner's rod (Hos. 4:12), and he argues that it has that connotation in this present context. This connection seems unfounded. According to *NIDOTTE*, vol. 2, p. 1088, the word is used to indicate a walking stick, a riding crop, small trees, and more. As indicated above, the reason why an almond tree is specified is because it was the first to bloom in the spring, and, according to Thompson (*The Book of Jeremiah*, p. 153), the city of Anathoth is known for its almond trees.

K. van der Toorn ("Did Jeremiah See Aaron's Staff," *JSOT* 43 [1989], pp. 83–94) has argued in favor of the view that Jeremiah was not having a vision of the branch of an almond tree, but rather was looking at a cultic object which represented Aaron's blossoming rod (Num. 17). He does not believe this rod was actually Aaron's. Indeed, he suggests that it was originally a fertility symbol, but later was associated with the story in Numbers. He further suggests that the boiling pot was also something that Jeremiah actually saw while he was on priestly duty at the temple. While van der Toorn has shown this is a possibility, it is certainly not proven.

1:13 / The interpretation offered here of the **boiling pot** is the standard one that the pot is imagined to be filled with water and that the evil or disaster that is about to be unleashed on Judah is identified with the boiling water rushing over the land. Holladay (*Jeremiah* 1, pp. 39–40) has an unnecessarily complicated interpretation of this image based on the unfounded idea that the pot is empty and that the heat is allowing the scraping off of crud, which he identifies with the sin of the people.

1:14 / Controversy has raged about the disaster that will be poured out from the **north.** With only a few exceptions (e.g., Egypt and the small nation states to the east of the Jordan), incursions into Israel would come from the north. But what, if any, particular threat did Jeremiah have in mind here? If, as seems most likely considering this oracle is embedded in the call narrative, this is an early word of God to the prophet, soon after his call in 626, then, it is argued, it would be too early to think of the Babylonians. Thus, some scholars (H. H. Rowley, "The Early Prophecies of Jeremiah and their Setting," *BJRL* 45 [1962–1963], pp. 198–234) pick up on a statement by the Greek historian Herodotus and suggest the Scythians (a sophisticated nuance of this position may be found in H. Cazelles, "Zephaniah, Jeremiah, and the Scythians in Palestine," in Perdue and Kovacs, pp. 129–49). However, doubt is now cast on Herodotus' assertion that the Scythians made such a deep penetration at this time. Whatever, the conscious understanding of Jeremiah at the time of the oracle, there is no doubt that in its present literary setting we are to understand the threat from the north to be associated with Babylon. As Childs has argued ("The Enemy from the North and the Chaos Tradition," *JBL* 78 [1959], pp. 151–61), perhaps the answer is that the north has by this time taken on mythological dimensions and that at first there was no specific identification that was made. For those who resolve the issue by dating the beginning of Jeremiah's ministry to later than 626, see C. F. Whitley ("The Beginning of Jeremiah's Ministry," *ZAW* 80 [1968], pp. 38–49) and Holladay (*Jeremiah* 1, pp. 39–40).

§3 *Former Bliss (Jer. 2:1–3)*

2:1–3 / God again commissions Jeremiah to speak an oracle to the residents of Jerusalem. The oracle reminds the Judeans of their former intimate relationship with God. Jeremiah uses the metaphor of marriage to make his point here. The beginning of the relationship between God and his people was like a honeymoon—pure **devotion.** The **bride,** Israel, followed the groom, God, through hard places like the **desert,** also called **a land not sown.** This language reminds the hearers of the wilderness wanderings (Exod. 13:7–Deut. 34:12). The picture presented here, of course, is an idealized one, considering the troubles that were experienced in the wilderness (e.g., Num. 13–14). According to DeRoche, the wilderness is not being idealized but rather "the attitude that Israel showed Yahweh wandering the desert" is being idealized ("Jeremiah 2:2–3 and Israel's Love for God during the Wilderness Wanderings," *CBQ* 45 [1983], p. 375; M. V. Fox, "Jeremiah 2:2 and the Desert Ideal," *CBQ* 35 [1983], pp. 441–50, takes a different view). Interestingly, Hosea had earlier used an idealized view of the wilderness to describe the restoration of the remnant after the judgment (Hos. 2:14–15). In any case, the description of Israel's early relationship with God as a marriage will set up Jeremiah's later charge that God's people have become whores.

Jeremiah then shifts from a marriage metaphor to an agricultural metaphor to describe the Lord's love for Israel. Israel is the **firstfruits** of the harvest. According to Pentateuchal legislation (Exod. 23:19; Lev. 23:10–14; Num. 18:12–13; Deut. 26:1–11), the firstfruits belong to God for use by the priests. They are not to be eaten by non-priests, but rather given to God as a gift. After all, God provides all the harvest. Indeed, there was a special offering of the firstfruits when the Israelites entered the land for the first time (Deut. 26:1–11), so this metaphor as well as the marriage metaphor may be reminiscent of God's early relationship with Israel.

Like the firstfruits, therefore, Israel was **holy** to God. To be holy meant to be set apart. Israel was special among the nations of the world in that they had an intimate relationship with God. This intimate relationship meant that any other nation who disturbed Israel would feel divine displeasure. Continuing the firstfruit metaphor, the text claims that anyone who **devoured** the Israelites would be declared guilty and **disaster** would overtake them. In other words, Israel was the recipient of God's special protection.

Additional Notes §3

2:2–3 / Jeremiah focuses on the marriage metaphor in this oracle. He is not the first or the last biblical author to utilize marriage as a fitting analogy of God's relationship to his people. The appropriateness of this image may be explained in part by the fact that marriage is an intimate and exclusive relationship between a man and a woman. Indeed, it is the only relationship that is restricted to one partner, at least according to the text that establishes the institution (Gen. 2:18–24). Second, both relationships may be described as a covenant (see Mal. 2:14), a relationship that is built on mutual love but finds expression in a legal form. Indeed, in Jeremiah 2:2, the word devotion is the Hebrew word *hesed,* a signature word indicating the love of covenant partners, and sometimes translated "covenant love."

Most often in the Old Testament, the marriage metaphor is used in negative contexts, particularly when Israel betrays the relationship. The prophet Ezekiel develops the metaphor of marriage to its greatest extent. He dedicates two long chapters to recounting the perversity of Israel's relationship to God using sexual terms (Ezek. 16; 23). The prophets exploit the marriage relationship most dramatically, but its contours can be discerned elsewhere in the Old Testament as well. In the Pentateuch, we hear of Yahweh's jealousy, an emotion that is only proper to an exclusive relationship like marriage (Exod. 19:3–6; 20:2–6; 34:14). Also, Israel's rebellion is described as adultery (Exod. 34:15–16; Lev. 17:7).

The Song of Songs celebrates intimacy between a man and a woman. Within the context of the canon, the relationship can only be understood as that of a married couple. We could justifiably treat the Song of Songs as an extension of the marriage metaphor in the Bible.

The use of the marriage relationship as a metaphor of the relationship between God and his people continues in the New Testament. Most notably, Paul in Ephesians instructs Christians that their connection with Christ is like a marriage (Eph. 5:21–33). The book of Revelation describes the final union between God and his people as a marriage (Rev. 19:6–8). See N. Stienstra, *YHWH Is the Husband of His People* (Kampen, Netherlands: Pharos, 1993).

2:2 / **how as a bride you loved me** is an idiomatic translation of the Hebrew, which is woodenly translated something like "the love of your honeymoon." God remembers Israel's early love, the love that characterizes the honeymoon period, before all the troubles of later life intrude.

§4 A Case against God's People (Jer. 2:4–13)

2:4–5a / This oracle has a lengthy introduction that emphasizes the divine origin of the words of Jeremiah. The prophet has no authority in his own right; he is a messenger, and thus we are not surprised that a common messenger formula (**This is what the LORD says**) is frequently used to introduce God's words in Jeremiah as well as other prophets. But even before the messenger formula is used, the oracle begins with a call to **hear,** not the word of Jeremiah, but **the word of the LORD.**

The addressee of the oracle is also specified. It is interesting to note that the audience is called **house of Jacob** with the parallel **all the clans of the house of Israel.** This language does not specify the southern tribes, but is language that calls to mind a united Israel, or perhaps the northern tribes. Of course, years before Jeremiah was born, the northern tribes had been exiled by Assyria (722 B.C.). It is unlikely that he addresses the northern kingdoms in exile or even the remnants that are still in the land. This epithet for the people of God at Jeremiah's time may be because Judah now stands for Israel, that is, they are all that is left. Another possibility is that the oracle refers to Judah in this way because it will now recall an experience from before the divided monarchy—the exodus and the wilderness wanderings.

2:5b / God questions the present generation concerning the actions of the **fathers,** that is their ancestors. They are the ones who moved away from him. The present situation did not begin in the recent past but in the far distant past. The Deuteronomic Historian (1 Samuel–2 Kings) describes the process of apostasy that Jeremiah now decries. God asks a question to challenge them (**What fault?**). The only answer is that there was no fault, no injustice, on God's part that explains their behavior.

They not only left God, but they also pursued something else. **They followed worthless idols.** At the heart of Jeremiah's charge against Judah is the fact that they have left God and pursued idols.

Jeremiah notes that a person becomes like his god. Judah's gods are empty and so they became empty as well.

2:6–8 / These verses pick up on the idea that God's people followed worthless idols, and not the true God. They did not even know that God was gone. The form of the question indicates that they should have missed him, considering how gracious he had been to them in the past. Far from the fault of verse 5, God delivered them from the bondage of **Egypt,** navigated them through the difficult terrain of the **wilderness,** and finally deposited them in the promised land, a land of great fertility. They entered this land of God's good gifts and **defiled** it. They turned it from the holy place where God dwelt with his people and turned it into an unclean locale.

In particular, and most horrifically, it was the leadership of God's people that ignored him and followed the hated Baal. Specifically named are the **priests,** the legal experts (scribes?), the political **leaders,** and the **prophets. Baal** is named for the first time in this book. Baal is a Hebrew/Canaanite word that simply means "lord" or "master." Baal, along with El, was the focus of worship of the Canaanites who were in the land when the Israelites first entered it.

2:9–13 / God now determines to prosecute God's people because of their rebellion. The verb **bring charges** (*rib*) is a legal term (see also Hos. 2:4–25; 4:1–3; Mic. 6:1–8). The theological background is the covenant, with its laws that Israel agreed to observe. Now the laws have been broken, and God has sent in his covenant lawyer, Jeremiah, to present his case against his people. Lurking in the background are the curses (see Deut. 27–28) that followed the law as a consequence of breaking the covenant.

Yahweh expresses his disbelief at Israel's apostasy by underlining its uniqueness. Nothing like this has ever happened before! Just go to **the coasts of Kittim** (Cyprus), which are to the west, and to **Kedar,** which is to the east, and one will not be able to find anything like this. The mention of Cyprus and Kedar serves as a merism where the two opposite directions are mentioned to indicate the whole world. Nowhere will anyone find another people trading in their national deities for another set of gods. What makes it all so tragic is that they have taken the true God, something real and glorious, and turned it in for something empty.

The oracle concludes with a summary of the people's sin that calls for punishment. Indeed, it is **two sins,** that is, a two-fold sin. They have **forsaken** the true God, **the spring of living water** and have also **dug their own cisterns.** This is a metaphor for the other gods that their own (and other nations's) imaginations have produced (i.e., Baal). In the first place, there is a contrast between the true God who is a spring of fresh water, and a cistern that holds dank, stale water. But in addition, these are broken cisterns. They think they will find life-giving water in these cisterns (gods), but they will be empty because broken and all the water will drain out.

Additional Notes §4

2:5 / The term **worthless idols** translates the Hebrew word *hebel,* well known from the book of Ecclesiastes. Its basic, non-metaphorical meaning is "bubble, vapor" (see T. Longman III, *Ecclesiastes,* pp. 61–65). While it may occasionally indicate transcience, it more often refers to emptiness or meaninglessness, as it does here. A more literal translation of v. 5c would be "they pursued emptiness and became empty," but the NIV makes explicit what is implicit in the language, that is, that the *hebel* is an idol.

2:8 / In Hebrew, the **leaders** are the "shepherds" of the people. This is a common metaphor for leaders (Jer. 23:1–3; Ezek. 34). God is the ultimate shepherd of his people (Ps. 23), but he appointed human leaders who were to take care of his people. However, at this time his shepherds were leading his people astray.

2:12 / God appeals to the **heavens** in his charge against his people with the expectation that they, as a witness to the covenant promises that the people made to God (Deut. 32:1; Isa. 1:2), will be horrified.

§5 The Way of the Lord or the Way of the Nations (Jer. 2:14–19)

The previous oracle commented on the nature of Judah's sin; the present text draws out the implications. This oracle, in essence, describes Judah's movement away from Yahweh as the source of its confidence to the nations. These nations, however, will not protect God's people; they will rip it apart. Due to the mention of Assyria as a potential ally in this oracle, we assume that it is one of Jeremiah's earlier oracles, since Assyria was in no position to help anyone after 612 B.C. when Nineveh fell.

2:14–16 / The oracle begins with two taunting questions, inquiring whether God's people are someone's **servant** or, in the intensified expression in the second colon of verse 13, **a slave by birth.** The latter expression derives from the fact that the children of slaves automatically became slaves. While slaves might be eligible to leave after seven years of service, this may not have been true for children born into slavery (Exod. 21:4).

God's people were supposed to be servants of Yahweh. Indeed, prophets are in particular called to be "servants of the LORD" (2 Kgs. 17:13; Jer. 7:25). Unfortunately, as the passage unfolds, it becomes clear that they are not bound to Yahweh, but are enslaved to other nations. In other words, they have turned away from the Lord and to other nations for help in their distress.

The third question of v. 14 makes it obvious that Jeremiah believes that this strategy of survival has backfired on God's people. He asks them if they are slaves, then why are they **plunder?** If Israel had been a faithful servant of Yahweh, then they would not be plunder to the nations. But their devastated and weakened state is testimony to their alliances with the nations that have not protected them.

Lions often represent powerful nations that feed off the people of God. Specifically, the Assyrians are likened to lions that have consumed vassal nations including Israel and Judah (Nah.

2:12–14 [ET 2:11–13]). Biblical and Near Eastern history record a number of times when the Assyrians had raided, **laid waste,** and **burned** towns in Palestine. Specifically, we mention the following Assyrian rulers: Tiglath-pileser III (745–727 B.C.), Shalmaneser V (727–722 B.C.), Sargon II (721–705 B.C.), Sennacherib (705–681 B.C.), and Esarhaddon (681–668 B.C.).

With the reference to **Memphis** (Heb. *Noph*) and **Tahpanhes,** Jeremiah brings Egypt into the picture as well. Memphis was an early capital of Egypt that was located relatively near modern Cairo, while Tahpanhes was in the eastern Delta region near Sinai and en route to Palestine. The point of the verse is that Israel and Judah have entered into alliances with Egypt with the result that they have been hurt, not helped. Ironically, the defeated and rebellious remnant of Judah will flee to Egypt and end up at Tahpanhes, Memphis, and other Egyptian locations (see 43:1–44:6).

2:17–19 / The second half of the oracle continues the interrogation of God's people. The first question suggests that they have brought this destruction on themselves. How? The answer is given in the next few verses with a play on the word **way** (*derek*). They have left the way of the Lord and have gone on the way to **Egypt** and **Assyria.** That is, Israel and Judah have put their trust in alliances with foreign nations and not with the Lord. This is the **wickedness** and **backsliding** that results in their severe punishment.

The fact that they wrongly go to Egypt and Assyria to drink water may connect this oracle to verse 13 of the previous oracle (or even be an argument that verse 13 ought to be part of this oracle). In other words, they should have all the water they need from the Lord who is the spring of living water.

Additional Notes §5

2:14 / Israel has become the **plunder** (*baz*) of the nations. Perhaps the word should be specifically understood and translated as prey, considering the animal metaphor that is developed in v. 15.

2:16 / The significance and even the meaning of the expression **shaved the crown of your head** is debated. It is true that shaving one's head can be a sign of humiliation or servitude in the ancient Near East (2 Sam. 10:4; Isa. 7:20; Jer. 41:5; 48:37; Ezek. 44:20). Some question the

Hebrew text here and suggest a repointing of the word so that it derives from a Hebrew word (*r*ʿʿII) which means "to break," thus "broke the crown of your head."

2:18 / Holladay (*Jeremiah* 1, pp. 95–6) suggests that **Shihor** is short for "Pool of Horus" and "refers to a body of water on the eastern edge of Egypt, either one of the eastern arms of the Nile or a lake like Lake Menzaleh." The **River** is a common way of referring to the Euphrates.

§6 Like a Whore (Jer. 2:20–28)

This section could be divided into subunits, especially since there is quite a variety of imagery used in it. However, most of the verses present a picture of God's people as a whore, and thus we will treat these verses as a single section.

2:20–21 / God's people are rebellious against their true master, Yahweh. Jeremiah uses a common image of rebellion when he accuses God's people of tearing off the **yoke** that bound them to God. He also represents them as dangerously asserting their independence: **"I will not serve you!"** Jeremiah then reverts to a sexual image and pictures them as having sex **like a prostitute.** That Jeremiah understands the sexual act as analogous to spiritual betrayal is clear from the references to **high hill** and **spreading tree** (Deut. 12:2; 1 Kgs. 14:13; 2 Kgs. 17:10; Isa. 57:5; 65:7; Ezek. 6:13; 20:28; Hos. 4:13). These refer to the locations of pagan shrines in ancient Palestine. God's people would go to these places and worship the idols of the Canaanites.

Jeremiah then changes metaphors yet again and speaks of God's people in viticultural terms. As a **vine,** they were planted as **sound and reliable stock.** Such a beginning would virtually assure a good plant, but no, they inexplicably became a **corrupt, wild vine.** This image is reminiscent of the "Song of the Vineyard" in Isaiah 5:1–7. Isaiah there speaks of God's special care and concern for his vineyard where he planted the "choicest vines." But while expecting good fruit, "it yielded only bad fruit" (5:2). God did everything necessary for God's people to turn out for the better, but they willfully turned degenerate.

2:22–25 / The guilt of God's people is so deep it cannot be easily removed. An analogy is drawn between **guilt** and a **stain** that is resistant to even the most vigorous rubbing and the strongest of soaps. The psalmist also uses the image of dirt or staining to communicate how sin and guilt spoil someone. In the light of sin, the psalmist implores God to "wash away all my iniquity and cleanse me from my sin" and again "cleanse me with hyssop, and I will be clean; wash me, and I will be whiter than snow" (Ps. 51:2, 7). Malachi describes the coming messenger of the covenant as one who will be like "a refiner's fire or a launderer's soap" (Mal. 3:2). But in Jeremiah, God denies the efficacy of soap; it will not remove the stain.

Their sin is that of idolatry, but they deny their involvement with **Baal.** Baal was the seductive god of the Canaanites. His connection with the fertility of the land and sexuality made him a popular object of worship. Again, God calls his people to a sober appraisal of their practices. Their **way** (note again the play on the word "way") **in the valley** was to worship Baal. They not only worshiped this false god, but they pursued him like a **wild donkey** in heat pursues sexual intercourse. A **wild donkey** does not have to work hard to have sexual intercourse with another **wild donkey** in heat, so Baal and his devotees don't have to work hard at promoting Baal's interests among God's people. They will come running. Note for instance the implied large following of Baal among Israelites during the time of Ahab and Jezebel (1 Kgs. 17–18). God's people cannot help themselves; they have loved *strangers* (i.e., foreign idols, Deut. 32:16) and cannot resist the temptation.

2:26–28 / Israel's behavior will lead to her disgrace. A **thief** works in secret, but is disgraced when found out. So Israel will be publicly humiliated. Jeremiah has a tendency to spell out in lists what types of people in particular are meant, and in this case, it is **they, their kings and their officials, their priests and their prophets.** All their leaders are implicated. Those who were to lead them to the Lord led them away. Again, the sin of idolatry is pinpointed. Instead of calling God their **father** and the one who brought them into existence, they give that title to **wood** and **stone.** The idols of the nations were made out of wood and stone. As Isaiah earlier proclaimed, these idols cannot save (Isa. 43:8–13; 44:6–23, see also Deut. 32:37–38). They cannot help their followers when they get into trouble.

Additional Notes §6

2:20 / The NIV translates the verb *tsoʿah* used with "whore" (*zonah*) as **lay down as a prostitute.** However, the verb, though rare and somewhat ambiguous in meaning, seems to have a more specific meaning, referring to spreading one's legs or bending over backwards (Lundbom, *Jeremiah 1–20,* pp. 277).

2:27 / A. Dearman suggests that Jeremiah sarcastically reverses ancient expectations when he has Israel call the **wood** father and the **stone** the one who gave them birth. He argues this on the basis of the fact that the wood is usually associated with Asherah, a female deity, and that the stone is a phallic symbol, representative of male deity (*Jeremiah/Lamentations*). See also the discussion of M. S. Smith, *The Early History of God* (2d ed.; Grand Rapids: Eerdmans, 2002), pp. 129–30.

2:28 / **as many gods as you have towns.** This may not be hyperbole, since it was ancient Near Eastern practice that every town had its own particular deity. Indeed, the title Baal simply means "lord." Each town had its particular manifestation of the god Baal, so we hear of Baal of Tyre, Sidon, Gad.

§7 Israel Accuses God; God Accuses Israel (Jer. 2:29–37)

2:29–37 / This oracle begins with God questioning the people who are bringing **charges,** that is, legal action, against God (see Additional Notes). The charges are unspecified but stem in all likelihood from the people's perception that God has not followed through on his covenant commitments. God immediately reverses the accusation and charges that they have **rebelled** against him. The specific nature of that rebellion is spelled out in the verses that follow.

God informs them that he tried to stem the damage that their rebellion caused by punishing them (v. 30), but they did not respond to the message of the **prophets.** Indeed, they killed the prophets. Often in the Old Testament the image of the **lion** is used to denote the ruthless, ravenous enemies of God and his people (Ps. 7:2; 10:9; Isa. 5:29).

God then seems to be answering the people's charge in part when he asks whether he has been a **desert** or **a land of great darkness** to his people. In other words, has he left them alone and deserted, struggling to find the resources they need to live and live well? He is incredulous that they have asserted their autonomy against him, saying they are **free to roam.** Indeed, he accuses them of having **forgotten** him. Israel forgetting God is as unbelievable as a **maiden** forgetting her **jewelry** (perhaps jewelry connected to her forthcoming wedding) or even a **bride** the **ornaments** that she wears at her wedding. Who has ever heard of such a thing? Of course, in biblical conception, forgetting is a matter not so much of knowledge as of obedience. They knew God existed, but they simply paid no attention to him. The images of v. 32 evoke the imagery of the marriage between Israel and God that we saw in 2:2–3. Though they have forgotten their marriage to God, they are still adept at **love.** However, the love in which they excel is illicit love. They can even teach the worst of women, presumably whores, how to improve their trade. We have here again a subtle allusion to the idolatrous practices of Israel.

They proclaim their innocence, though in reality they kill the **innocent poor** (2:34–35). The irony throughout this section is overpowering. They are telling God they are innocent while their clothing is smeared with the blood of their victims. The phrase **though you did not catch them breaking in** is the hint that lets us see their flimsy excuse. Exodus 22:2 states that if one kills an intruder at night, then one is not guilty of murder; it is a matter of self-protection. However, they are lying about this and so are guilty. Since they are making up flimsy excuses for their unethical behavior and denying they are sinners, God is determined to punish them.

In 2:36 the oracle again picks up on the theme of the **way** and accuses Israel of constantly **changing** their way. The reference to **Egypt** and **Assyria** indicates Israel's tendency to find protection not in God but in foreign alliances. They had earlier entered into a treaty with Assyria, but Assyria ended up destroying the northern kingdom (722 B.C.) and attacking the south (701 B.C.). During much of Jeremiah's ministry, particularly during the time of Jehoiakim (609–597 B.C.), elements within Judah's society were banking on Egypt's help in the light of increasing Babylonian threat. However, this too did not help Israel. The oracle ends with a reference to coming exile. God, who stands behind the great nations and movements of history, will not allow the people of God to survive. They will soon assume the position of captives being led off to a foreign land; they will leave **that place** (the promised land) **with hands on your head.**

Additional Notes §7

2:29 / The verb **bring charges** (*rib*) is a well-known legal term in biblical Hebrew. It is the language of the courtroom. The law is embedded in the covenant and is followed by blessings and curses that are the consequence of obedience or disobedience. When Israel breaks the law, God sends prophets to confront them. In other words, prophets may be understood as covenant lawyers. Jeremiah acts this way as he is sent to the people exposing them as lawbreakers, reminding them of the curses, and, at least at first, offering them the alternative of repentance.

§8 Like a Nomad in the Desert (Jer. 3:1–5)

3:1–5 / Jeremiah presents yet another oracle of accusation and judgment against the people. He begins by presenting an analogy of a husband who **divorces** his wife, who then marries another man. The prophet then asks the simple question whether he is able to remarry her, and the answer is a categorical no. The land would be **defiled.** The background to this passage is found in Deuteronomy 24:1–4, where the law clearly states that a man is not able to remarry a wife whom he divorced and who remarried, but then divorced her second husband. The analogy with Israel continues themes found in the previous chapter. Israel's first husband was God; she then acted like a **prostitute** with idols. Jeremiah by using this language is stating the seriousness of Israel's offense (see also Hos. 2:7). They may not come back. In Jeremiah we find a mixture of conditional and unconditional oracles, the present oracle is the latter. Their sin is so great that there is no chance at repentance.

The next verses continue the theme of Israel's spiritual wandering by describing it as a whore. He calls on Israel to look up to the **barren heights.** This is where the trade caravans would travel, a convenient place for prostitutes seeking clients (see Additional Notes).

In response, the **showers** have stopped. This particular manifestation of God's punishment has a point to it. Israelites were tempted to worship Baal in particular, and Baal was a storm god, the one who brought the rains and fertility. In other words, the Lord seems to say, if you worship Baal for rain and fertility, then I will withhold them to show who is really in control. We see a similar situation during the time of Elijah, when Ahab and Jezebel promote the worship of Baal with the result that God withholds the rains for a long period of time (see 1 Kgs. 17:1).

The people call God their **Father** and expect him to eventually calm down. Again, as at the time of Elijah, the people "waver between two opinions" (1 Kgs. 18:21). They call God their Father, but they continue to do **evil** by breaking the law. "Faith by itself, if not accompanied by action, is dead" (Jas. 2:13).

§9 Israel More Righteous Than Judah (Jer. 3:6–11)

3:6–11 / We now have a prose oracle that is set during the reign of **Josiah.** Jeremiah 1:2 indicates that Jeremiah's prophetic ministry began in Josiah's thirteenth year (626 B.C.) Since Josiah's reign came to a close with his death on the battlefield in 609 B.C., this oracle should be dated between these two dates. The oracles are not in chronological order so we cannot use this rare dating to fix the time of the surrounding oracles. Josiah was the first king to rule during Jeremiah's ministry, and he was a good one (see Introduction). Jeremiah's message here would have supported Josiah's attempt to clean up the religious practices of his people.

Once again, we see sexual imagery used to condemn Judah. In this case, the previous example of the northern kingdom (**Israel**) is cited. Earlier, they had turned against the Lord, and he responded by allowing the Assyrians to defeat them. In the language of the oracle, he divorced them. But instead of learning from this vivid historical example, Judah continued to behave similarly. Indeed, Judah was more **unfaithful** than Israel. The prophet Ezekiel radically develops this idea in his two allegories of the unfaithful sisters, Israel and Judah (Ezek. 16 and 23).

Additional Notes §9

3:1 / The verb rendered **return** (*shub*) here is also the word for repentance and will be used throughout the next few oracles.

3:2 / **Barren heights** may more precisely be translated caravan roads, the place where traders traveled from one locale to another, cf. Holladay, *Jeremiah* 1, p. 36. Most roads were located on ridge routes in Israel. There may be further allusion to the fact that Canaanite religious sites were located on high places (see Lundbom, *Jeremiah 1–20*, p. 302).

§10 Future Restoration (Jer. 3:12–4:4)

In the context of the preceding oracle, in which faithless Israel is said to be more righteous than Judah, it is possible that this oracle directed toward the north was intended for those northerners who were already exiled decades before by Assyria. However, they may also be directed toward all the people of God, including those who will be exiled in the future. Among other problems is the issue of dating these individual oracles. In any case, this oracle injects a note of hope that anticipates the full-blown promise of restoration found in chapters 30–33.

3:12–18 / The oracle begins with a call to **faithless Israel** that they **return** to God. As we have seen in 3:1, this verb can also be translated "repent." God is calling for his people to make a full turn from their guilty ways toward him. He then affirms his mercy toward them and the fact that his anger, fueled by their sin, will not last forever. The key to a change in God's attitude toward his people is dependent on their recognition of their responsibility, in particular the idolatry that they have practiced in traditional Canaanite worship locations (**under every spreading tree**). A similar statement of God's unwillingness to abandon his sinful people may be found in Hosea 11:8–11, when God movingly asks, "How can I give you up, Ephraim? How can I hand you over, Israel?"

If Israel does return, then God promises restoration to some of his people. In v. 14, we have the subtle introduction of the theme of the remnant. God will take **one from a town and two from a clan.** Not everyone will survive the judgment that God's people have brought on themselves. Those who do survive will come back to **Zion,** the spiritual center of Jerusalem, and God will give them shepherds (leaders) who will shepherd them. Ezekiel 34 describes the effects of bad shepherds on the people, and also looks forward to the day when God will put a new shepherd, associated with David, over his people (34:23–24). The beginning of the fulfillment of this promise may be seen at the time of Sheshbazzar and Zerubbabel and then later Ezra and Nehemiah (see the books of Ezra and Nehemiah). The New Testament associates Jesus with both David and shepherd imagery, and surely understands that he is the ultimate fulfillment of these prophecies.

The oracle concludes with two important prophetic themes: expanding holiness and the nations' recognition of God. In the early history of Israel, the most potent symbol of God's presence was the **ark of the covenant** (see Additional Notes). However, its loss will be insignificant in the future because all of Jerusalem will be holy. It is interesting to note that by the end of the book of Nehemiah, after the temple and the walls of Jerusalem are rebuilt, the whole city is called "holy" (Neh. 11:1). Zechariah 14 too ends with the vision of the entire city of Jerusalem pervaded by God's presence and holiness. Accordingly, the nations recognize God's glory and journey to Jerusalem to be in God's presence (Jer. 3:17). The picture of the nations gathering in Jerusalem to worship the Lord is found elsewhere in prophets (Isa. 2:2–4; 56:6–7; Jer. 12:15–16; 16:19; Mic. 4:1–3; Zech. 2:11; 8:2—23; 14:16–17). In the New Testament, the fact that the Gentiles were turning to Christ was surely thought to be a fulfillment of this Old Testament anticipation.

3:19–4:4 / This section begins with God's desire for intimate relationship with his people as well as a remembrance of their betrayal. God had given his people a **desirable land,** namely the promised land, which today we call Palestine. Deuteronomy 32:8–9 describes how God gave each nation their **inheritance.** As in our passage, biblical authors frequently comment on the peculiar beauty and desirability of Israel's portion (Exod. 3:8, 17; Lam. 2:15; Ezek. 20:6; Dan. 11:16, 41). God intended to establish an intimate relationship with Israel. They would call him **Father** and be like sons to him. But, changing the metaphor to one that has been common in the opening oracles, they were **like a woman unfaithful to her husband.**

The people of God are then described as recognizing their guilt from the **barren heights** (see Jer. 3:2). The rest of the oracle is a dialogue between God and his repentant people. We are to understand this dialogue as an oracle of hope for future restoration. God first calls them to **return**/repent (3:22), and he will **cure** them of their incessant unfaithfulness. They respond to this call affirmatively, describing their **idolatrous** sins and pointing to the Lord as Israel's salvation. They acknowledge the life-sapping hold that the false religion of Baal (**shameful gods**) worship has had on them. God then asserts that their sincere repentance will lead to their restoration and also the blessing of the **nations** (4:1–2), the latter allusive of the Abrahamic promise of Genesis 12:1–3.

The oracle ends with an ultimatum. On the one hand, they can repent with the implication of restoration. Two metaphors of repentance are used here. One is agricultural. Their hearts are **unplowed,** therefore hard-packed, ground and filled with **thorns,** prohibitive of productive growth. He calls on them to **break up** that hard ground of their hearts. Secondly, he demands that they **circumcise** their **hearts.** Externally, they would have been circumcised in the flesh (Gen. 17:14), but this was to be an external side of an internal reality (see Additional Notes). They were to obey the covenant and its laws from the heart (see Deut. 10:16 and Jer. 9:25). The alternative was not pretty. If they did not repent, then they would feel the burning **wrath** of God.

Additional Notes §10

3:14 / The verb translated **I am your husband** is formed from the Hebrew noun that means "husband." Interestingly, this noun is *baʿal,* the well-known name of the Canaanite god Baal. It is very possible that this image of God as *baʿal* ("husband" or "lord") of Israel is deliberately chosen as a polemic against Baal worship.

3:16: The **ark of the covenant** was made of a rather simple construction design (see Exod. 25:10–22). It was essentially a relatively small box that was 3¾ feet long, 2¼ feet wide, and 2¼ feet high. It also had rings attached to the side through which were slid poles that were used to carry the ark.

While the construction design was simple, its composition was not. The poles and the box were made of precious acacia wood and both were covered with gold. At each side of the ark were to be placed gold statues of cherubim. The cherubim are especially powerful spiritual beings who served the role of protectors of God's holiness. They are at the sides of the ark with their wings outstretched and touching each other, while their heads are bowed.

The reason for their posture is that the ark is the most potent symbol of God's presence in the tabernacle. Indeed, it is seen as the footstool of his throne (1 Chr. 28:2), perhaps even occasionally as the throne itself (Jer. 3:16–17). God the king sits in his earthly house on his throne and the cherubim whose wings support him look to the ground to shield their gaze from the radiance of his glory.

4:4 / Circumcision was established as a ritual in Genesis 17. It was a sign of the covenant between Abraham's descendants and God. Evidence indicates that other nations practiced different forms of circumcision, but the Bible gives it a new theological meaning. It was, as baptism is today, the outward sign of an inward spiritual reality. However, as with such external signs, they may, as here, be out of keeping with the realities of the heart and practice. In other words, God's people were betraying their covenantal commitments symbolized by the physical cutting of their foreskin. The call to **circumcise** the **heart** is a call to make inward what is already marked on their bodies, that is, covenantal faithfulness and obedience.

§11 A Lion from the North (Jer. 4:5–10)

4:5–6 / The prophet announces future judgment by insisting that warnings of the impending attack be issued. Other prophets also utilized the call to battle to warn of impending judgment (see Nah. 2:1). He evokes a sense of urgency when he urges that the **trumpet** be sounded and a **signal** be raised. These were signs of an attack (see Amos 3:6). Warning of an attack from the **north** first appeared in 1:13-14 (see commentary and notes).

4:7–8 / The threat is described as a **lion** coming out of his **lair** in order to destroy the land. The lion is a frequently used metaphor for an enemy, which we have already encountered in Jeremiah 2:15 (see commentary). Lions are ruthless and violent, and indeed this one is called a **destroyer of nations,** an apt description of an empire builder like Nebuchadnezzar who will ultimately destroy Jerusalem. However, there is a fuzzy boundary between the language describing the Lord as the one who will destroy Jerusalem and his unwitting human agents, so much so that it may be God, the Divine Warrior coming to punish with **fierce anger,** who is pictured as the destroying lion. The response of God's people should be lament, represented by the command to put on **sackcloth,** the traditional dress of one in mourning.

4:9–10 / The leaders—**prophets, priests,** and **king**—have been smug in their self-confidence. As Jeremiah will repeatedly point out, these leaders of the people above all others resist Jeremiah's message that judgment is coming because of the people's guilt. Therefore when destruction does arrive they will be the first to **lose heart, be horrified,** and **be appalled.** It will take them by utter surprise. False prophets fueled their previous self-confidence with a message of **peace** (6:14; 14:13; 23:16–17). What is interesting and troubling is that Jeremiah attributes this message of peace to the Lord himself. He says that God **deceived** the people through this message of peace. Perhaps we are to seek some understanding of this through 1 Kings 22, where we see that God does indeed put "a lying spirit in the mouth of the prophets" (v. 23) at the time of wicked king Ahab. This did not make Ahab do evil, but it certainly sealed his punishment. God did not leave Ahab without a witness to the truth in the person of Micaiah, but Ahab's sinful heart led him to believe the lying prophets from the Lord rather than the true prophet. Jeremiah, of course, plays the role of Micaiah in the present text. In any case, the leaders of the people believe that peace is in their future even when disaster is on the horizon (**the sword at our throats**).

Additional Notes §11

4:5–6 / The **trumpet** (*shofar*) was actually a ram's horn that was used as an instrument. The **signal** (*nes*) was likely some kind of battle flag or pennant around which troops would rally. Both the ram's horn and the battle flag were signals that a battle was soon to break out.

§12 Scorching Wind (Jer. 4:11–18)

4:11–18 / This oracle, consisting of a short prose introduction and then a poem, is directed toward God's **people** and specifically **Jerusalem.** The first metaphor is a **scorching wind.** The language describes the sirocco, "a hot 'east wind' off the desert, very strong, and often leaving destruction in its wake. The temperature rises sharply just before the wind reaches gale force, when it then clouds the atmosphere with fine sand, greatly reducing visibility" (Lundbom, *Jeremiah 1–20,* p. 343). The wind comes from the **barren heights,** the place earlier associated with the adulterous/idolatrous activities of God's people (Jer. 3:2, 21). The image is probably of an army moving with great speed and destructive force toward Jerusalem. However, we should not press the imagery to insist that this indicates an attack from the east. The sirocco's destructive force is the point of the analogy, not its direction. When the looming attack is mentioned explicitly, the direction is always said to be from the north. This wind clearly represents God's judgment. The other possibilities, such as refinement or chastisement (under the images of winnowing and cleansing), are explicitly ruled out.

The poetic portion of the oracle is an event-vision that reports the future attack as if it is happening in the present (Nah. 2:3–10 is another example). It begins by saying, **He advances like the clouds.** Who is the unnamed he? Again, we cannot answer this question if we ask concerning the prophet's conscious intention, for we are not certain when to date this oracle. He may not have known the identity of the people God was going to send against his people. But in historical retrospect, we know it was the Babylonians. The question goes even deeper, however, since we are not certain whether any human enemy is being described here. The imagery of this oracle suggests that God is in mind here. He is the one whose advance is elsewhere pictured on a cloud chariot (Ps. 18:7–15; 68:33; 104:3; Nah. 1:3) or a whirlwind (Job 38:1, but see Isa. 5:28 for a similar description of a human enemy).

Perhaps the best understanding is that it is God, the Divine Warrior, leading the tool of his judgment, the Babylonians, against his people. This would explain the plurals (**chariots/horses**).

The northern origin of this attack is made clear in v. 15. The voice proclaiming disaster comes from **Dan** (Tell el-Qadi), a site in the northernmost reaches of Israel. In the second colon the voice is from the **hills of Ephraim,** north of Jerusalem, but closer to it. The army is closing in on Jerusalem. The reason for this attack is clear from 4:18. **Your own conduct and actions have brought this upon you.** Jeremiah leaves the people in no doubt that it is their sin that leads to their destruction. It is a judgment that **pierces to the heart.**

However, embedded within the oracle, is a call to repentance. Verse 14 demands that the people **wash** their hearts of evil (see also Ps. 51:7; Jer. 2:22). This implies a note of conditionality to the prophecy at this stage, even though the oracle does not imply what would happen if they did repent.

§13 My Anguish (Jer. 4:19–22)

4:19–22 / We hear the piercing voice of a tormented speaker in 4:18. He yells out his **anguish** in pain. The speaker has not been introduced, though this passage (at least through v. 21) is taken by most to be the first of Jeremiah's laments (or confessions). The cry seems human as it describes the pounding of his **heart.** It bemoans the destruction that God himself is intentionally loosing among his people (v. 21). However, verse 22 may only be understood as a divine utterance. It is probably best, therefore, to understand these verses as the prophet's lament followed by an answer from God, but the ambiguity does remind us of the close connection between God and his spokesperson. Indeed, God was torn by what he states is the necessity of the impending judgment. (For a similar statement, see Hos. 11:8–11.)

The anguish is clearly evoked by the coming destruction. He describes the future as if it is the present when he hears **the sound of the trumpet,** even the **battle cry.** He envisions the destruction of the **tents.** Notice too that the speaker identifies with the people as he states "my tents."

Though it is horrible, there is a reason for the disaster to come. The people are **fools.** They have turned from God. They are God's children, to be sure, but they are ignorant children who have forgotten who their true father is. They are not only apostates, but they are also immoral. Through practice, they have gotten very good at **evil.**

Additional Notes §13

4:19 / **my anguish, my anguish** is literally, "my innards, my innards." The idea that his anxiety has physical ramifications permeates this verse. It was like getting kicked in the stomach.

§14 Chaos Will Reign (Jer. 4:23–28)

4:23–26 / Jeremiah uses creation language to describe the coming destruction. As a matter of fact, he describes it as a reversal of creation. Genesis 1:2 says that God created the *tohu wabohu,* that is, **formless and empty** matter. God then took this unformed blob and shaped the creation out of it. Sin reverses the order of creation and so God basically says that he is going back to square one. This thought is carried further when he says that the **light** (presumably the sun, moon, and stars created on the fourth day) of heaven is going to go out. Furthermore, the **mountains,** which are the height of stability in the creation, will actually begin **quaking** and **swaying.** This is a literary theme that occurs in a number of places in Scripture and is associated with the appearance of the Divine Warrior (Nah. 1:5), God, who comes to punish. Turning to the animate part of creation, we see that **people** and birds also are gone. The **fruitful land** turns into a **desert.** "The dissolution of Judah is itself an undoing of creation" (Goldingay, *Old Testament Theology, Volume 2: Israel's Faith,* p. 247).

4:27–28 / In verse 27, we find the divine declaration that God will punish, but **not completely.** This appears to be a subtle suggestion of the remnant motif, that is, the idea that God will leave some to continue the line of the promised people. The reference to the darkening of the skies is also a well-attested motif associated with the judgment of God. Among many other places, we witness this motif in Zechariah 14:6, "On that day there will be no light, no cold or frost." As Jesus looks forward to his apocalyptic return, he quotes Isaiah 13:10; 34:4: "the sun will be darkened, and the moon will not give its light; the stars will fall from the sky, and the heavenly bodies will be shaken" (see Mark 13:24–25 and parallels).

God says he will not **relent,** that is, change his mind. God is not above relenting. He will change his mind in the light of repentance. When the Ninevites repent in the book of Jonah, God relents and allows them to live. Jonah sourly accuses God "I knew you are a gracious and compassionate God, slow to anger and abounding in love, a God who relents from sending calamity" (Jonah 4:3). However, here the doom of God's people is sealed.

§15 The Devastated One (Jer. 4:29–31)

The last three verses of the chapter have a loose thematic connection, but poetically cohere well as a short three-stanza poem. It has somewhat diverse imagery, but it is action packed.

4:29–31 / The passage opens with the sound of **horsemen and archers** and a reaction of the inhabitants of the attacked **towns.** They flee the inhabited areas and, as was typical in such situations, seek hiding places in the rough terrain in the nearby countryside. **Rocks** likely refers to nearby cliffs and wadi walls, which had crevices and caves that provided suitable hiding places.

Verse 30 then addresses the people of God as the **devastated one,** under the figure of a woman who is extravagantly dressed. The contrast is striking. She is devastated but dressed in **scarlet** (the most expensive dye in antiquity), ornamented in **gold** jewelry, and wearing eye makeup (**paint**). She is dressed to seduce. She wants a lover but her **lovers despise her** and indeed want to kill her. Similar to Ezekiel 16 and 23, the lovers of God's people stand for those nations (Egypt) to which they looked for help against their attackers, when they should have turned to God, the true husband of God's people, for help (Jer. 2:1–3).

Finally, the imagery changes slightly again. God's people are still pictured as a woman, but instead of an unsuccessful seductress, they are a **woman in labor** (v. 31). This woman, though, will give birth to death. As she passes out of existence, she cries out **"my life is given over to murderers,"** namely those who are attacking her, God's tool of judgment.

Additional Notes §15

4:30 / The description of the woman (**devastated one**), who represents the people of God, is taken by many as a whore (Thompson,

The Book of Jeremiah, p. 232). Walton, Matthews, and Chavalas (*IVPBBCOT,* p. 646) dispute this, suggesting that the items of female adornment described in the passage were "not specifically associated with prostitutes but were simply used when a woman wished to be her most attractive." I believe the latter view fails to read the passage in context. She has lovers and already implied in Jeremiah is the idea that God is her husband. If she is not a whore, she is certainly an adulteress.

§16 Poor and Great, All of Jerusalem Depraved (Jer. 5:1–9)

This oracle is a dialogue between Yahweh and Jeremiah. Yahweh first challenges Jeremiah to go out into Jerusalem to discover a single righteous person (5:1–2). Jeremiah then argues that the good people are among the leaders, not the poor who are in the streets. He is quickly disillusioned (5:3–6), and finally, on this basis, God proclaims that his coming judgment is just (5:7–9).

5:1–2 / The challenge goes out, presumably to Jeremiah in the light of the response in verses 3–6, to find a righteous person, that is one **who deals honestly and seeks the truth.** If such a person can be found, then God says he will **forgive** the whole city. Such a statement is reminiscent of Abraham's bartering with God over the fate of Sodom and Gomorrah in Genesis 18. Indeed, there the agreement ended at ten non-sinners. If ten righteous people could be found in those cities, then God would spare it. However, for his beloved Jerusalem all that was needed was for Jeremiah to find **one person.** Verse 2 suggests that though people may sound like they follow Yahweh, sealing their agreements with an oath (**As surely as the LORD lives**), they really follow other gods and, thus, swear **falsely.** The second colon of the verse could be translated "they are swearing by The Lie," with the Lie standing for Baal himself. God's speech here is hyperbolic. Jeremiah and his circle are those who are on the Lord's side in this struggle. It does, however, remind us of Paul's citation of the Psalms when he states:

> There is no one righteous, not even one;
> there is no one who understands,
> no one who seeks God. (Rom. 3:10b–11)

5:3–6 / A voice, we presume it to be Jeremiah's, responds to Yahweh's challenge. It opens with a concession that, though God had tried to correct their sinful behavior, they nonetheless **refused to repent.** Then the prophet reflects that this might just characterize the **poor,** those who are not in leadership positions, who are ignorant. He turns his attention then to the leaders. But again, he discovers that they also have abandoned the Lord and his ways. The result is that they will be the recipients of God's judgment. 5:6 describes God's judgment as an attack by animal predators, the **lion,** the **wolf,** and the **leopard.**

5:7–9 / Finally, we hear God's voice again. This time he announces the appropriateness of his punishment. Since they are so evil, they are well-deserving of the judgment. They have given God no grounds to offer his forgiveness. God has given them everything they could possibly need, but they have committed idolatry by worshiping other gods. This latter is represented by the image of adultery again (see 3:6–10). Another animal image is used for their sin. God's people are like a **lusty stallion, each neighing for another man's wife.** The rhetorical questions lead the reader of these words to affirm God's decision to judge his people.

§17 Destroy the Vineyard (Jer. 5:10–13)

5:10–12 / The Lord speaks, first commanding an unspecified addressee to **ravage** the **vineyards,** but not completely. Jerusalem was surrounded by vineyards; terraces encircled the hills. These were mainstays of Judah's agricultural bounty. To destroy the vineyards was an economic and psychological blow against God's people. The prophecy almost certainly is appealing to a figurative meaning of vineyard as well. Israel is God's vineyard (Isa. 5). To ravage the vineyard is to ravage the people. However, God tells the destroyers **not to destroy them completely.** Here we have another reference to the remnant theme (see 3:12–18; 4:27–28). God's people will not be totally eradicated in this judgment.

5:13 / We likely hear Jeremiah's voice in this verse responding to the divine oracle. He informs the Lord that the people are not paying attention to the message of coming judgment. Why? Because other voices are saying that **no harm** will come to them. Who are these other voices? We hit on yet another major theme in the book, false prophets. Later (i.e., Jer. 28), we will have an up-close-and-personal encounter with one such prophet, Hananiah. Here Jeremiah simply says that they speak, but their words are empty. They are wind.

§18 Fire to the Wood (Jer. 5:14–19)

5:14 / The Lord **God of Hosts** is God's battle name. He speaks to Jeremiah and says that he will make Jeremiah's words a **fire** that will set the people, like **wood,** on fire. His message will consume them with its ferocity.

5:15–17 / The Lord continues by announcing the onslaught of a **distant, ancient,** and **enduring** nation. Again, we do not know for sure when in Jeremiah's life this particular oracle was uttered or what the conscious identification at that time was. In historical retrospect, we can clearly see that this language anticipates the coming of the Babylonians, a nation that fits this description very well. They spoke Aramaic and wrote in Akkadian, the latter strange to all but the most educated Hebrews. But more to the point, they were a powerful military force. They dealt death, so that the idea that their **quivers** were **like an open grave** was apt. Like locusts they will sweep in and **devour** crops, and people; they will devastate the cities.

5:18–19 / Again (see 5:10, also 4:27), we hear from God that the judgment to come would not involve a complete destruction of the people of God, though this will not be fully developed until later (Jer. 30–33). The oracle also anticipates the obvious question that will follow the judgment: **Why has the LORD our God done all this to us?** After all, the people likely grew up learning of their special relationship with Yahweh and the judgment will throw that relationship into question. The answer is clear and emphatic. They suffer because they betrayed God by worshiping other gods. They have broken the covenant. Since they have worshiped **foreign god**s, they will now serve **foreigners** in a strange land.

§19 A Foolish and Senseless People (Jer. 5:20–31)

This section may be further divided and may actually contain more than one oracle. Verses 20–25 address the foolish and senseless people who do not fear the Lord in spite of his great power as manifested particularly at creation. Verses 26–29 are a reflection on the great sin of the people that deserve the judgment that is coming. Finally, verses 30–31 express shock at the sinful behavior of prophets and priests and how the people readily accept such behavior. The function of the entire section is to justify the horrible fate that will soon befall the people of God.

5:20–25 / These verses are specifically addressed to the **house of Jacob** (used only one other place in Jeremiah [2:4], but frequently in Isaiah [2:5, 6; 8:17; 10:20]). One would think this is a reference to the whole nation, since Jacob is another name for Israel. However, this reference is sharpened in the second colon by the naming of **Judah,** a reference to the remaining southern part of the kingdom. The ignorance of God's people is described as unseeing **eyes** and unhearing **ears.** Interestingly the Psalms use this language to describe the idols (Ps. 115:6; 135:17).

God then questions the people as to their lack of **fear** for him. Perhaps we are to see here the influence of the wisdom tradition with its frequent refrain of "the fear of the Lord is the beginning of knowledge/wisdom" (Job 28:28; Prov. 1:7, 29; 2:5; 3:7; 8:13; 9:10; 10:27; 14:2, 26, 27; 15:6, 33; 16:6; 19:23; 22:4; 23:17; 24:21; Eccl. 12:13). Jeremiah denounces the people since they do not treat the Lord with the proper awe. Jeremiah now invokes creation themes in order to support this idea. God is the one who bounded the sea with the **sand** in order to make the dry land. The sea represents the power of chaos, but God firmly pushes back chaos to allow the order of creation to exist. Further, God is the provider of the life-giving **rains** (v. 24). This reference is particularly germane, since the people of God are tempted to worship a god like Baal who is a storm deity. Their **sins** have deprived them of **good,** like the crops.

5:26–29 / God through Jeremiah now expands upon the sins of the people by means of the metaphor of a fowler (**men who snare birds**). **Wicked men** exist among God's people who catch people in their **traps** as a fowler traps birds. They use **deceit,** just as bird traps, hidden in the environment, catch birds unaware. Those caught are killed and used for the profit of the fowler. These wicked men have become very **rich and powerful** through their evil behavior. In particular, sins against the **fatherless** and the **poor** are listed as especially egregious. These two classes of people were powerless in the society and were dependent on those who possessed power to protect them. God's law insisted that Israel protect the rights of orphans (Exod. 22:22–24; Deut. 10:18; 24:17, 19, 20, 21; 27:19). It also required assistance for the poor (Exod. 22:25–27; 23:6, 11; Deut. 15:11). These are offenses against God himself, and they justify his judgment. Chillingly, he concludes his description of the sins of the people with a rhetorical question: **Should I not avenge myself on such a nation as this?**

5:30–31 / The chapter ends with a special focus on the religious leaders, the **prophets** and the **priests,** and their horrible effect on the people. The prophets are only supposed to give messages that come from the Lord, but they **prophesy lies.** According to the Mosaic law, they deserve death (Deut. 18:14–22). The priests are the "servants" of Yahweh. They have no authority in and of themselves. However, Jeremiah tells us that these priests **rule by their own authority.** They are guilty because prophets and priests were responsible to lead the people to God. However, the **people** themselves are not guiltless. They are not unwilling subjects; rather **they love it this way.** Jeremiah leaves them with a question at the end of this oracle: **But what will you do in the end?** How will they respond? This may inject a note of conditionality into the oracle. Or it may be asking what will these self-satisfied sinners do when the end (the judgment) actually comes.

Additional Notes §19

5:24 / The **autumn and spring rains** (also known as the early and late rains) bring life-bringing waters to Israel. The rainy season begins in October-November and concludes in April. While Israelites were tempted to attribute these rains to Baal, Jeremiah rightly attributes their origin to God himself.

§20 *Jerusalem Attacked! (Jer. 6:1–8)*

The oracles in chapter six continue the difficulty of distinguishing individual oracles. Fortunately, the major effect on the reader is not dependent on proper division of the text or accurate dating of the original setting of the oracles. A further difficulty is determining who is speaking. Subtle clues indicate whether it is Jeremiah or God. This too, however, is not a major obstacle to understanding the message, since Jeremiah, after all, is Yahweh's spokesperson.

We take 6:1–8 as the first oracle and here Jeremiah employs an event-vision to describe the future judgment of God on his people. An event-vision describes a future occurrence as if it were a present event. See also 4:11–18.

6:1–3 / The call goes out to the **people of Benjamin** to get out of Jerusalem. The following context makes it clear that they **flee** from the capital because of an invading army. The invading army is not identified in the passage and may not have been known by Jeremiah for certain at the time the oracle was given, but later events revealed that it was the Babylonians under Nebuchadnezzar.

The call to flee the city extends to the south as we know from the warning signals that are coming from **Tekoa** and **Beth Hakkerem.** Tekoa is a small town to the south of Jerusalem, a bit beyond Bethlehem, less than a day's walk from the capital (ca. 10 miles). Beth Hakkerem is not located with certainty. The name of the city means "House of the Vineyard." The hills surrounding Jerusalem were terraced with vineyards. Even today, grapes are grown and wine is produced in the area south of Jerusalem.

Two different types of warning signal are mentioned. The trumpet, more precisely the "ram's horn," is associated with Tekoa. The NIV translation of the alarm associated with Beth Hakkerem (**raise the signal**) sounds like it might be a flag, but perhaps a fuller translation would be "raise up a smoke signal."

The enemy comes from the **north,** again a description that fits well with the Babylonian invasion. The mention of Tekoa and Beth Hakkerem to the south may be because that is the direction the residents of Jerusalem flee or because the Babylonian army circled the city and took the surrounding towns first.

The object of judgment is called the **Daughter of Zion** and described in feminine terms as **beautiful** and **delicate.** The contrast between this description and God's actions against it show the horror of the situation. He judges his beloved daughter for her sins.

In verse 3 Jeremiah employs the imagery of **shepherds** to describe the invasion. The shepherd was a natural figure of speech for the leaders of people both in Israel and in the surrounding nations. Pitching **tents** suggests a siege on the city as the idea of each **tending his own portion** uses the shepherd image to describe how the invading army will take over the surrounding agricultural and pastoral resources in order to supply their own needs during the siege.

6:4–5 / These verses are a quotation from the camp of the attackers. We can tell that it is a quote of the enemy rather than the besieged city because the objects of their attack are the city's **fortresses.** They are anxious to get started in their invasion, so much so that when they cannot get underway by **noon,** they attack during dark.

6:6–8 / God tells the attacking army to **cut down the trees** in order to build **siege ramps.** In an assault against the walls of an ancient Near Eastern city like Jerusalem, there were three methods: scale it with ladders and siege ramps, tunnel under it, and collapse it by undermining the wall's foundation. Here, we have reference to the first.

God then justifies his encouragement of the enemy by connecting its destruction with his judgment and his judgment with their oppression. Verse 7 expands on the theme of Jerusalem's evil. It overflows from the city like a **well** overflows with water.

This oracle ends with a warning from God that suggests that this may be a conditional oracle. He has not yet turned away from Jerusalem, but will do so soon unless there is a change of heart. Subsequent events make it clear that they did not respond to God's appeal for repentance.

Additional Notes §20

6:1 / It is unclear exactly to whom the **people of Benjamin refer**. Benjamin was the tribe to the immediate north of Jerusalem. Jerusalem was actually captured by David after the tribal boundaries were already set, and like Washington D.C., a city with no direct connection to a state, became a capital that had no strict tribal allegiance. Even so, of all the tribes Jerusalem was most closely aligned with Judah. However, it may be that a number of Benjaminites lived in Jerusalem. Or it may be that Anathoth, Jeremiah's home village, was located in Benjamin (see 1:1).

6:4 / The translation of the command **prepare for war** obscures an important aspect of the verb. It comes from the root *qdsh,* which means "to be set apart (as holy)" or "to sanctify" or "to consecrate." In other words, it refers to the religious rituals that are associated with the waging of warfare in the Near East. In historical reality, the Babylonians would have dedicated their military activities to Marduk and the other Babylonian deities, but perhaps the expression intends to remind us that it is the true God Yahweh who is waging holy war against his own people here.

§21 The Gleaning of Israel (Jer. 6:9–15)

We cannot be dogmatic about the division of this unit. We take our cue from the messenger formulas in verses 9 and 16 and by the general coherence of the resulting passage in verses 9–15. However, it is not always true that the messenger formula stands at the beginning of a single oracle. Question also arises concerning the speaker(s) of this oracle. From the content of the speech it appears that God begins speaking in verse 9, then Jeremiah in verses 10–11a. God finishes the oracle (vv. 11b–15).

6:9 / Presumably, God speaks in the first verse of the oracle, at least if we follow the clue of the messenger formula (**this is what the LORD Almighty says**). It is equally unclear who is being asked to **glean** Israel. Is it Jeremiah? More likely perhaps it is the foe from the north. This is additionally complicated by the third person reference followed by the second person reference. In any case, the gleaning metaphor is absolutely clear. The people of God were often likened to a vine or a vineyard (Isa. 5:1–2; Ps. 80:9–10; Gen. 49:11–12, 22). Destroying the vineyard is a frequent motif in the prophets. As Jeremiah 2:21 already has indicated, the vineyard has gone bad. Therefore, God will destroy the vineyard, already indicated in Jeremiah 5:10. In 5:10, however, God commanded that the vineyard not be completely destroyed. Here we find a more radical expression of judgment. The tool of God's judgment is here seen as the gleaner (**one gathering grapes**) who passes his hand over the vine again to knock *all* the grapes off the vine.

6:10–11a / As mentioned above, we understand these verses to be Jeremiah's words to God. He objects that no one will listen to him. **Their ears are closed** (see Additional Notes). However, even though they do not listen, he **cannot hold it in** because he is filled with God's wrath.

6:11b–12 / In response to Jeremiah's objection that no one will listen to him, God tells the prophet to take his pent up anger and pour it out on everyone. He names **children, young men, husband and wife,** and **the old**—everyone will feel the consequences of God's anger. Their property (**houses, fields**) and their **wives** will be turned over to **others,** a reference to the attackers.

6:13–15 / That everyone is culpable is indicated by the expression **from the least to the greatest.** In particular, however, the religious leaders (**prophets and priests**) are guilty. They are telling everyone that the problem is superficial. Unlike Jeremiah who warns of doom to come with the hope, at least initially, that they will repent, the other religious leaders are saying that there is peace **when there is no peace.** This message may sound pleasant and reassuring, but it keeps them from addressing their sins and thus avoiding the ultimate anger of God. They do not feel any shame for their **loathsome conduct** of misleading the people. Thus, they too will feel the anger of God's judgment.

Additional Notes §21

6:10: The NIV rather banally translates the third colon of v. 10 as **their ears are closed.** The Hebrew has the rich metaphor: "their ear has foreskin." In other words, they have uncircumcised ears. Circumcision is the ritual of cutting away the foreskin of the penis and was a sign of the Abrahamic covenant (Gen. 17:9–14). To be circumcised indicated one who was in covenant with God, and to have a foreskin meant to be outside of the covenant. Thus, we can see that the image of ears with foreskin means more than simply that they do not pay attention to God, it means that they are unclean, outside of the covenant.

§22 Refusal to Walk on the Ancient Paths (Jer. 6:16–21)

6:16–21 / After the messenger formula, the oracle evokes the metaphor of the path. God urges the people to find the **ancient paths,** which are identical with the **good way,** and then he urges them to **walk in it.** Here, as elsewhere in Scripture (notably Prov. 1–9), the image of the path or way or road represents life. There are multiple roads the journey of life can take, but the ancient/good path is the one that conforms to God's desire for the nation. Here is where they will find rest.

They are at the **crossroads** and are called upon to make a decision. The people's response is quick and to the point. They utterly refuse. With that, God says he set up **watchmen,** an obvious reference to the prophets (see use of this metaphor in Ezek. 3:17; 33:1–9). When they see trouble, they are to blow the **trumpet** (ram's horn) as a signal.

God then calls on the **nations** and the **earth** to play the role of covenant **witness** to the fairness of God's coming judgment. They are getting punished because they have rejected the law of the covenant (**my law**). As a result, the curses of the covenant are coming into effect.

Verse 20 assumes that God's people are still offering **incense** and **sacrifices** to God, but apparently, as will be emphasized in the temple sermon of the next chapter, without any real heartfelt worship. After all, if they really did love the Lord, they would demonstrate it by obeying his law. As a result, God will bring his judgment (**obstacles**) on the people (v. 21).

Additional Notes §22

6:16–21 / Y. Hoffman ("'Isn't the Bride Too Beautiful?' The Case of Jeremiah 6:16–21," *JSOT* 64 [1994], pp. 103–20) presents an odd argument in favor of seeing this oracle as not from Jeremiah. The heart of his point is that there are too many typical Jeremiah sayings. It is too like Jeremiah to be Jeremiah. Such a view contravenes itself.

6:20 / Statements like this verse (see also Ps. 40:6–8; Mic. 6:6–8) have been used to drive a wedge between the prophets and the priests. The context makes it clear that the prophets, especially one with a priestly background like Jeremiah, did not oppose the sacrificial cult, but rather exposed the superficial nature of the contemporary practice.

§23 *Attack from the North (Jer. 6:22–26)*

6:22–23 / Yet another messenger formula introduces an oracle that draws the people's attention to the northern enemy first mentioned in the second of two opening visions (1:13–17, compare 3:18; 10:22; 16:15; 23:8; 31:8; 46:10; 50:9). This **army** from the **north** is not specifically identified, but in the aftermath of fulfillment, it is to be associated with the Babylonians who attacked Judah from its northern boundaries.

The description of the army is fearsome. They are described as **cruel** and having **no mercy.** Intriguingly, their voice is likened to a **roaring sea.** We can understand this on a phenomenological level first. Powerful surf can generate anxiety or even fear to one near by. The crashing waves display a powerful and sometimes destructive force. In its ancient Near Eastern setting, though, there is little doubt but that the oracle exploits a mythological allusion here. The sea was representative of the supernatural forces of chaos. The Babylonians picture the anti-creation forces in the cosmos as personified sea (Tiamat), as did the Canaanites (Yam and Lotan = Leviathan). Other places in biblical literature also associate destructive and evil forces to a chaotic sea (Isa. 5:30; 17:12; compare Ps. 46; Dan. 7:1–9). Their object of attack is the **Daughter of Zion,** God's people living in Judah. See Jer. 50:41–43 for a similar oracle delivered against Babylon.

6:24–26 / These verses now describe the reaction of God's people to the on-coming army. In a word, they are paralyzed with fear. Their **hands hang limp,** an expression of utter terror and powerlessness. Their fear has the physical effect equivalent to **a woman in labor.** The image of the pain of a woman giving birth is frequently attached to the reaction to God's judgment in Isaiah (21:2–3; 26:16–21; 66:7–14), Jeremiah (13:21; 22:23; 30:6; 49:24; 50:43), and Micah (4:9–10). Labor pains also draw our attention back to the curse against the woman in Genesis 3. Childbirth in antiquity was not only painful, as it is today, but also there was a much larger possibility of losing a child or the mother's life during the birth process. Thus, it is an image of great distress.

God's advice is to begin the mourning process, and to mourn as if they lost their only son. Putting on **sackcloth,** rolling in **ashes,** and **bitter wailing** are all well-known mourning customs in ancient Israel.

§24 Jeremiah, Metal Tester (Jer. 6:27–30)

6:27–30 / In this final unit of the chapter, God addresses Jeremiah as a metal **tester,** or refiner. The **people** are **the ore,** and they are to be refined to see if anything valuable is still left. In particular, this image may be based on the refining of lead to see if any silver may be found. The oracle immediately continues with God pronouncing the results. They are **hardened rebels.** Therefore, they are base metals, **bronze and iron,** described as the "dross of silver" in Ezekiel 22:17–22. As the refining continues, it is impossible to separate the **wicked** people out from the righteous and therefore they are all **rejected silver,** worthy only to be discarded.

The text does not specify the process by which Jeremiah is to accomplish his refining work. It is possible that this is done by his preaching. As Lundbom (*Jeremiah 1–20,* p. 449) puts it so well, Jeremiah refines by "preaching Yahweh's fire-laden word to a people imbued with impurity."

§25 Jeremiah's Temple Sermon (Jer. 7:1–15)

Jeremiah's temple sermon is one of his most famous speeches. The core of its message attacks those who appear religious by participating in religious ceremonies, while not backing up their apparent beliefs with ethical lives. In other words, this sermon is an attack on the hypocrites of his day. We do not know the exact time before the destruction of the temple when this sermon was delivered. However, its strong conditional tone holds out hope that God's judgment might be diverted or at least mollified, and this may be a sign that it is relatively early in Jeremiah's ministry, before the people's categorical rejection led to an unconditional message of doom. See the commentary on Jeremiah 26 for a similar but not identical message delivered at the temple precincts.

7:1–2a / These opening verses are a superscription to the temple sermon. In the first place, it affirms that Jeremiah came to the temple precinct with a divine oracle. And then there is the divine command to Jeremiah to **stand at the gate** of the temple and **proclaim** the following **message**. The temple, of course, was the primary symbol of God's presence with his people. The gate would have been a busy place, giving Jeremiah opportunity to address many people. Of course, this location would have also attracted the attention of his fellow priests, who would be none too pleased with the tone of what follows.

7:2b–3a / Jeremiah now addresses the crowds that pass in and out of the temple area. He first of all demands that they listen to the **word of the LORD.**

7:3b–8 / The prophet gets right to the point. He calls on them to change their behavior, and, if they do, then God will allow them to **live in this place.** In other words, they will be able to avoid exile. The type of behavioral change required is specified in verse 6 in terms of social justice. It implies that they have been taking advantage of those (**aliens, fatherless,** and **widows**) who have no social network to fall back on. God had a special place in his heart for the powerless, and the prophet's charge indicates that the people are neglecting them. Indeed, the accusation that the people **shed innocent blood** may imply an accusation that more than neglecting the powerless was at hand in the community. Even more, they committed idolatry by worshiping **other gods** (v. 6).

However, it appears that the people are not responding to the word of the Lord and heeding the threat of judgment that looms over their head. Indeed, from what we know about the Babylonian threat at the end of the seventh and beginning of the sixth centuries B.C., we know that the takeover of Judah was not sudden. The people had plenty of warning and reason to worry. However, instead of listening to the divine oracle, they paid attention to **deceptive words,** most likely the words of false prophets. In particular, this leads them to chant "**The temple of the LORD, the temple of the LORD, the temple of the LORD.**" It appears that they were taking solace in the superficial trappings of religion. They knew that the temple represented God's presence on earth. They then wrongly reasoned that God would let nothing happen to his earthly residence. So they took solace in the presence of the temple. As events unfold, we see that this presumption is based on a misunderstanding of God's connection with the temple. 1 Kings 8, the dedication sermon of Solomon, makes it clear that orthodox Israelite faith did not believe that God lived in this structure.

7:9–11 / This passage expands on the moral and religious offenses of the people. The list of sins includes **stealing, murder, perjury, adultery,** and worshiping **other gods.** These are direct offenses toward the heart of God's covenant law as expressed in the Ten Commandments. Nonetheless, these people still come to the temple (**the house that bears my Name**) and claim it as a refuge against outside attack. Strikingly, God accuses the people of turning his temple into a **den of robbers.** The Judean countryside was filled with caves that occasionally served as a hideout for thieves. Since the people and priests congregating at the temple were such offensive sinners, that building was analogous to a hideout or hangout for criminals. These words are memorable to a Christian audience, largely because Jesus employs them in his charge against the temple economy of his own day (Mark 11:17; Luke 19:46). The people may think that God is not aware of their activities, but he challenges them by saying, **I have been watching!** (v. 11).

7:12–15 / Those presuming they are safe because their city, Jerusalem, houses the temple should have learned their lesson from what happened at **Shiloh.** Before the temple, God's home was represented by the tabernacle, a tent-like structure that conformed to the fact that the people of God were not yet firmly established in the land. During the judgeship of Eli, while Samuel was a youth, God punished Israel by allowing the Philistines to defeat its armies at the battle of Ebenezer and capture the ark. Presumably, at this time the city of Shiloh was also destroyed (Ps. 78:60). The ark was eventually returned, but its capture and Shiloh's fate should have been an object lesson to the residents of Jerusalem at the time of Jeremiah. The presence of God's dwelling was no guarantee that a people will escape judgment if it is deserved.

Additional Notes §25

7:12 / **Shiloh** is twenty miles north of Jerusalem at a site now called Khirbet Seilun. Archaeologists explored this site in the 1920s and 1930s (Danish) and in the 1980s (Israeli). Evidence of an eleventh-century destruction may well point to the defeat of the city by the Philistines (see Lundbom, *Jeremiah 1–20,* p. 468).

§26 Do Not Pray (Jer. 7:16–20)

7:16 / One of the essential functions of the prophet was to pray for the people. Abraham was the first person titled a prophet and he was called such in the context of praying for Ahimelech's life (Gen. 20:7). Pharaoh called on Moses the prophet to intercede with the Lord on behalf of Egypt (Exod. 8:8–15, 25–32; 9:27–35; 10:16–20), and Moses pleaded for Israel after they sinned by worshiping the golden calf (32:30–34). At the transition point of his ministry, when he went from being a judge to assuming a prophetic role, Samuel told the people "far be it from me that I should sin against the **LORD** by failing to pray for you" (1 Sam. 12:23). It is because the prophets had access to the divine council chambers that they were charged with interceding for the people. Jeremiah prays for the people (18:18–20), but God tells him not to do it (see also 11:14; 14:11–12). We will see that Jeremiah's intercession for grace transforms into a prayer for their punishment.

7:17–20 / The reason why God has commanded Jeremiah to stop his prayers for the people is because of their stubborn sin, particularly the sin of idolatry. They all (**children, fathers, women**) join in the worship of the **Queen of Heaven** (see Additional Notes) and other deities. This angers God. Verse 19 is an example of an interesting rhetorical device. The answer to the first question (**am I the one they are provoking?**) is yes, but by adding the second question (**Are they not rather harming themselves, to their own shame?**) God is saying: "You think I am angry, and indeed I am, but even more are they harming and shaming themselves." With that, God again announces his intense, certain, and extensive judgment on the land of Judah.

Additional Notes §26

7:18 / The **Queen of Heaven** is a reference to a female astral deity in the pantheon of the surrounding nations. The fact that the Hebrew word **cakes** (*kawwanim*) is an Akkadian loan word (*kamanu*), and its mention in the Gilgamesh Epic (vi, 59) as offerings to Ishtar, the goddess of love, war, and sex associated with the planet Venus, suggest that there is an association between this deity and the Queen of Heaven. However, it is possible that the direct reference is to her Canaanite reflection, probably Ashtart or Asherah (see Z. Zevit, *The Religions of Ancient Israel,* pp. 541–42). See also Jer. 44:17, 18, 19, 25 where the postexilic Jewish community in Egypt continues to offer worship to this deity. The fact that such worship takes place in Egypt may indicate that there is an Egyptian equivalent.

§27 Obedience, Not Sacrifice (Jer. 7:21–29)

7:21 / The oracle begins with an interesting admonition that requires a knowledge of the sacrificial system to understand. Of the three main sacrifices, burnt offering, grain offering, and peace offering, only the **burnt offerings** were totally dedicated to God and beyond any human consumption. It was an atonement sacrifice (see Lev. 1) and, though the skin was removed, the entire animal was burned on the altar. In this verse, God says that God's people may just as well eat the burnt offering, since it is doing them no good, thanks to their sin and lack of repentance.

7:22–23 / This passage is difficult to understand, though the NIV has made things easier by helpfully adding **just** to 7:22. The Hebrew states baldly "I did not give them commands about burnt offerings and sacrifices." The NIV adds "just" because God had given Israel such commands as they came out of Egypt (so Lev. 1–7)! This rhetorical device emphasizes just how angry God is with the people. The sacrifices were not the only, or even the most important, requirement, and useless unless they are an expression of heartfelt worship of Yahweh.

7:24–29 / We observed this pattern before. The people did not obey, and God sent prophets, but the people did not listen to the prophets. Now judgment will come. The sin of the people of the generation that came out of Egypt, has only grown worse in the present generation. God forewarns Jeremiah that when the people hear his message at the temple, they will reject it. Once again, God promises to cut off his people because of their rejection of him. **Truth has perished.** They have rejected Yahweh, the truth, and pursued a lie, false gods, particularly Baal. God tells them to cut off their hair (a sign of mourning and worse, see Additional Notes) and to lament on the barren heights where they sinned (Jer. 3:2, 21).

Additional Notes §27

7:29 / The word for **hair** in this verse is not the generic term. It actually means a diadem or a sign of consecration. It is related to the verb *nazar* ("to dedicate oneself") and the concept of the Nazirite vow (Num. 6:1–21). The Nazirite vow was a way for a non-Levite to be specially consecrated in service to the Lord. By telling the Israelites to cut their "consecrated hair," Jeremiah is using a metaphor to say that Israel's special relationship with God is over.

§28 The Valley of Topheth (Jer. 7:30–34)

God now explains the extent of Judah's disgusting idolatry, bringing home the appropriateness of his judgment. For judgment against the practices performed in Topheth, see also Jeremiah 19.

7:30–31 / The Judaeans had set up idols in the temple itself and they engaged in child sacrifice at a place called **Topheth,** located in the **Valley of Ben Hinnom.** This valley was immediately to the south and west of ancient Jerusalem. We do not know for certain what the word Topheth means or where it came from, but we do know that Josiah had desecrated this place earlier during his religious reforms (2 Kgs. 23:10–11). It had been a place where the foreign god Molech was worshiped. We presume that the place was rebuilt and put into practice probably during the reign of his apostate son Jehoiakim. Jeremiah cites it as a paradigmatic example of the sin and guilt of the people. God explicitly had forbidden human sacrifice as well as the worship of Molech (Deut. 12:31; 18:10; Lev. 18:21; see also Isa. 57:5, 9; Jer. 19:5; 32:35; Ezek. 16:20–21; 20:25–26, 31; 23:37, 39).

7:32–34 / Topheth will be transformed. It will be the place of burial for those who experience God's judgment. In ancient Israel, one was buried outside of the city walls, and for those living in Jerusalem burial was frequently in the walls of the valleys, like Ben Hinnom, lying right outside the city. Verse 34 carries a common theme indicating judgment; joyful sounds, like those of **a bride and bridegroom,** will come to an end.

§29 Exposed Bones (Jer. 8:1–3)

8:1–2 / This oracle is related to the previous one in its mention of exposed corpses. The exposure of corpses was a great ignominy in ancient Israel. A proper burial was greatly desired, but the oracle envisions the disinterment of the entire population of Jerusalem. The list that is given (**kings, officials, priests, prophets, and people of Jerusalem**) moves down the hierarchy, and specifies the leadership of the people of God before referring to the common people. The leaders, who were commissioned to lead the people toward God, were instrumental in their apostasy and downfall.

They worshiped other gods rather than the true God. Jeremiah mentions the astral deities (**sun, moon, stars**). God created these heavenly bodies, but, as later articulated by Paul (Rom. 1:22–23), the Israelites had taken a bit of creation and exalted it to the position of the creator. They had gone into the presence of these astral deities in order to love, serve, follow, consult and worship them during their lives, so God will let them continue to be in their presence (**they will be exposed to the sun**) in death. Their **bones** will be placed in the presence of the sun, moon, and stars, but the result will be that their remains will deteriorate (**be like refuse,** i.e., manure).

8:3 / **Life** is associated with Yahweh; **death** with other gods. Not only did the dead and buried (vv. 1–2) prefer death to life, but so do the people who still remain (**the survivors of this evil nation**). Such an attitude is illustrated by the thinking and actions of the people who are left in the land after the destruction of Jerusalem and the assassination of Gedaliah (Jeremiah 43–44).

§30 My Stubborn People (Jer. 8:4–7)

The next oracle denigrates God's people for their foolish stubbornness. Through a series of rhetorical questions and comparisons, it emphasizes their unwillingness to restore their broken relationship with their God.

8:4–5 / The oracle begins with two rhetorical questions. When someone falls they naturally get themselves on their feet again. When someone **turns away,** presumably from the right path, they try to **return** to go in the right direction. After these rhetorical questions, the oracle challenges the people with two probing questions that begin with **Why?** Their actions make no sense. They have refused to return (repent, see Additional Notes). They would rather listen and believe **deceit** than the truth. This deceit is a reference to the message of the false prophets who are telling them that there is no coming judgment and everything is just fine.

8:6–7 / The oracle portrays God as attentive to the possibility of their repentance, but to no avail. Their lack of response dumbfounds. They are determined in their sin **like a horse charging into battle.** The animal similes continue by comparing God's people with a variety of birds (**stork, dove, swift, thrush**). Birds know the proper time for an action (**their migration**), but the people do not know that they must heed the law and recognize that their sin makes this the proper time for repentance.

Additional Notes §30

8:4 / The verb for **return** (*shub*) is also the word for repentance and suggests that idea in this and other contexts in Jeremiah.

§31 The Deceit of the Religious Leaders (Jer. 8:8–12)

It is particularly the religious leaders who are to blame for the rebellion of the people. After all, it is they—wisdom teachers, prophets, and priests—who are to lead the people toward God, but do not. The role of prophets and priests are well known to readers of the Old Testament, but the exact status of wisdom teachers (**scribes**) is not as clear. Jeremiah 18:18 will mention the three groups again and associate them with what appears to be their main function, to "counsel." They give advice, and their advice is obviously supposed to flow from the law, but this is the bone of contention in the present oracle.

8:8–10a / These verses describe the offense of the wisdom teachers or **scribes.** Here, the term **wise** is used as a professional category (see Additional Notes for 9:24). The wise were those who were to teach and preserve the **law** and were likely those who copied the manuscripts. They were the interpreters of the law. The venue in which they worked is unclear. It could have been the court, the temple, the school—or all three. But the important point is that they neglected their primary responsibility. Since they rejected the law—the word of the Lord—they have no wisdom. Their interpretations are false, thus the reference to the **lying pens of the scribes.** They deserve punishment, and what is theirs will be lost. Their **wives** will be taken by others as will their **fields.** This is an indirect reference to the coming exile, when the Babylonians will displace the people of Judah and Jerusalem from their land.

Jeremiah certainly recognized that not all scribes had betrayed the Lord. Indeed, his closest allies and supporters were from among the scribal class (Baruch, Shaphan and his family; see in particular chapter 36).

8:10b–12 / After focusing on the wisdom teachers, Jeremiah's oracle now expands to include everyone (**from the least to**

the greatest), at least every religious leader (**prophets and priests alike**). No one is motivated by love of the Lord, but rather by commercial profit. When God's people are hurting or in distress, it is precisely the prophets and priests who represent the great Physician and heal the people. When the cancer (sin) is deep, the remedy is painful but necessary. However, these physicians treat the **serious** problem of the people's sin as if it were not. They tell them **"Peace"** when war is about to break out.

These quacks should feel great **shame.** They are supposed to be healers, but they do not heal. They rather settle for gain. Accordingly, God will punish them.

§32 Gather into the Cities! (Jer. 8:13–17)

8:13–17 / Some commentators (Holladay, *Jeremiah* 1, pp. 273–86) take verse 13 as part of the previous unit, but there is a catchword that links verse 13 and 14 (*ʾasap,* "to gather") that is obscured a bit by the NIV translation (**harvest** in v. 13; **gather** in v. 14). In any case, verse 13 cites the Lord as announcing that there will be no **harvest,** so starvation will threaten. Verse 14 begins a long quote of the people (through v. 16), which begins by announcing their intention to go into the **fortified cities** presumably from the countryside. At this time only large cities like Jerusalem had defensive walls, so people from villages in the countryside would seek refuge in these cities when threatened by foreign armies. Jeremiah's own Anathoth was a village in the vicinity of Jerusalem, and its inhabitants would look for shelter behind the walls of Jerusalem. The advantage of the city was, of course, the walls that kept the enemy out, at least temporarily. The disadvantage was that there were limited supplies in the walled city and once those ran out the people had no recourse but to surrender, often to a horrible fate.

The people here recognize that their **doom** is the result of their sin. Their hopes for **peace** have been dashed as the oracle envisions the onslaught of the enemy army. This is a foe from the north as is indicated by the reference to the snorting of the enemy horses from **Dan,** the tribe settled furthest north in the nation. The foe from the north remains unnamed (see §23 for identification of this force).

The section ends with a final word from God himself. He announces that he will send **snakes** among his people. This is likely a metaphor for the human enemy that God will send among them, the Babylonians.

Additional Notes §32

8:14 / Under a siege, a city would be vitally dependent on its water supply. If it were poisoned (**poisoned water**), inaccessible, or undrinkable for any reason, that city's fate was sealed.

§33 No Balm in Gilead (Jer. 8:18–9:1)

8:18–9:1 / This lament contains words of Jeremiah, God, and the people. It all, however, bemoans Judah's fate. Jeremiah begins by confessing his heartrending grief at the suffering of his people. He hears their cries **from a land far away.** Presumably this is a reference to people in exile, but it is unclear whether this imagines a future situation or a present reality. If the latter, it would likely be a reference to those who were taken in the Babylonian intrusion of 597 B.C. However, Jeremiah's grief does not center on their deportation, but rather on their quoted statement that questions God's presence in **Zion.** Zion is the hill where the temple was located, but sometimes it refers to the entire city of Jerusalem. Their present suffering leads them to question God's presence in Zion.

God asks a question in response, **"Why have they provoked me to anger with their images, with their worthless foreign idols?"** Here is the answer to their question. Of course God is not going to make his redemptive presence known to his people in the light of the fact that they have set up false gods in his place. Immediately following this quotation of God comes another word from the people: time has passed (**harvest summer**) and rescue still has not come. Indeed, because of their sin, their sufferings would continue for years to come.

Jeremiah responds to it all. He identifies with the people. He again uses the pervasive theme of Judah as a wounded person who needs a doctor (see M. L. Brown, *Israel's Divine Healer*, pp. 191–95). He is **crushed** as they are crushed. The people need a **physician,** but there is no **balm in Gilead.** Balm "was probably the resin of the storax tree, obtained by incision on the bark of the tree" (*IVP BBCOT*, p. 650). It was used in the treatment of wounds. God's people were wounded, but there was no medicine available to treat the wound. The lament ends with Jeremiah's confession that he cannot stop weeping for those killed (9:1), presumably during the Babylonian attack, among his people. In this regard,

Jeremiah uses a vivid metaphor. He wants his head to turn into a **spring of water** with his eyes providing the spouts (**my eyes a fountain of tears**). There are not enough tears for the devastation that has come on his people.

Additional Notes §33

8:18 / This verse presents major difficulties in the Hebrew as can be witnessed by the chaotic interpretations offered by the ancient versions. The NIV takes the verse as a bicolon, but it is better taken as a tricolon (see Lundbom, *Jeremiah,* p. 530 and Holladay, *Jeremiah* 1, p. 288). One minor emendation (*ʿale* repointed to *ʿaloy*) leads to the following translation:

My cheerfulness is gone (*ʿaloy*);
grief has come on me.
My heart is sick.

9:1–26 / The Masoretic Text of the Old Testament numbers the verses in this section as 8:23–9:25. We will follow the English versification used by the NIV in what follows.

§34 The People Are Liars (Jer. 9:2–6)

9:2–6 / The division between oracles is difficult throughout this section, but is particularly hard with this passage. No two commentators seem to agree. The fact that 9:1 and 9:2 begin with the same grammatical construction (**Oh, that**) might lead us to put these two verses in the same oracle (so Lundbom, *Jeremiah 1–20*, pp. 534–39), but the tonoe of 9:2 sets it apart from what precedes. In verse 1, Jeremiah expresses his emotional devastation at the fate of his people. In verse 2 the speaker expresses disdain toward the people. The two thoughts are not utterly irreconcilable, but the latter fits in better with verses 3–6 that follow.

Another ambiguity has to do with the speaker. Does the oracle begin with Jeremiah's lament or God's or are we to understand the prophet and his God sharing the same voice? In any case, the speaker desires to be far from the people because of their sin. Their spiritual unfaithfulness is metaphorically likened, once again (2:20, 23–24; 3:1–5, etc.), to sexual infidelity. **They are all adulterers.** The expression and the thought is the same as found in Hosea 7:4, and Jeremiah may be quoting or alluding to his earlier prophetic colleague.

The next few verses focus in on one particular transgression by the people—their lying. Their lies are weapons. Indeed, their tongues are **like a bow** from which they shoot lies like arrows. A similar thought is found in Psalm 64:3–4 where the wicked person's tongue is compared to a sword and then implicitly to a bow. Even those in the most intimate of relationships must be on their guard against deception. Friends and brothers betray each other. Implicit is the message that those who betray God will also betray their closest human relations, thus undermining community.

§35 Should I Not Avenge Myself? (Jer. 9:7–11)

9:7–11 / The messenger formula (**this is what the LORD Almighty says**) likely signals a new oracle, though verse 8 continues the topic of deceitful speech. The similar topic may, however, explain why the two short oracles are found together in the final form of the book of Jeremiah.

God begins to speak, describing himself as a refiner of metals (**I will refine**). The image of refiner was used already of Jeremiah in 6:27–30. The principle here is that the people need to be tested as metal is tested to see if they are pure or not. They are impure. They are sinful. Therefore, God will refine them to remove their impurities.

The sin is again **deceit,** and as in verse 3 the tongue is described as shooting arrows that harm others. What is said sounds sweet (**each speaks cordially to his neighbor**), but behind the pleasant words is the intention to hurt. With **his heart he sets a trap.**

It is sometimes difficult to tell who is speaking here, but because of the close relationship between God and his prophet, it is not always important to differentiate. It is likely, though, that Jeremiah is the speaker of verse 10. He is the one who takes up the **lament** for the desolation and abandonment of the land, the the result of God's judgment, which took the form of an incursion of the Babylonian army.

At the end of the oracle God states a determination to destroy **Jerusalem** as well as the surrounding countryside (**Judah**). It will be made such **a heap of ruins** that wild animals like **jackals** will take up their homes there.

§36 *Why? (Jer. 9:12–16)*

9:12–16 / This prose oracle asks the question, **Why? Why** has the land been punished so thoroughly? Who is so wise to give an answer? The Lord finally gives the answer, but not because the question is difficult. They have broken the **law** and deserve the curses of the law, which are quite clearly listed in Deuteronomy 28 and elsewhere. They not only have resisted the true God, however; they have also served the **Baals,** the gods of their predecessors in the land. Their judgment is first described by the metaphor of drinking **bitter food** and **poisoned water.** The land that God gave them was a land flowing with milk and honey, but because of their sin, they will be cut off from this provision and given something horrible instead. Furthermore, they will not be allowed to stay in the land, but the Lord will **scatter** them widely as described as an explicit curse in the covenant law (Deut. 28:25, 36–37, 64–68).

Additional Notes §36

9:12 / **What man is wise enough?** The question does not presuppose a negative answer. As mentioned above, the question is not that difficult and, furthermore, may be paralleled by Hosea 14:9:

> Who is wise? He will realize these things.
> Who is discerning? He will understand them.

In other words, this is not so much a rhetorical question as a challenge.

9:14 / Baal is a Hebrew word that means "master" or "lord." It reflects a Ugaritic word (*b*ᶜ*l*) that has the same meaning, but in Ugaritic is a proper name for the most active God in the Canaanite pantheon. The plural (**Baals**) is used because there were different geographical manifestations of this God. These gods were Yahweh's chief rivals in the land for the affection of the people.

9:15 / **Bitter food** (*laʿanah*) is more specifically wormwood, which is the bitter-tasting leaf of a shrub. It was used for medicine, but would not make a pleasant diet. Wormwood also evokes mourning or expresses a sense of bitterness. For **poisoned water,** see Additional Notes for 8:14.

§37 Wail, O Women! (Jer. 9:17–22)

9:17–19 / These verses are addressed by the Lord to the wandering people of God. They advise that **wailing women,** professional mourners, be called. Why? Because disaster and death are about to arrive because God will judge them for their sins. The devastation will be so great that **eyes will overflow with tears.** They will have to leave their land because its destruction will be so great.

9:20–21 / The next section addresses the wailing **women.** They should teach their **daughters how to wail.** The cause for lament will not be short-lived but will survive to the next generation. Death will kill off not only the old, but also the **children** playing out in public.

9:22 / The oracle ends with a divine pronouncement concerning **dead bodies of men** lying in the **open field** like **cut grain.** Their bodies will not be collected and honored in burial, but will be like **refuse** (i.e., manure), fertilizing the ground. Burial was considered an important closure to one's life. It was appalling to contemplate a dead body rotting in an open field.

Additional Notes §37

9:21 / The reference to death climbing through the window may well have a mythological background. The Baal myth in Ugaritic has an episode where Baal and Kothar wa-Hasis, the craftsman god, argue over whether or not to build windows in his house. The text is broken, but he seems concerned that someone will enter his house to destroy him and his. As it turns out, Mot, whose name means Death, does sneak in and capture him in the following section. The Baal text may be read in M. D. Coogan, *Stories from Ancient Canaan* (Philadelphia: Fortress, 1978), pp. 86–115.

§38 Boast Only in the Lord and Uncircumcised of Heart (Jer. 9:23–26)

The chapter ends with two short oracles, the first poetic and the second in prose.

9:23–24 / In the New Testament Paul may be alluding to, or quoting from, this passage in Jeremiah, when he says: "Let him who boasts boast in the **LORD**" (1 Cor. 1:31, see also 2 Cor. 10:17). However, the context of the New Testament passage is different because the apostle seeks to encourage an audience *not* characterized by **riches,** power (**strength**), or **wisdom.** Jeremiah is warning those who are wise in the eyes of the world, those who have riches, and those who have power not to put their confidence in these things. Indeed, riches, power, and wisdom can easily blind people into thinking they do not need the Lord. Jeremiah addresses a complacent Judean audience who are depending on their own resources rather than on God himself.

In this passage God declares himself on the side of those possessing ethical strength—**kindness, justice,** and **righteousness**—rather than on the side of those with material wealth, power, riches, and wisdom.

9:25–26 / The final oracle of chapter 9 attacks the Judeans' presumption of safety in the sign of circumcision. We observed in Jeremiah 7 that the people presumed on the temple as a sign of God's presence and blessing. Here the prophet uncovers their confidence in circumcision for blessing. Circumcision was established in Genesis 17, at the time of Abraham, as a sign of the covenant. It marked them as God's people. Though they did not act like God's people by obedience, they felt that God would still carry through on his part of the promise to take care of them.

Jeremiah here uncovers their misunderstanding of what it means to be circumcised with a comparison to the circumcision practices of the surrounding nations (see Additional Notes below). Most of the surrounding nations, including those listed in verse 26—

Egypt, Judah, Edom, Ammon, Moab, and all who live in the desert in distant places—practiced some form of circumcision. The shock value for Jeremiah's Judean audience was that they were listed with these pagan nations (and not even in a prominent position). They are being compared with those who are both **circumcised in the foreskin** (v. 25) and also **uncircumcised** (v. 26). The people of God may have practiced complete circumcision, but they were not really circumcised because it was not reflected in their life and behavior.

Additional Notes §38

9:23–24 / For the relationship between Jeremiah and 1 Corinthians, see G. R. O'Day, "Jeremiah 9:22–23 and 1 Corinthians 1:26–31: A Study in Intertextuality," *JBL* 109 (1990), pp. 259–67. H. H. Drake Williams III ("Of Rags and Riches: The Benefits of Hearing Jeremiah 9:23–24 within James 1:9–11," *Tyndale Bulletin* 53 [2002], pp. 273–82) points out that James 1:9–11 is dependent on the Jeremiah passage and that this helps the reader of James to identify the rich as Christian and the boast in Jeremiah as heroic.

9:24 / Jeremiah's use of **wise man** (*hakam*) is different than that in the book of Proverbs. In the latter, wisdom is integrally associated with righteousness and thus an unmitigated positive category. The only true wisdom is a wisdom bequeathed by God himself (Prov. 1:7). However, Jeremiah knows of wise men whose purposes are at odds with God (Jer. 18:18). Whether he uses this term in a purely professional sense is a matter of debate. The safest way to understand the expression here is to think of these people as those who are wise in their own eyes.

9:25–26 / This passage has been debated through the centuries. The difficulty has to do primarily with what seems to be a contradiction between vv. 25 and 26 (in Hebrew vv. 24–25, see Additional Notes for 9:1–26 above). On the one hand, the nations listed in v. 26 are said to be circumcised in the flesh, but in v. 26, they are described as uncircumcised. The NIV tries to solve the tension by adding "only" in v. 25 and "really" in v. 26, giving the impression that all these nations practiced the same form of physical circumcision, but were also united in not having that circumcision affect their relationship with the true God. In an interesting article, however, R. C. Steiner ("Incomplete Circumcision in Egypt and Edom: Jeremiah [9:24–25] in the Light of Josephus and Jonckheere," *JBL* 118 [1999], pp. 497–505) has picked up a suggestion by Rashi, modified by Erhlich, which argues that the circumcision practiced by nations like Egypt was physically partial. "The Egyptian procedure involved either the excision of a triangular section from the dorsal face of the foreskin or simply a longitudinal incision along the median line of the dorsal face allowing retraction of the foreskin and exposure of the glans." Thus, they were circumcised, yet according to the Israelites, uncircumcised.

§39 The Supremacy of Yahweh (Jer. 10:1–16)

10:1–5 / The chapter begins with a diatribe against idolatry, which is reminiscent of the biting sarcasm used by Isaiah (40:18–20; 41:7, 29; 44:6–23; 46:5–7). After the admonition to listen to the divine oracle (vv. 1–2a) the passage begins with the call to avoid the **ways of the nations,** which are further defined as **signs in the sky.** The latter is a reference to astrology, the use of astral phenomenon to determine the future. This method was used to read the minds of the gods concerning the future and, if that future was not desirable, then proper ritual steps could be taken to ward off danger. Divination of all sorts, including astrology, was practiced by the nations that surrounded Israel and was part of their religious practice against which Jeremiah inveighs.

Verse 3 begins a motive clause explaining why God's people should not learn the ways of the nations and in the description it becomes obvious that more than astrology is meant. The warning is against pagan religion in general. The warning presupposes that idolatry was a temptation, and most of the Old Testament testifies that Israel frequently turned against the Lord and toward false religion. But such a move is stupid; idols are not gods—they are objects made by humans. Jeremiah reminds the hearers that the idol before whom people bow is simply an ornamented piece of wood. Isaiah develops this bit of sarcasm further when he describes the craftsman taking a piece of wood and using half of it to warm his hands and cook his bread, while creating a god out of the other half (Isa. 44:15). Further, this "god" can only stand upright if fastened with a nail! How ridiculous to worship it as a powerful deity.

Of course, the finished product is more than a lump of wood. It was the practice of ancient Near Eastern peoples to ornament their deities with precious metals (**silver and gold**).

The sarcasm continues with an analogy between the idols and a **scarecrow in a melon patch.** Birds may be frightened of scarecrows, but human beings know better. In this way, Jeremiah makes the biting observation that humans should know better than they do about idols. There is nothing there but fakery. They cannot even move themselves and therefore are worthless, not able to help or hurt a person.

10:6–10 / The previous unit warned against idolatry by describing the folly of worshiping human-made objects. While this theme continues in the present verses, the argument is augmented by the description of the superiority of the true God, Yahweh. Verse 6 begins with a general statement to the effect that Yahweh is unique among the gods. He is **great** and his reputation (**name**), founded on his acts in history (i.e., the exodus), show that he is **mighty in power.**

This is all the motivation that people need in order to worship (**revere**) Yahweh, who is here, appropriately in the light of the contrast being drawn with the religions of the surrounding peoples, called the **King of the nations.**

However, somewhat surprisingly, Yahweh is not then compared with the false gods immediately, but rather with the **wise men of the nations,** who get their instruction from senseless idols. These idols are indeed beautiful, being ornamented by the finest materials. But while they are inert, the true God is living and eternal. This is not a God to disturb because he can destroy the nations.

10:11–16 / God thus commands Jeremiah to tell **them** (the people of Judah) that the false gods, represented by idols, will **perish.** In one sense, the gods of the nations never existed to begin with, so how can they perish? Two answers are possible. The first is that they do exist. They are not deities, but lesser and malevolent spiritual beings (the New Testament will refer to them as demons). The second answer is that even though the gods do not exist, it is their worship that will perish. In any case, it is the true Creator who deserves their worship, and this section describes Yahweh as the ones who made the heavens and the earth.

Verses 12–13 describe God's power and wisdom (see the prayer in Dan. 2:20b–22) in the context of creation and the storm. The latter may be particularly appropriate in that the leading gods of the surrounding nations, who so tempted the Judeans to worship them, are the storm gods Baal (from Canaan) and Marduk (from Babylon). They are not the ones who bring the storm and life-giving rain; it is Yahweh. A similar polemic may be seen in the conflict in the Elijah-Elisha narrative (1 Kgs. 17–2 Kgs. 7) and in a place like Psalm 29.

Verses 14–16 contrast the fraud and resultant worthlessness of idols made by a goldsmith with the true God who is the creator of the world and the one who has aligned himself with his people (see Additional Notes on v. 16).

Additional Notes §39

10:1–5 / A. L. Oppenheim (*Ancient Mesopotamia,* pp. 183–98) provides a compelling picture of the "care and feeding of the gods."

10:9 / The reference to silver from **Tarshish** and gold from **Uphaz** likely intends to underline the high quality or rarity of the precious metals, but there is some question about both terms. Tarshish is best understood as a reference to a geographical location in southern Spain and thus about as western a location as could be imagined by an ancient Israelite. It was the western location to which Jonah wanted to flee from the great eastern city Nineveh where God commanded him to go (Jonah 1:1–3). Uphaz is more difficult, only appearing in Daniel 10:5, also in reference to precious metal. Some commentators (see Thompson, *Jeremiah,* p. 324) want to change it to the more common reference, Ophir (Gen. 10:29; 1 Kgs. 9:28; 10:11; 22:48, and more) based on the Syriac, but this is more likely a scribal change from something obscure to something more common. Whatever the location, the point of the reference is to underline just how precious the metal is.

10:11 / This verse is written in Aramaic, perhaps because it was a well known saying. Contrary to earlier scholarship, the presence of Aramaic does not require a late date of composition.

10:12–16 / These verses are repeated in 51:15–19.

10:16 / **Portion of Jacob:** the noun here translated "portion" (*kheleq*) comes from a verb that means to divide up and is often used of land or plunder that is divided up and apportioned (see *NIDOTTE,* vol. 2, pp. 161–3). Someone's portion becomes their possession. Thus Yahweh is the possession of Jacob, another name for Israel; God gives himself to his people. For a similar thought, see Num. 18:20; Lam 3:24; Ps. 16:5; 73:26; 119:57; and 142:5.

§40 The Future Exile (Jer. 10:17–22)

10:17–18 / The oracle addresses those who **live under siege.** It is not clear whether they are presently under siege (either in 597 [more likely] or 586 B.C.), that is, the inhabitants of Jerusalem at the point when the Babylonian armies surround their city, or whether Jeremiah is addressing them prophetically as those who will be under siege in the future. In any case the message is clear; the siege will end badly. God (**"I"**) will **hurl** them out of the land. The verb hurl denotes an angry, violent action.

10:19–22 / At this point Jeremiah speaks a woe oracle. It appears that the first person speaker is Jeremiah, but the prophet is here representative of the people of God. The speaker is injured with an **incurable** wound. The reference to the destroyed tent is indicative of the destruction of habitation in the promised land, and the absence of sons represents the dissolution of family life. Shepherd is a common metaphor (Ps. 23; Ezek. 34) for the leaders of Israel who instead of providing wise guidance are there called senseless with the result that the flock, the people of Judah, will be scattered, presumably as a result of the exile and the following diaspora.

Finally, there is a call to listen for a coming report, presumably a report of coming war from the north. While the enemy is not specified, the fulfillment of this prophetic oracle comes when the Babylonian army sweeps down on Jerusalem from the north. It will eradicate the towns of Judah, making it desolate, a place fit only for the habitation of wild animals like **jackals.**

Additional Notes §40

10:19–22 / The form of this passage is that of a woe oracle, a common linguistic vehicle for a judgment speech in the prophets (see also Isa. 5:18–19; Amos 5:18–20; 6:1–7; Mic. 2:1–4; Nah. 3:1–3, to name only a few). Much research has been devoted to this form of prophetic speech, which appears to be a form of speech commonly heard in funeral processions (1 Kgs. 13:30; Jer. 22:18; 34:5; Amos 5:16; about which there is an extensive bibliography, one of the most extensive being W. Janzen, *Mourning Cry and Woe Oracle* [New York: de Gruyter, 1972]). As mourners followed a dead body on its way to the gravesite, they would express their grief by crying, *"hoy, hoy."* The association of this word with death probably led the prophets to use it as they foresaw destruction coming. In many of the prophetic uses, *hoy* no longer marks an expression of lamentation, but it is used sarcastically against those who deserve God's judgment with the sense of "you are as good as dead."

10:19 / The metaphor of the incurable **wound** is used elsewhere in the prophets, Jeremiah 8:22; 30:12; 46:11, Micah 1:9; Nahum 3:19. It is an expression of complete and certain death.

§41 *Jeremiah's Prayer (Jer. 10:23–25)*

10:23–25 / The chapter ends with a prayer to the Lord. The most natural reading is to take the prayer as that of Jeremiah, who first voices his belief that the Lord is sovereign over the affairs of humankind. His language here is very similar to that found in Proverbs 16:9:

> In his heart a man plans his course,
> but the LORD determines his steps.

This sovereignty works itself out in God's punishment, and Jeremiah requests temperance in language reminiscent of Psalm 6:1–3. If God punishes in anger, nothing will be left. On the one hand, he asks for mercy toward himself, while calling down God's wrath on the pagan nations that have harassed Judah.

§42 Betraying the Covenant (Jer. 11:1–17)

At the heart of Jeremiah's charge against Judah is the accusation that it has broken the covenant and now faces the impending implementation of the curses. In particular and most strikingly, it has broken the covenant by its worship of foreign gods as specified by the following oracle.

11:1–8 / The Lord now instructs Jeremiah to accuse the people of Judah that they have broken the covenant. Prophets often functioned as lawyers of the covenant as God commissioned them to accuse his people of breaking the covenant by disobeying the laws of the covenant. Here Jeremiah is acting as a lawyer; elsewhere in the prophets we actually see the use of specifically legal or courtroom terminology in support of their task (e.g., Mic. 1:2; 6:1–8).

The covenant that is specifically in mind here is the Mosaic covenant established on the occasion of the exodus from Egypt (Exod. 19–24) and renewed before entering the promised land (Deuteronomy). On the other hand, though this covenant with its emphasis on law (the **terms of the covenant,** v. 4) and the attendant curses that flowed from disobedience (**cursed is the man who does not obey** [v. 3]; see, for instance, Deut. 28), surely intends us to focus on the Mosaic covenant, the other covenants (especially the Davidic covenant [2 Sam. 7]) may also be in mind.

Through the generations, God has warned his people not to continue breaking the covenant (v. 8). This is likely a reference to the prophets who preceded Jeremiah with a message of repentance and a call back to covenant obedience.

11:9–13 / This passage presents the specific charge of covenant betrayal, and it gets at the heart of the divine-human relationship. They are following in the pattern of past wayward generations in their worship of false deities. They thus break the very first of the commandments: "You shall have no other gods before me" (Exod. 20:3). Indeed, the number of their gods exceeds the number of towns in Judah. This may be a reference to the fact that a god like **Baal** (whose name simply means "lord") had specific manifestations in different cult places. Furthermore, with the worship of Baal came the acknowledgement of a host of other deities including prominent ones like El, Asherah, Anat, Dagan, and so on. The altars set up to worship these gods outnumber the streets. The worship was pervasive, but even so, such attention will not help. These gods will be ineffective as their false worshipers face the coming judgment of the true God as he sets the covenant curses into motion.

11:14–17 / God surprisingly directs Jeremiah not to pray for the people (**Do not pray for this people nor offer any plea or petition for them**). It is arguable that the primary role of the prophet was to intercede for them in prayer. Abraham is the first one who is called a prophet (Gen. 20:7) in a context of intercession for Abimelech the king of the Philistines. The admonition not to pray for the people just underlines the anger God feels toward the people because of their sin. They have reached the point beyond which prayer can help. The language is similar to Proverbs 1:28, which envisions people who ignore Woman Wisdom until a crisis, after which they come running to her. She responds coldly: "Then they will call to me but I will not answer; they will look for me but will not find me." In Proverbs, this may be taken as an encouragement to the students to seek Wisdom before it is too late. In Jeremiah, it probably underlines the fact that God has no real expectation that the people will change their minds.

Verse 15 points out the people's hypocrisy. They are in the temple, but they are plotting evil there. They perform sacrifices (see Additional Notes on **consecrated meat**), but their joy comes from their practice of evil.

In spite of the fact that this is God's special people, their evil will mean their judgment. Verse 16 must point to Israel before it sinned, since **a thriving olive tree** is not only beautiful, but productive. Hosea 14:6 also uses the image of the olive tree to refer to Israel. However, in spite of the nation's original beauty, God will judge it. God's angry appearance may be implied in **"the roar of a mighty storm."** Perhaps the storm is thought to be accompanied by lightning by which God burns down this tree which he planted but will now destroy because of the people's idolatry.

Additional Notes §42

11:4 / Jeremiah uses the metaphor of an **iron-smelting furnace** to describe Israel's experience under Egyptian bondage. The image is used in the same way also in Deuteronomy 4:20 and 1 Kings 8:51. This image fits into a broader metaphor of refining applied to other referents (Prov. 17:3; Isa. 24:1). In reference to Israel in Egypt the metaphor first of all would point to the unpleasantness of the experience. However, though unpleasant, even horrific, iron is subjected to smelting specifically to make it malleable in order to transform it into something useful.

11:4 / The phrase **you will be my people, and I will be your God** and near variants speaks to the heart of the covenant relationship. One or both sides of this expression appear in Genesis 17:7; Exodus 6:6, 7; 19:4, 5; Leviticus 11:45; Deuteronomy 4:20; 2 Kings 11:17, and elsewhere. See discussion in O. P. Robertson, *The Christ of the Covenants* (Phillipsburg, N.J.: P and R Publishing, 1980), pp. 45–52.

11:5 / The expression **a land flowing with milk and honey** refers to the promised land that God gave the Israelites. The expression appears first as God speaks to Moses at the burning bush (Exod. 3:8). As we know from the use of milk and honey in the Song of Songs (see 4:11), these are sensuous liquids that denote the lushness of the land. Milk is a staple and suggests abundant pasturage, whereas honey is a luxury. The phrase also occurs in Jer. 32:22.

11:9 / The betrayal of the covenant, a political metaphor with roots in ancient Near Eastern treaties between nations, is described with a military term here, **conspiracy.** We should not read into this the idea that it was organized and secret.The point is that any violation of a covenant, even when it is akin to open revolt, is the equivalent of a conspiracy to overthrow a legitimate and acknowledged authority.

11:15 / Even in the midst of a judgment speech, Israel is here called God's **beloved** (see also Deut. 33:12; Ps. 60:5; 108:6; 127:2; Isa. 5:1; Jer. 12:7). Perhaps this name also underlines the evil of the people's behavior.

The expression **consecrated meat** refers to the meat of sacrifices. Perhaps in particular it would refer to the *shelemim* sacrifice which would have been consumed by the worshipers (Lev. 3).

§43 God Protects His Prophet (Jer. 11:18–12:6)

This passage speaks of a plot against Jeremiah. It begins with Jeremiah's complaint (11:18–20) and ends with God's judgment against those who are plotting against him (11:21–23). Then the text continues with another complaint (12:1–4), followed by a divine response (12:5–6). Jeremiah was an unpopular person because while other prophets were claiming that God would bring peace, Jeremiah was saying that defeat was inevitable and the result of the people's sin (see Jer. 27–28). Jeremiah 18, 26, and 36 provide other accounts of the people's desire to get rid of this prophet of doom.

11:18–23 / At first it is a bit unclear as to the identity of those plotting agains Jeremiah. The text refers simply to their plot and the fact that God showed Jeremiah what they were doing. However, the Lord's judgment proper is directed specifically toward **the men of Anathoth,** Jeremiah's home town (1:1), which was filled with family members and fellow priests (12:6). Perhaps the fact that his opponents were intimates accounts for Jeremiah's surprise at their plots. As priests, they may have been upset with Jeremiah as a supporter of Josiah's move to centralize worship, thus putting many village priests out of work.

Jeremiah calls on God to save him and avenge himself on them, and God obliges. He does so by issuing an oracle that calls for the death of them and their families. The plotters had called for the end to Jeremiah (**let us cut him off from the land of the living,** v. 19), but God's judgment will see to their end (**not even a remnant will be left to them,** v. 23).

12:1–6 / This event caused Jeremiah to reflect on his life and his work (12:1–4), which itself elicited a response from God (vv. 5–6). The connection with 11:18–23 is found in the reference to family members (those who lived in Jeremiah's hometown of Anathoth) who have betrayed the prophet (see 11:21; 12:6). It appears that the plot evokes Jeremiah's lament in 12:1–4.

Jeremiah speaks to God in the first of his so-called "confessions" and begins with an affirmation of God's righteousness in a judicial sense (**when I bring a case before you**). This legal language again reminds us of the fact that prophets were covenantal lawyers. God's righteousness would imply that he renders the innocent innocent and the guilty guilty. However, Jeremiah proceeds by questioning precisely that point. As he sees, wicked people prospering, he wonders whether the divine judge really does give people what they deserve.

Jeremiah is not the first or only person who has questioned the righteousness of God in this way. Psalm 73 describes the turmoil that another pious person felt in the light of the prosperity of the wicked, and of course Job and Ecclesiastes (7:15–18; 8:10–12) wrestled with the same doubts over just retribution. And why not? The very structure of the covenant seemed to underline the blessings that would come on the righteous who obeyed God and the curses that would afflict those who did not (Deut. 27–28). A book like Proverbs also pointed to the good life for the wise and the reverse for the wicked. As for Jeremiah, his questions arose in his own situation where he was obeying God's command to speak the divine word to a sinful people who not only rejected his message but wanted to harm him. Where was God's righteousness in this situation?

Jeremiah considers this a test of his faith. Reality does not conform to what his faith dictates should be the case, and so he reminds himself that God reads his heart (Jer. 1:5; Ps. 139). He calls for God's justice, which would include the slaughter of the prosperous wicked. His call that they be treated **like sheep to be butchered** should be read in the light of the fact that they were treating him that way (11:19). He connects the sins of the wicked with the difficult situation that the land is in. One might remember the situation during the time of Ahab and Jezebel, when God caused the land to experience a horrible drought because of their Baal-worshiping ways (1 Kgs. 17–19).

As a final attempt to motivate God to act against the wicked, he names their indifference, a frequent theme in the psalms (Ps. 10:11; 73:11; 94:7). They don't believe that God knows what they are doing and so they think they can get away with all kinds of injustice.

God responds directly to Jeremiah's complaint in verses 5–6. He appears to be chiding him for his complaints. God basically says: "If you are lamenting now, you are in trouble, because you have not seen anything yet!" Now Jeremiah is worn out racing with men, but what about in the future when he must race horses? Jeremiah is stumbling in the open country (when the persecution is relatively light), what about in the future when the going gets tough (running in the thickets by the Jordan). Now Jeremiah's persecutors are his family, what about later when it is the King of Judah and his officials (Jeremiah 36)? God ends with a warning not to trust even his own family, who indeed has already betrayed him. The point here is that his own family mirrors the general rejection of his endeavors.

Additional Notes §43

11:19 / Jeremiah, in connection with the persecution he was experiencing, described himself as **a gentle lamb led to the slaughter.** T. Fretheim (*Jeremiah,* pp. 189–90) rightly surmises that by this image Jeremiah "considers himself to be innocent of these plans to take his life, perhaps too trusting of his antagonists," but the image does not suggest that Jeremiah "claims vicarious import for his suffering" (in this sense unlike Isa. 53:7; John 1:29, 36).

The NIV follows the MT with its rendering **the tree and its fruit,** the word *lakhmo* translated "fruit" being literally "bread, food." Some want to emend the text to "its sap" (*lekho*), either by dropping the letter *mem* or treating it as an enclitic *mem* (Lundbom, *Jeremiah 1–20,* p. 636). The difference in meaning may be negligible. To destroy Jeremiah "tree and fruit" or "tree and sap" may simply mean "totally," but commentators sometimes argue that the latter indicates that Jeremiah was young and unmarried at this time and thus to destroy him was to destroy all future offspring.

12:2 / This verse describes the wicked as those whom God has **planted,** who have **taken root** and **bear fruit.** This is the reverse situation envisioned in Psalm 1 (see also Jer. 17:7–8) where it is the righteous who are said to be planted near the water. They are the ones who bear fruit, while the wicked are like chaff.

12:5 / The **thickets by the Jordan** would refer to the jumble of reeds, bushes, and other vegetation on the banks of that river that would provide tremendous obstacles to walking, not to speak of running.

§44 God Abandons His People (Jer. 12:7–13)

Though the NIV treats this section as part of Yahweh's answer to Jeremiah's complaint (along with 12:5–6), it is necessary to see a change of subject in these verses. God turns from Jeremiah's situation with his own family to God's own situation with the people. Just like those who should love and trust Jeremiah have determined to hurt him, so the same is true of Yahweh's people.

12:7–13 / The oracle begins with the consequence of the rebellious actions of the people. God will **abandon** them. He will **forsake** his house (v. 7), which could specifically point to the abandonment of the temple, where the people presumed that he lived (see Jer. 7; Ezek. 8:1–11:25), but the verse goes on to talk about how he will abandon his **inheritance,** which would mean the people themselves. Verse 7 concludes when Yahweh says that he will not simply abandon them, but will allow their enemies to prevail over them. We can feel the torment of God in this decision as he describes his wayward people not only as his inheritance, but as **the one I love.**

At this point, Yahweh uses a number of metaphors to describe the situation. His people are **like a lion** that roar at him (v. 8). They have set themselves fiercely against God and would harm him if they could. This has only elicited Yahweh's **hate** and determination to see them punished. In another metaphor, Yahweh likens his people to **a speckled bird of prey.** As a bird of prey, the implication is that his people are intent on hunting and hurting others. The fact that a speckled bird is specified might simply be a way of noting that they stand out. But although they are a bird of prey, they will be attacked by other birds of prey, representing nations, most notably Babylon, that will successfully hunt them. To heighten the image of violence toward Judah, the oracle invites the **wild beasts** to join in on the feast on the body of Judah.

Verse 10 uses the image of **shepherd** to denote the leaders of the enemy army. These shepherds will swarm the land and destroy

God's **vineyard,** a metaphor for the promised land (Isa. 5:1–7). The fertile land that God gave Israel will turn unproductive because of the **destroyers** who will sweep the land. In v. 12, the destroyers are associated, perhaps even identified with the **sword of the LORD** (see also Jer. 47:6–7). The point is that God is behind the enemy army that is in actuality the tool of his judgment.

Additional Notes §44

12:9 / Thompson (*Jeremiah,* p. 357) would date this oracle to 602 B.C., a time when the Babylonians, Arameans, Moabites, and Ammonites were raiding Judah (2 Kgs. 24:2) in anticipation of the fuller attack of 597 B.C. If so, these are the nations who should be identified with the **birds of prey** that ravage Judah. We should note that the Septuagint translated **speckled bird of prey** as "hyena's lair." If this represents the original text correctly, then the idea is that the birds of prey will pounce on the hyena and the dead carcasses in the lair as soon as they detect an opening.

§45 Uprooting and Reestablishing the Nations (Jer. 12:14–17)

12:14–17 / In the final oracle of the chapter, the Lord turns his attention to those who take advantage of Judah in the moment God judges them. The key word of this oracle is the verb **uproot** (*ntsh*), which is significant because of its mention in the commission of Jeremiah (1:10, see also 18:7–8). Those **wicked neighbors,** like Edom (see Obad. 10–14 and Ps. 137:7), who take advantage of Judah, will themselves be uprooted.

Nonetheless, this oracle looks beyond judgment to salvation. Even the nations, if they acknowledge God and stop trying to convert the people of Judah to the worship of **Baal**—even the nations will be reestablished. This more universal vision may be traced back to Genesis 12:1–3 where the promise of God to Abraham is that he will blessed and also be a blessing to the nations. However, this future blessing is contingent on obedience, because if they are disobedient (**if any nation does not listen**), then uprooting will be a permanent condition.

Additional Notes §45

12:14 / God will **uproot the house of Judah among them** as he uproots the lands that took advantage of Judah. While "uproot" is typically used negatively, this usage seems positive. That is, the exiled Judeans will be returned to their land. In this way, this oracle anticipates fuller development found in the Book of Consolation (Jer. 30–33).

12:16 / Since, as far as we can tell from the biblical record, it was Tyre and Sidon in particular who **taught my people to swear by Baal,** Lundbom (*Jeremiah 1–20,* p. 664) suggests that this oracle was originally directed toward them and then applied more broadly to all the evil neighbors of Judah who aided the Babylonians.

§46 *The Ruined Linen Loin Belt (Jer. 13:1–11)*

This passage records the first of Jeremiah's symbolic actions. While most of the prophet's prophecies are verbal utterances pure and simple, a surprising number of times these words are accompanied by actions that illustrate the message (according to Fretheim, *Jeremiah,* p. 204, other symbolic actions include 16:1–9; 18:1–11; 19:1–15; 25:15–29; 27–28; 32:1–15; 43:8–13; 51:59–64).

13:1–11 / This particular prophetic action begins with the divine command to Jeremiah to **go and buy a linen belt** and put it around his waist. The belt is linen because Jeremiah is a priest (or the son of a priest) and priests wear linen undergarments. "Belt" may be a misleading translation anyway (see Additional Notes). What is clear is that this garment is worn around the waist tightly and touches the skin. This position illustrates the original relationship that the people enjoyed with God (v. 11).

Jeremiah is to buy the linen belt, put it on, but then not let **water** touch it. The latter probably signifies washing; in other words, Jeremiah is to put on the linen belt and then not wash it. This garment represents God's people in their relationship with God and right away it starts getting grimy, just like the people in their relationship with God.

But more instructions follow. Jeremiah is to travel to **Perath** and bury the linen belt in a **crevice.** Perath is a town not far away from Jerusalem, though its name sounds like the name for the Euphrates River (see Additional Notes) and may indeed represent that river which defines the area of land controlled by the great Mesopotamian powers including Assyria and the Babylonia.

After an unspecified, long period of time, Jeremiah is told by God to return to Perath and get the linen belt. Not surprisingly it is **ruined and completely useless.** Again, it is clear that the analogy is drawn with the people of God, who started out in a close intimate relationship with God, but ended up ruined. It is particularly Judah's pride that is ruined. The people of God should not feel pride since they should have known their proper place of subservience to the Lord. But apparently they did not and this oracle indicates that God will cut them down to size. In addition, idolatry, the worship of false gods, also makes them useless like the linen belt (v. 10).

Additional Notes §46

13:1 / The **linen belt** (*ʾezor pishtim*) may better be understood to be a loincloth, a kind of undergarment that extends from the waist to the knees. This one is made of linen because Jeremiah is a priest (Exod. 28:39; 39:27–29; Ezek. 44:17–18).

13:4 / Jeremiah is commanded to take and bury the garment at **Perath,** which is a simple transliteration of the Hebrew. As it happens, this word is often used as a name for the mighty Euphrates River, but on those occasions the Hebrew word for river is often associated with it. To understand this as a literal command would also mean that Jeremiah would have had to travel 700 miles round trip two times, which is possible over an extremely long period of time. It is better to understand this as a reference to the city also mentioned in Joshua 18:23 (Parah), chosen not because of its promience, but because the name sounds like the name of the river Euphrates.

§47 Wine Jars (Jer. 13:12–14)

13:12–14 / God tells Jeremiah to go out to the people with a new message. This message begins with what would be taken as a rather stupid statement: **Every wineskin should be filled with wine.** The response would be incredulity. Of course, every wineskin should be filled with wine. After all, what other purpose were they made for?

At this point there may be a subtle but devastating critique of God's people, but the text does not bring it out. As the wineskin was obviously made in order to hold wine, so Judah was made to be God's obedient people, but they weren't acting that way.

In any case, the oracle develops in another direction. The wine jar metaphor suggests **drunkenness.** Jeremiah is to tell them that they will be filled with drunkenness. This picks up on the recurrent theme of the "cup of wrath" (see Jer. 25:15–38; see also comments at 48:26–28). It is another way of saying that they are about to experience the devastating power of the anger of God. The various leaders of Judah (**the kings who sit on David's throne, the priests, the prophets**) as well as **those living in Jerusalem** are specified.

§48 Light Turns to Darkness (Jer. 13:15–17)

13:15–17 / In this next oracle, Jeremiah begins by calling his hearers, the people of Judah, to **pay attention.** He claims to speak for the Lord, and calls on them to acknowledge the Lord by giving him his proper **glory.** But there is a time limit of unspecified duration for them to do this. Soon God will bring his judgment on the people, the judgment signified by a coming **darkness.** In this darkness, the people will fall down. The people expect **light,** but because of their refusal to give glory to God, God will bring **thick darkness,** even **gloom.**

Listening means more than simply hearing the words of Jeremiah. The Hebrew word (*shm*ᶜ) implies acting on that message, in other words, repenting. Jeremiah imagines his reaction to the strong possibility that they will not repent—he will weep secretly and bitterly. If they do not repent, it will be because of their arrogant attitude (v. 15), their **pride** (v. 17). Pride keeps them from acknowledging God's glory because to do that entails recognizing their own subordinate place in the world. Perhaps he will weep **in secret** because he knows that weeping at their appropriate judgment is not becoming. But he will weep on account of their rebellion and its consequences, for even in the midst of the judgment, these people are referred as **the LORD's flock.**

Additional Notes §48

13:15–17 / Throughout this section it is hard to determine who is speaking, Jeremiah or God, but that may be the genius of the oracle. Jeremiah, as prophet, speaks the very words of God.

13:16–17 / The imagery of **darkness, thick darkness,** and **deep gloom** points to judgment. Most moderns living in an age of electric lights have no real experience of deep darkness, which can be quite dangerous. But perhaps the image as it is used in contexts of judgment also point to primeval darkness, the darkness of the world when matter was first created ("darkness was over the surface of the deep" [Gen. 1:2]), and thus the image suggests a reversion to a pre-creation state. It is also interesting to note that while the people of God thought that Day of the Lord would be a day of light, it would turn out to be one of darkness for them (Amos 5:18–20).

§49 King and Queen Mother—Divested (Jer. 13:18–20)

13:18–19 / This brief oracle is directed to the **king** and **queen mother.** The king is probably Jehoiachin and his mother, Nehushta, daughter of Elnathan of Jerusalem, the queen mother. They are mentioned as going into exile (Jer. 22:26 and 29:2). The fuller story is found in 2 Kings 24:8–17, with reference to the events of 597 B.C. The mother of the king was often a very influential person, and this would be even more so in the case of Jehoiachin, who was only eighteen or nineteen during his brief tenure as king.

This oracle is addressed to them before these events and asks them to step down in humiliation from their thrones. Eventually, all of Judah will experience exile. The exile of 597 is a foretaste of what happens more definitively in 586 B.C.

13:20 / The queen mother is specifically addressed in verse 20 (see Additional Notes). She is told to look up and see the attacking army **from the north.** No matter what was in the mind of Jeremiah when he received the oracle, it is clear from its fulfillment that this refers to the Babylonians. Interestingly, in this case it is the queen mother who is the shepherd who fails her flock, the people of Judah.

Additional Notes §49

13:19 / The **cities of the Negev** refer to the southernmost cities of Israel. Sometimes it refers to the wilderness area far south of Jerusalem. At other times it refers simply to the area south of Bethlehem. In any case it would include important cities like Beersheba and Arad. It is unclear whether this indicates that the Babylonian army penetrated deep into Judah or whether it signifies that another nation, say Edom, was already taking advantage of Judah's problems.

13:20 / With Lundbom (*Jeremiah 1–20,* p. 682), we understand this verse to conclude the present oracle rather than introduce the next one, as many other commentators and versions understand it. The written (*ketib*—as opposed to the spoken *qore*ʾ) Hebrew uses imperatives in the feminine, and thus addresses the queen mother. Some (Fretheim, *Jeremiah,* p. 210) believe that the feminine is used in reference to Jerusalem as "mother city."

§50 God's Unclean People (Jer. 13:21–27)

This oracle is replete with various images of accusation and judgment directed toward the people of God. The verses are otherwise loosely related, though the metaphor of the people's prostitution appears in verses 22 and 26–27.

13:21–27 / The passage begins with a taunt questioning Judah's reaction when those countries it considered allies would end up taking over. The history of Judah during Jeremiah's ministry records different periods when the kings were helping or hoping for help from Babylon (Josiah and we may presume Jehoahaz, though the latter's reign was brief) or from Egypt (Jehoiakim, Jehoiachin, Zedekiah). But these **special allies** will not help, indeed they will even dominate the people of God. As a result, the people will experience pain, a pain that is like the extreme pain of a **woman** in labor (Jer. 4:31; 6:24; 22:23; 30:6; 48:41; 49:22, 24; 50:43).

Jeremiah then articulates the question that the people of God were asking themselves and would ask themselves when the exile actually took place: **Why has this happened to me?** Jeremiah is blunt in his response: sin, pure and simple. It is because of the people's sin that they experience the type of punishment that is likened to sexual abuse: they will be stripped and raped.

Jeremiah then uses a well-known metaphor to describe Israel's inherent tendency to sin. It is as much their nature as dark skin is natural to an **Ethiopian** and spots to a **leopard.** God's people are stubborn in their evil. Verse 24 then presents another image of judgment, the scattering of **chaff.** Unlike a well-rooted tree (Ps. 1), chaff is rootless and blown about by the wind; a metaphor for the kind of scattering God's people will experience as they are exiled to foreign countries.

Verse 25 then names the sin. They have forgotten God and worship **false gods.** Jeremiah often holds up idolatry as the apex of the people's sin (see 10:1–16; 11:1–17). Thus, verses 26–27 again describe the punishment that God will bring on the people. By their idolatry, they have committed spiritual adultery, so their punishment is described like that levied on a prostitute, namely public humiliation. The section ends with a **"woe"**-saying, connecting the oracle with mourning rituals (see 10:19–22). In ancient Israel, mourners would follow a body to burial crying, "woe." It is a way of saying that Jerusalem is as good as dead. As the passage began, so it ends with a question. This one implicitly charges the people of Jerusalem with ritual impurity because of their sin.

Additional Notes §50

13:26 / In the ancient Near East, a harlot could be punished by exposure. Here Jerusalem is charged with being a spiritual prostitute for worshiping other gods. She will experience the appropriate punishment. There is a near parallel phrase in Nahum 3:5.

§51 The Drought (Jer. 14:1–10)

Boda ("From Complaint to Contrition: Peering through the Liturgical Window of Jer 14,1–15,4," *ZAW* 113 [2001], pp. 186–97) has persuasively argued that the unit 14:1–15:4 reflects a transformation from lament to penitential prayer. He believes that the chapter reflects a public liturgy led by Jeremiah to unsuccessfully avert God's coming judgment anticipated by a drought. While there are debates whether 14:1–16 and 14:17–15:4 are connected, he rightly points to the allusion to drought, the major subject of the first pericope, in 14:22b, to show that the two sections are united. The two sections have a similar structure since both begin with a statement about a disaster (14:2–6; 14:17–18) and then continue with a communal lament (14:7–9; 14:19–22). After this, each ends with a proclamation of judgment (14:10; 15:2b) followed by a "prose dialogue between prophet and Yahweh" (14:11–16; 15:1–2a, 3–4).

14:1–10 / The passage begins (v. 1) with a typical introduction (see Jer. 7:1; 10:1; 11:1, 46:1; 47:1; 49:34, etc. [though the syntax is slightly different in some of these]) to a prophetic oracle (**word of the LORD**) and identifies the subject of the oracle as a drought. The oracle proper is in verses 2–6.

We do not know anything about this drought outside of the oracle, and the chapter does not situate it in time. However, as Jeremiah's oracles as a whole point to an impending national catastrophe that we know as the Babylonian exile, this drought was probably understood to be a divine anticipation of that judgment.

The oracle proper begins with a description of the great grief that has come on the land of Judah and in particular Jerusalem (14:2–3). It is immediately clear that the problem is a lack of water caused by a drought. The land of Judah has minimal fresh water supplies and the rainfall is normally not overly abundant. A drought could cause great hardship in the land. Even the **nobles,** the richest of the land, can obtain no water and their riches are of no help. They, like the farmers described next, **cover their heads** as a sign of sadness. The farmers' ground is hard and **cracked** from lack of rain. And the hardship and suffering is not limited to humans: the animals (**doe, wild donkeys**) have no water. The situation is indeed dire.

After the oracle, Jeremiah speaks on behalf of the people (vv. 7–9). He pleads with God to have mercy on them in spite of their sin. He acknowledges the justice of God, but appeals to God's reputation in an attempt to prod God into action. God is like a **stranger** in the land, a **traveler** who only spends the night. But because of the covenant, the people believe that God is "**among us**" and that they have a special relationship with God and "**bear your name.**" On these grounds, the prophet, on behalf of the people, appeals to God not to **forsake** them.

God responds to the peoples' plea with a cold shoulder (v. 10). He knows this people. They **wander.** They may repent now, but their attention is short lived.

Additional Notes §51

14:1 / Though we do not have knowledge of precisely when this **drought** takes place, we should not be surprised that Jeremiah describes it as a judgment of God. After all, Leviticus and Deuteronomy both cite drought as one of the consequences of breaking the covenant (Deut. 28:22–24; Lev. 26:18–20), and the apostate time of Ahab experienced a horrible drought in response to its worship of Baal (1 Kgs. 17:1).

14:3 / **Cisterns** were huge hollowed out pits in the ground where rainfall was stored. That there was no water in a cistern meant that the drought was long and severe.

§52 False Prophets (Jer. 14:11–16)

14:11–16 / In the following verses, God speaks another oracle. This oracle is of uncertain connection with the previous one in 14:1–10 concerning the drought. The present oracle begins with a statement of his determination not to rescue the people from the judgment of **sword, famine and plague** that is about to overtake them. God then instructs Jeremiah not to **pray** for the people.

We have already seen this charge in 7:16–20 and 11:14–17 and have pointed out there that this flies in the face of the typical prophetic task. One of the prophet's main jobs was to pray for the people, but here God tells Jeremiah to stop, again indicating that the people's judgment is certain. God is turning a cold shoulder toward them, so even if they **fast** and **cry** out, God will not listen. This attitude is reminiscent of Proverbs 1:28 where Woman Wisdom will not respond to the people's repentance. They simply had waited too long.

Jeremiah steps in to defend the people. He tells them that **prophets** are preaching peace to them. They are not warning them about the coming judgment, but precisely the opposite.

God speaks to this issue by calling them lying prophets. They are not sent from God. The people should have recognized them as false according to the criteria laid down by Deuteronomy 13 and 18. The problem of false prophets in the time of Jeremiah is a large one (note in particular Jer. 23, 27–29).

Additional Notes §52

14:12 / The phrase **sword, famine and plague** (and its variant "sword and famine") is formulaic in the book of Jeremiah (5:12; 11:22; 16:4; 21:7, 9; 24:10; 27:8, 13; 29:18; 32:24, 36; 34:17; 38:2; 42:16–17; 44:12–13, 18, 27). It may flow from Deuteronomy 32:24–27, which describes the types of divine punishment that would come on Israel for their idolatry. Certainly all three were present in war and its aftermath, so it well represented the coming catastrophe at the hands of the Babylonians.

§53 Yahweh Weeps and Jeremiah Complains (Jer. 14:17–22)

Verse 17 introduces the following verses with "you will speak this word to them." In keeping with the dynamic of the prophecy as a whole, the "you" must be the prophet Jeremiah and the speaker God, and the oracle begins with what is clearly a message of God (vv. 17–18). However, even though the next speech introduction is not until 15:1, there is what appears to be an unmarked change of speaker in verse 19. In other words, Jeremiah is commanded as prophet to speak in the name of Yahweh in verses 17–18, but then without warning Jeremiah seems to speak hard words to God on behalf of the people.

14:17–18 / Jeremiah is commanded to speak God's words. That these are God's words (contrary to Lundbom, *Jeremiah 1–20*, p. 712, and others) seem indicated by the reference to Judah as **my virgin daughter—my people.** This way of referring to Judah is very intimate and rather shocking in light of the fact that the general context contains oracles that emphasize God's great anger at their sin. The whole oracle is a strong statement of God's great anguish over the suffering of the people. God reveals the **tears** that he sheds for them and the wound that they suffer. His people are dying everywhere, both country and city. Also, **prophet** and **priest,** those supposed to be particularly close and in service to God, have been exiled. The latter reference may indicate that this oracle comes from the period after 597 B.C. when the early phase of the exile takes place at the time of Jehoiachin. The reference could conceivably be to the time of Zedekiah (586 B.C.).

14:19–22 / In verse 19 the shift in tone is signaled by the fact that the **"I"** of verses 17–18, namely God himself, is now referred to in the second person. Someone, presumably Jeremiah speaking on behalf of the people, charge God with rejecting Judah. This passage is a bit enigmatic because the people have not really shown any inclination toward the type of repentance noted in verse 20. It may be that Jeremiah, as an intercessor, tries to stand in the place of the people to appeal to God and his **covenant.** Verse 22 asserts hope in Yahweh and rejects the false gods. This section reads like a lament in the tradition of Psalm 77.

Additional Notes §53

14:19 / Jeremiah asks if God **detests Zion.** In the covenant blessings of Leviticus 26 God promises not to detest them if they obey his laws (26:11), but in the curse, he guarantees that he will detest them if they disobey (26:30), though he promises not to completely despise them (26:44).

14:22 / The word translated **worthless idols** more literally means "nothings." It refers to the false gods of the nations whose worship lures God's people away from Yahweh, but they are empty, of no account. The word (*hebel*) is well-known from the repeated refrain in Ecclesiastes that repeats it, "meaningless, meaningless."

§54 Not Moses, Samuel, or Jeremiah! (Jer. 15:1–4)

15:1–4 / At the end of the previous chapter, we heard Jeremiah speaking as a covenant mediator, interceding on the people's behalf with God. This passage presents God's negative response to his appeal. Jeremiah's prophetic intercession stands in the great tradition of **Moses** (Exod. 32:11–14, 30–34; Num. 14:13–19) and **Samuel** (1 Sam. 7:5–11; 12:17–23). But God tells Jeremiah that even if these worthy individuals were trying to save this people from divine wrath, they would fail. Jeremiah's appeal, thus, does not stand a chance. God wants them away from his presence. He then describes their fate as **death** by war (the **sword**), famine (**starvation**), and exile (**captivity**). The four kinds of destroyers refers to war (**sword**) and its aftermath as the bodies are eaten by the wild animals of the region (**dogs, birds,** and **beasts of the earth**).

Their doom was sealed during the reign of **Manasseh** (ruled ca. 687–642 B.C.). He was the son of Hezekiah, a king typically judged as relatively faithful to Yahweh and elsewhere (2 Kgs. 21:24) known as the grand father of the other good king of the time period, Josiah, a contemporary of the early Jeremiah. Nonetheless, though bracketed by good kings, Manasseh is judged as the worse of the worse by the historian in 2 Kings 21. It is in 2 Kings 21:13 that God pronounces "I will wipe out Jerusalem as one wipes a dish, wiping it and turning it upside down." Even after Josiah's religious reforms, God reasserts his intention to destroy Judah (2 Kgs. 23:26–27).

§55 No Pity for Jerusalem and Jeremiah's Lament (Jer. 15:5–10)

The prose oracle of Yahweh is followed by a poetic one on which is appended a very brief (v. 10) lament from Jeremiah.

15:5–10 / The divine oracle begins with a series of three rhetorical questions (v. 5) that imply not only that Jerusalem will be destroyed, but no one will care. Their destruction will be because they have **rejected** God.

God does not simply let them be destroyed, he actively destroys them. He will **winnow** them, invoking an agricultural image of separating the wheat from the chaff. Normally the protector of socially vulnerable people (Deut. 14:29; Ps. 68:5), here God will create, rather than protect **widows.** Indeed, we might compare the penalty associated with the failure to protect the widow in Exodus 22:22–24. It is also interesting to note the metaphor used to describe the multiplication of the widows. That they will be as numerous as **the sand of the sea** is an obvious play on the promise to Abraham that his descendants will be that numerous (Gen. 22:17; 32:12; 41:49). Blessing has become curse.

But not only will women become widows (see also Lam. 5:2c), but they will also die. A mother of **seven** (a symbolic number for completion) will **breathe her last** and die.

All this talk of mothers and widows reminds Jeremiah of his own mother to whom he addresses a personal lament (v. 10). He bemoans the fact that even though he has not angered people by his financial dealings, he is hated by all because of his message.

Additional Notes §55

15:5 / These rhetorical questions are reminiscent of Nahum 3:7, but there the context is an oracle against the dreaded Assyrians. How far has Jerusalem come when it is treated like that pagan nation?

§56 The Lord Speaks to the Prophet (Jer. 15:11–14)

The divisions of the oracles and the responses continue to be difficult as, on occasion, does discerning the addressee. In verses 11–12 it is clear that God is responding to Jeremiah's lament in 15:10, and in verses 13–14 we presume that the oracle continues to address Jeremiah.

15:11–14 / In any case, God first of all assures Jeremiah that in spite of the fact that he is a "man with whom the whole land strives" (v. 10), God will **deliver** him **for a good purpose.** That good purpose might refer to Jeremiah's ministry. God backs this up and asks an enigmatic question about metals. Can a man break **iron** or **bronze**? Of course not, but what does the iron and bronze stand for? The iron is from the **north** and this is the key to recognizing that it stands for Babylon, the enemy from the north (1:13–15; 4:6, etc.). But what about the bronze? The reference is not at all clear until we read in the following oracle (15:20) that Jeremiah is a wall of bronze. Thus, God assures Jeremiah that his prophetic message of judgment at the hands of the Babylonians will not falter. The people cannot change their fate in spite of their protests to the contrary.

The most difficult aspect of this oracle comes as we move to verses 13–14. We might expect that these verses are directed toward the people of Judah (especially since a similarly worded oracle directed toward Judah may be found in 17:1–4), but, as mentioned, the pronominal references do not change and there is not a new antecedent. The best explanation is that Jeremiah is now addressed as a member of the community. The wealth of the community will be dissipated because of sin (v. 13) and the community will be taken into exile (v. 14) because of God's anger. For a different take on the relationship between 15:11–14 and 17:1–4, see M. H. Floyd, "Prophetic Complaints about the Fulfillment of Oracles in Habakkuk 1:2–17 and Jeremiah 15:10–18," *JBL* 110 (1991), pp. 397–418.

§57 *Jeremiah's Complaint and Divine Response (Jer. 15:15–21)*

15:15–21 / Jeremiah then appeals to God for protection and also for vengeance against those who tried to undermine and harm him. He reminds God of the suffering he has endured in his ministry. He reminds him of his passionate reception of God's words to him (v. 16). The metaphor of eating words (**when your words came, I ate them**) refers to the internalization of the message. He had distanced himself from evil people (cf. Ps. 1). But why does he, a righteous person, find himself in such pain? Is God deceptive, promising blessings to his faithful people, but giving them nothing or even a curse in return?

God responds by calling on Jeremiah to repent. He must be a worthy spokesperson for God. God in return will make him a **wall of bronze** to the people. This means that they can attack but to no avail. Because of the rarity of some of its ingredients, bronze is a relatively precious material, and walls are not typically made out of any metal.

Additional Notes §57

15:16 / Holladay (*Jeremiah* 2, p. 26) interprets Jeremiah's statement about consuming God's words as a reference to the discovery of Josiah's law in the temple in 622 B.C., but this seems a far too specific understanding of what is to be taken as a metaphor of the internalization of God's message.

15:18 / How can a **brook** be **deceptive?** The image that Jeremiah has in mind is the appearance of a brook with its refreshing waters turning out to be either a dry riverbed or a simple mirage. Both could be encountered in the wilderness. In Jeremiah 2:13 we hear that God asserts that he is **the spring of living water,** but here Jeremiah, on the basis of his experience, questions whether God is truly life-giving.

§58 *Don't Marry, Don't Mourn, and Don't Celebrate (Jer. 16:1–13)*

This unit, which is related to the one that follows at the end of the chapter, presents three prohibitions in the light of the judgment that is coming and which itself is the result of the people's sin. These prohibitions lead to behaviors on Jeremiah's part that are resonant with prophetic significance and therefore should be considered a prophetic sign-act that incarnates the words he is speaking. These prohibitions seem to be directed to Jeremiah himself. Certainly, this is true of the first prohibition.

16:1–4 / Jeremiah receives a **word of the LORD** that prohibits him from marrying and having children. The times are not right to have a family and bring children into the world. Suffering is certain in the light of the people's sin. The description of the children who would be **like refuse lying on the ground** and their **dead bodies** becoming **food for the birds of the air and the beasts of the earth** is not metaphorical but a realistic description of the carnage after a battle.

In an ancient Israelite culture, as distinct from ours, the lack of a wife when one is of marriageable age, would be considered quite odd. It would call attention to itself. People would ask, "Why isn't Jeremiah married?" And the answer would be something like "He thinks the world is going to end." In other words, Jeremiah is asked to act in a way that will incarnate the words of judgment he announces with the hope that it will elicit response and even repentance. Of course, such a demand on the prophet is heavy, leaving him without intimate human companionship during the difficult period. On the other hand, the prospect of war and the resultant famine and disease is not an acceptable alternative. One of the trials of a prophet is the awareness of the tragedy to come.

16:5–7 / Jeremiah is further forbidden to go to a **funeral.** This prohibition centers on an important social obligation. Not to go to a friend's funeral is an action bound to raise questions. However, God has withdrawn his **blessing, love,** and **pity** from his people. The deaths are not to be mourned because they are a part of the divine judgment. They deserve it. And no one will escape, both the powerful wealthy (**high**) and the poor (**low**).

16:8–9 / Thirdly, Jeremiah is not to go to a celebration where there is **feasting** and drinking. This is not a time to celebrate, but a time of mourning. As judgment comes, no one will feel like going to a party.

16:10–13 / By his words and actions, Jeremiah was telling the people that God had decreed judgment for them. Marriage, funerals, and parties were out of synch with the times. This message will elicit questions from the people. They ask what they had done wrong. Jeremiah tells them that they have broken the law, and in particular they have committed idolatry. **Idolatry** breaks the first and second commandments. This was a longstanding problem stretching back to the fathers and mothers of the present generation, but God tells them that the present generation is not being punished for their forebears' sins, but for their even worse sin. Since they want to serve other gods, God will throw them out of the land, where they can do so **day and night.**

Additional Notes §58

16:5 / The **house where there is a funeral meal** is the translation of two Hebrew words (*bet marzeakh*). The *marzeakh* is a word that only occurs twice in the Hebrew Bible (see Amos 6:7), but is found in Ugaritic and other extrabiblical literature and has occasioned extensive discussion (see M. Pope, *Song of Songs* [AB; Doubleday, 1977], pp. 216–21, for an extensive discussion and bibliography). It seems to be a pagan mourning rite that asserts the forces of life in the face of death and includes ritual eating, drinking, and sometimes sexual activity. The occurrence of this word here indicates the depths to which Israel's religious traditions have been degraded.

16:6 / Cutting oneself and shaving one's head refer to pagan mourning practices (see Lev. 19:27–28; 21:5; Deut. 14:1). The first is reminiscent of the god El's reaction to the news of Baal's death at the hands of Mot in the Ugaritic Baal epic. The fact that the prophets of Baal cut themselves with knives and swords when Baal did not throw fire down from heaven on Mount Carmel may also be explained by this mourning ritual (1 Kgs. 18:28).

§59 A New Exodus after a Double Judgment (Jer. 16:14–21)

It could be that the oracle that begins in verse 14 and includes verse 15 is a continuation of the thought of the previous unit (it begins with *laken,* translated **however** by the NIV, but it could also be translated "therefore"). We will treat it as part of a complex that comprises the second half of the chapter. In our analysis, verses 14–15 envision a future salvation, then verses 16–18 is a judgment oracle. Verses 19–20 is a prayer of Jeremiah, followed by verse 21, which is a divine response.

16:14–15 / With the phrase **the days are coming,** this oracle looks to the future. It envisions a change to the standard oath formula. Right now when people take an oath they swear by the Lord who brought the Israelites out of their bondage in Egypt. In the future, people will swear by the Lord who will bring the Israelites out of captivity in the **land of the north** (Babylon) and other nations where they have been taken. Jeremiah, in other words, utilizes exodus imagery to describe the future deliverance after the coming judgment. For other prophets who use this imagery, see Isaiah 40:1–11; 52:10; Hosea 2:14–15.

16:16–18 / With the words **but now** the oracle moves from future salvation to present distress. No escape is forthcoming from the present judgment. God will send **fishermen** to catch them and **hunters** to track them down. The use of these two metaphors makes clear that punishment will be comprehensive. As Lundbom (*Jeremiah 1–20,* p. 773) puts it: "The combined operation, in any case, will be comprehensive, with the fishers going after a large-scale catch and the hunters chasing down fugitives holed up in mountain rocks and caves." Most likely these are references to the Babylonians (**the land of the north**) and any others whom God uses as an instrument of his judgment.

God will not spare them his judgment, but will **repay them double** for their sin. If understood literally, this remark could raise issues about God's justice. On what grounds could God judge them more severely than their sins deserve? But that is not the point. After all, it could be argued that their sin deserved death. This language of double punishment, however, does underline the seriousness of their sin and the anger of God. The sin, after all, is **idolatry,** the most heinous of all transgressions.

16:19–21 / The preceding oracle elicits a prayer from the prophet. He affirms God as his place of protection, using imagery common to the psalms (**my strength, my fortress, my refuge**). He looks forward to a time when not just Israel, but the nations will come and confess their former allegiance to **false gods** and **worthless idols.**

It is unclear whether verse 20 is a continuation of Jeremiah's prayer or the beginning of a divine response, but verse 21 is clearly the latter. God will teach the nations his **power** and **might** (presumably by means of his judgment and perhaps also by the future deliverance described in verse 16–18), and in this way they will acknowledge him.

§60 *Indelible Sin (Jer. 17:1–4)*

17:1–4 / This short oracle does not have an introduction but begins with a statement of Judah's indelible sin. It is written permanently and deeply on a tablet with **flint** (see Additional Notes). The use of such a writing instrument may indicate that the tablet is stone or metal, rather than the less durable clay. In any case, the tablet represents their **heart.** They sin not just externally but from the innermost part of their being. It is also indelibly inscribed on the **horns of their altars.** The altar is at the heart of their worship ritual, and their false religious practices show just how deep their sin goes. The horns of the altar refer to the protrusions on each corner whose function is unclear (some people think it allows for the tying down of the animal, but the animal is dead by the time it is on the altar), but its symbolic value is clear. Again, the sin in focus is idolatry, and in verse 2 false altars and **Asherah poles** are cited as prime examples of that idolatry.

Because of their sin, the **land** that God gave them as well as the **wealth** with which God blessed them will be taken away. The passage ends with an allusion to the future exile that will result from God's **anger.**

Additional Notes §60

17:1–4 / Note that similar language is directed toward Jeremiah, perhaps as a representative of the people, in 15:11–14.

17:1 / While Judah has engraved its sin on its heart, later God will write his law on their heart (Jer. 31:33). The Hebrew word translated **flint** (*shamir*) may be diamond, referring to the diamond point of an engraving stylus. In any case, it is a very hard stone (see *NIDOTTE,* vol. 4, p. 167).

17:2 / **Asherah poles** were trees or poles that represented the Canaanite goddess Asherah. False religious practices took place in their vicinity. See Exodus 34:13; Deuteronomy 12:3; 16:21; 1 Kings 15:13; 18:19; 2 Kings 21:7; 23:4 (also Jer. 2:27).

§61 Wisdom Sayings (Jer. 17:5–11)

The next passage is not a prophetic oracle but rather a collection of wisdom sayings attributed to Yahweh. They are not specifically addressed to contemporary issues, but their teaching certainly applies to the issues facing Judah in the days when Jeremiah was preaching. The first saying contrasts those who trust God with those who rely on human resources. The second talks about the deceitfulness of the human heart that lies open before Yahweh. The third describes the person who gains material wealth through illegitimate means. This section is distinguished from what follows since these sayings are attributed to Yahweh himself, followed by a speech directed to Yahweh from the prophet himself verses 12–16.

17:5–8 / These verses contrast those who trust in human resources with those who trust in God. The former are cursed and the latter are blessed. Contrasting images describe both classes of people. Those who trust humans are **like a bush in the wastelands.** In other words, they languish and are not fruitful. On the other hand, those who trust the Lord are **like a tree planted by the water.** In language reminiscent of Psalm 1's description of the righteous man, this image illustrates how these people thrive and are fruitful. The purpose of this wisdom saying is to encourage people to trust God and not themselves. In light of the military danger facing Judah, those who took this lesson to heart would turn to God for protection and not to their own weapons and defenses nor to political alliances with nations like Egypt.

17:9–10 / In one of the most famous sayings found in Jeremiah, the Lord addresses the self-deceptiveness of human nature (the **heart**). Human beings may think that their actions are ethical, but God knows better. He will ultimately reward people according to what they deserve. This aspect of human nature was illustrated early in the Garden of Eden when Adam and Eve made their own moral judgment about eating the fruit of the tree of the knowledge of good and evil rather than following God's prohibition. Their heart deceived them into thinking that the act was morally permissible, when in fact it was not.

17:11 / Yahweh speaks specifically of those who get rich without working hard for it, perhaps as a specific illustration of the self-deceptive nature of the human heart. The image that is used is that of a **partridge** who hatches eggs that it did not lay. The book of Proverbs also speaks negatively about the gaining wealth without working for it and also states that such gain will be temporary (Prov. 11:4, 18; 13:11; 21:6; 22:16, cf. Ps. 73:3–6, 12).

§62 *Another Lament by the Prophet (Jer. 17:12–18)*

Clearly the speaker changes indicating a transition from a divine oracle to a prayer addressed to Yahweh, certainly to be understood as uttered by the prophet. There is, however, the question of the literary unity of verses 12–18. The first two verses are hymnic in tone and the rest is a lament. While some (Thompson, *Jeremiah,* pp. 423–26; Frietheim, *Jeremiah,* pp. 261–63) separate the two parts (Lundbom [*Jeremiah,* pp. 792–802] divides the text even more finely), it is best to understand the hymn to be an introduction to the lament as in, e.g., Ps. 89.

17:12–13 / The prophet's prayer begins with praise of Yahweh by honoring the place where he has chosen to make his presence known on earth. The **sanctuary** is the temple located on Mount Zion, which was thought to be the place where the divine king had his **throne** (Isa. 6:1–3; Jer. 14:21; Ezek. 1:26–28; 43:2–5). Elsewhere the ark of the covenant, originally located in the Holy of Holies, was called his footstool (1 Chr. 28:2; Ps. 132:7). Two cherubim statues held outstretched wings over the ark with their heads face down, so as not to be overwhelmed by the glory seated above them.

Jeremiah knew that God was not held hostage in the temple (see Jer. 7 and 26). Even so, as long as God made his presence known there, the temple could be honored and, of course, the temple on earth represents the heavenly temple that was always glorious.

The hymnic introduction continues in a way that begins to turn toward the subject of the petition (another reason to think that hymn and petition belong together). Yahweh is called the **hope of Israel,** the one who can lead Israel from death to life. Those who turn their back on Yahweh, however, will be put to **shame,** the same verb found in verse 18 where Jeremiah asks God to put to shame his persecutors and to keep him from shame.

The destruction of the traitors is described as being **written in the dust,** which is an apt end for those who turn away from Yahweh, who is described as the **spring of living water.** Even the record of their passing is transitory as letters formed in dust.

17:14–18 / In these verses, Jeremiah turns to petition. The rest of the passage is indisputably to be classified as one of Jeremiah's confessions (see also 11:18–12:6; 15:10–11, 15–21; 18:18–23; 20:7–13, 14–18). Jeremiah knows where his problems can be solved. He asks God to **heal** him and to **save** him. He does so on the basis of the fact that he praises God. Because he praises God, he expects God to take care of him.

The next verses help us understand from whom Jeremiah wants salvation—his detractors. We have seen it elsewhere and will see it again; there are those who hate Jeremiah for his message. They want to see him harmed. They taunt him and challenge the validity of his oracles. They do not want see his words come to pass.

In verse 16 Jeremiah affirms that he has not shirked his responsibility to lead (**shepherd**) the people by means of the prophetic word. The **day of despair** could be either the day of his despair (as a result of those who persecute him) or the day of the nation's despair (that will arrive with the Babylonian army). It is probably the former, since the rest of the prayer calls on God to bring his judgment against his enemies.

Additional Notes §62

17:16 / Many other versions and commentaries take the same tack as the NIV in rendering the first colon as a statement that Jeremiah did not avoid his role as a **shepherd.** However, it is more in keeping what we know about Jeremiah as well as the form of the verb *ʾws* to render it something like "I did not insist on shepherding after you" (so Lundbom, *Jeremiah,* p. 799). In other words, this is another statement of Jeremiah's reluctance to be a prophet.

§63 Observe the Sabbath (Jer. 17:19–27)

God now directs Jeremiah to issue a challenge concerning the **Sabbath.** To many modern readers, Sabbath observance may seem almost trivial in relationship to the other charges God through Jeremiah levels at Judah: murder, child sacrifice, idolatry. However, the Sabbath was considered the sign of the Mosaic covenant (Exod. 31:13, 17). In a sense it was the pinnacle of the law during the Old Testament period. It was established at creation (Gen. 2:1–3) and mandated as the fourth commandment (Exod. 20:8–11; Deut. 5:12–15). To neglect the Sabbath, in short, was a serious affront to God and his authority (see Longman, *Immanuel in Our Place,* pp. 161–84).

17:19–21a / God commands Jeremiah to go to every **gate** of the city, especially making sure to go to the gate where **the kings of Judah go in and out** of the city. All city gates were public areas, and they were portals in and out of the city, so that virtually everyone who could walk would have to pass through them. While God tells Jeremiah to get the message out to the entire city, he is particularly to go to the main gate where its leaders conducted court or business.

17:21b–23 / These verses reassert the commandment, found in the Pentateuch, that the people were not to engage in work on the **Sabbath.** Commerce in the trade of materials and agricultural supplies would pass through the gates where Jeremiah was to speak. Verse 23 indicates that in the past, and certainly up to the present, the people of Judah were not observing this requirement.

17:24–27 / In spite of the past neglect of this important law, God calls on them to begin to observe the Sabbath. This renewed command comes with blessing and curse as the law in general did in the Mosaic period (see Deut. 27–28).

The blessing comes in the form of the continuance and prosperity of the people of Judah and their Davidic kings. In terms of the latter, we are reminded that David was promised that one of his descendants would remain on the throne forever. The blessing describes Judah and Jerusalem as it was meant to be, prosperous and coming to Jerusalem with **their sacrifices to praise the LORD.**

However, the description of the consequences of disobedience is as horrifying as the picture of the results of obedience is inviting. God will cause the gates, again where Jeremiah is speaking, to burn with **fire.** This fire will extend to the palaces of those leaders who ignored the divine command to observe the Sabbath.

As we know, the people of Judah did not listen to this warning and they were exiled. It is sad to realize that even after they are restored to Jerusalem that Sabbath observance continued to be a serious problem as Nehemiah notes in Nehemiah 13:15–21.

Additional Notes §63

17:18 / Since it is distinguished from **all the other gates of Jerusalem,** the **gate of the people** must be a specific gate. We do not know of this gate from other sources. From its name we would expect that it is the gate that was used by all the people, but then we hear that kings go through this gate. Lundbom (*Jeremiah 1–20,* p. 805) points out that some think that this might refer to a temple gate rather than a city gate and that its name indicates that it is where non-priests enter. But this does not go well with the expression **other gates of Jerusalem.**

§64 Jeremiah's First Trip to the Potter (Jer. 18:1–23)

Though observed by Jeremiah rather than performed by Jeremiah, we now hear of another prophetic action that illustrates the prophet's verbal message. Jeremiah 18:1–4 narrates the action while 18:5–10 interprets the general significance of the action. Verses 11–12 apply the teaching of the general principle specifically to Judah and Judah's negative response to God's call for repentance. A poetic oracle registering surprise at the people's unwillingness to change follows along with a statement of their coming destruction (vv. 13–17). A plot against Jeremiah motivated by the people's distaste for these negative oracles is disclosed (v. 18), and finally another lament of Jeremiah (vv. 19–23), bemoaning the plots against him and calling on God to punish the plotters.

18:1–4 / God begins by telling Jeremiah to go to the house of the **potter** where God will give the prophet a **message.** Jeremiah responds obediently and observes the potter at work. The basic method of throwing a pot is the same today as it was in antiquity. The potter would place a clay on a **wheel** and as it revolved would use his hands to mold the clay into a useful shape. However, on this occasion things did not go according to plan, and the hoped-for pot was misshapen. The remedy was easy enough: start over again. We are to imagine that the potter took the misshapen pot, smashed it down again, and then molded it into another pot.

18:5–10 / As promised, the word of the Lord came to Jeremiah, and we next hear the divine oracle delivered on this occasion. It is addressed to **the house of Israel** and challenges them to consider themselves like the **clay** and the **potter** to be like God. The language of the oracle here changes, but the implication is clear. God is sovereign over the nations and particularly over Israel (here standing for Judah). If he perceives that the pot, which is Israel, is misshapen (that is, sinful), then he can crush it and start over. The language by which the oracle continues goes back to Jeremiah's commission in Jeremiah 1:10, where God appoints Jeremiah "over nations and kingdoms to uproot and tear down, to destroy and overthrow." On the other hand, and again reverting to the language of Jeremiah 1:10, God can also choose that a nation or kingdom is **to be built up and planted.**

However, these decisions are conditional upon the response of the nations and kingdoms. If those announced for judgment repent or those who are established sin, then all bets are off.

18:11–12 / Germane to Judah and Jerusalem in this oracle is the former condition, namely repentance. Because of their sins, they are now marked for judgment. But if they repent, then disaster can be averted. God calls on them to repent, to turn away from their sins and avert the coming judgment.

However, Judah will have none of it. They persist in their sins. In language surely put into the mouths of the inhabitants of Judah in order to state what their actions demonstrated, we hear them say: **It's no use. We will continue with our own plans; each of us will follow the stubbornness of his evil heart** (v. 12).

18:13–17 / The next section begins with **therefore** (*laken*) indicating that the following divine oracle is in reaction to the refusal to repent of the previous verse. In a word, God registers consternation at their stubbornness, followed by a renewed commitment to punish them.

Not even the pagan nations have ever heard of such a thing. That thing is substituting false gods (**idols**) for the true God. The nations do not betray their (false) gods. Such a situation is described as **a most horrible thing** (*shaʿarurit*). A variant form of this word (*shaʿarurah*) is used in Jeremiah 5:30 and 23:14 in reference to prophets giving false prophecies. **Virgin Israel,** a term of continuing endearment, has done the unexpected by worshiping false deities and refusing to repent.

The unexpected should not happen. **Snow** is always on the **rocky slopes** of the high mountains of Lebanon. **Cool water** always flows from distant sources. And Israel should repent and worship the one true God, but it doesn't!

They have **forgotten** God, which means they do not worship and obey him. Rather they participate in idolatrous worship rituals. They **burn incense** to other gods. In this way, they have stumbled on the **ancient paths** and have taken side roads. The metaphor of the path reminds the reader of the two-path theology of Proverbs (see Longman, *Proverbs,* pp. 59–61). The path is the journey of life. Walking on the ancient paths would signify living according the Yahwistic tradition, while taking the **bypaths** would be cutting a new way. The last colon of verse 15 underlines this last point by referring to the paths **as roads not built up.** Of course, one cannot travel well on such ill-formed roads.

Thus, the final two verses of the oracle move to judgment. God declares that their **land will be laid waste.** Though not specified, this certainly refers to the destruction of Judah by the Babylonian army. As a result, they will be the object of scorn or ridicule.

God then says he will be like a **wind from the east,** the sirocco with its tremendous, life-sapping heat. By showing them his **back** rather than his **face,** he indicates that he will depart from them during the **day of their disaster,** when the punishment comes. They will see his back as he walks away from them to let them suffer the consequences in his absence.

18:18 / All of a sudden we hear from "**they,**" clearly a reference to the people who were the recipients of the pronouncement of divine judgment delivered by Jeremiah. They plot against him. They will verbally attack him, probably by undermining his reputation, plus they will ignore what he says. Of course, what is most damaging to them is that they **pay no attention** to the charge of sin he has leveled against them and will not respond to his call to repentance.

Their reasoning is fascinating and often commented on because it seems to list three functionaries who are pivotal in teaching the people the will of Yahweh. These three groups include the **priest,** the **wise** teacher, and the **prophet.** Of further interest is the association between these three and their respective media of divine revelation. The priest is associated with the **law,** charged to teach the people the law from the moment of its and their inception (Deut. 33:10). The wisdom teacher is associated with **counsel.** This description of the wise is consonant with that we get in the book of Proverbs. They are able to give advice to others. Finally, the prophet has the **word,** short for the word of God. The prophets speak oracles given to them by God. As the people reject Jeremiah and his message, they encourage each other by saying that they still have these vehicles of divine revelation. Get rid of Jeremiah and there will still be a conduit to the divine. However, the broader context of Jeremiah leads us to believe that these priests, sages, and prophets are not legitimate; rather, they say only what the people themselves want to hear.

18:19–23 / Jeremiah responds to this plotting by accusing them before Yahweh. Jeremiah thus utters another of his laments or confessions (11:18–12:6; 15:10–11, 15–21; 17:14–18; 20:7–13, 14–18). He first calls Yahweh's attention to these plotting words. He has done **good** for them, by preaching God's message to them and giving them the opportunity of repentance, which would spare them from punishment. But they repay this good with **evil.** They seek to undermine the prophet, a fate described as digging a **pit.** It is as if Jeremiah is walking on the path of life but that these wicked people have set a trap, a pit into which he will fall.

But Jeremiah has done more than speak God's words of warning and issued the call to repentance to them. He has also come before God and prayed on their behalf. In so doing, Jeremiah has fulfilled the intercessory role of the prophet. The prophet was charged with appealing to God on behalf of the people as well as presenting God's judgment to them. We can see this with Abraham (Gen. 20:7), Moses (Exod. 33:12–23), Samuel (1 Sam. 12:3), and others.

Since they have responded to Jeremiah's good with such evil, his prayer of intercession on behalf of the people turns into an imprecatory prayer, asking for God's judgment against them. The language that follows is similar to the curses of the psalms calling for the destruction of the enemy. First, he asks that God allow their **children** to experience **famine** and that they themselves will be struck down by the **sword.** In this way, their wives will become grieving widows. Of course, the content of these curses fit well with the coming punishment since it describes the aftermath of a battle like that which Judah will experience at the hands of the Babylonians.

Additional Notes §64

18:13 / Schmitt ("The Virgin of Israel: Referent and Use of the Phrase in Amos and Jeremiah," *CBQ* 53 [1991], pp. 365–87) has made the argument that **Virgin Israel** should be understood in a construct genitival relationship, thus "Virgin of Israel," and as a specific reference to the city of Jerusalem, not the entirety of Israel (see also 31:4, 21).

§65 A Clay Jar: Judgment against Topheth (Jer. 19:1–20:6)

Jeremiah 18 narrates a trip to the potter where a lesson is drawn from the relationship between the potter and the clay he molds into a vessel. No chronological relationship is explicit between chapters 18 and 19 and the sequence may simply be the result of the common theme of the potter. In this passage, however, Jeremiah purchases a finished pot and takes it to the valley of Ben Hinnom, also known as Topheth, where horrible and idolatrous rituals were performed. He identifies the pot as symbolic of the apostate nation of Israel and then smashes it. This ritual reminds us of the Egyptian execration texts. These are texts on which the names of Egypt's enemies were written and then smashed in anticipation of the destruction of the nations themselves. Walton (*IVPBBCOT,* p. 656) also notes a possible literary connection that goes back to the Sumerian Lament over the Destruction of Sumer and Ur which compares the citizens of destroyed Ur to broken pots ("Its people like potsherds littered its sides" [*COS* 1:163, 536, line 211]). After speaking at Topheth itself, Jeremiah returns to the temple where he also speaks of Judah's coming judgment. Finally, in response especially to Jeremiah's speech at the temple, a priestly official, Pashhur has the prophet beaten. As a result, Jeremiah delivers a judgment speech against Pashhur and takes the opportunity to deliver yet one more oracle against Judah.

19:1–6 / The chapter begins with the divine directive to Jeremiah to **purchase a clay jar from the potter.** The clay jar may be more specifically a flask (the Hebrew term *baqbuq*) may be onomatopoetic for the sound that liquid would make coming out of the vessel (*NIDOTTE,* vol. 2, p. 655). The clay jar will be a prop for yet another prophetic symbolic action. He takes the **elders of the people** and the **priests** out to the Valley of Ben Hinnom. That he could convince these important individuals in Judean society to accompany him indicates that Jeremiah was something of a force to be reckoned with and could not be easily ignored.

For the **Valley of Ben Hinnom** see commentary on Jer. 7:30–34. We do not know the Potsherd Gate except in this one occasion, but the name describes broken pieces of pots littering the exit to the "dump." The gate may have gone by a variety of names including the Dung Gate (Neh. 2:13; 3:13, 14; 12:31).

Upon his arrival at this location, God instructed Jeremiah to deliver an oracle that announces a future, horrible punishment upon the people. It is so bad that it will make **the ears of everyone who hears it tingle.** The reason for the punishment is given as idolatry and the reason for the choice of this location for the delivery of the oracle is now clear. This place has been dedicated to the worship of foreign deities, in particular to Baal. Specifically, they have offered their own children as sacrifices to their false god here.

In the context of the announcement of judgment, we hear a second name for this place, **Topheth** (see also Jer. 7:30–34). This word in Hebrew means "spit" and is clearly a pejorative name expressing contempt for the place. It is of great interest to note that 2 Kings 23:10 tells us that Topheth was desecrated during the reforms of Josiah. "He desecrated Topheth, which was in the Valley of Ben Hinnom, so no one could use it to sacrifice his son or daughter in the fire to Molech." Here, the child sacrifice is associated with Molech rather than Baal, but the principle is the same. Since Jeremiah is speaking this judgment speech at least in part to the kings of Judah (19:3), it suggests that Jehoiakim rebuilt the place and started using it again. Whatever its name—Topheth or Valley of Hinnom—Yahweh through Jeremiah announces a name change. In the future it will be called the **Valley of Slaughter.** The slaughter will be that of the Judeans who practice such horrific rites. This prophetic judgment has already been narrated in 7:30–34 and the theme will be revisited in 32:35.

19:7–9 / In these verses Jeremiah continues to relate Yahweh's judgment against his apostate people. He will **ruin** their **plans.** The plans probably point to their intention to continue worshiping false gods and offering child sacrifice to them, perhaps as a misguided attempt to stave off disaster. He will frustrate these plans by allowing their enemies (who will turn out to be the Babylonians) to have victory over them. They will meet the most horrible of ends. They will not only die in battle, but they will not even receive proper burial. Their bodies instead will be exposed on the battlefield and be picked at by birds and animals of prey. In other words, God will use his creatures, both their human enemies as well as the animals of land and air, to accomplish his judgment. But it is not only the death of the ungodly people of Judah that will result; the **city** of Jerusalem itself will be destroyed. Those who hear about it will be horrified and speak poorly of the city, which at a better time was "beautiful in its loftiness, and the joy of the whole earth" (Ps. 48:2). Finally, Jeremiah, on behalf of God, describes the horrors of the coming siege. The inhabitants of the city will run out of food and then eat their children (see 2 Kgs. 6:24–31, for such a description during an earlier siege) and then one another. From 2 Kings 25:1–7, we learn that the siege began against Jerusalem on January 15, 588 B.C. (Hebrew translates: "on the tenth day of the tenth month of the ninth year of Zedekiah's reign") and did not end till all the food ran out on July 18, 586 B.C. (by the ninth day of the fourth month of Zedekiah's eleventh year; see also Jeremiah 52:6).

19:10–13 / At this point Jeremiah was to take the **jar** and smash it. This action anticipates what will happen to the city and its citizens. They too will be smashed through an act of divine judgment. Jeremiah also makes the point that the defilement caused by idolatry is not just restricted to Topheth, this location of child sacrifice outside the city, but extends to the entirety of Jerusalem. As a result, God will make Jerusalem like Topheth, a place of ruin. After all it was not just at Topheth that they **burned incense on the roofs to all the starry hosts and poured out drink offerings to other gods.**

19:14–15 / The chapter ends with Jeremiah leaving Topheth after the prophetic action of breaking the clay jar that represented Judah, and delivering a brief related oracle to all the people at **the court of the LORD's temple.** In this way, the audience for his words expands. By standing on ground made holy by the Lord's presence, Jeremiah's words grow in solemnity.

The oracle is not only brief, it is to the point. God will bring on Jerusalem and its surrounding villages **every disaster I pronounced against them.** Whether this previous pronouncement points immediately to words that Jeremiah has already spoken to the people specifying siege, defeat, death, exile, or whether it refers to the divine words pronounced in covenant curses such as those found in Deuteronomy 28 is beside the point. The former derives from the latter. The stated purpose is also straightforward.

The people have not obeyed God's words as they have been stated through the law.

20:1–6 / The text now narrates the reaction of a powerful official (**chief officer in the temple of the LORD**) to Jeremiah's judgment speech, most likely the one just delivered in the temple precincts. This official is named **Pashhur,** the son (in the sense of descendant) of **Immer.** We know from the genealogy of 1 Chronicles 9:12 that Pashhur was a priest himself. He is not the same Pashhur as in Jeremiah 21:1.

Priests were guardians of the holy space (Longman, *Immanuel in Our Place,* pp. 117–60), and so Pashhur was surely within his rights to punish someone whom he thought was a false prophet (Deut. 17:12). However, since Jeremiah's prophecy was not false, the story condemns Pashhur. It does so by having Jeremiah deliver a personal judgment speech against the priest. He renames Pashhur, **Magor-Missabib.** The new name means "terror on every side," and is an expression used eight other times in Psalms, Isaiah, and Jeremiah. "Such an expression depicts a hopeless state of terror where survival itself is threatened" (*NIDOTTE,* vol. 1, p. 840). This encompassing horror will not only be the experience of Pashhur, but of all of Judah. Pashhur thus embodies the sins and will illustrate the punishments that come on the land of Judah as a whole. This oracle is significant because it is the first specification of **Babylon** as the instrument of God's judgment. Elsewhere permutations like "foe from the north" are used.

Additional Notes §65

19:7 / There is a sound play between **I will ruin** (*baqqoti*) and the word for **clay jar** (*baqbuq*), which seems intentional (Lundbom, *Jeremiah 1–20,* p. 836; Fretheim, *Jeremiah,* p. 283).

§66 *Jeremiah's Lament (Jer. 20:7–18)*

As we have just heard (20:1–6), Jeremiah's message was not met with repentance but resistance. He is not proclaimed as a messenger of God come to save the nation from destruction, but he is met with violence because the religious and political authorities believed he was seditious and a false prophet. This complaint records the prophet's reaction to his circumstances. Using the lament form familiar at least in general structure and tone to what we find often in the psalms of disorientation, Jeremiah records his anger toward God and those who persecute him. However, also like the lament psalms found in the Psalter, Jeremiah registers his confidence in God as his protector. Typically, however, in laments that move from sorrow to joy, the latter is the mood with which the composition ends. Here, as is typical with people who are in mental and physical torment, it moves back and forth and ends as it begins—with sadness concerning his circumstances. Jeremiah's other laments may be seen in 11:18–12:6; 15:10–11, 15–21; 17:14– 18; 18:19–23.

Though the beginning of the lament does not explicitly suggest that this lament is in direct reaction to the events of 20:1–6, the connection may be seen in the reference to Magor-missabib (20:3), which is the Hebrew behind the expression **"Terror on every side!"** (v. 10).

20:7–10 / Jeremiah starts out with a strong accusation against God. The verb translated **deceived** (hiphil of *pth*) could alternatively be translated "persuaded" (see NIV footnote) or even "seduced" or "lured," but in any case the charge against God is quite negative (for the argument that it is persuade and not seduce, see D. J. A. Clines and D. M. Gunn, "'You Tried to Persuade Me' and 'Violence! Outrage!' in Jeremiah xx 7–8," *VT* 28 [1978], pp. 20–27). That the proper translation is either "deceived" or "seduced/lured" rather than "persuaded" is strengthened by the second colon, which accuses God of violence (**you overpowered me and prevailed**). The charge against God is either deception or rape (seduced and overpowered together suggest the latter). In answer to the protest that God cannot deceive or violate in this way due to his nature, it should be noted that Jeremiah is expressing his heart, not giving an accurate picture of the nature of God. On the other hand, we do elsewhere have the suggestion that God at least allows deception and violence to take place in order to further his plans (see 1 Kgs. 22 for the role of Micaiah).

Today in the West at least, shame is not always a negative thing, indeed it sometimes creates celebrity and brings wealth to people. This was not true in the ancient Near East, a culture that was obsessed with maintaining honor and avoiding shame. Jeremiah experiences the latter as he is **ridiculed** and mocked. The mocking comes from people who reject his message of impending destruction and judgment. We can almost picture the scene as Jeremiah announces his message and people respond with insults.

In what may be one of his most famous statements, Jeremiah acknowledges that he contemplated not delivering the divine message. However, though tormented, he admits that he could not help himself. God's word is **like a fire** in his innermost person (**my heart** and **my bones**). It is harder for him not to speak than to speak, a classic case of being "between a rock and a hard place."

But everyone is against him, passersby as well as his friends (20:10). The former are saying **"Terror on every side! Report him! Report him!"** The first phrase is the same as the name Jeremiah gave to Pashhur (20:3), Magor-missabib. The people seem to be repeating Jeremiah's message, and the context suggests that they say it with contempt toward the prophet. It motivates them to report him, presumably to the political and religious authorities. They want to shut him up. Indeed, it is likely no accident that their hope to **deceive** (from *pth*) him and **prevail** (from *ykl*) over him repeats the language by which he accused God in verse 10. But it is God who has prevailed; thus the next section marshals his divine resources against his hostile friends.

20:11–13 / The mood shift between verses 10 and 11 is sudden and unexplained. However, this abruptness is typical of laments in the Psalms as well and could also be explained by the turbulent psychology of someone who undergoes persecution. Though they have tried to **prevail** over him (v. 10), they will not succeed (v. 11), because God has prevailed over him and that means God is with him as a **mighty warrior.** That, of course, signifies that the plans of Jeremiah's enemies will be thwarted (**stumble**). Instead of shaming the prophet (vv. 7, 8), they will be **thoroughly disgraced** and experience **dishonor.**

Jeremiah, who is **righteous** himself, invites God to explore his **heart and mind.** As God does so, Jeremiah understands that he will see his commitment to him and then will take **vengeance** on the enemies. This sentiment is familiar also from Psalm 139, in which God is urged to examine the motives of the psalmist and then take action against those who hate him. Indeed, Jeremiah himself has already stated his confidence in God's future vengeance against his enemies in Jeremiah 11:20 (see Freitheim, *Jeremiah,* p. 294).

Jeremiah's confidence in God's determination to save him from persecution leads him to praise the Lord with song and ask all those who hear him to join in. Why? Because he saves the **needy** (in this case Jeremiah himself) from the hands of the **wicked** (namely, the prophet's detractors).

20:14–18 / Though Jeremiah's lament had a brief respite in verses 11–13, his speech ends with an expression of complete depression. Jeremiah goes beyond a death wish by saying that he is sad that he was ever born. Ecclesiastes 5:3b–5 also describes a life not worth living using similar language (for translation and commentary, see Longman, *Ecclesiastes,* pp. 163–65). Furthermore, the sentiment and some of the language are similar to Job's lament (Job 3), where he expresses his distress over the immense suffering that has come into his life.

Verses 14–15 begin by pronouncing a curse on the day **he was born.** It recreates the day when a messenger came to his father with the news that he was born. The joy of that day contrasts with the sadness of Jeremiah's present condition. Verses 16–17 then carry the argument further by moving to pronounce a curse on that man who brought the news. So hard has his life become that Jeremiah wishes great suffering for that man, the kind of suffering that came on Sodom and Gomorrah (**the towns the Lord overthrew without pity,** see Gen. 18). Why is this man being cursed? Because instead of announcing with joy Jeremiah's birth, he should have performed an abortion. It would have been a mercy had he never been allowed to be born and suffer in the way that he is suffering. He wishes his mother's womb had been his grave. Considering that Jeremiah acknowledged he was called to be a prophet in the womb (Jer. 1:5), this statement also throws a note of sarcasm on his prophetic task.

Additional Notes §66

20:11 / The image of God as a **mighty warrior** is a pervasive one in the Bible (Longman and Reid, *God is a Warrior*). Here Jeremiah claims that the warrior is with him personally in his battle against those who try to subvert his prophecy. It seems to be a pattern that the Divine Warrior makes his presence known to his prophets on the occasion that the kings become apostate (see 2 Kgs. 6:8–23 for the appearance of the God's angelic army for the rescue of Elisha).

20:14–18 / Most commentaries (Fretheim, *Jeremiah,* p. 296) include a discussion as to the formal status of vv. 14–18. They are a curse, but the question remains whether this curse is a prayer to God. Certainly within these verses there is no indication that God is invoked, but that the curse is part of a prayer seems obvious from the larger context (v. 8). Another general question concerning these passages has to do with why Jeremiah curses the day he was born and the messenger? I think the answer lies in seeing what the stronger alternative would be. He does not curse father or mother, thus breaking the fifth commandment, nor does he curse God himself, at least directly, thus breaking the third commandment. See parallels in Job 3 and 10. See also the discussion by J. Lundbom, "The Double Curse in Jeremiah 20:14–18," *JBL* 104 (1985), pp. 589–600.

§67 God Rejects Zedekiah's Request for Prayer (Jer. 21:1–14)

The setting of Jeremiah's next judgment oracle is more definitively described than some of the previous ones. Zedekiah, the last Judean king (597–586 B.C.), sends two individuals, Pashhur and Zephaniah (the second is a priest, but the first may be as well) to Jeremiah to request that the prophet intercede with the Lord for them. We can get even more specific about the date because the prophet's response to the priests' request includes a mention of "the Babylonians who are outside the wall besieging you." Thus, this oracle's setting is during the relatively short period of time after the siege of Jerusalem began but before its destruction (588–586 B.C.). Other episodes within the book of Jeremiah tell us that Zedekiah tried to undermine the prophet's ministry, but we might imagine that the situation has become so dire that the king wants to try almost anything to reverse his fortunes. The fact that he turns to Jeremiah indicates that he thinks that he is a true prophet, and it is indeed the role of the prophet to pray for God's people. However, Jeremiah's response indicates that it is too late for the nation as a whole and for the king himself. However, the people as individuals have the opportunity to either stay hard and die in the city or repent and surrender to Nebuchadnezzar.

21:1–2 / Jeremiah speaks his next oracle in response to an appeal from King Zedekiah, who sends **Pashhur** and a priest named **Zephaniah** (see Additional Notes) as his ambassadors. Now that his back is against the wall, the king, who has mistreated Jeremiah, asks him to pray to the Lord with the hope that the Lord will perform **wonders** and deliver them from the Babylonians, who, we soon learn (v. 4) are besieging the city.

A king asking a prophet to intercede with the Lord in this kind of situation is not at all unusual. After all, the prophet served as the conscience of the king and as one who could represent the king's interests to the Lord. However, as soon becomes evident, the king has waited too long to take this positive stance.

21:3–7 / The judgment oracle proper promises that the Babylonians who are presently besieging the city will succeed. At present the forces of Judea are fighting against the Babylonians, but God confirms that their fighting will be of no avail. Soon the Babylonians will be inside the walls of the city. God then reveals that it is not just the Babylonians who are fighting the Judeans, but God himself, in what may be described as reverse holy war, which will assure the defeat of Jerusalem. Indeed the language of God's military power (**with an outstretched hand and a mighty arm**) is reminiscent of God's victory over the Egyptians at the time of the exodus (Exod. 6:6; Deut. 4:34; 5:15; 7:19; 9:22; 11:2; 26:8). God's exodus power is here being used against them. The devastation that the siege will cause on the inhabitants of Jerusalem are summarized by the phrase **plague, sword and famine,** all typical consequences of military siege of walled cities. For those who survive the siege itself, including king Zedekiah, there is only further suffering. Nebuchadnezzar will put them to death.

21:8–10 / In these verses, the Lord through Jeremiah addresses the people directly. There is still a glimmer of qualified hope; there is still the possibility of choosing **the way of life** rather than **the way of death.** This language is reminiscent of the two-path theology in Proverbs, especially found in the first nine chapters. God's way is the way that leads to life, but to reject that way lands a person on the way to death. Jeremiah's language is also reminiscent of that of Moses, who places before the Israelites a choice between life and death (Deut. 30:11–20). In the long run, they have chosen death.

The choice is to either surrender to the Babylonians and live under their authority or else to resist and die in the city. Because of the sins of the people, there must be punishment, but still there is a choice. Either way, the city will be destroyed. It is in the light of oracles like this one that we can understand why Jeremiah was accused of being a Babylonian collaborator. But he is not pro-Babylonian; he is pro-God and he knows that God is using the Babylonians, at least temporarily, to effect punishment on Judah.

21:11–14 / The next oracle is pronounced against the **royal house of Judah.** This would include the king and his royal predecessors, whom chapter 22 names individually. There is no specific mention of a date, but the presumption is that this is an oracle that was delivered during the time of Zedekiah (21:1).

In this oracle God demands that the officials who are addressed do their job with integrity (**administer justice every morning**). Dearman suggests that morning was the typical time for court cases (*Jeremiah*, pp. 206–7). As part of their task of administering justice, they would be responsible for making sure that those who have been exploited (**robbed by oppressors**) were protected. The implication of the demand is that these officials were not fulfilling their duty. Therefore Yahweh threatens judgment in the form of **fire.** In this case, the threat of fire may turn out to be literal since the destroyed city of Jerusalem was put to fire (2 Kgs. 25:9).

Verse 13 contains a frequently attested formula of judgment (**I am against you**) that declares God's displeasure with his people (see also Jer. 50:31; 51:25; Nah. 2:13; 3:5). Specifically, the oracle seems addressed against **Jerusalem.** The city name is added by the NIV (compare NRSV), but is not in the Hebrew (see Additional Notes). Rather, the object of judgment is described as those who **live above the valley on the rocky plateau.** This description is appropriate to Jerusalem, which is surrounded by three valleys.

The object of judgment is further described by their arrogant response. God has said he is against them and they say **"Who can come against us?"** Perched on the plateau above the valley, they feel a totally unjustified security. If the oracle is dated to the time of 21:1, then their confidence is nearly inexplicable since the Babylonian army completely surrounds them. Irrational bravado is not unknown in such circumstances, however.

In the light of their indifference, God repeats his intention to punish them for their wicked actions. Again, the instrument of judgment is fire; in this case the picture that is drawn is a forest fire that consumes everything in its wake.

Additional Notes §67

21:1 / **Pashhur son of Malkijah** does not appear to be the same person as Pashhur son of Immer in the account found in 20:1–6. It may be that the present Pashhur is also a priest, based on the genealogy of a Pashhur son of Malkijah found in 1 Chronicles 9:12 (see also Neh. 11:12). He is also mentioned in Jeremiah 38:1 (which context indicates that he may have been from the royal house). As for **the priest Zephaniah son of**

Maaseiah, he appears again in 29:25, 29, as well as in 37:3. In the light of the story in chapter 29, he may have had some sympathy toward the prophet. He is described as being taken prisoner by the forces of Nebuchadnezzar in 2 Kings 25:18 (compare Jer. 52:24).

21:5 / When God himself announces that he will fight against his own people (**I myself will fight against you**), we have what might be described as reverse holy war. In the curses of the covenant, God promises to fight on behalf of his obedient people, but to side with their enemies when they are disobedient (Deut. 28). Precursors to such divine warfare may be seen at Ai (Josh. 7) and before that in the Philistine victory over Israel under the leadership of Eli's wicked sons (1 Sam. 4–5). For more on this, see Longman and Reid, *God is a Warrior,* pp. 49–52.

21:13 / The NIV supplies the name **Jerusalem,** which is not found in the Hebrew, though the language almost certainly is an indirect allusion to that city. We say almost certainly because the Hebrew is a bit ambiguous. Literally, it is rendered "I am against you, oh inhabitant of the valley, rocky plateau." Jerusalem was on a rocky plateau surrounded by valleys. It is possible to construe the literal Hebrew as "you enthroned above the valley" (so Thompson, *Jeremiah,* p. 470).

§68 Oracles concerning the Kings of Judah (Jer. 22:1–23:8)

The previous chapter issued an oracle against Zedekiah, and now the prophet continues the diatribe against Judah's kings. At first the oracle is addressed to the "king of Judah" without specification (22:1–10). After this initial speech Jeremiah addresses Shallum (22:11–17 also know as Jehoahaz, who ruled for only a few months in 609 B.C.). Then (22:18–23) he turns his attention to Jehoiakim (609–597 B.C.), followed by Jehoiachin, who ruled only a few months in Jerusalem before he was taken away in captivity to Babylon and replaced by Zedekiah, the last king of Judah (597–586 B.C.). In essence, these oracles cover the post-Josianic kings who ruled during the period of Jeremiah's prophetic activity.

22:1 / God instructs Jeremiah to go to the **palace** in order to deliver a judgment oracle against the kings of Judah. This move makes sense, of course, because the recipient of judgment is more likely to hear the oracle this way. However, it is also clearly dangerous for Jeremiah because an offended king could turn against the prophet easily and powerfully.

22:2 / The oracle is addressed primarily to the king, but includes the entire royal apparatus (**you, your officials and your people**). The **gates** were probably gates that led to the palace.

22:3 / The oracle demands that the king take care of the vulnerable, which includes victims of crimes (**the one who has just been robbed**), the **alien,** the **fatherless,** and the **widow** (Exod. 22:21; Lev. 19:33; 25:14, 17; Deut. 23:16). It was the king's duty to protect those who could not protect themselves and also create a society that was harmonious for law-abiding citizens. That God through Jeremiah felt it necessary to issue such a proclamation about a requirement found in the law (Exod. 22:22; Deut. 10:18; 27:19), implies that the kings of Judah were not taking care of their responsibilities in this regard. They were also not to **shed innocent blood** (Deut. 19:10; 27:25). The particular action behind this expression is not clear. Is it because they are putting to death people who do not deserve it or does it refer to child sacrifice? It may refer to the fact that they have allowed social conditions to deteriorate to the point where people were being killed by wrongdoers.

22:4–5 / God's demand comes with blessing and curse, similar to the law of the covenant (see Deut. 27–28). If the kings obey, then the Davidic dynasty will be allowed to continue without interruption. If the kings do not obey, then the palace itself will be destroyed.

22:6–7 / The prophet uses a geographical metaphor to describe the present status of the temple as well as its potential condition, contingent on the lack of obedience of the kings. **Gilead** and especially **Lebanon** had breathtakingly beautiful landscapes and heavily forested areas. The palace had been built out of timber brought from the cedar forests of Lebanon. Solomon's palace went by the name "Palace of the Forest of Lebanon" (1 Kgs. 7:2). If the kings rebel against God, this plush building will become **like a desert,** a desert which will not sustain life. In verse 7b a related image is used, that of a ghost town. God will accomplish this transformation by sending against them destroyers who will tear down the building. Jeremiah's prophecy was fulfilled in the Babylonian destruction of the city that included the dismantling of the palace.

22:8–9 / Finally, in this first general oracle against the kings of Judah, the prophet imaginatively recounts a conversation that would take place once God's judgment has been executed against his disobedient royal house. Foreigners who pass by the future ruins will ask each other the reason for such a horrific destruction. Even the Gentiles will know the reason—this horrible fate has come on those who broke the covenant especially by committing idolatry.

22:10–12 / Jeremiah now begins a series of prophetic judgment speeches against the kings of Judah who followed Josiah on the throne. The first begins with a poetic oracle telling people not to weep for the **dead king,** but rather for the exiled king. This enigmatic reference is explained in the following verses where we learn that the dead king is Josiah, while the exiled king is his son who is here called **Shallum.** With the exception of 1 Chronicles 3:15, this person is elsewhere referred to as Jehoahaz. That kings often go by more than a single name, sometimes taking on a throne name, may be seen in other places (The Assyrian king, Tiglath-pileser, is called Pul in 2 Kgs. 15:19 and 2 Chr. 5:26).

Jehoahaz was the son and immediate successor of Josiah, who is consistently regarded as a good king in Scripture and by Jeremiah. Indeed in verses 15–17 Shallum's evil is contrasted with the good character and actions of Josiah (**your father**). Josiah's death at Megiddo was a huge setback for Judah and especially the pro-Yahweh forces. It may be that the fourth son, Shallum, was placed on the throne because of his pro-Babylonian, anti-Egyptian stance (see further Introduction: Historical Context).

We get the brief story of the rise and rapid fall of Jehoahaz in 2 Kings 23:31–35 and 2 Chronicles 36:1–4. We learn there that he was twenty-three years old. We also are informed that when Neco dethroned him he took him to Egypt where he died. It is from Kings that we characteristically hear that he "did evil in the eyes of the LORD, just as his fathers had done" (2 Kgs. 23:32). We are not given the details, though the presumption is that he allowed illegitimate religious practices to continue. The Jeremiah passage confirms the historiographic tradition when it tells us that he was taken away and died in the place of his exile.

22:13–23 / In 609 B.C. Neco removed Jehoahaz from the throne, presumably because like his father he was pro-Babylonian, and placed his second son **Jehoiakim** there. Neco's decisions, the animosity between Jehoiakim and Jeremiah (Jer. 26 and 36), together with Jehoiakim's later actions, suggest he was pro-Egyptian. It would make sense that Jeremiah was pro-Babylonian because his task included trying to convince Judah to submit to Nebuchadnezzar, while Jehoiakim's hope to be free of their influence was based on potential aid that would come from Egypt.

It was not very long before Nebuchadnezzar projected his influence into the area. If the tradition preserved in Daniel 1:1–3 is taken seriously, he was able to exact tribute from Jehoiakim beginning in 605.

Jehoiakim waited until 597 to make his move and we do not know what induced him to do so (2 Kgs. 23:36–24:7). He rebelled against Nebuchadnezzar, which at a minimum indicated that he did not pay annual tribute. When he heard of this, the Babylonian king mobilized his troops and began the long march toward Jerusalem. Before he reached the city, however, Jehoiachin was king. It is unclear whether he is co-regent with Jehoiakim or the sole king, or what forces led to Jehoiakim being thrust to the side.

The different biblical texts are also difficult to harmonize in terms of Jehoiakim's end. It is unclear whether Jehoiakim was killed by the Babylonian forces in Jerusalem (as implied by the oracles that he will have the burial of a donkey—dragged away and thrown outside the gates of Jerusalem) or was deported (2 Chr. 36:6). In either case, his end was not a happy one.

His sad end, according to Jeremiah (vv. 13–17), has to do with ethical shortcomings unrecorded in Kings or Chronicles, though it appears that this king was in it for his own profit. In saying that he made **his countrymen work for nothing** in the construction of his palace, 1 Kgs. 11:28 states that he, like Solomon before him, illegally pressed Judah's citizens into forced labor. It implies that he got what he deserved because unlike his father before him, he was an oppressor.

The oracle that Jeremiah utters concludes with the statement that Jehoiakim's death will not be met with mourning. Typically when a person dies, they have those who survive whose grief leads them to say **alas** (*hoy*). Both relatives (**my brother, my sister**) as well as subjects (**my master**) would express their grief at his death. However, Jeremiah envisions that his death will be greeted with indifference at best and joy at worst. Also he will have a contemptible funeral like that of a **donkey.**

Verse 21 reminds the king that the prophet had tried to convince him and get him to change in a way that would have saved him from his fate. But he **felt secure** as he sat in his temple, here called **Lebanon** because the building was constructed from the finest cedars from that area. But judgment will transform his confidence and security into pain.

22:24–30 / As might be expected, the next oracle of judgment is directed toward Jehoiakim's successor and son, **Jehoiachin.** This is the first mention of this king in the book; he is even absent from the superscription (1:1), which surprisingly moves from Jehoiakim to Zedekiah.

The historiographic tradition (2 Kgs. 24:8–17; 2 Chr. 36:9–10) informs us of the brief reign of this king. As explained in the previous section concerning his father Jehoiakim, the exact conditions under which Jehoiachin came to the throne (either as solo or coregent) are unknown to us. What we do know is that he became king at the age of eighteen and had to immediately deal with a Babylonian siege of Jerusalem. He only lasted three months (in the year 597 B.C.), and when Nebuchadnezzar took the city, the

Babylonians took treasures from the temple and palace and exiled the king, his mother, wives, and many others including the 7000 troops. From the book that bears his name, we also know that Ezekiel was a part of the exiled group (Ezek. 1:2). There is an interesting and telling contrast with Ezekiel concerning this king, but Jeremiah has a decidedly negative attitude toward him.

The book of 2 Kings (25:27–30) also informs us that Jehoiachin lived long into the exile and was released from prison in the year that Evil-Merodach (also known as Amel-Marduk the son of Nebuchadnezzar) became king. This event is dated to 562 B.C.

Jeremiah's oracle speaks as if Jehoiachin is still on the throne, which is also true of the others. It may well be that what we have here is a selection of oracles that come from the respective time periods of the kings that are addressed. The oracle begins with a vivid speech purportedly directed to the king (**you, Jehoiachin**). Even if the king were identified with God as closely as a **signet ring** (see Additional Notes) is to the person wearing it, God would distance himself from him and turn him over to Nebuchadnezzar. As we have already observed in our historical review, this is precisely what happened. Jehoiachin was indeed exiled and never came back to Judah.

At this point Jeremiah speaks a poetic oracle (vv. 28–30) that begins by comparing the king to **a despised, broken pot.** Clay pots were easily broken and were unusable. If we judge by the millions of potshards that litter the surface of tells today, they probably grew to be quite a nuisance to the ancient inhabitants, since they do not disappear with time.

Progeny and succession were matters of great concern to ancient kings, including those of Judah, a land ruled by a single dynasty for its entire history. However, Jehoiachin would be like a childless king; though he had children (2 Chr. 3:17), they would never rule.

23:1–8 / Following the oracles against the kings of Judah, Jeremiah delivers a final statement of judgment against the **shepherds** who are destroying and scattering the sheep of God's pasture. This is followed by an oracle of future salvation of the people and the arrival of a new **King** who will rule his people with righteousness.

The initial proclamation against the shepherds is delivered in the form of a **woe** oracle, a form that we have already encountered in 22:18 (see Additional Notes on 10:19–22). The shepherd is a not uncommon metaphor for political and religious leaders (Num. 27:17; Ps. 78:70–72, see especially Ezek. 34). The fact that these shepherds destroy the **sheep** (which stands for their subjects) is particularly damning since real shepherds go to great lengths to take care of and protect their sheep. Rather than keep these sheep together for their protection, they have **scattered** them, making them easy prey. For this the leaders will be punished. However, the punishment of these evil shepherds signals the beginnings of salvation for some of the sheep, described as the **remnant**, yet another potent concept frequently encountered in the prophets. The remnant refers to the faithful people of God who survive the coming judgment and who will provide the foundation of the rebuilding of God's people.

Finally, God speaks to a future (signaled by the phrase **the days are coming**) godly leadership of the people of God. The oracle speaks in terms of a future Davidic ruler. The metaphor of the **Branch** (*tsemakh*) derives from the idea of the people of God as a tree that has been chopped down; from its stump comes a shoot or a branch, and, as W. Kaiser (*The Messiah in the Old Testament*, p. 156) points out, may emanate from 2 Samuel 23:5, where David states that God will bring to fruition (from the verb *tsmkh*) his salvation. The idea of the Branch is developed as a messianic theme also in Isaiah 4:2; Zechariah 3:8 and 6:12. While from a New Testament perspective we rightly understand this salvation oracle to be ultimately fulfilled in Christ, who is the righteous shepherd and descendant of David, the immediate effect on Jeremiah's audience may have been to anticipate a righteous human king. The name **The LORD Our Righteousness** formed from the divine name Yahweh plus the word *tsedeq* is a play on the name of the last king of Judah Zedekiah (English "zedeq" from the Hebrew *tsedeq* and "iah" from a short form of Yahweh). The idea is that Zedekiah is not the righteous king; another will come in the future.

Finally (vv. 7–8) Jeremiah invokes another important prophetic theme of the time, the second exodus, to talk about the future salvation of the remnant. The future judgment will cause many Judaean's to depart from the promised land. The future return is likened to the original entry after liberation from Egypt.

Additional Notes §68

22:15 / **Cedar** was an expensive and precious wood imported from Lebanon. It was an indication of luxury and great wealth. The fact that the king built his house in such a luxurious manner during a time of threat indicates his callousness to the needs of the people.

22:24 / A **signet ring** (*khotam*) was a ring that could make an impression when pressed into soft clay. The ring would have an identification symbol, and sometimes the name, of the wearer. Its impression would mark an object as belonging to the person. Thus, the signet ring was a precious object that was closely identified with the owner and conferred the owner's authority. The closest parallel use of this word may be seen in Haggai 2:23 where Zerubbabel is likened to a signet ring.

22:26 / Jeremiah reports that God will **hurl** Jehoiachin and his mother into exile. The verb translated "hurl" (*hiphil* of *twl*) is used frequently in Jonah 1, but more interesting for its use here are those instances where it "describes the Lord's decisive and violent judgment against officials and nations" (Isa. 22:17; Jer. 16:13, Ezek. 32:4). See *NIDOTTE,* vol. 2, p. 359.

§69 Prophets Who Lie (Jer. 23:9–40)

Jeremiah now trains his sight on false prophets. The rest of the chapter collects various prose and poetic oracles pronouncing judgment on those who claim to speak God's word when in actuality they do not. Jeremiah was not the only one offering a "word of the LORD." The false prophets bear a special burden of God's anger because they make it more difficult for the people to discern the authentic divine message. Jeremiah 28 will recount a particular conflict between Jeremiah and a false prophet named Hananiah.

23:9–12 / Jeremiah describes his mental anguish in the light of the judgment (**the LORD and his holy words**) he is pronouncing. The prophet is shaken to the core, as is represented by the broken **heart** and shaking **bones.** He has lost his capacities like a **drunk** whose mind is clouded by drink and has lost control over his bodily functions.

The description of the objects of God's judgment at first is general. They are described as **adulterers** who fill the land. Adultery here is likely meant literally of those who break their marriage vows in pursuit of illegitimate sexual relations, but also metaphorically of those who depart from their exclusive relationship with Yahweh to pursue other gods (see also 3:1–5; 9:2). The NIV clarifies what the Hebrew text leaves unidentified until verse 11 by supplying **prophets** in verse 10. But whoever specifically are the adulterers the results include a drought that leaves the land **parched** and **withered.**

The objects of judgment are the religious leaders of Judah, the **prophet and priest,** though for most of the chapter it is the former who is described as leading people in the wrong direction. Prophets and priests are those who are especially commissioned to direct the people to a proper relationship with God, but here at the center of holy space (**my temple**) they ply their evil deeds.

Thus, verse 12 announces their judgment. At first metaphors of the **slippery** path and **darkness** are used. The **path** metaphor, already well known in Jeremiah and elsewhere such as in Proverbs, describes life as a journey. The godly walk the straight path that leads to life. Here the wicked are said to slip right off and go into the darkness. God has **disaster** for them, a time of **punishment.**

23:13–15 / In yet another oracle against the prophets, Jeremiah speaks against both northern and southern varieties of false prophets. **Samaria** was the capital of the former northern kingdom (defeated by Assyria in 722 B.C.). It was also a name sometimes given to the entirety of the northern kingdom. Thus, when Jeremiah says that he witnessed this atrocity (**I saw**), he is speaking metaphorically in order to be vivid. These northern prophets spoke in the name of **Baal,** the detestable deity of the Canaanites whom the Israelites were supposed to displace (see 1 Kgs. 18). By speaking in the name of a god other than Yahweh, these prophets are false even if what they say comes true (Deut. 13:1–5).

The prophets of **Jerusalem,** the capital of the southern kingdom of Judah, are no better. These prophets were still operating, and Jeremiah accuses them of committing **adultery** and walking in lies. Their lies refer to their prophetic speeches and their adultery should probably be taken both literally and figuratively since they commit adultery in their exclusive relationship with Yahweh by worshiping other gods.

Thus, God pronounces that they are like **Sodom** and **Gomorrah** (Gen. 18:16–19:28). That is, they are evil through and through and well-deserving of the most horrific judgment.

That judgment is pronounced in verse 15. God will make them eat **bitter food** (specifically wormwood) and drink **poisoned water.** For the significance of this see the similarly worded judgment in Jer. 9:15.

23:16–22 / Yet another oracle against false prophets follows in this section. It is addressed to the audience of those prophecies, and God tells them quite simply not to listen to their prophecies. Apparently, they claim that the Lord has told them that peace, not war, is coming, and this is the opposite of what God has truly been saying through Jeremiah. A message of peace would calm the people down so they will not consider repentance. God tells the people that this message is not coming from heaven, but rather from the prophet's own imagination.

To make the point that he is not speaking through them, he tells the people by means of a rhetorical question (v. 18) that these prophets have never sat in on the divine council. This reference to the divine council refers to the place where God meets with his angelic hosts in order to affect the future. Prophets hear the word of the Lord by attending these meetings. A remarkable illustration of this may be found in Isaiah 6, where that prophet is translated to the heavenly realms to appear in the very council chamber of God.

In verse 19, Yahweh switches to judgment language. His anger at these false prophets will issue forth in punishment. He will send a **storm** against the wicked. His anger will energize his carrying out of his plan. The plan that apparently is in mind here is the plan to use the Babylonians to judge his sinful people. The false message of the false prophets will not hinder the coming judgment. The people will understand this clearly in the future; namely, after God puts the plan into effect. This oracle will be repeated in a different context in 30:23–24.

This particular oracle ends with the reiterated assertion that these false prophets did not come from the Lord. They had not come to his divine council chamber, because if they had they would turn away from their **evil deeds.**

23:23–24 / The connection of these two verses to what comes before and after is not clear, nor is its connection specifically to the issue of false prophecy. However, the rhetorical questions it raises are relevant to any context where divine judgment may be doubted. The first question, **Am I only a God nearby and not a God far away,** has an obvious positive answer. Using modern theological language, the oracle affirms both God's transcendence and his immanence. The second question, **Can anyone hide in secret places where I cannot see him,** requires a negative answer. No one can hide from a God who is nearby and faraway. The third question, **Do not I fill heaven and earth,** also demands a positive answer and follows from the first two. The relevance of these questions is that no one can hope to escape from the judgment of God.

23:25–32 / Yet another oracle, this time in prose, against false prophets follows, first with a description of their illicit activity and then with a pronouncement of judgment that has a stereotypical introduction: **I am against the prophets who.**

God begins by proclaiming that those who **prophesy lies,** fabricated by their own imaginations, have not escaped his notice. They claim to have a **dream** of divine origin, but God denies that he gave them this dream. Indeed, these false dreams are instruments of false religion. They will turn the people against Yahweh.

While dreams are sometimes legitimate vehicles of divine revelation in the Bible (e.g., Joseph's dreams in Gen. 37 or Daniel's dreams), the text seems to make a distinction here between prophets who claim dream revelation and those who have "**my** [God's] **word.**" It is the difference between **straw** (useless) and **grain** (nutritional). God's word is like **fire** and a **hammer,** two images that suggest devastating judgment. We may presume that the false message of the lying prophets concerned peace and not judgment.

23:33–40 / The sixth and final oracle against false prophets here begins as a divine statement to Jeremiah and prepares him to respond to questions that the **people, or a prophet or a priest** might ask. This question might come from any Judean, but the prophet and priest are specified from within that broader group because of their special leadership role and because they are particularly culpable for the present bad spiritual state of the nation. The expected question addressed to Jeremiah is "**What is the oracle of the LORD?**" The word oracle (*massa*ʾ) denotes a word of divine revelation mediated through a prophet concerning a coming judgment. To this question Jeremiah is to respond, speaking for God. In the response, then, the "**I**" is God, not Jeremiah, and the "**you**" refers to the questioners. In sum, Jeremiah is to tell them that there is no oracle (**What oracle?**). They come looking for an oracle that will alert them to what is coming in the future, but because of their sin and particularly because of the multiplication of illegitimate prophetic messages, God grows silent. The situation may be analogous to the time that God stopped speaking to Saul even through the Urim and Thummim (1 Sam. 28). God shows his anger and determined judgment by cutting off communication.

Jeremiah, who continues to speak for God, proceeds to address the issue of false prophecy. If anyone presumes to speak in the name of Yahweh and present an oracle of God, then they will be punished. Since God is not in the business of giving oracles (except presumably through Jeremiah), then all other claims of divine revelation are false. The message is similar to Zechariah 13:2–6. Admittedly obscure, the text says that the prophecy by definition is false and deserving punishment.

Jeremiah seems to address a situation where everyone is claiming prophetic revelation. Each person turns to **his friend or relative** to ask for the **LORD's answer.** But they better not claim that there answer is an oracle of the Lord, because they don't have an oracle. Thus, if they claim they have one, they are lying.

Because there is such pervasive false prophecy, God promises to punish them. He will **cast** them out of the **city** (Jerusalem) and give them everlasting shame. This, of course, is an obvious reference to the exile.

Additional Notes §69

23:9 / The first-person speaker is ambiguous. Is the "I" Jeremiah or God? Certainly in v. 11 it is God who is the first-person speaker. However, in v. 9, since the Lord is spoken of in the third person, we would think that it is pointing to Jeremiah. The simile of a drunk soldier could conceivably be used of God (as it is in Ps. 78:65), but it also fits with the prophet. We have in this oracle a good example of the fluidity of the prophet's speech with the divine word. It is often hard, if not impossible, to discern clearly between the two voices. After all, Jeremiah purports to speak in the name of Yahweh.

23:18 / The concept of the **council of the LORD** is found in 1 Kgs. 22:19–23; Job 1–2; 15:8; Ps. 82; Isa. 6:1–3. It is also implicit in the divine plural found in Gen. 1:26 and 11:7. It is difficult to determine just how much of this language we should accept at face value. Fretheim may be correct to say that this group of angels is "a consultative body, not just a group to which God delivers edicts" (*Jeremiah,* p. 336).

23:23–24 / The Greek of the Septuagint is different here in that it does not have the form of a rhetorical question, thus reversing the thought of the Hebrew (MT). The MT asks a rhetorical question that has the force of affirming both the otherness (transcendence) as well as the involvement (immanence) of God, while the Greek ("I am a God at hand, says the Lord, and not a God far off") simply affirms his immanence. The following two verses read better with the MT rather than the Greek reading. See W. E. Lemke, "The Near and Distant God: A Study of Jer 23:23–24 in its Biblical Theological Context," *JBL* 100 (1981), pp. 541–55.

23:33 / *Massa*ʾ (**oracle**) was formerly translated "burden," by commentators who followed the ancient versions (Greek, Peshitta, Vulgate) and attended to the noun's etymology (from the verb *ns*ʾ, "to lift up"), but J. A. Naude ("*Massa*ʾ in the Old Testament," *Proceedings of Die Ou-Testamentiese Werkgemeenskap in Suid-Afrika* 12 [1969], pp. 91–100), among others, has persuaded most scholars that the word marks the beginning of a prophetic oracle (see Nah. 1:1; Hab. 1:1). Specifically, the word describes a prophecy predicting the divine destruction of a nation.

§70 Good Figs, Bad Figs (Jer. 24:1–10)

The next six chapters are written in prose. In this first revelation, Jeremiah receives further divine insight concerning Judah and its future. The time period is likely soon after the exile of Jehoiachin and some of the leading citizens of Judah in 597 B.C. (24:1), but certainly before the final exile of 587/86 B.C. God describes his people with two images, those who went into exile (the good figs) and those who stayed in Judah (the bad figs). The text only mentions that the vision came to Jeremiah, not that he actually reported it to the people. If he did (which is likely) inform the people of this vision, it would be to make the people who remained after the 597 B.C. exile feel badly about their condition. While there is no indication that the hope of the vision was the repentance of the people, it may well be implied.

24:1–3 / The chapter begins by setting the context for the vision that the rest of the chapter reports. The temporal location of the vision is **after Jehoiachin son of Jehoiakim king of Judah and the officials, the craftsmen and the artisans of Judah were carried into exile.** For details of the historical setting see the Introduction: Historical Context.

From the language of the vision it appears that Jeremiah's vision is evoked by two actual baskets of figs that were in the **temple,** though there seems no specific connection between the message of the vision and the temple itself, except for the fact that it was a public place. These baskets of figs are only differentiated by their quality. The first is from the earliest of the two annual crops of figs and are high quality, the second is so bad (presumably rotten) that they could not be eaten

God initiates the vision by drawing Jeremiah's attention to the baskets of figs by asking, **What do you see, Jeremiah?** Jeremiah's response is to the point; he sees the two baskets of figs and notes their differing quality (see similar dialogue in Jer. 1:11, 13).

24:4–7 / God begins by identifying the recent exiles, those from 597 B.C., which would include **Jehoiachin,** Ezekiel, and others, as the **good figs.** These people will find God's favor and protection. Verse 6b then applies the words from Jeremiah's prophetic commission to them (see 1:5–10). He **will build them up and not tear them down;** he **will plant them and not uproot them.** He then describes his relationship to them using the covenant formula: **they will be my people, and I will be their God.** They will **know God,** which implies more than simple head knowledge, but also obedience, something lacking in the present generation that remains in Judah.

24:8–10 / The final paragraph of this divine oracle now identifies the **poor figs.** They include king **Zedekiah** whom the Babylonians chose to replace Jehoiachin after 597 B.C.. Elsewhere in the book we can see how **Zedekiah** (who ruled from 597–586 B.C.) resists the message of God as delivered through Jeremiah (Jer. 21; 32:1–5). It also includes all others who remain in Judah and, interestingly, it also specifies those who live in **Egypt.** The mention of Zedekiah, who was carried away in 586 B.C. would lead us to believe that this oracle comes from before that time, but the mention of those who live in Egypt makes us think of the flight to Egypt mentioned in Jeremiah 42–43 and the exilic time period. Perhaps we have a preexilic oracle that has been redacted in the postexilic period in order to retain its immediate relevance. Another possibility, suggested by Fretheim, *Jeremiah,* p. 348, is that the reference is to Jehoahaz, who was deposed by Neco in 609 B.C. (2 Kgs. 23:34). In any case, these people are to be judged, as opposed to the fate of the early exiles.

The contrast between Jehoiachin and those exiled with him, and Zedekiah and those exiled with him is not easily understood. After all, the first group wasn't exiled because they were better than those who remained and we nowhere hear of a massive repentance of those who went first to Babylon. The logic of the oracle may be that the first exiles are the good figs because they are already in the process of the refining fires of exile. On the other hand, the survivors who are still in the land continue to sin. Their judgment is still in the future. In any case, the purpose of the oracle is certainly to accentuate the guilt of the generation that remained in the land until 586 B.C.

Additional Notes §70

24:2 / The **fig** tree was a staple of the Israelite economy. It also was frequently used as a symbol of fruitfulness (Hos. 9:10) and shelter (Mic. 4:4; Zech. 3:10). The latter concerns not just the fruit, but the tree which casts a shade under which a person might find protection from the sun. The fruit alone or on the tree might figuratively represent fruitfulness. However, a rotten fig is is useless.

§71 The Seventy-Year Punishment (Jer. 25:1–14)

The next oracle begins like many others. After dating it to the fourth year of Jehoiakim, it proceeds to condemn the people of God for not obeying the Lord, particularly in the matter of their worship of other gods. After rehearsing their sin, the oracle pronounces their punishment: destruction at the hands of Nebuchadnezzar, king of Babylon.

Many of the themes of this textual unit are found earlier in Jeremiah. Indeed, this section may well be seen as a grand summary statement of what has gone before.

Though the broad outlines of this oracle are so far well-known from previous ones, a new twist comes at the end. Here Jeremiah looks beyond the punishment of his people. After "seventy years," God will punish the tool of his vengeance, the Babylonians themselves. Interestingly, though the naming of seventy years suggests an end to the punishment of God's people, this particular oracle does not talk explicitly about their eventual restoration (but note 29:10–14).

25:1–3 / The first verse provides a date for this oracle in a typical Israelite fashion, that is in association with the years of a king's reign. Specifically, it is dated to Jehoiakim's **fourth year,** which is cross-dated to Nebuchadnezzar's **first year.** We know that Jehoiakim followed his brother Jehoahaz on the throne. The latter had had a very short reign that lasted only months following the death of his father, Josiah. The year is now 609 B.C. Thus, the fourth year of Jehoiakim would be 605 B.C., which correlates with the date that we can infer from ancient cuneiform documents for Nebuchadnezzar's first year as king upon the death of his father Nabopolassar.

The audience for this oracle is no less than **all the people of Judah** and **all those living in Jerusalem.** By this time, they had heard many of Jeremiah's divinely inspired oracles, since, as he tells them, he started his prophetic preaching in the thirteenth year of Josiah. Since the latter began his relatively long reign in 640, this would place the origin of Jeremiah's preaching in 627/26 B.C. This information conforms to that which we have in the superscription in 1:1–3.

25:4–7 / The people had been warned repeatedly concerning the coming judgment. God had sent the prophets who are his **servants** (see also 2 Kgs. 17:13; Jer. 7:25) to present them with an ultimatum. The prophets told them to turn away from their sins, their **evil ways** and **evil practices.** The worse of these is their worship of false deities (**other gods**). The worship of idols (**what your hands have made**) fundamentally breaks the covenant with Yahweh. They have broken covenant and now deserve the judgment of destruction and exile (see Deut. 28). The prophetic message was conditional. If the people of God turned away from this despicable practice, then they would be able to **stay in the land.** But they **did not listen** (implying disobedience) to this message and so they angered God to the point where judgment against them was certain.

25:8–11 / In consequence of their refusal to repent even in the face of the prophets' appeal, God will punish them. The punishment will come in the form of the "enemy of the north," which has been alluded to since chapter one (see vv. 13–16). Here, Nebuchadnezzar leads the people of the north and the identification of the enemy with Babylon is certain. Historically we know it was Babylon that repeatedly invaded Judah culminating in the destruction of the temple and the essential end of the monarchy in 587/586 B.C. Nebuchadnezzar is here called God's servant in a manner similar to the language used by the prophets themselves. From what we know about Nebuchadnezzar he had no awareness that he was God's servant when he conquered Judah. The language suggests that God can use the most powerful people even when they are not conscious of it.

The language of verse 10 describes the extent of the destruction by listing the wonderful things that will come to a close at the time of judgment. There will be no joy or gladness in the promised land, no rejoicing at weddings, no grinding of grain to produce food to enjoy, and even the lights will disappear along with the people. Nebuchadnezzar's arrival will initiate a seventy year period of destruction in the land.

25:12–14 / At the end of seventy years, God's instrument of judgment, the Babylonians, will themselves be judged for their guilt. Their guilt is not specified. Though used by God in his judgment of Israel, the Babylonians were not conscious of this fact and were motivated rather by their devotion to their own gods, particularly Marduk, and their own desire for empire. For their own sins, the Babylonians will be destroyed and **will become a desolate wasteland.** This is exactly what happened to the political entity called Babylon. In 539 B.C., the native Babylonian dynasty led by Nabonidus and his son and co-regent Bel-shar-usur (the latter mentioned in the Bible under the name Belshazzar [see Dan. 5]) were defeated by the Persians under Cyrus the great. What historians call the Neo-Babylonian Empire, the third such empire centered in Babylon in ancient times, came to a close and never reemerged. While the hegemony of the Babylonians was devastated, the land in the vicinity of Babylon did not immediately become a wasteland, and the Persians and then the Greeks controlled it for centuries. The reference to the **things I have spoken against it, all that are written in this book and prophesied by Jeremiah** surely includes the oracle in chapters 50–51 (for which see commentary).

Additional Notes §71

25:1 / The correlation of the **fourth year of Jehoiakim** with the first year of Nebuchadnezzar's kingship creates a problem when compared with the correlation between the third year of this Judean king and Nebuchadnezzar's first year in Daniel 1:1. In addition, it is claimed that the Babylonians did not come to Jerusalem until the fifth year of Jehoiakim (Jer. 36:9). A surface reading of the Babylonian Chronicle appears to support this opinion. According to Hartman and Di Lella (*The Book of Daniel* [New York: Doubleday, 1978], p. 48), the second-century author of Daniel was confused and misled by his understanding of 2 Chronicles 36:6–7 in connection with 2 Kings 24:1.

D. J. Wiseman (*Notes on Some Problems in the Book of Daniel* [Wheaton, Ill.: Tyndale, 1965], pp. 16–18) countered this argument by reminding us that there were two systems of dating current in the ancient Near Eastern world, both of which can be found in the Old Testament. The passages may be harmonized by assuming that Jeremiah utilized the Judean method of chronological reckoning, which counts the first year of a king's reign as the first year, and that Daniel used the Babylonian system, which counts the first year as an "accession year."

Wiseman then persuasively argued that the Babylonian Chronicle fails to mention the siege of Jerusalem because it is preoccupied with "the major defeat of the Egyptians" and a "successful incursion into Judah by the Babylonian army group which returned from the Egyptian border could be included in the claim that at that time Nebuchadnezzar conquered 'all Hatti'" (Wiseman, *Notes,* p. 18).

25:4 / Jesus tells a parable about a landowner who rented his vineyard to wicked tenants who refused to pay rent (Matt. 21:33–45). At the conclusion of the story it is clear that the wicked tenants are the Pharisees to whom Jesus is speaking, and they represent the people of God or the leaders of the Old Testament people of God. The refusal to pay rent is analogous to Israel's refusal to obey God's law. The servants whom the owner sends to collect the rent are horribly abused. These servants are to be understood as God's **servants** the prophets as here in this passage. God's people treated the prophets horribly, and Jeremiah was no exception.

25:11 / Jeremiah announces that God's devastation of Judah will last for **seventy years.** This number raises some difficult questions. We know that the exile of Judah comes to a close in 539 B.C. Strictly speaking, we would expect then that the beginning of the horror could be situated at 609 B.C. However the exile begins in earnest in 587/86 B.C. What are we to make of this apparent anomaly?

In the first place, we may note that it is this prophecy (also found in Jer. 29:10) that motivates Daniel to begin to pray for restoration (Dan. 9). We are to presume from this that Daniel understood the seventy years as nearing completion at this time. However, in response to his prayer Daniel receives a prophecy that announces future events that will happen during a period of "seventy 'sevens'" (Dan. 9:20–27), perhaps to be understood as an extension of the originally stipulated time period.

In any case, it is possible that the seventy years are thought to begin in 605 B.C., the time when Daniel 1:1–2 places Nebuchadnezzar's first incursion into Judah, and the deportation of Daniel and his three friends. Certainly 597 B.C. when Jehoiachin, Ezekiel, and other leaders were deported, the exile has begun in earnest, even though 587/86 B.C. is a watershed year. Seventy also may be considered a symbolic number representing completion since it is a multiple of seven and ten.

25:13 / It is interesting that the Septuagint situations the oracles against the nations found in chapters 46–51 at this point in the text.

§72 The Cup of God's Wrath (Jer. 25:15–38)

The next oracle centers on the theme of the cup of God's wrath (see also 49:12; 51:7). Clearly, vv. 15–29 treat this theme explicitly, but there are reasons to connect the remainder of the chapter with this oracle as well.

God commands the prophet to take a cup that represents his wrath to all the people who will receive his punishment (vv. 15–16). Jeremiah obeys and then names the nations to whom he goes. As we follow the list, we see that it includes all the nations of the ancient Near East, beginning with Judah and ending with a reference to Babylon (Sheshach), which will at least initially be the one who will carry out the judgment against the other nations. No one escapes God's judgment (vv. 17–26). Verses 27–29 record God's demand that the nations drink the cup. The remaining part of the chapter (vv. 30–38) presents a series of oracles that do not explicitly mention the cup, but are to be understood as accompanying the ritual drinking.

Though described like a symbolic action that would typically have been acted out by a prophet, it is unlikely that Jeremiah actually traveled to all these nations to compel their leaders to drink from a cup. It is most likely that this is a dramatic description of an important literary theme.

25:15–16 / God now directs Jeremiah to undertake a dramatic ritual that will illustrate his determination to judge not only Judah and Jerusalem but also many of the surrounding nations. Specifically, God tells Jeremiah to take **the cup filled with the wine of his wrath** and make the nations listed in verses 17–26 drink from it. The results will be devastating because it will stagger them and make them go mad. While some people believe that the cup of God's wrath is a kind of poison because it leads to death, it is better to see it as inducing a state of extreme drunkenness that leaves them powerless to resist the **sword** (military might) that is coming against them. Certainly that is the case in this text since the liquid is said to be the **wine** of God's wrath.

It is impossible that Jeremiah literally went to all the nations listed in the following paragraph and literally asked their kings to drink from this cup. The time and energy it would take would be staggering! Not only that, but it is inconceivable that Jeremiah would get an audience with the king of Egypt (see below, v. 13), not to speak of his actually drinking from such a cup.

Fretheim suggests it is either a development of the common prophetic metaphor (see Additional Notes) or a vision. Fretheim prefers the latter, but as there are no indications of the latter, the former is more likely (see Fretheim, *Jeremiah,* p. 359).

25:17–26 / Jeremiah follows through on God's command given in vv. 15–16 to take **the cup** of his wrath to the nations. He begins with God's own people in **Jerusalem and the towns of Judah.** Because of their sins, they will get the same treatment as the pagan people who follow in the list. Their political leaders, **kings and officials,** are specifically named. The region will be turned into a **ruin** and **the object of horror and scorn and cursing.** What will happen to them at the hands of Babylon, in other words, will be devastating.

Next in line are the Egyptians. All parts of Egyptian society are named in the list of those who will be the object of God's wrath, beginning with **Pharaoh** and including his entire administration and population. Interestingly, even the **foreign people** who live there are named (v. 20a). Their mention may simply be a way of talking about the extent of the destruction that is coming.

After the Egyptians come the nations that most immediately surround Judah. For **Uz,** see Additional Notes. The **Philistines** refer to the people who live in the coastal areas and low foothills of the Shephelah in an area to the southwest of Jerusalem. Four of its chief cities are mentioned by name (**Ashkelon, Gaza, Ekron, Ashdod**). Then the three nations to the east of Judah are named moving from south to north (**Edom, Moab, and Ammon**). To the north we hear of the Phoenician seacoast towns of **Tyre** and **Sidon.** Suddenly the list shifts to the Arabian peninsula in its mention of **Dedan, Tema, and Buz.** Then it moves to the far, far east in mentioning powers which have their center in what is today Iran (**Zimri, Elam, and Media**). The list then ends with the people who live in the far north and here a place called **Sheshach** is mentioned, a name that is clearly a code word for none other than Babylon.

25:27–29 / These verses record God's judgment speech that accompanies the ritual of drinking from the cup of wine that represents God's wrath. He introduces himself by his Divine Warrior name **LORD Almighty** (or, "Lord of hosts," in reference to his heavenly army). God commands them to **drink, get drunk and vomit,** rendering them impotent to resist the **sword** that will destroy them.

Even if they don't agree to drink the cup, they must. In other words, whether they drink it or not the judgment is coming on them. This ritual is not a magical act that effectuates the punishment, but rather a prophetic illustration of what is surely coming on these people.

The divine reasoning of verses 28–29 may be summarized as follows: if God judges his own people for their sin, how can the other nations that surround Judah escape punishment? They cannot. They will all feel God's wrath.

25:30–38 / God then tells Jeremiah to utter the following pronouncements against those many nations who have drunk from the cup of his wrath. Verses 30–31 communicate God's anger against the nations by describing his **roar** and **shout** against them. The roar (*shʾg*) is that of a lion. As in Amos where Zion is specified (see 1:2), God roars from a **high place.** The Amos passage also speaks of God's thundering, thus presenting both a lion, as well as a storm, metaphor to represent God's destructive anger toward his people.

A third metaphor for God's loud noise directed toward the objects of his judgment is the shout of those who **tread the grapes.** This is not an angry or threatening **shout,** but rather a joyful shout. It fits the present context, though, as the analogy that is drawn is between the grapes and the bodies of those against whom God brings judgment. In other words, God shouts for joy as he tramples the bodies of those who have sinned against him. As the juice flows out of the grapes, so the blood flows out of their bodies. The analogy between treading grapes and the divine judgment against sinners is developed at greater length in Isaiah 63:2–6, which provides the literary background to the picture of the final judgment given in Revelation 19:15. As we move from Jeremiah 25:30a to 25:30b–31 we see an expansion of the object of God's judgment from **"his holy dwelling"** and **"his land"** to **"the nations"** and **"all mankind."**

Verses 32–33 begin with the introduction to what appears to be a separate oracle. Here the prophet calls the hearers attention

(**Look**!) to the spreading disaster that results from a devastating **storm** that we are certainly to identify with God's judgment as it works itself out initially through the agency of the Babylonian army. The devastation will be so massive and sudden that bodies will be everywhere and there will be no time to bury them all.

The judgment poem that concludes the chapter (vv. 33–38) centers on the metaphor of the **shepherd.** Here the shepherd clearly refers to the leaders, political and religious, of God's people (**the flock**). Their demise is spelled out because of their special responsibility for the present crisis. Their job was to keep God's people pure and on the path of godliness, but they did just the opposite. God, who is again likened to a **lion** (v. 38), will destroy shepherd and pasture (flock).

Additional Notes §72

25:18 / The verse describes the devastating effects of God's anger on Judah and Jerusalem that come as a result of drinking God's cup of judgment. Jerusalem will be a ruin and an object of horror, scorn, and cursing. At the end of the verse is an intriguing clause that simply states: **as they are today.** Clearly that means that Judah and Jerusalem already exhibit the horrifying conditions described in the verse, but it is less clear exactly how to understand it. Fretheim (*Jeremiah,* p. 358) suggests that this indicates that this is an oracle that was delivered to an exilic audience. If this is so, it makes one wonder why God now wants to get them to drink the cup to make them a ruin. Thompson (*Jeremiah,* p. 516), may be right when he says that the phrase "suggests that at the time of writing some aspects of this judgment, at least, were apparent." Or else perhaps we should "split the difference" and say that the phrase is an exilic addition to a preexilic oracle.

25:20 / The location of **Uz** is difficult to determine. It is only mentioned in three other places. The first occurrence of the word Uz is as the name of a descendant of Esau, thus pointing to a location east of the Jordan in connection with Edom (Gen. 36:28 and 1 Chr. 1:42). The second, and the best known, reference to Uz is in Job 1:1, as the place where Job lived, though this reference does not give us any information as to where Uz is located. For our purposes the most interesting reference is in Lamentations 4:21:

> Rejoice and be glad, O Daughter of Edom,
>   you who live in the land of Uz.
> But to you also the cup will be passed;
>   you will be drunk and stripped naked.

Here we note the parallelism between Edom and Uz in the context of the theme of the cup of God's wrath. The Genesis and Lamentations passages point to the area of Edom as connected to Uz, while the Job reference does not dispute it. The only hesitation we have to making a strict identification of the two areas as identical is that they are both mentioned in this context.

25:26 / The name **Sheshach** is a code name for Babylon. The code is known as *atbash,* where the last letter of the alphabet stands for the first, the second to last for the second, and so on. With such a system Babel becomes Sheshach. See also 51:1.

§73 A Second Temple Sermon (Jer. 26:1–24)

26:1–6 / This oracle is dated in the first verse to **early in the reign of Jehoiakim** (609–597 B.C.). Assuming that this means before 605 B.C., then the oracle would be before Babylon became an active threat toward Judah, and even then only if one accepts the testimony of Daniel 1:1–2 that Nebuchadnezzar threatened Jerusalem in the third year of Jehoiakim's reign. The following oracle is marked as a word from the Lord and is directed to Jeremiah who is to take this message to the people.

Specifically, Jeremiah is told to go to the temple **courtyard** to deliver the oracle. We have already had one sermon with this setting (ch. 7), and there are a number of similar themes with the sermon delivered at that time, though they do not appear to be variants of the same sermon. That Jeremiah would deliver two sermons at the temple courtyard is hardly surprising considering the importance and significance of that place. It was a public place as well, and so he could, at least by representation, reach **all the people of the towns of Judah.**

The divine intent of this oracle is clearly repentance. God wants the people to hear the pronouncement of judgment and then turn back and obey him (**perhaps they will listen**). If they do, he will relent; that is, he will not bring on them the disaster that Jeremiah is about to announce. The **evil way** of the people, as is evident in other places in the book, begins with idolatry, an act that fundamentally breaks the covenant, and includes other ethical and religious infractions.

While God explicitly states to Jeremiah his intention to bring the people to repentance, it is implicit in the public oracle itself. The conditionality of the prophecy of the people's doom is seen in the conditional nature of the grammar (**if, if, then**). Their doom is certain if they do not listen and follow God's law. If they do not, then he will make **this house** (the temple built during the Solomonic period) **like Shiloh** (Jeremiah made a similar argument in the earlier temple sermon [Jer 7:12–14]). It will not only be the temple that is destroyed, but also the **city** of Jerusalem where it is located.

The divine oracle has a tone of pessimism concerning the possibility of repentance since it mentions that the people have not listened in the past to **my servants the prophets, whom I have sent to you again and again.**

26:7–9 / This section narrates the reaction of **the priests, the prophets and all the people** to the words of Jeremiah. They vociferously attacked Jeremiah both physically (they **seized him**) and verbally. They demanded the death penalty. The priests and the prophets represented the religious establishment of the day, which did not confront but rather comforted the people in the midst of their distress (see the interplay between Jeremiah and the false prophet Hananiah in chs. 27–28). Perhaps they demanded the death penalty simply out of rage, but they may have thought that Jeremiah blasphemed God by suggesting that God's house, the temple, would be destroyed. Thus it is possible that their hatred toward Jeremiah was generated by a misplaced religious devotion. Freitheim thinks the charge is false prophecy, which also entails the death penalty (*Jeremiah,* p. 369), but this seems an unlikely charge considering it takes time to determine whether a prophecy is false or not.

26:10–11 / Through their charge and the demand for punishment, the priests and the prophets evoked a response from the **officials of Judah.** From their actions, this rather general term indicates some kind of civic authority responsible for adjudicating such a case. They came from the **royal palace,** which again would indicate civic leaders associated with the government. As is well established elsewhere in the Old Testament, such legal proceedings took place at the gate of the city and in this case a particular gate named **New Gate** is mentioned. From its mention in 36:10, it appears that this gate is in the vicinity of the temple. Furthermore the same context may fill us in on the identity of some of the same officials of Jehoiakim who are simply spoken of under the general category of "official" (36:11–15).

To this group of officials (as well as all the people) the priests and prophets repeat their charge of sedition and perhaps blasphemy and call for the death penalty again.

26:12–15 / These verses present Jeremiah's defense to the charge that he has prophesied against Jerusalem. His defense is actually quite simple: God has given him the message that he is proclaiming. Indeed, his confidence in the message is such that he uses this occasion to urge the people to listen and obey the oracle. He also underlines the conditional nature of the prophecy. There is still time to change the outcome. Judgment is contingent on the people's staying the course in their sin. If they reform their ways, then God will **relent.** From the perspective of the people, their future is still open to them. Repentance will avert complete disaster; rejection will bring the Babylonian army.

With his responsibility to communicate God's message to the people out of the way, he now turns to his own fate. On the one hand, he tells them to do what they want with him. However, there is more than an implicit threat in the comment that if they hurt him that they will bring the guilt of **innocent blood** on themselves. Such an act in and of itself would bring the death penalty from God (Exod. 23:7; Deut. 19:10, 13). Thus, his ultimate defense is that his words are the words of God himself. He is a prophet and therefore a messenger of God.

26:16–19 / After listening to Jeremiah's defense, the officials along with all the people conclude that he is innocent. He has spoken the truth in the name of the Lord (see the tests of the prophet in Deut. 13 and 18). Then what appears to be a group within the broader group of officials, namely some of **the elders of the land,** step forward and speak further on behalf of Jeremiah. They cite the precedent of the prophet **Micah** who prophesied during the time of **Hezekiah** (715–687 B.C.). His message was just as negative toward the land of Judah as was that of Jeremiah. His message also stated that Jerusalem would be destroyed and the temple razed (**the temple hill a mound overgrown with thickets**).

However, they add, Hezekiah did not have Micah put to death, but rather he listened to the message and repented. Thus, during the reign of that great king there was no destruction of Jerusalem though that could easily have happened considering the incursion of the Assyrian king Sennacherib that took place in 701 B.C. during his reign.

While this episode with Micah the prophet is not mentioned in Kings in the records of the time of King Hezekiah, the verse itself is nearly identical to Micah 3:12. Hezekiah's reaction had been the proper one. However, even though these elders carry the day and Jeremiah is spared at least momentarily from imprisonment or worse, there is no record of Jehoiakim, a broader group of Judah's officials, or even the prophets and priests being persuaded to repent. The elders' final words are ominous (**We are about to bring terrible disaster on ourselves!**)

26:20–23 / After Jeremiah escapes a difficult legal and political situation, we are given the story of another prophet, otherwise unknown, by the name of **Uriah son of Shemaiah from Kiriath Jearim.** We do not get a specific description of the oracle he delivered, only the statement that contained the **same things against this city and this land** as that prophesied by Jeremiah. The purpose of recounting this story appears to be to inform us just how serious was the situation Jeremiah faced. This prophet who spoke the same message as Jeremiah also aroused Jehoiakim's anger. Before that king could arrest Uriah in Jerusalem, Uriah escaped to Egypt. However, Jehoiakim had his men pursue him to Eygpt. It should be remembered that Jehoiakim maintained a pro-Egyptian, anti-Babylonian policy, so it was probably not the best place for a political refugee to flee. Uriah was brought back to Judah, where he was executed and given an ignominious burial.

26:24 / In the concluding verse, we hear of one factor that may have differentiated Uriah from Jeremiah, at least from a human perspective. **Ahikam son of Shaphan** interceded for Jeremiah. Ahikam is mentioned in 2 Kings 22:12, 14, 22, as is his father Shaphan (2 Kgs. 22:3, 8, 9, 10, etc.), as officials during the reforms of Josiah. We might presume that their support for Josiah would make them favorably disposed toward Jeremiah. They likely walked a political tightrope with Josiah's son, Jehoiakim, but had enough power to do so. Of further interest is the fact that Ahikam is later mentioned as the son of Gedaliah (Jer. 40:5, 6, 7, 9, etc.), the Babylonian appointed governor of Judah during the early exilic period and a man with whom Jeremiah also had a close relationship.

Additional Notes §73

26:10–11 / That the civic authorities (**the officials of Judah**) take the lead here in the proceedings seems like it might be out of keeping with Deuteronomy 17:8–13. Perhaps because the priests and the prophets are bringing the charges, another group, the palace officials, assumes that responsibility.

26:18 / As mentioned above, this snippet of Micah's prophetic message is found in Micah 3:12. The verse appears in the context of an oracle where there is a strong contrast between Micah, who is "filled with power, with the Spirit of the LORD, and with justice and might" (Mic. 3:8), and the prophets "who lead my people astray, if one feeds them, they proclaim 'peace'" (3:5). This dynamic between Micah and the false prophets of his day is being replayed at the time of Jeremiah, who here is accused not just by priests but also by (presumably) false prophets.

Micah is identified as a Moreshite—from a town called Moresheth-gath [Mic. 1:1, 14], a town identified with "Tell ej-Judeideh, a rather imposing mound, in the foothills of southwestern Judah, favored with an elevation of 1,000 feet above sea level and a view of the undulating coastal plain to the west. It is located about twenty-one miles southwest of Jerusalem," see B. K. Waltke, "Micah," in *The Minor Prophets,* edited by T. E. McComiskey (Baker, 1993), p. 594.

§74 *Jeremiah Versus the False Prophet Hananiah: (Jer. 27–28)*

In the midst of a turbulent time, Jeremiah's message was not the only one that was being heard in Jerusalem. Other prophets with different messages were also active. Hananiah is an example of a rival prophet, and in chapter 28, these two will almost come to blows.

The book of Deuteronomy anticipated the presence of false prophets. False prophets are those who are not sent by Yahweh, though they might speak in his name. Deuteronomy 13 and 18 provide the people with two tests by which they were to determine whether or not they should listen to a prophet. Deuteronomy 13:1–5 describes a situation where a prophet presents a message that comes true, but then urges the people to follow a god other than Yahweh. Even though the message came true, the prophet is by definition false because he represents a false deity. On the other hand, Deuteronomy 18:14–21 addresses the situation of a prophet who speaks in the name of Yahweh, but whose message does not turn out to be true. By definition, this prophet cannot really be a prophet of Yahweh since Yahweh never speaks falsehoods. Such false prophets were to be killed.

Even with such clear instructions, we can still imagine that discerning a true from a false prophet would have been difficult "on the ground," particularly in the light of the second criterion for true prophecy. After all, it may have taken some time for the prophecy to come true, though typically it is reported that there are short term signs of the veracity of a prophet's message. In any case, we should keep these deuteronomic laws in mind as we read chapters 27 and 28.

27:1–7 / The event to be described in chapter 27 takes place **early in the reign of Zedekiah.** In the next chapter the time is more specifically described as the fourth year of this king, who ruled for eleven years (see 28:1, which describes the fourth year as the same year). The fourth year of Zedekiah was 593 B.C.

Zedekiah had become king of Israel in 597 B.C. (2 Kgs. 24:18–20). He was placed on the throne by none other than Nebuchadnezzar after a revolt by Jehoiakim. Jehoiakim had departed the throne before Nebuchadnezzar could come with his army to put down this insurrection, but Jehoiachin, Jehoiakim's son, was on the throne, so Nebuchadnezzar defeated him and deported him to Babylon. He placed Jehoiachin's uncle, Mattaniah, who received the throne name Zedekiah, in his place. The Babylonian king must have had some reason to think that this king would be more malleable than the others, but we here learn that by the fourth year of his reign Zedekiah was contemplating revolt. We learn in Jeremiah 51:59 that he was called back to Babylon perhaps in order to renew his oath of loyalty (Provan, Long, and Longman, *A Biblical History of Israel,* p. 280). At this time, Jeremiah wrote an oracle against Babylon which he had delivered by an official named Seraiah.

God then directs Jeremiah to perform a symbolic act to accompany his prophetic word. He is to make a **yoke** and put it on his neck as he goes around town. Jeremiah in a yoke would draw considerable attention, with people asking why he is doing such a preposterous thing. Of course, by this time, late in his ministry, Jeremiah already had quite a reputation for doing bizarre things to get attention to his message. A yoke symbolizes submission and control. Just like an animal is yoked in order to harness its energies for its owner, so, according to Jeremiah, Nebuchadnezzar will make the nations submit and bring them under his control. The yoke is the center of attention throughout chapters 27 and 28 (see also Jer. 2:20; 5:5; 30:8).

God directs Jeremiah to first **send word** to the leaders of **Edom, Moab, Ammon, Tyre and Sidon,** the small nations that surround Judah. He is to do this through the envoys or ambassadors who have come to Jerusalem to meet with Zedekiah. They are listed from south to north with the first three to the east of Judah and the last two on the coast to the north. We may presume that these nations are meeting together in Jerusalem to contemplate some kind of mutual venture against the Babylonians.

The message that God sent through Jeremiah to these emissaries who are to take back to their royal masters is that their fate in regard to Babylon is sealed, at least for a time. God prefaces his message with a reminder that he was the one who created the **earth** and its **people** and the **animals.** He is in charge and can dispose of people and nations as he so chooses, and he has decided to deliver these nations to Nebuchadnezzar, people and animals alike. This message reminds us of Nebuchadnezzar's vision of the tree in Daniel 4 where he is the tree and all the birds and animals find refuge in that tree (vv. 9–12), similarly illustrating his sovereign control over all creatures.

Verse 7 indicates, however, that there is a time limit on even this great king's power. He will subjugate the known world during his reign and that of his son and his grandson, but then his nation's time will come when other nations and kings will then subjugate it. In historical retrospect, we can identify that time as 539 B.C., when Persia under Cyrus the Great put an end to the Neo-Babylonian Empire.

27:8–11 / Verses 1–7 describe the best-case scenario for these five small nation states that surround Judah. If they submit to Babylon, then they will become its vassals, but will survive intact. But if they resist Nebuchadnezzar's yoke, then they face warfare and deportation (vv. 8–11). The harm that will come to these nations is described by the familiar triad of **sword, famine and plague** (or by some combination of them, all the result of warfare: 5:12; 11:22; 14:12–18; 15:2; 16:4; 18:21; 21:7, 9; 24:10, etc.).

The oracle makes clear that, while Nebuchadnezzar is the instrument, it is God himself who is delivering the punishment. Thus, no escape is possible if resistance is encountered.

Anticipating the prophetic conflict to be described in chapter 28, God warns these leaders not to listen to their **prophets, diviners, interpreters of dreams, mediums or sorcerers.** This is a laundry list of those who claim to know the future. Scripture permits some of these roles, but some, like the last two, are absolutely prohibited (see Deut. 18:9–13). They are lying to these leaders and leading them astray. The only hope for these five nations is to submit to the yoke of Babylon.

27:12–15 / Jeremiah then delivers the above message to Zedekiah, then king of Judah. He too should submit (**bow your neck**) to Nebuchadnezzar (**the king of Babylon**). Surrender is the passport to survival; to resist means death for the king and for many of his people. Rather than providing a long list of mantics, as above with the foreign leaders, Zedekiah is warned not to listen to prophets with a different message. They may claim to speak in the name of Yahweh (thus meeting the requirement of Deut. 13:1–5), but they are telling lies, so they obviously are not really speaking at God's initiative (thus failing the test of Deut. 18:21–22). For heeding the false message of the prophets, the king will die. For giving the false message in the first place, the prophets themselves will perish.

27:16–22 / Now Jeremiah turns to the priests and the people to warn them about the false prophets and their dangerous message of hope. The prophets were apparently claiming that God told them that **the articles from the LORD's house** would be returned to Jerusalem soon. We learn about the capture of some of these articles, which included gold and silver dishes, silver pans, and gold bowls, in 605/604 B.C., at the time Daniel and his three friends are brought into captivity (Dan. 1:2), though the most immediate reference here must be to the capture of the articles at the time when Zedekiah's predecessor, Jehoiachin, was taken into captivity in 597 B.C. (2 Kgs. 24:13). Ezra 1:9–11 mentions 5,400 total articles that were eventually returned at the end of the exile.

The articles were significant, not because of their value as precious metal, but because of their symbolic significance. They represented the presence of Yahweh, especially because Israelite religion was aniconic, imageless. In ancient Near Eastern theological thinking, the Babylonian king's ability to take these objects would have represented either Yahweh's collaboration with the king or his defeat by the king.

By saying that the articles would be returned, these prophets were giving false hope that the situation with Babylon will get better, not worsen. Such ideas would hinder any possibility of sincere repentance that would lead to the survival of Judah.

But Jeremiah knows that the Lord has not decreed the return of the articles. Indeed, he knows that apart from repentance the situation will grow worse. Not only will the articles not be returned, but further damage will be done to the temple and even the palace. So far only the small and easily removable items, not large scale and integral parts of the temple structure, like the pillars and the Sea, have been taken. Jeremiah 52 narrates the taking of these large temple objects at the time of the fall of Jerusalem.

The **pillars** are described in 1 Kings 7:15–22. They were bronze and were each 27 feet tall and 18 feet around. On top of the pillars were capitals that themselves were seven and a half feet tall and carefully designed like lilies. It is uncertain whether these pillars were connected to the temple structure or free standing, but their removal would be psychologically staggering. After all, they were named Jakin ("he establishes") and Boaz ("by strength"), names that would indicate establishment.

The **Sea** was equally formidable and symbolically significant (1 Kgs. 7:23–26). It was a tremendous laver shaped like a lily, holding 11,000 gallons of water. This water was likely used in ritual lustrations which were part of temple rites. The significance of this structure can be seen in its name, the Sea (*yam*). The sea was a symbol derived from ancient Near Eastern mythology that stood for the forces of chaos. In its present form, the Sea symbolized God's control of the waters of chaos. If destroyed or removed, however, it would represent the return of chaos on a social and a cosmological level.

The **movable stands** are described in 1 Kings 7:27–37. These stands may actually have been watercarts (DeVries, *1 Kings* [WBC; Dallas, Word, 1985], p. 110) used to transfer water to the Sea.

The **other furnishings** of the temple would have included ten bronze basins, various altars, lampstands, and more.

Thus, unless there is repentance, these items plus items from the palace will be carted off to Babylon as a symbol of an utter subjugation. Even in the midst of such a devastating oracle, however, God gives a glimmer of hope, to be developed further later, that **he will bring them back and restore them to this place.**

In chapter 27, Jeremiah had spoken in general of prophets who were misleading the leadership and people of Judah through their false words of hope. Now we meet one, Hananiah son of Azur, a prophet from Gibeon. The chapter recounts a public dispute between Jeremiah and Hananiah that took place before priests and people at the temple, the house of the Lord.

The events of the previous chapter were rather ambiguously dated as early in the reign of Zedekiah. The following conflict is described as taking place in the fifth month of the same year, namely the fourth year of Zedekiah. The fourth year could be dated approximately to 593 B.C. The fifth month would be sometime during August or September.

28:1–4 / Like Jeremiah in the previous chapter, Hananiah claims to speak in the name of Yahweh, here described as **the LORD Almighty, the God of Israel.** His oracle picks up on the yoke theme that was integral to Jeremiah's prophetic message. Indeed, we will soon see that Jeremiah is still wearing the yoke as he is delivering his prophetic message. Unfortunately, due to the vague dating reference at the beginning of chapter 27, we have no definite idea how much time Jeremiah has been wearing the yoke.

Hananiah acknowledges that there is a yoke of Babylon imposed on Judah. After all, articles from the temple as well as captives had been taken just four years before. Nevertheless, Hananiah proclaims that God intends to break this yoke **within two years** and bring the articles and people, in particular the captured former king Jehoiachin, back from Babylon.

28:5–9 / Jeremiah responds in a surprising way. Rather than growing defensive, considering he has been presenting a different divine message, he greets Hananiah's prophecy warmly yet with suspicion. Jeremiah would love to be wrong and see his people return to the land. He takes no pleasure in the destruction of his people. He hopes for and is open to God changing his mind and speaking through Hananiah. Thus, he reacts with an **Amen,** "so be it." An alternative interpretation understands Jeremiah's statement as ironic (Lundbom, *Jeremiah 22–36,* p. 333). It is difficult to read tone from the text.

Even so, Jeremiah is suspicious. After all, he has been hearing a different divine voice. More to the point, he knows that prophets are typically not in the business of bringing exclusively good news. After all, they are covenant lawyers (see comments at 2:9, 29; 11:1–8; 12:1–6), that is, they are the ones God sends to his people when they have broken their covenantal obligations and run the risk of bringing the curses of the covenant on themselves. It is true that prophets do speak words of hope. Even Jeremiah himself has words of restoration (see chapters 30–33). However, the difference is that this hope follows judgment and repentance. Hananiah's message as we know it does not require the repentance of the people and, from what we know of Jeremiah's message at this point and up to the destruction of Jerusalem, there has been no significant repentance on the part of the people. Thus, Jeremiah's does not completely deny the validity of Hananiah's words, but he does say in effect he'll "believe it when he sees it."

Of course, in a sense, Jeremiah's caution could also be directed toward a prophet of doom. The two tests for a prophet are that he speaks in the name of Yahweh (something that Hananiah does do) and that what he says comes true. However, it is also true that often prophets will have short-term predictions or signs that come true that intend to give confidence in the face of long-term prophecy. In 1 Kings 13, for instance, when the unnamed prophet pronounces the ultimate destruction of Jeroboam's altar, something that will not happen for centuries, his words are accompanied by damage to the altar and the paralysis of Jeroboam's arm. Here we have no similar demonstration of divine presence.

28:10–11 / Hananiah appears not to appreciate Jeremiah's suspicion and he enacts a prophetic drama himself. He rips off the **yoke** that is on Jeremiah's neck and smashes it. The act intends to symbolize God's removal and destruction of the yoke of bondage that Nebuchadnezzar has on Judah. Again, Jeremiah reacts coolly. The text simply says that he **went on his way.**

28:12–17 / It is not long (**shortly**) before Jeremiah's caution gives way to certainty thanks to a divine oracle. Jeremiah is directed to confront Hananiah and reject his claim to divine authority. Indeed, his actions have made matters worse. Rather than a wooden yoke like the one he broke from around the neck of Jeremiah, God will now place an **iron yoke,** one not as easily removed or broken. The oracle reaffirms the message that Jeremiah had been giving in the previous chapter. All the nations and even the **wild animals** will be subject to Nebuchadnezzar. The reference to wild animals is best to be understood as prophetic hyperbole. Wild animals, after all, are wild and thus virtually impossible to subjugate. If he can control the wild animals, he will easily control the inhabitants of these nations, including Judah. The language here is strikingly similar to the vision that Nebuchadnezzar himself has in Daniel 4.

But Hananiah will not escape with simply being wrong. What he has done deserves death. He has spoken falsely in the name of the Lord, and "a prophet who presumes to speak in my name anything I have not commanded him to say must be put to death" (Deut. 18:20). However, Judah's leaders were not sympathetic to Jeremiah or the will of Yahweh at this moment in history, so God must execute his judgment himself. Hananiah soon died; we don't know how. His death should have been taken as a confirmation that God was speaking through Jeremiah. It was the type of short term prophetic word that should have given rise to confidence concerning his longer term more national message. Though the text does not inform us of crowd reaction, we unfortunately have no reason to think that Judah or even a substantial part of the population changed their minds.

Additional Notes §74

27:1 / The NIV and most modern translations (see NJB for an exception) emend the Hebrew (MT) which has Jehoiakim rather than **Zedekiah.** However, the events of chapters 27–28 take place during Zedekiah's reign and unless one is willing to believe that God anticipated this event by a number of years, the MT is unlikely to be correct. Perhaps a scribe was thrown off by the beginning of chapter 26. There are some Hebrew manuscripts, along with Arabic and Syriac references, which do attest the name Zedekiah, though the Dead Sea scrolls support the MT.

27:6 / This oracle shocks because God calls Nebuchadnezzar **my servant.** How could a pagan king be the servant of Yahweh? The answer is that the king is a servant without being aware of it. God is using Nebuchadnezzar for his purposes. In other words, when Nebuchadnezzar subjugates these nations and Judah itself, he thinks it is a result of his power and the power of his chief god Marduk, but in reality it is because God has delivered them into his hand (see Isa. 45 and Dan. 1:1–2 for a similar dynamic).

27:7 / This verse indicates that Babylon's dominance will not last forever. The verse specifies that Babylonian power will last beyond Nebuchadnezzar's time through that of **his son** and **grandson.** We can and should understand this phrase as simply meaning for an extended period of time. While Nebuchadnezzar's son, Amel-Marduk (mentioned in 2 Kgs. 25:27 [Evil-Merodach]) did succeed him in 562 B.C. and ruled for two years, he was deposed and replaced by Neriglissar, who may have been his son-in-law. As a matter of fact, there were to be three more rulers after Neriglissar before the fall of Babylon in 539 B.C.

28:1 / Hananiah comes from **Gibeon,** a town in Benjamin, that has been identified archeologically with el-Jib and investigated by the archeologist J. B. Prichard in the 1950's and 60's. Joshua 21:17 lists it as a priestly town. While it is interesting that a number of jar handles have been discovered there inscribed with the name Hananiah, it needs to be remembered that this was a common name (Lundbom, *Jeremiah 22–36*, p. 330).

§75 Letters to Babylon and Back (Jer. 29)

Chapters 27 and 28 describe a prophetic conflict concerning the status of the 597 B.C. exiles to Babylon and the future of those who remain behind. Jeremiah represented the view that the former would stay in exile and the latter were under judgment. Hananiah attacked Jeremiah and optimistically stated that all would end well in just a short period of time. The present chapter continues the same note of prophetic conflict. However, rather than two prophets in contact physically, we have here the exchange of letters between Jeremiah who is in Jerusalem and Shemaiah, a prophet in Babylon.

29:1–3 / The chapter begins by introducing the body of the chapter as a letter from Jeremiah in Jerusalem to the leaders of the exiles, specifically the **elders, priests,** and **prophets,** and indeed to everyone. Verse 2 makes it clear that these are the exiles who were taken in 597 B.C. along with **King Jehoiachin,** his mother, and other royal officials as well as skilled craftspeople. That the letter is not addressed to Jehoiachin may indicate that Jeremiah does not recognize him as the leader of the exiles. Indeed, Jeremiah believed that God worked through Nebuchadnezzar and sovereignly removed Jehoiachin from the throne and replaced him with Zedekiah. Jeremiah would have liked to have seen Jehoiachin remain in exile and Zedekiah be a good vassal of Nebuchadnezzar, not because of any love for the latter, but because it would have indicated that these leaders understood that their plight was a just punishment for their sins and the sins of their people.

The letter was sent through two royal emissaries, **Elasah son of Shaphan** and **Gemariah son of Hilkiah.** Elasah is mentioned only here, but **Shaphan,** his father, is well known from his role as the king's secretary in the reforms of Josiah as recorded in 2 Kings 22. In Jeremiah, he is mentioned in relationship to his sons. Besides Elasah, we hear about Shaphan's other son Ahikam who supported and protected Jeremiah (26:24; 39:14, see also 2 Kgs. 22:12). Gedaliah the future governor of Judah after 586 B.C. is the son of Ahikam and the grandson of Shaphan (40:5, 9, 11; 41:2; 43:6). In Jeremiah 36, we read about Shaphan's son Gemariah and the latter's son Micaiah (see vv. 10–12), who tried to get King Jehoiakim to take Jeremiah's prophecy seriously. Since Shaphan and all his sons and grandsons were members of the royal court and also sympathetic to Jeremiah, we can safely assume the same for Elasah.

While Shaphan was Josiah's secretary, **Hilkiah,** mentioned as Gemariah's father, was high priest. Since he is given a different parentage, it is unlikely that this **Gemariah** is the same as the one just mentioned who is described as the son of Shaphan. Of course, this Hilkiah may not be the famous high priest who discovered the law book (2 Kgs. 22). After all, we observed that Jeremiah's father was a certain Hilkiah from Anathoth (see 1:1), who most likely was different than the high priest. However, here it is more likely since Gemariah was most likely not the brother of Jeremiah. Moreover, since Shaphan was Josiah's secretary, it is likely though not certain that Hilkiah was the deceased king's priest.

The bottom line is that these royal messengers came from backgrounds that make it likely that they were sympathetic to Jeremiah's message. In this way, we understand why royal messengers might be willing to do the prophet a favor. While they were on an official embassy to Nebuchadnezzar on behalf of King Zedekiah, they also carried a message from Jeremiah to the exiles.

29:4–9 / The letter was not from Jeremiah per se, but rather from none other than **the LORD Almighty, the God of Israel.** The letter is addressed to all the exiles. Of interest in the description of the addressee is the fact that God tells them that it was he (**all those I carried into exile**) that sent them to Babylon, again making clear that it was God's ultimate responsibility and that Nebuchadnezzar was the unwitting tool of his judgment.

The message is forcefully stated. The exiles will be in Babylon for a long time. They are not coming back in the near term. Thus, they should settle in by building **houses** and planting **gardens.** They should **marry,** have children, and then find spouses for their children. They should not hold back on having children but should numerically increase while they are in Babylon. These commands imply that their exile will be multigenerational.

Perhaps even more striking is God's command to pray for **the peace and prosperity** of the **city,** Babylon, where they are in exile. One would think that it would be hard to pray for one's enemies who had just deported them. However, the command is not totally altruistic. The divine reasoning appeals to the exiles' self-interest and once again indicates that their stay is not temporary. As Babylon prospers, so will they.

Finally, God warns the exiles against the fraudulent hope offered by the false prophets. Interestingly, these prophets are not speaking a divinely-inspired message, but rather they are having or at least reporting dreams that the people want them to have, hopeful messages of return to their homeland. But it is all a chimera.

29:10–14 / A second section of the divine oracle in letter format is introduced by a shorter formula: **this is what the Lord says** (compare v. 10 with v. 4). The tone of the message also changes from present judgment to future salvation.

Indeed, the duration of the judgment is specified as **seventy years.** After that period of time in Babylon, God will come to the exiles and return them to their homeland. It is hard, even in historical retrospect, to know the precise significance of seventy. Even the original hearers may have wondered if this number was symbolic for a long, but unspecified period of time, since seven is a well known symbolic number for completion and seventy is, of course, seven times ten. Then there is the difficult question of knowing when this seventy-year period of judgment began (for more detailed information see note at 25:11 and also *DBI,* pp. 774–75).

In spite of the surprising ambiguity of the number seventy, God's statement here clearly indicates that the judgment is for a specified period of time. God is not abandoning his people in Babylon forever. God still has **plans** for Israel in his redemptive purposes. Of course, in their present situation the exiles would think that God has intentions only to bring harm on them, but through Jeremiah he informs them that he is not done with them. Of course, from what is said in vv. 4–9 the recipients of the letter would not see this change from judgment to redemption, but perhaps their children or grandchildren would.

Verse 12 suggests that this transition will be initiated by the people's repentance. They must first **seek** God, and when they do, God will allow himself to be **found** by them. Repentance precedes restoration (contra Fretheim, *Jeremiah,* pp. 405). Perhaps we should understand these verses as motivating Daniel to articulate repentance in Daniel 9, set at a time when it was felt the seventy years were about to expire (see G. Wilson, The Prayer of Daniel 9: Reflection on Jeremiah 29," *JSOT* 48 [1990], pp. 91–9).

29:15–19 / While the message of the letter is ultimately positive, the short term outlook is bleak. Thus, God expects that the people will not immediately accept the divine oracle delivered by Jeremiah. This attitude seems to explain best the anticipated response from the people who will say, **The LORD has raised up prophets for us in Babylon.** The reference is surely to false prophets who were mentioned in vv. 8–9 and will reoccur in vv. 20–32 where a number of them will be specified by name. In any case, God's message concerning these prophets is clear. Do not listen to them because they are speaking lies.

Rather, the immediate future will not bring redemption but future judgment. This judgment to be directed against those still in the land is described using a, by now, well-used formula: **sword, famine and plague** (see note at 14:11). The people remaining in Judah are likened to inedible **figs.** It is not as if God had not warned them of this coming judgment. Indeed, he had sent them true **prophets,** called his **servants,** prophets like Jeremiah, to come and warn them. But they have rejected their message.

29:20–23 / In the previous paragraph, God has expressed his anger with false prophets in general. Now he turns his attention to two particular prophets: **Ahab son of Kolaiah and Zedekiah son of Maaseiah.** These prophets are named nowhere else. It is interesting to note that another person designated son of Maaseiah occurs in this chapter beginning with v. 25. However, there is no way to know whether the same Maaseiah is meant in both instances.

In any case, these particular prophets are only important as specific cases of a general principle. They are lying in the name of the Lord and thus are breaking the law stated in Deuteronomy 18:14–21; the penalty for such was death. It does not appear that the exiles are in the mood or the position to put these prophets to death. However, God's will cannot be thwarted, so again Nebuchadnezzar will be the unwitting tool of his anger. God will hand them over to Nebuchadnezzar who will put them to death. It appears that false prophecy is only one of the serious crimes that these men commit against God and their fellow citizens. They are also committing adultery and thus are breaking the seventh commandment.

What God desires and Nebuchadnezzar accomplishes is only justice. Indeed, the names of the prophets will be associated with a curse: **the LORD treat you like Zedekiah and Ahab, whom the king of Babylon burned in the fire.**

29:24–32 / The sequencing of events of this chapter's ending episode is a little convoluted, but the gist may still be discerned. It appears that a person named **Shemaiah,** who is identified as coming from an otherwise unmentioned place named Nehelam, has sent letters back to Judah from Babylon where he lives in exile, to a priest named **Zephaniah** as well as to other unnamed priests and all the people (a public letter?) of Jerusalem. Though Shemaiah is a popular name in the Bible, this particular Shemaiah is otherwise unknown. Zephaniah, the priest, however, is mentioned in 2 Kings 25:18 and Jeremiah 52:24, as the "priest next in rank" to the high priest Seraiah, as taken into exile in 586 B.C. We presume that Shemaiah writes to him because his duties included disciplining false prophets. He is also mentioned in Jeremiah 21:1 as part of a delegation of two (including Pashhur) sent by King Zedekiah to Jeremiah to encourage the prophet to pray for the protection of the people. While Jeremiah does not apparently accede to their request, there is nothing in that episode that indicates ill will on the part of Zephaniah toward the prophet. Later in chapter 37, Zephaniah will also be part of a second embassy to Jeremiah (see commentary).

After receiving the letter, Zephaniah shares its contents with the prophet, but does not act on Shemaiah's request. This leads Jeremiah to write two letters, one to Shemaiah and the second one to all the exiles.

The sequencing is odd, though, since the text begins by giving what seems to be a section of Jeremiah's letter to Shemaiah (vv. 25–29), which cites the contents of the latter's letter. Only after that does it mention that Zephaniah shares the letter with Jeremiah (v. 29). Finally, we hear the contents of Jeremiah's letter to all the exiles.

Shemaiah's letter to Zephaniah blasts the priest for not handling the "Jeremiah problem." He implies that Jeremiah has unsettled the exiles by telling them to **build houses and settle down; plant gardens and eat what they produce** (v. 28). He points out that it was for this very reason that Zephaniah was appointed to deal with **any madman who acts like a prophet** (v. 26). He references Jehoiada, an apparent rival for the office, as he berates the priest (see Additional Notes) for not putting him in **stocks and neck-irons,** apparently the punishment for such prophetic sedition (see 20:1–3).

It is interesting and perhaps a sign that we are getting only part of Jeremiah's letter to Shemaiah that this report only includes a reprise of what Shemaiah wrote to Zephaniah. We expect the letter to go on and condemn him. Rather it breaks off, and, after reporting that the priest shared the letter with Jeremiah, recounts a second letter he wrote to all the exiles. This letter does condemn Shemaiah. Because he has falsely prophesied, God will punish him and his descendants. He will not live to see the future day of salvation, the **good things** God will do for his people. Precisely what those good things are is the subject of the next section of the book of Jeremiah, the so-called Book of Consolation (chs. 30–33).

Additional Notes §75

29:2 / The **queen mother** is Nehushta, daughter of Elnathan of Jerusalem. She is mentioned in Jeremiah 13:18 and Jeremiah 22:26 as going into exile. The fuller story is found in 2 Kings 24:8–17, with reference to the events of 597 B.C. The mother of the king was often a very influential person, and this would be even more so in the case of Jehoiachin who was only eighteen or nineteen during his brief tenure as king.

29:17 / The **fig** tree was a common domesticated tree that produced delicious fruit. The "features of fruitfulness and shade make the fig tree a ready symbol for God in covenant relation to his people" (*DBI*, p. 283). Thus, rotten figs symbolize an intimate relationship with God gone bad. For the fig image, see also Jeremiah 24.

29:26 / Shemaiah berates Zephaniah the priest by implying that perhaps the job of policing wayward prophets should have been given instead to Jehoiada. Jehoiada, of course, is a very famous priest name from the past since God used a Jehoiada as part of the process of deposing Athaliah and replacing her with Joash her son (2 Kgs. 11–12; 2 Chr. 23–24). Lundbom (*Jeremiah 21–36*, p. 364) believes this reference is to the famous priest and that he set up the office that Zephaniah now holds, thus he translates "Yahweh made you a priest under Jehoiada." At issue here is the translation of the preposition *takhat* which can be translated "under" or, like the NIV and the majority of modern translations HSB, REB, NAB, NJB, **in place of**, or like the NRSV, "instead of."

§76 The Book of Consolation (Jer. 30–33)

30:1–3 / The Book of Consolation begins with a general statement of hope for the people of Judah who have so far heard a message predominantly of judgment. It is identified as a divine oracle to Jeremiah (**This is the word that came to Jeremiah from the LORD** and **This is what the LORD, the God of Israel says,** vv. 1–2a). Jeremiah is further instructed not only to speak this message, but to **write in a book all the words** that God has spoken to him. Such a command underscores the importance of the message as well as a need to preserve it long term. Perhaps as well it gives the message a certain measure of assurance. It is a word that the faithful could come back to and remind themselves of God's continued involvement with them.

The actual oracle is introduced with a formula that looks to a time in the vague future (**the days are coming**). The future event is simply described as a return of the people of Israel and Judah back to the promised land from their exile.

The fact that both the people of Israel and Judah are mentioned is of interest. It may indicate that the earlier exiles from the northern kingdom preserved some measure of identity at this stage in their captivity. Or it could simply be a way to refer to those who were exiled in 605, 597, and who will be exiled in 586 as now representative of both (and perhaps some northerners had escaped to the south after 722 B.C.). In any case, the future will certainly bring a return to Jerusalem and Judah beginning in 539, but no distinct return of northerners. By referring to the land as that which God gave the **forefathers** connects the future return to the promise given to Abraham (Gen. 12:1–3) and maintained by the other patriarchs, Isaac and Jacob.

30:4–11 / A second oracle initially reverts to lament and judgment but then turns at the end again to hope. It too is introduced by the double introduction identifying it as a divine oracle (**These are the words the LORD spoke concerning Israel**

and Judah and **This is what the LORD says**). The second phrase introduces a number of the oracles in chapters 30–31 (see 30:12, 18; 31:2, 7, 15, 16, 23 [with expansion on the divine name]). Toward the end of these oracles the reader gets a reminder of the divine origin of the oracle with the phrase **declares the LORD** (30:10, 17, 21; 30:14, 16, 17, 20). The latter also occurs in 31:32, 34, 37.

Notice again (see comment on 30:1–3) that the object of the oracle is referred to as **Israel and Judah** and not just Judah alone.

The oracle proper begins by anticipating the horror of conquest. Dramatically, it notes the high level of terror in society by imagining cries of fear. There is no peace; turmoil is in the air. The oracle then cites a familiar metaphor for fear, but gives it an interesting twist. Fear is often represented as a having the same effect as a **woman in labor,** particularly in Isaiah and Jeremiah (Isa. 21:2–3; 26:16–21; 66:7–14; Jer. 13:21; 22:23; 49:24; 50:43). It is an apt image because of the extreme pain and anxiety connected with childbearing since the time of the Fall (Gen. 3:16).

However, the interesting twist here is provided by the introduction to the metaphor. It begins by asking a rhetorical question, **Can a man bear children?** The obvious and expected answer is, "Of course not!" But then the oracle goes on to ask why strong men are grasping their midsections like women in labor. The answer is that the fear is so great, even on those **strong men** who would be responsible for providing military defense, that they would act like a woman experiencing labor pains. Their emotion is also etched on their face since fear causes their face to go pale.

The day that is coming will be unprecedented in its horror. Judah will be the object of great harm. But the final colon of v. 7 shifts the tone from judgment to salvation, noting that there will be light after the darkness (**he** [Judah] **will be saved out of it**).

Verses 8–11 form a subunit within the larger oracle. It begins with a variation on the formula (**in that day**) that indicates that the following statement refers to events in the indeterminate future as well as a reminder that this is a divine oracle (**declares the LORD Almighty**). In the oracle per se, God announces his intention to break the yoke off the neck of his people. The metaphor of the yoke as a metaphor for political oppression is one with which readers are familiar from chapter 28, in the fight between Jeremiah and Hananiah. The latter's claim that God was going to break the yoke from the neck of his people rang hollow because he proclaimed that freedom would come in short order and before further judgment. But God himself here announces their future freedom from political oppression (**no longer will foreigners enslave them**) with the language of the removal of the yoke from their necks and the bonds presumably on their limbs.

Their forced service to a foreign power will give way to a service to the Lord and his representative, the **king** in the line of **David.** "Liberation in the biblical view is a change of masters" (Lundbom, *Jeremiah 21–36,* p. 390). It is interesting to reflect on the latter part of this promise given the history that follows. In time, Judah will indeed be permitted to return to the land, but a Davidic king does not begin to rule from a Jerusalemite throne. Upon the failure of a human kingship upon the return, these royal oracles (as well as the royal psalms) began to be understood to have messianic significance. The exact nature of the messiah was differently construed in the Intertestamental period. The New Testament, however, would identify Jesus Christ as the one who fulfills the expectation of a Davidic king.

From this flows the admonition of v. 10ab. While the oracle begins by remarking on the cries of fear heard in the land (v. 5), God encourages them not to fear. Salvation follows judgment. God is in control. He will save them and reestablish **peace and security** in the land. He also indicates a restoration of the covenant relationship between them when he says **I am with you.** God's presence, disrupted by the sin of his people, will be restored.

Thus, there will be a distinction between Judah and the other nations of the world. God will bring judgment against all of them (see the oracles against the foreign nations in chs. 46–51), but while God will **completely destroy all the nations,** he will not completely destroy Judah. Their judgment is indeed punishment for their sin, but it is a chastisement, not an execution. See the similar oracle to verses 10–11 in 46:27–28.

30:12–17 / This oracle develops in a similar way to the preceding one. In other words, it begins with an emphasis on the coming judgment on Judah for their sin, but then at the end gives a note of hope of restoration.

The oracle begins with a dire diagnosis. God's people have suffered a wound and it is a wound that cannot heal (see Additional Notes). There is no one who can heal them. Switching to a legal metaphor, they also have no one to take up their case (**there is no one to plead your cause**).

When faced with foreign aggression in the past, Judah has sought help from other nations, forming political and military alliances. The history of the immediate preexilic period is a period of shifting alliances, but most often Judah sought the alliance of Egypt in order to counterbalance the threat from Babylon. Certainly this was the position of Jehoiakim and Jehoiachin. Zedekiah was actually placed on the throne by Babylon in the expectation that he would be a compliant vassal. However, even he sought foreign alliances that ultimately brought the might of Babylon to his doorstep. In spite of their efforts, though, when push came to shove, no **allies** were there to help them against Babylon.

In any case, even if they had allies, it would not have helped. After all, it was ultimately God himself who brought destruction to Judah. He turned from being their warrior to being their **enemy** (see Lam. 2). He fought against his people because of their sin as he warned in the covenant curses of Deuteronomy 28.

Such treatment should have been expected. Rebellion against God brings punishment. It is in that spirit that the oracle asks the reason behind Judah's cry over their incurable wound. Of course the pain of the wound lead to cries, but the question asks why they are crying out in surprise. God did it because of their sins.

But this is not the end of the story. This oracle ends similarly to the previous one (compare vv. 11 and 16–17). Ultimately, God himself will be their physician and heal their wound. No one else cares for them (**Zion**), but God will take care of them. On the other hand, the nations who presently **devour** Judah will themselves be devoured. Certainly this will be the case of Babylon. They presently have the upper hand against Judah, but it will not be too long before they themselves are plundered and destroyed. This end comes in 539 B.C. at the hands of the Persians.

30:18–22 / The previous two oracles all started with statements of judgment before turning to an expression of future redemption. The present oracle is positive from beginning to end. This oracle has the same structure as the previous two. It begins with that announcement: **This is what the LORD says,** and then toward the end has a reminder of speaker (**declares the LORD**). The latter does not bring the oracle to a close, but continues with a final statement.

The oracle begins with the so-called "restoration formula" (**I will restore the fortunes of,** see Additional Notes at 30:3). This refers to a return to the land from captivity and a material and spiritual prosperity on the part of the people. The reference to **Jacob's tents** is an anachronistic reference to the dwellings of the people of God. God will show compassion (verbal root *rkhm*) to his people. The latter clearly constitutes a return of covenant love on the people. That compassionate attitude of God will have concrete consequences. The **city,** destroyed in 586, will be rebuilt. The city, of course, is Jerusalem. The second colon of this parallelism specifies that one particular building, here translated the **palace** (*ʾarmon*), will be restored. But it is unclear that the specified building is the palace. The Hebrew word can be translated "citadel" (NRSV), "mansion" (REB), "stronghold" (NJB). If the correct translation is palace, then this would be a similar type of hope as that expressed in 30:9. However, as far as we know, if it is palace, this prophecy remains unfulfilled. It is more likely to be taken in the sense offered by the NRSV.

The response from the people will be songs of thanksgiving and joy. In terms of the latter, one thinks immediately of Psalm 126, a psalm that even uses the restoration formula (*shub ʾet-shebut,* "restore the fortune," see note to 30:3 and note v. 18):

> When the LORD brought back the captives to Zion,
> we were like men who dreamed.
> Our mouths were filled with laughter,
> our tongues with songs of joy.
> Then it was said among the nations,
> "The LORD has done great things for them."
> The LORD has done great things for us,
> and we are filled with joy.
> Restore our fortunes, O LORD,
> like streams in the Negev.
> Those who sow in tears
> will reap with songs of joy.
> He who goes out weeping,
> carrying seed to sow,
> Will return with songs of joy,
> carrying sheaves with him.

Then God expands upon how he will restore the fortunes of his people. For one thing, their population will expand (**I will add to their numbers**). Of course, the seminal Abrahamic promise (Gen. 12:1–3) speaks of descendants and as that promise is exegeted, it entails a large population (as numerous as the stars of heaven and as the sand on the seashore (Gen. 22:17, see also 32:12; 41:49). Of course, the wars and exile have taken a toll on their population, but with the restoration this diminishment will be reversed.

In addition, God will change their dishonor into **honor.** They will no longer be shamed by their subservient position as the vanquished, but in their restored relationship with God and the consequent material prosperity, they will again have dignity.

A bit more enigmatic is the prediction that **their children will be as in days of old.** Whether this refers to the number or quality of their children and their lifestyle or all of the above is not clear. Or perhaps with Fretheim (*Jeremiah,* p. 424) we should take this as a reference to the children of Israel and as referring "to the reestablishment of both northern and southern kingdoms (see v. 3) as a single community or 'congregation' (see 31:1)." In any case, their **community** shattered by the events of judgment will now be restored before God. Rather than using other nations to subdue his rebellious people, God assures them that in the future time of their restoration, God will punish those who do try to oppress them.

Verse 21 turns attention to their future leader. He will be a native (**one of their own**) and not a foreign oppressor. The leader will have an intimate relationship with the Lord. Both of these qualities are specified as important for a leader (see Deut. 17:14–20).

The oracle ends (v. 22) with the formula that indicates an intimate covenant relationship between God and his people (**you will be my people, and I will be your God**). This relationship had been disrupted because of the people's sin. Hosea had told the story of the naming of his son Lo-Ammi, which means "not my people." "Call him Lo-Ammi, for you are not my people, and I am not your God" (Hos. 1:9). But even Hosea predicted a better day:

> I will say to those called 'Not my people,' 'You are my people';
> And they will say, 'You are my God.' (Hos. 2:23b)

30:23–24 / The chapter concludes with a judgment oracle speaking of the coming storm of the Lord (this oracle is a repeat from 23:19–20). This **storm** will devastate the wicked. Nothing can stand in the way of the Lord's wrath. There is no mention of the specific objects of God's anger here. The audience is addressed in the second person (**you**) and the assumption is that this refers to the people of Judah. In the future, they will understand how God's storm-like judgment comes on the wicked. But does this understanding come by means of experience, in that they are the objects of violence, or by means of observation, where they observe God's wrath coming on the heads of their oppressors (so Fretheim, *Jeremiah,* p. 424)? Lundbom takes it as a general statement and reminder to the remnant of Judah that they need to beware lest wrath come on them again (*Jeremiah 21–36,* p. 411).

31:1–6 / This salvation oracle begins with the eschatological formula **at that time,** signaling a future, but unspecified time. In that future date, God will reestablish his covenant relationship with his people as expressed in his announcement that he will be their God and they will be his people (see also 30:22). Interestingly, he refers to all the **clans** (or families) **of Israel** as the object of his covenant affection. In one sense, this reference is a variant of the phrase "all the people of Israel" or "all the tribes of Israel," but it is also an acknowledgement of the family structure in Israel. As verse 6 makes clear, this oracle envisions the restoration of all Israel, north and south.

The oracle continues with a declaration that it is the Lord who is speaking, followed by a reference to those **who survive the sword.** Surely this is a reference to what elsewhere might be called the remnant, those who endure beyond the coming moment of judgment. God proclaims that these survivors **will find favor in the desert.** The term favor (or grace) describes a disposition on the part of God to treat people better than they deserve. The mention of the desert fits in with a theme that we find in other prophets (Hos. 2:14–16; Isa. 40:1–5) that God's coming judgment is in essence a reversal of redemptive history. God had previously brought Israel into the promised land from the desert. Now because of judgment he is going to hurl them out of the land and into what is theologically and metaphorically the desert, though in actuality it will entail a deportation to Babylon. But this oracle says that God will meet the survivors of the judgment and will restore them to covenant relationship. This restoration in essence will grant them relief (**rest**) from the troubles of the exile.

That this message of restoration is not a new thought is signaled at the beginning of verse 3 when it reminds Israel of a message from the Lord **in the past.** Again using language associated with the covenant, God reminded them that he has loved them with an **everlasting love** and has had an intimate relationship with them characterized by **loving-kindness** (*khesed*). For this reason, there will be a restoration that is described here as a rebuilding and a replanting. This language echoes part of God's commission to Jeremiah recorded in 1:10. In addition, note the intimate reference to Israel as a **Virgin** (compare 18:13, where the term refers specifically to Jerusalem; see Additional Notes there).

Such a restoration will cause celebration to begin, a celebration characterized by song and dance (v. 4b). Most significantly, there will be a restoration of worship on **Mount Zion.** God will make his presence known at that sacred location once again. It is significant that it is the **watchmen** who are on the **hills of Ephraim** that will issue the call to worship in Zion. Ephraim is the main tribe of the former northern kingdom. Thus, this verse envisions a restored and reunited Israel all worshiping together in Zion, something that has not happened since the schism in 931 B.C.

31:7–9 / This oracle of salvation begins with the introduction: **This is what the LORD says.** What follows is a call to celebrate the return from exile and includes a prophetic depiction of the return itself.

In good psalmic fashion, the oracle begins with an invitation to **sing with joy** concerning Jacob, one of a number of names used to refer to the people of God. **Jacob,** of course, is the name of the patriarch whose name was changed to Israel. Though they certainly were not the strongest or most cultured of nations at the time, they were **foremost** from a theological perspective, since they were the people that God had chosen and the ones on whom God would now renew his favor.

Along with their praises, the people are to ask God to **save** his people (but see Additional Notes on 31:7). In the second colon, the people are more precisely described as the **remnant of Israel.** In other words, they are those who survived the judgment of the exile. These are the ones who will return to the promised land.

Verses 8–9 anticipate that return by imagining God bringing them back from the **land of the north,** a term (along with near variants) used often in Jeremiah to indicate Babylon (1:13–15; 4:6; 6:1, etc.). But these people will come not only from the north, but also from **the ends of the earth.** The trauma of defeat and exile sent the Judeans not only to Babylon but to many other nations, most notably Egypt as will be seen in Jeremiah 41:16–44:30.

All the remnant will return. They are described as a **great throng** of people. It will include even those with disabilities (**the blind and the lame,** see Isa. 35:5–6; Mic. 4:6–8; Zeph. 1:19–20) as well as pregnant **mothers,** two classes of people who normally would find it difficult to travel in such a way. God will see to it that even they make it back safely.

As these return, they will be **weeping.** The reason for their weeping is not given but is rather assumed. While it is not impossible that they will be weeping for joy, it is more likely that they will be weeping over their guilt. This better explains why they pray as they return. Of course, the fact that they do **pray** shows a right relationship with the Yahweh, no matter what the explanation.

Further supporting the idea that their weeping is mournful rather than celebratory is the fact that God says he will comfort them by leading them beside **streams of water.** Though the language is not identical, the picture is similar to that in Psalm 23.

The motivation for acting compassionately toward weeping Israel is that God is **Israel's father** and **Ephraim** is his firstborn son. While Israel may stand for the entirety of the land, north and south, it is interesting that that term and especially Ephraim in verse 11 are ways of referring to the northern portion. Jeremiah's vision is of a united, whole Israel.

31:10–14 / While some treat these verses along with the previous section as a single divine oracle (Fretheim, *Jeremiah,* pp. 431–3), there is a change of addressee and a new introduction (**Hear the word of the LORD,** v. 10a). The addressees are now the **nations.** In this oracle the Lord now informs the nations of his good intentions toward his people.

The first announcement to the nations is that the Lord who **scattered** Israel, his flock, will now gather and protect them like a **shepherd** protects his sheep. The shepherd image is a familiar one in Scripture, one that is used of leaders, human and divine, who care for and protect their subjects (Num. 27:17; 2 Sam. 7:7; Ps. 78:70–72; Ezek. 34). In Jeremiah, we have earlier seen that Israel's incompetent leaders were likened to senseless shepherds (Jer. 10:21, see also 50:6). For that reason, these shepherds will be destroyed (Jer. 25:34–36) and they will be replaced by others (Jer. 3:15; 23:1–3), who better reflect the divine shepherd.

Switching metaphors, in verse 11 God will **ransom** his people. He will **redeem** them from **those who are stronger,** militarily and politically (Babylon), than they. For that reason, they will celebrate and enjoy a new measure of agricultural prosperity. Indeed, they will be like a **well-watered garden** themselves. That is they will be brimming with life and growing, as opposed to a dry, dying garden.

In the spirit of Psalm 126 (see also Ps. 30:11), which describes the transition from weeping to joy among those who are returning from exile, **God will turn their mourning into gladness.** Such joy is accompanied by **dancing.**

Interestingly, in the last verse of the oracle, the **priests** are specified as receiving God's **abundance.** Thus, the priests who survive will reap the reward. This is notable particularly since the priests have received their share of blame for the judgment that will come on Israel because of their sin. In an unusual move, the final parallelism moves from specific (priests) to general (people). However the point is clear, the entire remnant will enjoy prosperity.

31:15–22 / No two commentators agree on the extent of the next oracle. Some divide this oracle into many smaller units, treating, for instance, verse 15 as a very short oracle. While this is possible, there are characteristics that appear to unite these verses. For instance, in verse 15 we hear that Rachel is weeping, then in verse 16 the Lord requests that the weeping stop. It appears that this oracle, like some of the previous ones, begins with a reflection on judgment to be followed by the promise of redemption. The focus seems to be on the northern kingdom.

The oracle begins with God acknowledging a mournful weeping from **Ramah.** Ramah is located in Benjamin (Josh. 18:25; Judg. 4:5; 19:15, though there are other Ramahs). The significance of this Ramah in this context appears to be the fact that it was a deportation center (so Jer. 40:1). Thus, from here, the Israelites were shipped off to exile in Babylon. No wonder it was a place of great weeping.

Rachel stands for the northern tribes, since the tribes that descend from her two sons, Joseph and Benjamin, namely Manasseh, Ephraim, and Benjamin, are well known northern tribes. These are the children of Rachel for whom she weeps. They are no more because they are now carried off into exile. There is a tradition that Rachel's tomb is in this region in Benjamin (1 Sam. 10:2). Genesis 35:19 records her burial on the way to Bethlehem, though a number of scholars believe that this refers to a Benjamite site near Kiriath-jearim (see D. T. Tsumira, *1 Samuel,* p. 284). For the use of 31:15 in the New Testament, see the Additional Notes.

The Lord responds to this aggrieved weeping with a voice of hope. He comforts Rachel by telling her to stop weeping. The motivation clause, however, is difficult to understand. What is her **work?** It might be a reference to her labor during exile. Conceivably, it might refer to a work of repentance. More likely it refers to the restoration of the children themselves (see Additional Notes). But we must admit the reference remains enigmatic. Even if the work has an ambiguous reference, the reason for hope is not. That is centered on the return from the exile. Specifically, it says that the addressees' children will return to their land.

Now referring to the northern tribes by reference to the most dominant of those tribes, **Ephraim,** one of Rachel's sons, the Lord again acknowledges that he hears their moaning. At that point, the oracle quotes Ephraim's complaint (vv. 18b–19). Ephraim states that God has disciplined it and done so as if Ephraim is an **unruly calf** (see Additional Notes). It takes rough treatment to tame such a calf, but Ephraim acknowledges that God has been successful in his discipline. Now Ephraim wants to be restored to God's good graces. Verse 19 presents the sequence of events. It begins with Ephraim's straying from God's way. But then they repent and feel the shame caused by their rebellion.

As verses 16–17 respond to Rachel's weeping, so verses 20–22 respond to Ephraim's moaning. Verse 20 begins by giving God's reaction to Ephraim's repentance. He acknowledges Ephraim's status as his **son** (see 31:9). And like a son, though he has to discipline him as a son, God never completely abandons his love for him. Indeed, he remembers him, which implies more than cognitive retention. It implies that God will act graciously toward Ephraim. This graciousness will flow from his great **compassion.** The language describing God's strong emotions toward Israel is quite striking and belies the false stereotype of the Old Testament God as cold and merciless (see Hos. 11:8–9).

Then in verse 21 God tells them to plot the route of their return. **Virgin Israel** (see 31:4 and Additional Notes to 18:13) is told by God to return to their towns. The unfaithful daughter is to stop wandering and return home.

The oracle ends with an enigmatic proverb citing a new thing God will bring on earth: **a woman will surround a man.** While there are a number of possible alternative interpretations, the following understanding seems best. In the first place, a few facts seem clear about this verse. The gender of the woman is emphasized (*neqebah*) and the strength of the man is underlined (*geber* may be understood as warrior or strong man; *zakar* would be used to emphasize the male gender). It appears that what we have here is something of a reversal of roles. We might expect the strong man to surround the female, whether surround is taken as a reference to a sexual embrace and/or protection. The reversal is likely the reason why it is called new. But what does it mean? Since Israel is likened to a woman in this oracle (Rachel; Virgin Israel), we might understand this as indicating that Israel has embraced God, thus expressing her repentant attitude that has turned from faithless wandering.

31:23–26 / The next salvation oracle (**This is what the LORD Almighty, the God of Israel, says**) describes the situation of the people of Judah after their return from captivity. It envisions a time when the people come back and utter the following blessing: **"The LORD bless you, O righteous dwelling, O sacred mountain."** Such a request for blessing shows that the returnees will have their hearts in the right place. They turn to the Lord for their well-being and they direct their hopes in the right direction. The meaning of **righteous dwelling** is a bit ambiguous, however. The Hebrew for dwelling is literally "pasturage" (*nawah*). This word can refer to the land in general, to Jerusalem, or specifically to the temple. If the latter, then the oracle anticipates its rebuilding after the exile. The fact that "righteous dwelling" is in apposition to **sacred mountain**, certainly a reference to Zion, may support that idea, though the thought might be moving from general (**land**) to specific (**temple mount**). The Hebrew expression here translated **righteous dwelling** (*neweh-tsedeq*) occurs in Jeremiah 50:7 as well, but NIV translates "true pasture" in that context where the reference is to the Lord himself.

Judah's economy, both farming and shepherding, will be reinvigorated. There may well be significance to the fact that farmers and shepherds, who often compete over the use of land, will get along together in the restored Judah. God is there to reenergize those who languish in strength.

Verse 26 gives us unexpected information. The first person speaker (**I**), most likely we are to think of Jeremiah, wakes up from sleep. He comments that his **sleep was pleasant.** Perhaps we are to see a connection with verse 25, where God says he will **refresh the weary.** But it is still strange to hear that the prophet is waking from sleep since we have not been told that he was asleep to begin with! Fretheim (*Jeremiah,* p. 439) suggests that the reference is actually to the people of God who are waking up from their sleep of sin and death to new realities.

31:27–30 / The next salvation oracle invokes God's commission to Jeremiah in 1:10: "See, today I appoint you over nations and kingdoms to uproot and tear down, to destroy and overthrow, to build and to plant." The time for uprooting Judah will be over in the future (**the days are coming**) to be replaced by a time to plant. This oracle is directed toward both the north (**the house of Israel**) and the south (**the house of Judah**).

There will also be a change of accountability or at least a perception of change. In the future a new proverb will replace an old one. The old one (see also Ezek. 18:2; Lam. 5:7) recounts how children will suffer the consequences of the (evil) actions of the generations that preceded them:

> **The fathers have eaten sour grapes,**
> **and the children's teeth are set on edge.**

Perhaps this was what the people were saying as they were in exile. And certainly the prophets as well as the history recounted in Joshua through 2 Kings (the so-called Deuteronomistic History) did blame the ancestors for the sins that led to the exile. However, the prophets, and especially Jeremiah, also accused the generation right before the exile for their plight as well. Their repentance would have spared them the exile. However, for the generation born during the exile, this proverb would be literally true.

In any case, this old proverb will be replaced by a new one: **whoever eats sour grapes—his own teeth will be set on edge.** In other words, as the prophet explains, **every one will die for their own sin.** Such an understanding of personal accountability would certainly increase one's own interest in ethical behavior. As Hezekiah illustrates, one might be relieved to realize that the punishment for one's sin would come on future generations (Isa. 39). And Qohelet states the same concern as a principle: "When the sentence for a crime is not quickly carried out, the hearts of the people are filled with schemes to do wrong" (Eccl. 8:11). Indeed, the transition from the old proverb of paying for the sins of the parents to the new principle of personal accountability is also reflected in the difference between the delayed retribution of Samuel-Kings and the immediate retribution theology of Chronicles. Perhaps then it is no surprise that the old proverb was important in the preexilic period and the new one is important for the post-exilic period.

31:31–34 / With these verses we come to the heart of the Book of Consolation. This salvation oracle may be the most well-known and profound statement in the book of Jeremiah. They are so important to the development of the covenant idea of the Bible that we discussed its place in the rest of the canon in the Introduction (The Covenant). In the following comments, we will focus on its meaning within the book of Jeremiah, though this will necessitate a preliminary discussion of the background of the language Jeremiah uses here.

Again, the opening words of the oracle anticipate an unspecified future time when the conditions that are described in what follows will come to fruition (**the time is coming**). While vague in terms of time reference, the formula also makes it clear that fulfillment is certain.

What follows is the startling promise that God will make a **new covenant** with the people of God (**the house of Israel** and the **house of Judah**). The next few verses go on to describe the new covenant in contrast to what is implicitly understood to be the old covenant. It is explicitly called the covenant that God made with the present generations **forefathers** at the time when he brought them **out of Egypt.** Of course, the most immediate reference is therefore the Mosaic, also called Sinaitic, covenant, narrated in Exodus 19–24, with reaffirmations in Deuteronomy, Joshua 24, and elsewhere. In the Introduction, we considered the likelihood that the oracle, while focusing on the Mosaic covenant, actually considers all the previous covenants in contrast to the new covenant.

In any case, the transition from the old covenant to the new covenant is motivated not by some flaw in the old covenant, but by the inability of God's people to keep it. They **broke** the **covenant.** Their breaking of the law of the covenant is what has required the prophets, including Jeremiah, to preach judgment against them. Heightening the perversity of the rebellion of the people of God, is the fact that God has acted toward them like a **husband** toward a wife. The marriage metaphor of the relationship between God and his people emphasizes his love and caring concern for them. In spite of that, they have spurned him (see Ezek. 16; 23; Hos. 1; 3).

While verse 32 states that the new covenant will not be like the old covenant, verses 33–34 more positively express the nature of the former. The verse begins by stating that the law will be placed in their **minds** and written on their **hearts.** The latter expression ("hearts") in particular likely intends to contrast with the Ten Commandments that were written on tablets of stone. This is not an absolute contrast between the old and new covenants. In the first place, we should notice that the new covenant does not eradicate the law. Further, the old covenant's provisions were not strictly external (remember the tenth commandment ["You must not covet"] among other things). The old covenant was not simply an external religion expecting only appropriate external behavior. It, too, was a religion of the heart (Deut. 6:6; 10:12, 16; 11:18; 30:6, 14). We are probably to read this as intensification rather than a new administration.

It is after making this strong expression of the internal nature of the new covenant that God then proclaims, **"I will be their God, and they will be my people."** This is the covenant formulary. It expresses the covenant relationship in a nutshell. A memorable moment when God uses this formulary is Exodus 6:6–8, where it becomes the basis for why God will bring the people out of bondage in Egypt and into the land promised to Abraham.

Verse 34 then goes on to conclude that a **teacher** is no longer necessary in the divine-human relationship. No longer is a human covenant mediator necessary. Moses was such a teacher, a mediator of the relationship between God and his people, as was Joshua, Samuel, and many others. After the exile, Ezra and Nehemiah would mediate between God and humans. But when the new covenant goes into effect, there will no longer be a need for such pivotal figures.

This does not mean that all teachers are now obsolete, only those that help establish one's relationship with God. Teachers still have a role and are spoken of positively in the New Testament period (Rom. 12:7; Gal. 6:6; 1 Tim. 2:7; 3:2; 2 Tim. 1:11; 2:24). They can strengthen and deepen one's understanding, but they are no longer necessary for one to come to know God in the first place and to establish a relationship with him.

As McComiskey points out (*The Covenants of Promise*, p. 87), the idea that in the future people will not need a covenant mediator is similar to the idea behind Joel 2:28–29: "The prophet Jeremiah pictured the same great era as Joel, when even the most lowly believer will have the same rights of access to God as did the prophets who ministered under the old covenant."

The oracle ends with a motive clause for why they do not need a teacher in the sense of a covenant mediator. God will **forgive** them for their evil deeds. He will not **remember** their sins any more. The fact that he will not remember their sins does not mean that God will erase his memory of them. To remember is to act upon something. To not remember is to not act upon it. He will not treat them as if they are sinners.

While Jeremiah 31:31–34 is the only place where we find the term **new covenant**, a future and "everlasting" covenant is anticipated in Jeremiah 32:27–44; 50:4–5; Ezekiel 37:15–28. The term new covenant is found later at Luke 22:20. At the Last Supper, Jesus passes the cup of wine to his disciples while saying, "This cup is the new covenant in my blood, which is poured out for you." Thus, Jesus inaugurates the new covenant (see Introduction:

the Covenant). The New Testament also quotes and develops the significance of this passage in 1 Corinthians 11:25; 2 Corinthians 3:5–14; Hebrews 8:8–12; 10:16–17.

31:35–37 / In the next oracle God describes himself in terms of his work at creation. On the fourth day of creation, God made the **sun, moon,** and **stars** to rule over the day and night. Here the verbs are not the same and there is not an explicit mention of the creation itself, but rather how he assigned them specific tasks of illumination during the day (sun) and the night (moon and stars). The next poetic line playfully identifies God as the one who also is responsible for the world's waters (**the sea**). The celestial bodies and the earthly seas both are under God's control and do what they do only because he set the world up that way (v. 35 says that he **appoints** [literally "gives"]) and **decrees** them.

In verse 36 God assures the future remnant that the **descendants of Israel** will be a nation before him for as long as the sun, moon, and stars shine and the seas pound the shores with their waves. Thus God expresses his continual commitment to future restored Israel by likening it to his continual commitment to keep his creation working according to its normal rhythms (Gen. 8:22; 9:8–17).

A similar oracle follows which also connects creation to God's commitment to Israel. God will not reject Israel as long as the heavens remain unmeasured and the foundations of the earth be searched out. The point is that that moment will never come. God makes such a statement in spite of the fact that he is aware of their rebellion. **All that they have done** is surely a reference to their sin. Even so, God will remain committed to Israel.

31:38–40 / The final unit of the chapter is a prose oracle of salvation. Again it is introduced by the formula that indicates a future date that remains unspecified (**the days are coming**). The content of the oracle concerns the rebuilding and expansion of Jerusalem. That city had been destroyed but the future age of redemption will see its restoration and more. Not all of the landmarks given are mentioned elsewhere or known (**Gareb** and **Goah**), but some are. The **Tower of Hananel** is mentioned in Nehemiah 3:1; 12:39; Zechariah 14:10. The **Corner Gate** is cited in 2 Kings 14:13; 2 Chronicles 25:23; 26:9; Zechariah 14:10. **The valley where dead bodies and ashes are thrown** is a descriptive reference to the Hinnom Valley to the southwest of the city (see Jer. 19). The **Kidron Valley** is to the east of the city between it and the Mount of

Olives. The **Horse Gate** is found in 2 Chronicles 23:15; Nehemiah 3:28. The order of these landmarks "is a walking tour of the city's boundaries before its destruction, beginning in the northeast quadrant and proceeding in counterclockwise fashion until it ends up where it began" (Lundbom, *Jeremiah 21–36*, p. 490).

The theological significance of this passage is that Jerusalem will be expanded and the entirety of it will be considered **holy,** not just the temple precinct. Furthermore, the city will be rebuilt for God (**for me,** v. 38).

And in keeping with the previous oracles where God affirms his continuing and perpetual commitment to Israel, he promises that the city **will never again be uprooted or demolished** (see the language of Jeremiah's call in 1:10). Indeed, the city of Jerusalem is with us to today. However, this promise apparently does not intend to assure an untroubled history, since that city has been the center of strife and turmoil quite often in its long history.

32:1–15 / The narrative begins by giving the date of the event that follows. It is **the tenth year of Zedekiah, the eighteenth of Nebuchadnezzar,** clearly within months of the downfall of Jerusalem. Indeed, the siege of Jerusalem has begun. According to Jeremiah 52:4–5, the Babylonian army arrived at the gates of Jerusalem in the tenth month of Zedekiah's ninth year. Thus we are to imagine this story taking place within the walls of Jerusalem which was encircled by the Babylonian army. Furthermore, Jeremiah himself has been confined **in the courtyard of the guard of the royal palace of Judah.** The prophet was thought to be a collaborator since he advocated the view that Zedekiah ought to capitulate to Nebuchadnezzar. As verses 3–5 state, he was preaching that there was no way Zedekiah could hold out against the Babylonians. God will hand the city and its king over to their enemies. Zedekiah's fate will be deportation to Babylon. The divine ultimatum was clear through Jeremiah, **"If you fight against the Babylonians, you will not succeed"** (32:5). But Zedekiah did not accept this advice. It is even possible that Jeremiah 37 reports the specific episode that led to his arrest. During a break in the siege, precipitated by the withdrawal of the Babylonian army to deal with an apparent threat from the Egyptians, Jeremiah tried to leave Jerusalem to go home to Benjamin to deal with some real estate issues (perhaps the one resolved here). He was arrested as if he was going over to the Babylonian side.

Zedekiah's question "**Why do you prophesy as you do?**" reveals a fundamental misunderstanding of who Jeremiah is. It is not as if Jeremiah has a choice. As a divine spokesperson, he must speak the words God has given him.

In response, Jeremiah surprisingly tells of yet another divine oracle. It begins by God informing Jeremiah that **Hanamel** his cousin (**son of Shallum your uncle**) is going to make a real estate offer. As we think about the political, military, and theological circumstances, this offer is one that should be refused. However, by anticipating the visit by Hanamel, God is preparing Jeremiah to receive the offer favorably.

Hanamel appears at Jeremiah's place of confinement, and as expected in conformity with the divine forewarning, he offers his land near his ancestral homeland in Anathoth (see Jer. 1:1) to him for sale. However, the offer may be too soft a word since Hanamel explains it is **his right** to do so. Indeed, the divine oracle suggests it is **his right and duty** to do so. Since Jeremiah does not hesitate to buy the land, perhaps Hanamel was spared the onus of having to remind Jeremiah of the fact that it was his duty. After all, we are not hearing of an ordinary land transaction here, but rather an act of redemption. Hanamel is asking Jeremiah to **redeem** the land in the technical sense. Apparently, as nearest relative to Hanamel, Jeremiah must perform the function of the redeemer (*goʾel,* from *gaʾal*) as described in Leviticus 25:23–25:

Of course this does not automatically mean that Jeremiah would actually accept the offer. After all, we have the example of the unnamed kinsman-redeemer in Ruth 4 who refuses to redeem Ruth's land because in this case it would also entail taking Ruth as a wife. Fortunately, Boaz was next in line and more than willing to marry Ruth.

But Jeremiah knows that this is from God and so he accepts the offer and pays **seventeen shekels** of silver for the land. The modern reader then gets a glimpse at real estate procedure in the early sixth century B.C. in Palestine as they sign and seal the deed, have it witnessed in duplicate (a sealed and unsealed copy). This was a publicly transacted deal with those present functioning as witnesses. In principle, modern readers will find much that is familiar in this transaction!

In any case, Jeremiah entrusts his sealed and unsealed copies of the deed into the care of his trusted assistant and scribe, **Baruch,** who appears for the first, but certainly not the last, time in the book of Jeremiah (see 36 [throughout]; 43:3, 6; 45:1, 2). The reference in 36:4 indicates that by the time of this episode, they have been long standing associates, for at least eighteen years.

He publicly commands Baruch to take them both and place them in a clay jar for long-term safekeeping. At this point, Jeremiah delivers the prophetic punch line of the story. God has announced: **Houses, fields and vineyards will again be bought in this land.** Thus, this seventeen-shekel parcel of land in Anathoth is an earnest of future land possession. God is not permanently abandoning his people. There will be a return. Fretheim (*Jeremiah*, p. 456) has rightly seen this episode as an answer to Zedekiah's "Why?" question in verse 3 when he says, "Judgment must fall upon Jerusalem, because it is only through that refining fire that any hope for the future of the people of God becomes possible. Life can come only through death."

32:16–25 / After Jeremiah buys the land, he then prays to God. His prayer praises God for his power manifested both in acts of grace and judgment. But the ultimate purpose of the prayer is to pose a question to God.

He first extols God as the creator of the heavens and earth. Interestingly, Jeremiah states the God accomplished creation by his **great power and outstretched arm.** With the exception of Jeremiah 27:5, elsewhere this formula is used only in reference to warfare with special, but not exclusive, reference to God's acts of violence associated with the exodus (Exod. 6:6; Deut. 4:34; 5:15; 7:19; 9:29; 11:2; Jer. 21:5; 32:21). The creation account itself (Gen. 1) describes creation as taking place by the power of God's word. It is true, however, that in poetic and prophetic contexts the idea of conflict at creation does occasionally appear (for instance as in Ps. 74). Perhaps this formula is used here because Jeremiah is about to describe the great power and outstretched arm of God in reference to the Babylonian attack on Jerusalem. But the most immediate application of the remembrance of the creation is the conclusion that **nothing is too hard** for God. That God does wondrous things is associated with creation also in Job (9:10; 37:5), but is most often found in contexts of God's violent rescue of Israel particularly at the exodus (Exod. 3:20; Mic. 7:15).

Jeremiah then turns attention to God's acts of retribution. The prophet says that, on the one hand, God shows love to thousands, but he brings judgment due fathers on their children. See similar statements in Exodus 20:5–6; 34:7; Deuteronomy 5:9–10. Apparently, Jeremiah's generation is still in "those days" when the fathers eat sour grapes and "the children's teeth are set on edge" (see 31:29). As applied to the present generation, it is not as if they were not guilty themselves, but it is also true that they were suffering for the long-standing sins of their ancestors. The destruction of Jerusalem was long delayed only by the gracious forbearance of God. After all, Jeremiah goes on to say, everyone gets what they deserve (**you reward everyone according to his conduct and as his deeds deserve**).

Starting in verse 20 Jeremiah recounts the events associated with the exodus and the conquest, also as manifestations of God's **outstretched arm.** God's miraculous signs and wonders would have included the plagues and most pointedly the crossing of the Red Sea. The exodus was the paradigmatic salvation event of the Old Testament period, but, as Jeremiah indicates, it was not unique. God continued to make his gracious power known to his people up **to this day,** thus leaving them with even less of an excuse for their reprehensible behavior. God gave them the promised land, a bountiful land (**flowing with milk and honey**). However, in spite of God graciousness, they were disobedient. They broke his law and thus the covenant. As a consequence of breaking the law of the covenant, they now experience the curses (see Deut. 27–28). God has brought **disaster.** At this point, Jeremiah appeals to current events in Jerusalem. The Babylonians raise **siege ramps** that will allow them to breach the city defenses. The present situation is a time of **sword, famine and plague** (5:12; 11:22; 14:12; 16:4; 21:7, 9; 24:10; 27:8, 13; 29:18; 32:36; 34:17; 38:2; 42:16–17; 44:12–13, 18, 27). God has announced it and it is happening at the present: **the city will be handed over to the Babylonians.**

The point of the sermon, the underlying question, comes at the very end. Though the city will be taken, Jeremiah tells God that he chose this moment to command him to buy the field from Hanamel. Jeremiah's prayer is a respectful and subtle way of inquiring into the unexpected ways of his unpredictable God. The next verses provide God's response and this will allow the opportunity to once again speak of future hope.

32:26–44 / God responds to Jeremiah's prayer (vv. 17–25) in this section. There are two introductory rubrics in this speech found at verse 26 (**Then the word of the LORD came to Jeremiah**) and verse 42 (**This is what the LORD says**), both emphasizing that these are God's words to Jeremiah. In addition, we will also see a decisive transition in verse 36.

God's response also begins with divine self-identification emphasizing God's sovereignty over all humanity (**I am the LORD, the God of mankind**). Thus, as we will see, he is the one who determines how events will play out in the present and the future. Indeed, he echoes Jeremiah's affirmation found in verse 17 with a rhetorical question that also highlights his ability to do anything, even things that look impossible from a human standpoint (**Is anything too hard for me?**).

It is because of his sovereignty and ability to do anything that the hearer can be certain that what he announces as happening in the future will indeed take place. Thus, verse 28 begins with **therefore** and goes on to state that **this city,** namely Jerusalem, will indeed fall to the Babylonian forces that are now (see v. 24) besieging it. Indeed, he adds the gory details that the city will be set on fire. Specifically mentioned are the **houses** of the **people.** We have heard often how the leaders (kings, nobles, priests, and prophets) have gone astray, but the people are not therefore exonerated or not held responsible for their offenses against God. They are idolaters who have sinned against God in the worse imaginable way, because there is nothing worse than false worship. They practiced a personal religion which apparently included **burning incense on the roofs** of their houses and also **pouring out drink offerings to other gods.** Archaeology has shown evidence of widespread worship of other gods in Palestine during the monarchical period. This evidence may be interpreted in a number of different ways, but the one thing that is clear is that the people of Israel often availed themselves of false worship (for the evidence, see Z. Zevit, *The Religions of Ancient Israel* and R. Hess, *An Introduction to Approaches to the Study of Israelite Religion*).

Verses 30–35 develop the description of the pain and utter disappointment God feels toward his people due to their idolatry and worship of false gods. It begins with a hyperbolic statement that the people **have done nothing but evil** and have **done nothing but provoke** God. Whatever good they have done is now so totally obscured by their wickedness that it can no longer be seen. Specifically, God says that it is **what their hands have made** that so enrages him. In the context, this phrase surely refers at least primarily to the construction of idols that they worshiped in the place of the true God. Again, the whole spectrum of society (**they, their kings, and officials, their priests and prophets, the men of Judah and the people of Jerusalem**) has participated in this wickedness. The sin is so extensive, continuous (**from the day it was built**), and profound that God must remove it from his sight.

Rather than facing him in worship, they turned their backs on him. And it was not as if they were not warned. Verse 35 says that he **taught them again and again, but they would not listen or respond to discipline.** We may read into this statement the fact that God sent countless prophets and even let them taste some less severe punishments before the present when he was about to lower the boom, so to speak, on top of their heads. After all, not only did the people practice abominable religious practices in their personal religion (see v. 29), there was also a perversion of the national religion (**They set up abominable idols in the house that bears my Name,** v. 34). They also set up altars to the false God Baal in the Valley of Ben Hinnom, the valley to the southeast of the city. They actually practiced a form of child sacrifice associated with the pagan god Molech there. God never asked for such a heinous practice in his own worship. For similar condemnation of this practice, see commentary at 7:30–34 and 19:1–6.

A decisive transition takes place in verse 36, though this is obscured by the translation of the NIV (see Additional Notes), by not translating the conjunction that begins the verse. The conjunction makes the logic of the paragraph more obvious, but with or without it we have a transition from a past oracle that has present ramifications to a present oracle that looks to a change in divine attitude and action toward Jerusalem.

By sword, famine and plague it (Jerusalem) will be handed over to the king of Babylon. This message has resounded through the book (see Additional Notes and cited passages at 14:12), but now there is a new divine oracle (**this is what the LORD, the God of Israel, says**), an oracle of salvation that begins in verse 36. While he does not reverse the coming punishment of destruction and exile, this new divine word looks forward to the future when God will bring his people back from the many lands to which they will have been scattered. The primary place of scattering will be Babylon, but others will wander down to Egypt, and we know from a postexilic book like Esther that some made it eventually to Persia.

Not only will they be brought back to **live in safety,** but God will reestablish his covenant relationship with them. This is evident from the citation of the covenant formula: **They will be my people, and I will be their God** (v. 3; see earlier in 24:7; 30:22; 31:1, 33). Instead of being scattered in their attention between the true God and false gods, as they were in the past, they will be focused on Yahweh (**singleness of heart and action**). The result is that they will **fear** God. To fear God means to recognize one's proper place in the universe. It is to acknowledge that there is a being who is greater than oneself; indeed a being who has the power of life and death. The emotion is not as extreme as horror, but neither is it as slight as respect. Closer than the picture of horror or respect is that of knee-knocking awe. Such awe would lead to good consequences for that present generation as well as those that succeeded them. The book of Proverbs describes the good consequences that come on the wise and their descendants, wisdom being described as fear the Lord and staying away from evil (Prov. 1:7). Of course, Israel should by then be well aware that godless action results in both immediate and delayed punishment. The postexilic book of Chronicles is written in a way as to emphasize the former (sin now and suffer now) and the exilic history Samuel-Kings emphasizes the latter (sin now and later generations will suffer).

Verse 40 calls this restored relationship an **eternal covenant** (see also Isa. 55:3; 61:8; Ezek. 16:60; 37:26) to be connected to the new covenant of 31:31–34, and it further states that God will **inspire** them to **fear** him by reward. He will treat them so well, that they will fear him. For such a reason, he will bring them back to the land and **plant** them there (see 1:10). This passage clearly looks forward to the restoration from the exile and more.

The final paragraph of the chapter (vv. 42–44) also describes the transition from divine punishment (**great calamity**) to divine blessing (**prosperity**). God is as good as his word in both punishment as well as restoration.

The description of the divine blessing connects to the episode earlier in the chapter where Jeremiah buys the field of his cousin Hanamel (vv. 1–15). The Babylonians will turn the land into a **desolate waste,** but in the future real estate transactions will be a part of normal life. This restoration will extend from **Benjamin** (just north of Jerusalem) down to the Negev and, of course, include Jerusalem and its surrounding villages and towns. For the phrase **restore their fortunes,** see Additional Notes at 30:3.

33:1–26 / Chapter 33 is the fourth and final portion of the so-called Book of Consolation. It is related to the previous chapter by mention of Jeremiah's captivity (33:1), first mentioned in 32:2. It is the same period of captivity but the second time that God's word came to him.

The chapter may be divided into two sections. The first half has to do with the restoration of the people at large (vv. 1–13) and the second (vv. 14–26) with the restoration of the leadership.

33:1–13 / As mentioned in the previous paragraphs, Jeremiah was still a prisoner of Zedekiah in the **courtyard of the guard** (see 32:2) when this divine word came to him. Again (see 32:17), God introduces himself as the creator of the heavens and earth, a way in which he reminds the reader of his control over the creation and its affairs. He invites hearers to ask him (**call on me**), and he will answer them. The phrase **great and unsearchable things** is a reference to future events. Humans cannot know for certain what will happen in their future, but God can, and here he will, choose to reveal what will happen. As in the immediately preceding oracles, God begins by describing the period of judgment that is presently underway. The siege of Jerusalem has required that its inhabitants dismantle houses, even the palace, in order to provide defenses against the attacking Babylonians who have raised **siege ramps** to storm the walls. But these drastic defensive measures will not prevail. God's anger over his people's sins and his judgment of them will render their attempts to defend themselves futile. Instead, **dead bodies** will fill up these defensive structures. God has abandoned his people (**I will hide my face**) and he was their only hope of rescue (see Ezek. 9–11 for a graphic picture of God abandoning his holy place).

The oracle does not stop with judgment but goes on to talk about the restoration to follow it. Thus, this oracle is in keeping with the tenor of the Book of Consolation as a whole. Verse 6 uses the metaphor of a wound and its healing (**health and healing**) to talk about the judgment and restoration, and indeed the analogy is apt (see the study of this type of metaphor in Jeremiah in M. L. Brown, *Israel's Divine Healer*, pp. 191–95). In specific reference to the present verse, Brown comments "this divine healing translates out to the return of the Judean and Israelite captives (v. 7a), the rebuilding of the cities of old (v. 7b), and the purification from and forgiveness of past sins (v. 8). Repentance would lead to the return of the wearied exiles, the rebuilding of their ruined cities, and the reconciliation of their spiritual lives."

The restoration of God's people and their purification, as well as the rebuilding of the city, will bring God **renown.** It is the praise not of God's people in view here, but of the nations. It may well be significant that the words for fear here (**be in awe,** *pkhd* and **tremble,** *rgz*) are not the one used positively in Proverbs for the beginning of wisdom (*yrʾ*). However, many commentators from the past (Calvin) and the present (Dearman) suggest that this may refer to the future conversion of the nations. In any case, the verse does remind us that Jeremiah's call (1:10) was not just to Judah but to the nations.

33:14–26 / This oracle, which has many similarities with 23:5–6, looks to the future (**the days are coming**), perhaps even from an exilic perspective. The oracle looks forward to the restoration of the Davidic king and the levitical priesthood, so it may presuppose its current absence. In terms of the former, the oracle looks forward to the coming of a **righteous Branch.** This Branch will come from David's line, and clearly looks forward to a coming king. The emphasis on righteous (*tsedeq*) may be a play on the name of the last king of Judah, Zedekiah, in order to contrast with that king. The future will bring a just king in contrast with what the end of Judean history witnessed after Josiah. In the future too Judah and Jerusalem will be restored and allowed to live in safety. For a similar oracle anticipating the restoration of the line of David as a Branch, see Isa. 11:1; Zech. 3:8; 6:12. In these places the Branch has clearly taken on messianic significance. The branch image is also used for the remnant in Isa. 4:2 and 6:13.

Verse 17 makes clear what the Branch image refers to and also indicates that the promise is perpetual. **David will never fail to have a man to sit on the throne of the house of Israel.** This promise emanates from the Davidic covenant of 2 Samuel 7 and takes on added urgency with the loss of kingship in Judah as a consequence of the exile. The New Testament understands that Jesus is that son of David who is perpetually on the throne in fulfillment of this promise.

But there is another aspect to this promise of continuity with past covenants. Not only will there be a new David, there will be continuity with the promise to Levi as well. In response to Phinehas's zeal in protecting the purity of Israel, he is given this promise: "He and his descendants will have a covenant of a lasting priesthood, because he was zealous for the honor of his God and made atonement for Israel" (Num. 25:13). It is on this basis that Jeremiah looks forward to the continuation of the priesthood.

The next paragraph associates these perpetual promises to David and to Levi by associating them with the perpetual promise to Noah, here referred to as **my covenant with day and my cove-**

nant with the night (v. 20). This appears to be a reference back to Genesis 9 where God promises Noah that he will maintain the rhythm of creation. It is only if this covenant is broken, which it cannot, that he will break the covenants with David and Levi.

Interestingly, the reaffirmation of the covenant of kingship and priesthood is expressed in the terms of the Abrahamic covenant in verse 22. The promise to make the descendants of David and the Levites **as countless as the stars of the sky and as measureless as the sand on the seashore** is reminiscent of a similar promise concerning Abraham's descendants found in Gen. 15:5; 22:17; 26:4, though the language is not exactly similar.

The impact of this promise of the continuation and flourishing of the kingship and the priesthood must be understood on the background of the horrible failure of these institutions in the period before the exile. The appointed kings and the priests have not been faithful, but rather have led Israel down the primrose path of idolatry. 2 Chronicles 36:14 describes the priesthood on the eve of the exile in these terms: "the leaders of the priests became more and more unfaithful, following all the detestable practices of the nations and defiling the temple of the Lord, which he had consecrated in Jerusalem." God's continuing gracious involvement with them is a sign of his mercy and love.

The Book of Consolation then concludes with a final word to Jeremiah (vv. 23–26), in which God once again proclaims his intention to restore his people whom he has judged. The reference to **these people** in v. 23 are the surrounding nations who are questioning God's continuing involvement with his chosen people. The reference to the **two kingdoms** refers to the former northern kingdom that was deported by the Assyrians in 722 B.C. and the southern kingdom of Judah whose judgment has been the focus of the oracles of Jeremiah. God's treatment of them strikes outsiders as rejection. And this perception has led them to treat God's people with disdain.

But God now lets Jeremiah know that rejection is not his ultimate intention with regard to his people; God looks to restoration by once again alluding to the Noahic covenant (**my covenant with day and night and the fixed laws of heaven and earth**), the Abrahamic covenant (**descendants of Jacob; descendants of Abraham, Isaac and Jacob**), and the Davidic covenant (**descendants of David my servant and will not choose one of his sons to rule**). Restoration is as sure as the regularities of the cosmos.

Additional Notes §76

30:3 / The phrase translated **"I will bring back from captivity"** in Hebrew is *weshabti ʾet-shebut* and is often referred to as a "restoration oracle." NIV handles this phrase inconsistently between 30:3 (but see NIV footnote) and 30:18 where it is translated **"I will restore the fortunes."** The text translation of 30:3 depends on an old understanding of the nominal object as derived from *shbh* ("to capture") rather than *shub* ("to return"). The footnote at 30:3 is to be preferred. The restored fortunes of the people would indeed refer to a return to the land from captivity, but also much more.

30:6 / The oracle remarks that faces of strong men turn **deathly pale** with fright. The Hebrew does not have "deathly," but it is not a misleading rendition. Most translations render Nahum 2:11 and Joel 2:6 in the same way in similar contexts, but the Hebrew is different (for which see T. Longman III, "Nahum," in T. McComiskey [ed.], *The Minor Prophets,* vol. 2 [Baker, 1993], 807–8).

30:12 / The metaphor of the incurable **wound** is used elsewhere in the prophets, Jeremiah 8:22; 10:19; Micah 1:9; Nahum 3:19. It is an expression of complete and certain death.

30:14 / The word **allies** here is more precisely rendered "lovers" (see NRSV, NJB). The concept behind the idea of allies as lovers has to do with the marriage metaphor used for the relationship between God and his people. It is to her husband, God, that Judah should turn for help, but instead they prostitute themselves by going to political allies like Egypt (see the extended use of this metaphor in Ezek. 16 and 23). Also, the language of love between political allies is also reminiscent of the language of ancient treaties (W. Moran, "The Ancient Near Eastern Background of the Love of God in Deuteronomy," *CBQ* 25 [1963], pp. 78–79).

31:7 / The NIV well translates the MT as an imperative (**save**), but the Targum and Septuagint take the verb as a perfect form ("he has saved"). As Lundbom (*Jeremiah 21–36,* p. 423) suggests in favor of the MT, "nothing precludes a cry of gladness occurring simultaneously with a plea of salvation," but he also notes that the Dead Sea Scrolls (4QJer^{c}) supports the reading of the verb as a perfect.

31:15 / This verse is cited in the infancy narrative of Jesus in Matthew (2:18) in reference to Herod killing the young boys in the city of Bethlehem in an attempt to eradicate the expected Messiah. In this case, rather than just the northern tribes, Rachel would stand for the bereaved mothers of Bethlehem.

31:16 / God promises that Rachel will receive a reward for her work. Fretheim (*Jeremiah,* p. 435) offers the following possible explanation of this difficult saying. He states that the analogy that is drawn is between Israel returning from exile and Jacob and Rachel returning from years of work for the Laban. The reward the latter bring back to the promised land are their children. While insightful and possibly correct, the textual evidence for thinking of the children as reward for their work is very thin in Genesis (Fretheim cites Gen. 30:18 and the naming of Issachar).

31:18 / The phrase **unruly calf** may be translated literally, "like a calf not trained." An untrained calf would not wear a yoke and would indeed be unruly. However, the literal translation allows us to see the connection with the earlier prophecy of Hosea who describes Ephraim as a trained heifer (Hos. 10:11). Note the change in gender between the two. While these references are close, it is not clear that the Jeremiah passage derives from Hosea or vice versa. Not only is the gender of the animal different, the image is developed differently in both cases. In Hosea, the message is that Ephraim is a trained heifer, and for this reason God will put a yoke on her. In Jeremiah, Ephraim is not trained, and so God will have to train it.

31:31 / Rata (*The Covenant Motif in Jeremiah's Book of Comfort*, p. 90) points out that *khadashah* ("new") can also be translated and understood as "renewed," reminding us that the new covenant has continuity with the old covenant.

32:36 / The NIV omits the conjunction at the beginning of this verse that provides a transition to a new temporal horizon. Perhaps it is because it is missing in the Greek, but there is no textual note to that effect. In any case, the Masoretic Text begins, "And now therefore" (see NRSV and most other versions). In other words, we move from a previous oracle that describes what is happening in the present (the siege of Jerusalem) to a present oracle that proclaims what will be new in the future (its deliverance).

§77 Zedekiah: Capture but Peaceful Death (Jer. 34:1–7)

This section of Jeremiah goes back and forth between the time of the last king of Judah, Zedekiah, and the third to last king, Jehoiakim. Chapter 34 was set at the time of Zedekiah, chapters 35–36 during the kingship of Jehoiakim, and now we are back to the time of Zedekiah. Chapters 37 and 38 present accounts of times when the prophet was placed in prison and even threatened with death because of his message. Jeremiah was preaching repentance and surrender to Babylon, since Babylon was God's instrument of judgment. Thus, he was seen as someone who collaborated with the enemy and thus a danger to king and society. An interesting aspect of these stories is the nature of the private conversations between Jeremiah and Zedekiah. Publicly, Jeremiah boldly announced the message of judgment that God gave him. Privately, he begged Zedekiah to better his conditions. Publicly, Zedekiah rejected the projection of doom that Jeremiah preached and treated him as if he was not a true prophet of God. Privately he sought the prophet out and asked him to pray for him and the country, and hoped that he would get a more positive message.

34:1–7 / This oracle is dated during Nebuchadnezzar's siege of Jerusalem. From the historical reports found in 2 Kings 25 and Jeremiah 39 and 52, we learn that the siege lasted from the tenth month of the tenth year of Zedekiah's reign until the fourth month of the eleventh year when the Babylonian army breached the city's wall, a period of approximately a year and a half. The oracle came sometime during this period of time. Zedekiah who had become king when he was twenty-one was in his early thirties at this time. Verse 7 tells us that Jeremiah delivered this prophecy before the fall of **Lachish and Azekah,** two fortified cities to the west of Jerusalem in the Shephelah guarding one of the direct routes to Jerusalem. This bit of information may point to a time relatively soon after Nebuchadnezzar's incursion into the region (see Additional Notes).

God commanded Jeremiah to go to the king and tell him that the city's fall was assured and was coming soon. The city will be burned and the king himself will be captured. However, in verses 4–5 the king is told that he will not violently die but will have a proper burial where people will be able to mourn his loss.

From the historical reports in 2 Kings 25; 2 Chronicles 36, and Jeremiah 39 and 52 we learn that indeed Zedekiah was not killed when the city was taken. However, his suffering must have been great. Once captured, Nebuchadnezzar took him along with his sons to his staging area in Riblah in what is today Syria. He then killed the sons and afterward blinded the king. He then sent the king into exile in Babylon. We never hear about his end. Indeed, when the book of Kings wants to present a note of hope at the end of its historical narrative, it reports the release from prison of his predecessor Jehoiachin, taken into exile in 597 B.C. For some reason, we do not hear about Zedekiah. Perhaps he has already died in prison, as is reported by Jeremiah 52:8–11.

Additional Notes §77

34:7 / Intriguingly, **Lachish and Azekah** are mentioned on an ostracon that has been dated to the period of the Babylonian incursion toward Jerusalem. Lachish tablet IV ends with these ominous words:

> And let (my lord) know that we are watching for the signals of Lachish, according to all the indications which my lord hath given, for we cannot see Azekah.

Perhaps this letter comes from the period of the fall of these two fortress cities that likely would have meant that Jerusalem was now vulnerable to a full-blown attack by the Babylonian army.

§78 Reversing a Godly Decision (Jer. 34:8–22)

34:8–11 / The next oracle comes in the context of the royal decision to free Hebrew slaves. To understand the story and the oracle we must begin by reviewing the slave laws of the Torah (Exod. 21:1–11; Lev. 25:39–46; Deut. 15:12–18, though see S. Chavel, "'Let My People Go!' Emancipation, Revelation, and Scribal Activity in Jeremiah 34.8–14," *JSOT* 76 [1997], pp. 71–95, for the view that Jeremiah 34 does not follow Pentateuchal legislation). If Israelites became impoverished, they could sell themselves into slavery. However, this slavery was only temporary since the law stipulated that slave owners must free their Hebrew slaves in the Sabbatical Year. While it was possible for Hebrew slaves to become permanent slaves, this decision was theirs and not the slave owners. These slave laws were associated with other laws concerning the return of land to original owners, the canceling of debts, and the fallowing of the ground. Such laws worked against perceived economic self-interest on the part of the wealthy elements of society; observance, therefore, would be the result of confidence in God as well as concerns for others in the society.

We do not know exactly when the decision to release the slaves took place during Zedekiah's reign. Speculation has centered on the time when Jerusalem's fate looked dire. Perhaps Zedekiah and the people were frightened and tried to take steps to rectify their situation with God. Fretheim (*Jeremiah,* p. 489) disagrees saying that such a motivation does not fit well with God's approval of the decision, but that consideration hardly seems relevant. After all, God had sent Jeremiah to his people in order to confront them with the horrific consequences of their sin if they did not repent. It seems to be precisely the divine intent to scare Judah into obedience. This time it worked, but only temporarily. If this is the correct time period, then it is likely that this event and oracle should be dated sometime during 588 B.C., within a year of the final destruction of Jerusalem.

The decision to release the slaves took the form of a **covenant** between Zedekiah and the people of Jerusalem. Covenant is a term that is used for human legal agreements as well as the divine-human relationship. The covenant carries potential punishments for disobedience to the terms of the agreement, and below in vv. 18–20 we will learn of a ritual that brought that reality home to the participants in the agreement. But the use of the term covenant here also alerts the reader that the present situation, as bad as it is, simply represents an even more dire betrayal. Just like Israel will go back on this agreement to release the slaves, so they have repeatedly disobeyed the even more important and fundamental covenantal relationship between them and God.

And indeed, the text reports that they **changed their mind.** No good reason is given. Indeed, no reason at all is reported. They just changed their minds and **enslaved them again.** It is possible to imagine a scenario that would make some sense of this. We know, for instance, that the Babylonians temporarily withdrew their siege of Jerusalem because of reports that the Egyptians were coming to help them (ch. 37). This is probably what is meant in 34:21a, which refers to the withdrawal of the Babylonian army. Perhaps the withdrawal of the Babylonians led the residents of Jerusalem to think everything was fine and so they could again oppress their fellow citizens for their own economic benefit. However, since the text does not state a reason, we are speculating. The point of the passage is clear enough. They did not follow through on their commitment to do the right thing; they betrayed their covenantal agreement.

34:12–16 / Once the situation has been set in the previous verses, we now hear the oracle that came to Jeremiah from God. God begins by reminding his hearers why Israel has such a culturally enlightened perspective on slavery. They were slaves in Egypt and he released them (**out of the land of slavery**). Since they knew the hardship of perpetual slavery, God would not let his people experience that again. Why not completely abolish slavery? We are not told here or in the slave laws of the Torah. In the light of modern experience of slavery, particularly in the American past, most moderns find the institution intolerable. We need to remember that in its ancient context this type of slavery was an alternative to debtors' prisons or abject poverty. If such a relationship were conducted in a proper fashion, it could have been a positive societal institution, a temporary state to help individuals and families get back on their feet. But as far as we know it was never enacted in such an enlightened way. It was then, as in more recent days, an oppressive and exploitative institution.

Based on God's rescue of Israel from Egyptian slavery, verse 17 rehearses the law as we know it best from Exodus 21:1–11 and Deuteronomy 15:12–18. Slavery in Israel was to be temporary (see Additional Notes). However, Israel apparently rarely observed this law of release. It was not only the present generation that did not properly release slaves, but also the **fathers,** that is, previous generations.

The oracle then recounts the events already described in verses 8–11. Here it describes their original action as a result of repentance and as doing what **was right** in God's sight. It also adds the additional information that the covenant that Zedekiah made with the people to release the slaves was ratified in the temple (**the house that bears my Name**). To break a solemn agreement between two human partners was bad enough, but that the agreement was made in sacred space makes it so much worse.

34:17–22 / Now that the people's sin has been described, God announces their fate. God will give them **freedom** though they did not grant freedom to the slaves. But this is a freedom they will not want. It is a freedom to fall **by sword, plague and famine** (for this formula of siege and defeat, see Additional Notes on 14:12). Rather than the "joy of the whole earth" (Ps. 48:2), they will be **abhorrent to all the kingdoms of the earth.**

Verses 18–20 then recount the ritual performed at the time of the making of the covenant that promised release to the Hebrew slaves. It involved cutting a **calf** in two and then the parties walking through the halves. This is a self-maledictory oath. That is, the parties who are making the agreement and walking through the halves are saying that if they break the agreement they will become like the mutilated calf. And by breaking their agreement, everyone—**leaders, court officials, priests, and all the people**—have confirmed their own destruction. For the biblical and ancient Near Eastern background, see Additional Notes.

Verses 21–22 names **the army of the king of Babylon** as the tool of this devastating destruction. They have **withdrawn,** probably fueling a false sense of optimism in Jerusalem, but they will be back and will **lay waste the towns of Judah so no one can live there.**

Additional Notes §78

34:14 / This verse cites the principle that Hebrew slaves should be released every seven years. The relevant laws are Exodus 21:1–11 and Deuteronomy 15:12–18, which specify such a release from slavery, though neither is quoted precisely. The other relevant law is found in Leviticus 25:39–46, which legislates a release during the Year of Jubilee without recognizing a release during the seventh year. On the surface of it, Leviticus seems harsher than the laws of Exodus and Deuteronomy and many efforts have been made to harmonize the three. Milgrom (*Leviticus 23–27* [AB; Garden City, N.Y.: Doubleday, 2001], pp. 2251–53) discusses the options at length and points out that the Leviticus code actually undermines the whole institution of the slavery of fellow Israelites by insisting that they be treated as a "hired worker" (Lev. 25:40), which would mean that they could pay off their debt by means of their work. While questions remain as to the harmonization of these slave laws, it is clear that Jeremiah's generation were breaking the law by enslaving their fellow citizens longer than the law allowed.

34:18 / To confirm the covenant to release the slaves between Zedekiah and the people of Jerusalem, they walked between the halves of a **calf they cut in two.** This is reminiscent of a scene in Genesis 15:9–20 where God directed Abraham to cut a number of animals in half. Afterward, he passed between the halves as God confirmed the covenant he made with Abraham. To understand this ancient ritual we can cite similar rituals from ancient Near Eastern texts that describe this behavior as a self-malediction. There are texts from Alalakh, Mari, and Hatti dating back to the second millennium B.C. (see discussion in V. P. Hamilton, *The Book of Genesis 1–17* [NICOT; Grand Rapids: Eerdmans, 1990], pp. 430–34).

§79 Recabite Obedience (Jer. 35:1–19)

35:1–2 / Jeremiah 35 describes a symbolic-act prophecy (see Jer. 18)—that is, a prophecy that is accompanied by a dramatic action that illustrates the verbal oracle. The events of this chapter are dated to the reign of **Jehoiakim,** which scrolls back the time from the previous oracle that dated to the last few months of the reign of Zedekiah. We know that Jehoiakim reigned from 609–598 B.C. Later in the chapter Jonadab, the leader of the Recabites, will state that they are in Jerusalem because of the siege of the Babylonians. While this conceivably could be a reference to a siege mentioned in Daniel 1:1–3, which took place in 605 B.C., it is more likely that it is in reference to the later attack of the Babylonians in 597.

35:3–11 / The symbolic-act concerned a family known as the Recabites, named after the patriarch, now long dead, named Recab. We know nothing about this family beyond what is described in this chapter. Further, their chosen lifestyle and expression of devotion to Yahweh is like none other that we know. Their principles are nowhere expressed in Scripture, and where they got the idea to live as they lived (beyond the fact that v. 6 mentions that it was established by **Jonadab son of Recab,** see Additional Notes) is also unknown to us.

Their life regulations included the following: (1) they were not to drink wine (v. 6); they were to live in tents or live the life of unsettled people (**you must never build houses, sow seed or plant vineyards; you must never have any of these things, but must always live in tents,** v. 7). In other words, they maintained the life of **nomads** (or Bedouins) even after the people of God were established in the land.

God never required such a mode of living; these seem to be human laws. Whether their mode of life was right or not is not the issue in this chapter, however. It rather has to do with the quality of their obedience. About the latter there is no doubt.

The obedience of the Recabites is illustrated when Jeremiah invites them to **one of the side rooms of the house of the LORD.** He brought the whole family together with the leader of the present generation, a man named **Jaazaniah son of Jeremiah, the son of Habazziniah.** The historical concreteness of this episode is highlighted by the mention of the fact that the room was **the room of the sons of Hanan son of Igdaliah the man of God,** that as next to **the room of the officials, which was over that of Maaseiah son of Shallum the doorkeeper.** This detailed description allows readers to picture the event more concretely in their mind.

After bringing them into the room, Jeremiah places **bowls full of wine** before the men of the family and tells them to drink the wine. They refuse and give as their reason the command that they received from their forefather Jonadab (vv. 6–7). They have been scrupulous in their observance of this regulation, and they have no intention to depart from their obedience now.

It is interesting to read this story against the background of 1 Kings 13. There God sent an unnamed prophet to confront Jeroboam the son of Nebat on the occasion of his dedication of the calf shrine at Bethel. After delivering the oracle of the future destruction of the shrine, the prophet refuses the invitation of the king to eat and drink, saying that God had told him not to eat or drink until he returned from the northern to the southern kingdom. On the way home, however, an old prophet greets him and invites him to eat and drink. When the unnamed prophet declines, the old prophet claims that he has a new prophetic word that would allow the unnamed prophet to eat and drink. The unnamed prophet does so, but is condemned for listening to the false words of the older prophet. He should have known that a later divine oracle would not contradict an earlier expression of God's word.

As Jonadab hears Jeremiah invite him to drink wine, he does not waver. This prophet must not be heeded because he contradicted the lifestyle to which he has devoted his life. The only reason why they are even in Jerusalem (and not living in tents) is because of the siege, which may date this to 597 B.C.

35:12–19 / Verses 1–11 describe the symbolic-act and in the remaining verses of the chapter (vv. 12–19), we learn of its prophetic significance. This message is not for the Recabites but rather for **the men of Judah and the people of Jerusalem.** It appears that this oracle came from a time when God through Jeremiah was still allowing for the possibility of repentance, slim as that might be.

This episode is orchestrated so the people **might learn a lesson and obey** God. If they do heed this conditional prophecy, then they **will live in the land.**

The argument of this oracle is "from the lesser to the greater." The Recabites are utterly devoted to the teachings of their forefather. He said do not drink wine, so when Jeremiah offers them wine, they refuse. This obedience to conscience is commended, but the point is that this requirement is one imposed by a human authority figure. While the Recabites obey their forefather, the rest of the people do not obey God himself. And this is in spite of the fact that God has continued to warn them through his **servants the prophets.**

Since there is a difference between the people and the Recabites, there will also be a difference in terms of their future. First, since the people did not listen and obey God, they **will be punished with every disaster I** (God) **called on them.** For a list of such horrible punishments, see Deuteronomy 27–28. On the other hand, since the Recabites obeyed the requirements of their forefathers and thus have followed their conscience, there will always be a descendant of Jonadab son of Recab serving God. Though we do not know the future of this family, the principle is clear: obedience brings blessing and disobedience brings curse. Freitheim suggests that 1 Chronicles 2:55, which mentions Recab, is an indication of the family surviving to the postexilic period (*Jeremiah,* p. 496). Lundbom refers to a lively tradition that develops about the family that may be found in the Mishnah, Talmud, and Midrashim, as well as an early Christian writing from somewhere between the first to sixth century A.D. called "The History of the Blessed Sons of the Recabites." But these latter may not have much of historical value.

Additional Notes §79

35:6 / The requirement that the Recabites never drink wine comes closest to a known religious practice from the Old Testament, namely the lifestyle of the Nazirites who are described in Numbers 6:1–21. The Nazirite vow was a self-imposed lifestyle that included avoidance of the dead, a refusal to cut one's hair, and a prohibition on drinking wine and other fermented drinks. Indeed, not only must the Nazirite avoid wine, but even grapes. The Nazirite vow was the way a non-Levite could take on a special level of consecration for either a temporary period of time or for a lifetime (Samuel and Samson were Nazirites). However, while there is a similar avoidance of alcohol, there is no indication that the Recabites practiced the other aspects of the Nazirite vow, or that the Nazirites lived in tents rather than houses.

The Recabites are best understood against the background of other groups through history who have frozen a particular cultural form. In modern times, one might think of the *hasidic* Jews who still wear the dress that was current in Polish ghettoes rather than wearing modern styles. Or among Christians we might think of the Amish who wear shirts without buttons and ride in a horse-driven buggy. The Recabites seem to consider the lifestyle of the nomad as appropriate to their religious expression. It may be that they equated the settled agricultural lifestyle too close to that of Baal worshiping Canaanites.

The **forefather Jonadab son of Recab** is the man known as Jehonadab son of Recab in 2 Kings 10:15–17. He is mentioned as an ally of Jehu during his purge of the Baal-worshiping king Ahab and his wife Jezebel. Again, this points to the extreme anti-Canaanite stance that this family has taken.

35:11 / The Recabites have moved into Jerusalem because of the threat of the invasion. Fretheim (*Jeremiah,* p. 495), who offers many helpful insights into this chapter, suggests that this is a sign of unfaithfulness and contradicts the earlier statement that they have been faithful to **everything our forefather Jonadab son of Recab commanded us.** He then further argues that this illustrates the need to adjust one's ethical principles in the light of circumstances. However, there is no good reason for his statement that it was obvious "they could not pitch tents in the city." Why not? There is no necessity to the belief that they were living in houses.

§80 Jehoiakim Burns the First Jeremiah Scroll (Jer. 36)

The next story is one of the most gripping and vivid of the book. It also has interest as a book that gives a rare glimpse at the preparation, presentation, and development of a biblical book, though at the end of the story the scholar is still left with many questions. For this chapter, see J. A. Dearman, "My Servants the Scribes: Composition and Context in Jeremiah 36," *JBL* 109 (1990), pp. 403–21.

36:1–7 / These verses describe the instructions that are given to Jeremiah, who then gives instructions to Baruch, his scribe. The first part of the story (see 36:9) is set in the **fourth year of Jehoiakim,** which would be a year after the first siege of Jerusalem according to the dating found in the first verses of the book of Daniel (therefore late 605–604 B.C.). Of course, this first siege was simply an initial sign of Babylonian presence and power in the area, but it was significant enough that Jehoiakim turned over to the Babylonians some of the temple vessels as well as a number of the young, noble men of the kingdom. Perhaps it was this that led Jeremiah to think that the king might listen to the warnings that were recorded in the scroll that he sent to the court through Baruch.

God's opening words to Jeremiah (vv. 2–3) indicate that this event took place early enough that the prophecy was couched in a conditional rather than an unconditional fashion. In other words, there is the expressed hope that the scroll will induce the king to begin a national repentance. The motivating force of such repentance would be the warning of destruction that the oracles described (**every disaster I plan to inflict on them**). All the oracles from the beginning, during **the reign of Josiah,** to the present were to be included in this scroll. The superscription (1:1–3) says that Jeremiah's prophetic ministry began in the thirteenth year of Josiah's reign (626 B.C.), so we are talking about a time period of about two decades. However, we have also observed that there are not a lot of datable oracles in the book from the earlier part of this time period and in any case the scroll was probably selective.

Jeremiah was to **take a scroll and write on it.** How the oracles have been preserved up to this moment is unclear. We are not to necessarily take this as the first writing down of the oracles, though no doubt the majority of oracles were initially delivered in an oral form. It may be that this new scroll was a collation of previously written down oracles.

The reader has already encountered **Baruch** in chapter 32 where he served as the scribe in the real estate transaction described in that chapter. Though that story comes earlier in the book, the present episode takes place at an earlier point in time. Baruch functions here too as Jeremiah's scribe by first writing down in the new scroll what Jeremiah dictated to him. Again, this does not necessarily indicate the first writing down of the oracles, since Jeremiah might have been reading previously written down versions of the oracles.

But Jeremiah has already been restricted (**I am restricted; I cannot go to the LORD's temple**) in terms of his movements presumably because of his challenging words and actions. He is not allowed to go into the temple area, so he asks Baruch to deliver the material. His restriction may be because he had delivered a scathing sermon at the temple (see Jeremiah 7 and 26, the latter of which is dated to "early in the reign of Jehoiakim"). However, his restriction is not because he is imprisoned but because he is in hiding (v. 19).

Baruch was to go to the temple and read the scroll in the presence of the people. The hope was that they would respond with repentance and beseech the Lord to spare them of the fate that their sins deserved.

36:8–10 / Baruch followed Jeremiah's instructions exactly and read the words of the Lord from the scroll to the people at the temple. (Some time had passed since the original divine command to make a scroll [compare 36:1 with v. 9]). He did so at a time when public **fasting** was taking place. Perhaps this was a special occasion of fasting specifically to beseech the Lord at a time of great need. The fact that this special religious observance was in process would mean that the temple area would have been jammed. If the fasting were for the dire situation in which Judah found itself, then one would expect that the people would be particularly open to this message. The specific time is named as the **ninth month of**

the fifth year of Jehoiakim, which means it has taken a few months for the preparation of the scroll since the divine command came to Jeremiah in Jehoiakim's fourth year (36:1).

Baruch read the scroll from the room of a man named **Gemariah.** This Gemariah was likely different from the one in 29:1–3, because in that text Gemariah's ancestor is called Hilkiah while here it is **Shaphan.** However, the other person named in that context is Elasah who is called the son of Shaphan and so perhaps this Gemariah is brother to Elasah. In any case, it appears that Gemariah is part of a circle of powerful families that have had a close tie to the prophet (and likely to Josiah's earlier reforms). The location of Gemariah's room is specified as near **the entrance of the New Gate of the temple,** this location also being named in 26:10–11.

36:11–19 / In this paragraph, **Micaiah,** the son of Gemariah, and therefore also a descendant of Shaphan, plays an important role. He was apparently in charge of his father's room, from which Baruch was reading the oracles, since his father will later be found in the room of Elishama the secretary (or scribe), whose office was at the royal palace.

Micaiah went to the palace and reported the prophet's message to a broad circle of officials, and they set the wheels in motion to bring this scroll to the attention of the king. The members of the broader circle (**Elishama the secretary, Delaiah son of Shemaiah, Elnathan son of Acbor, Gemariah son of Shaphan, Zedekiah son of Hananiah,** as well as **Jehudi son of Nethaniah, the son of Shelemiah, the son of Cushi**) are listed by name and they were likely well known to their contemporaries. However, though many of these names are known elsewhere from the Bible and on occasion from extrabiblical sources, we can rarely be sure that these other attestations of the name are the same individuals as those listed here (see Additional Notes to vv. 12 and 14).

But before they send the message on to the king, they politely ask Baruch to repeat the scroll that he had been reading to the people to them. Baruch does so, and when they hear the message of judgment for sin, they respond with fear and determine that the king should also hear these oracles. They also confirm with Baruch that the message came from Jeremiah. Baruch confirms that he served as the scribe of the message. Apparently, the identity of the prophet is a significant piece of information for those who hear his word.

It is clear that the group knew that this message would likely not be well received by the king. They warn Baruch to go into hiding and to take Jeremiah with him.

36:20–26 / This paragraph describes the third reading of the scroll, this time to King Jehoiakim himself as well as to others of his attendants. The reading took place in his **winter apartment,** which had a fire burning. While he was willing to hear the oracles at the urging of the officials listed in verses 11–14, he did not like what he heard. He showed his displeasure by taking a knife and cutting off portions of the scroll as they were read and throwing them into the fire. The text specifically says that neither the king nor his attendants demonstrated **fear** as they heard these words, contrasting them with the earlier group of officials who did react in that way (36:16). At least some of the earlier group were in attendance as the king read the scroll; Elnathan, Delaiah, and Gemariah are specifically said to have tried to stop the king from burning the scroll. Politics and religion may both play a part in the different reactions here. The ones who fear obviously believe that Jeremiah is a true spokesman for God, and they may also be promoting a more pro-Babylonian policy, while King Jehoiakim was well-known to be anti-Babylonian (after all, he was put in his position by the Egyptians).

In any case, the king not only destroyed the scroll, he ordered one of his sons, **Jerhameel,** along with **Seraiah son of Azriel** and **Shelemiah son of Abdeel** to go out and arrest Jeremiah and Baruch. However, the latter had followed the advice of the other officials and hid himself. The text takes the divine perspective and tells us that **the LORD had hidden them.**

36:27–32 / The king had cut up and burned Jeremiah's scroll out of anger and maybe as an attempt to extinguish the possibility that the curses that his oracles announced could actually come to be. However, it is impossible to extinguish the Word of God. It is not as easy as burning it in a fire. The Word transcends the medium on which it was written.

Thus, we are not surprised to hear God say to Jeremiah after Jehoiakim had burned the scroll, **Take another scroll and write on it all the words that were on the first scroll.** Jehoiakim has not escaped judgment; he has actually increased it. He burned the scroll because he did not like the message that the king of Babylon would destroy the land. But now Jeremiah is told that Jehoiakim will have a more severe penalty: **He will have no one to sit on the**

throne of David; his body will be thrown out and exposed to the heat of the day and the frost by night. I will punish him and his children and his attendants for their wickedness; I will bring on them and those living in Jerusalem and the people of Judah every disaster I pronounced against them, because they have not listened.

The historical books report that when Jehoiakim revolted against the Babylonians in 597 B.C. Nebuchadnezzar mobilized his army against him. However, by the time the Babylonians actually reach Jerusalem, it is Jehoiachin not Jehoiakim who is on the throne. Jehoiakim has been deposed, even though he appears to have been alive when the Babylonians arrive (2 Chr. 36:6–7). The texts are unclear as to what happened next, though Kings (2 Kgs. 24:6) supports the idea that he was killed in Jerusalem (and buried there) rather than deported to Babylon. His son Jehoiachin, though, was deported to Babylon, and Nebuchadnezzar put his uncle Zedekiah (who was also Jehoiakim's brother) on the throne.

Additional Notes §80

36:12 / **Elnathan son of Acbor** is known from 2 Kings 22:8–10 as the father of Jehoiachin's wife and also from Jeremiah 26:22–23, where he was sent by King Jehoiakim to Egypt to track down a prophet named Uriah. When he found Uriah, he brought him back to Jerusalem, where Jehoiakim had the prophet executed. Elnathan plays a much more positive role in this chapter, since he is part of the group that will encourage Jehoiakim to listen to the scroll and will try to dissuade the king from burning it (36:25).

36:14 / **Jehudi son of Nethaniah, the son of Shelemiah, the son of Cushi** is given an extraordinarily long patronymic. The reason may be because the final reference (Cushi) indicates that he is a Cushite, or Ethiopian.

36:18 / Baruch tells the officials that he wrote down Jeremiah's words **in ink on a scroll.** Lundbom reports that "black ink for writing was made from carbon, usually being soot scraped from cooking vessels or else specially prepared, and then mixed with a solution of gum and water and dried into cakes" and that "pens were made from a piece of thin rush (*Phragmites communis*), but from one end on the bias and then frayed to form a brush" (*Jeremiah 21–36,* p. 602).

36:23 / A **scribe's knife** was normally used to prepare papyrus for writing, but here it is used to destroy the scroll that contained Jeremiah's oracles.

36:26 / **Jerahmeel** is called a son of the king, though it is debatable whether that means he is a biological son or whether the phrase is a title for a servant of the king. In any case, it is interesting that archaeologists have uncovered a seal impression of a Jerahmeel who is called the king's son. Thus, this individual joins Baruch son of Neraiah and Gemariah son of Shaphan as being attested in contemporary seal impressions.

§81 Jeremiah in Prison during the Reign of Zedekiah (Jer. 37:1–38:28)

Scholars are split over the relationship between chapters 37 and 38. Carroll (*Jeremiah,* pp. 678–79) and Fretheim (*Jeremiah,* p. 519) suggest that they are variants of the same story of Jeremiah's imprisonment at the instigation of the pro-Egyptian party in Judah and eventual release. They believe that the differences are the result of variants that arose in the context of oral tradition. However, Holladay (*Jeremiah* 2, p. 282) argues that the differences are too great to be accounted for in this way and believes that they are different stories. Lundbom (*Jeremiah 37–52,* pp. 64–5) does not discuss the issue, simply assuming that they are two different accounts.

37:1–2 / The first verse announces a new time period different from the previous chapters. We have moved from the time of Jehoiakim (609–597 B.C.) to the time of Zedekiah (597–586 B.C.). The introduction of Zedekiah also reminds the reader that he had been placed on the throne by none other than Nebuchadnezzar. Jehoiakim had revolted against Babylon and had been removed from the throne by the time Nebuchadnezzar's army arrived in Jerusalem. Jehoiakim's nineteen-year-old son Jehoiachin was on the throne and was quickly unseated and deported to Babylon. Nebuchadnezzar chose another member of the royal family to take his place with the hope that he would be more amenable to Babylon. As we read on in the story, we recognize that the time is actually quite late in Zedekiah's reign. The Babylonian army already has Zedekiah's Jerusalem under siege (v. 5, **the Babylonians who were besieging Jerusalem**). Zedekiah had not remained loyal to Babylon, but revolted at a time he thought he might successfully pull away from their control (2 Kgs. 24:18–25:26).

From Jeremiah and God's perspective, matters had not changed a bit in the transition from Jehoiakim to Zedekiah, for Zedekiah and his officials paid no attention to **the words the LORD** had spoken through Jeremiah the prophet. They did not heed the warnings and did not repent, so the pronouncement of judgment was still in effect.

37:3–5 / Even though Zedekiah paid no attention to Jeremiah's message by not responding to it with repentance, he nonetheless sent an embassy of two men to request that the prophet pray to the Lord for the nation (**Please pray to the LORD our God for us,** v. 3). This request indicates that the king had some measure of respect for Jeremiah. It was an essential duty for a prophet to pray for the people of God. We can see this in the first mention of "prophet" in reference to Abraham (Gen. 20:7), where his role as prophet is linked to his prayers. As Samuel transitions from judge to prophet-figure, he asserts that he would not fail to pray for the people (1 Sam. 12:23), and Moses' effective intercessory prayer plays a major role in the Golden Calf incident (Exod. 32–34).

The people whom Zedekiah sent are **Jehucal son of Shelemiah** and the **priest Zephaniah son of Maaseiah.** We learn very little about them from this story since they are only said to deliver the message. However, in 38:1, we will see Jehucal again, this time calling for Jeremiah's death. On the other hand, Zephaniah, the priest, has made appearances at 21:1; 29:25, 29, and we will read about him again in 52:24. In the last reference we learn that Zephaniah is not an ordinary priest, but "the priest next in rank" after the "chief priest." The account in chapter 21 tells us that he was involved in an earlier embassy to Jeremiah from Zedekiah along with Pashur son of Malkijah, a known adversary of Jeremiah. However, in the story in chapter 29 we see that Zephaniah himself was either well-disposed toward Jeremiah or at least tolerant. There we learn that an exile named Shemaiah had accused Zephaniah of not tending to his priestly duties by clamping down on Jeremiah. Indeed, Zephaniah had shared this letter with Jeremiah, prompting a response on the part of the prophet back to Shemaiah.

For these reasons, Lundbom (*Jeremiah 37–52,* p. 55) may well be right that Zedekiah has sent a "good-cop, bad-cop" combination to Jeremiah. Jehucal hated him and Zephaniah may have been sympathetic.

The occasion for the royal request for prayer is the withdrawal of the Babylonian army from the walls of Jerusalem. They did this to respond to a threat from the Egyptians who had mobilized their armies and were on the march from the south. The Pharaoh at this time was Hophra (also known as Apries, see Jer. 44:30), who had taken the throne in 589 B.C. and had likely concluded some sort of treaty alliance with Zedekiah that may have given that king ill-founded confidence to revolt in the first place.

But what exactly is going through the king's mind when he asks Jeremiah to pray for the nation on the occasion of the withdrawal of the Babylonian army? In the earlier encounter in chapter 21, Jeremiah announced sure defeat and did not mention the possibility of withdrawal. Could Zedekiah be inquiring as to whether the divine message has changed? It may be best simply to think that Zedekiah was asking Jeremiah to pray that God would make this withdrawal permanent.

Another aspect of the setting of this story has to do with Jeremiah's freedom. At this time, the text makes a point to say the prophet has not yet been put in jail. As we will see, his status is about to change.

37:6–10 / But instead of prayer, Jeremiah responds with yet another oracle of judgment directed toward Zedekiah. After all, God had earlier forbidden Jeremiah to pray for the people as a way to express the depth of their sin and the certainty of their destruction (7:16; 11:14; 14:11).

The message is simple. The Babylonian withdrawal is temporary. The Egyptians will retreat and the Babylonians will take up their siege again. Nothing will prevent them from their ultimate victory because God has determined that it will happen. As a matter of fact, Jeremiah declares, even if they defeated the Babylonian army and only left wounded men, those **wounded men** would breach the walls and burn down the city. No apparent success, no matter how great, should be a cause of any hope to the people of Jerusalem, especially this involvement of Egypt. To think otherwise would be for the leaders of Judah to **deceive** themselves.

37:11–15 / During the time of the Babylonian withdrawal, however, Jeremiah was arrested and thrown into a prison. He was arrested as he was leaving the city to go get his **share of the property** among the people in **Benjamin.** We can safely assume that this refers to the property that he eventually bought from his cousin Hanamel in his ancestral homeland of Anathoth. The account of that transaction is in chapter 32 and took place during a later phase of the Babylonian siege of Jerusalem. Perhaps a relative had died and he was going to see to his claim. Since he is prevented, as we will see, from progressing northward, this transaction will take place later when he is imprisoned.

He left Jerusalem through the Benjamin Gate (see Additional Notes). The gates of ancient Jerusalem, as with all ancient cities, were fortified and secured, and thus it is not surprising that the **captain of the guard** was located there and vigilant for any suspicious activity. Jeremiah's leaving the city was considered suspicious because he was thought to be a Babylonian collaborator by many, perhaps even a spy.

The arresting officer was a man named **Irijah son of Shelemiah, the son of Hananiah.** Irijah is named only here, and Shelemiah and Hananiah are very popular names for many individuals in the book of Jeremiah and elsewhere in the Old Testament, so we can proceed no further in our identification of them.

The claim was that he was **deserting to the Babylonians,** but Jeremiah vociferously denies the charge. Even so, he was arrested and turned over to certain unnamed officials who beat and imprisoned him. Though the officials were unnamed, they can probably be identified with foes that are named elsewhere, as for instance those listed in 38:1.

37:16–21 / Jeremiah spent a long time in a vaulted cell in a dungeon. This location surely was unpleasant but nothing like the cistern into which he will be thrown in the next chapter. In any case, it is here that Zedekiah makes another private overture to the prophet. First he had him brought to the palace so he could ask him personally and not go to the prison house himself. The question is surprising considering how he has been treating the prophet. He asks him **"Is there any word from the LORD?"**

It is clear Zedekiah was hoping for something different than what he heard. The oracle was short and to the point: **you will be handed over to the king of Babylon.**

The text does not record Zedekiah's response to this harsh oracle. Rather Jeremiah now has a private request for the king. He wants the king to better his condition. Jeremiah pleads that he has committed no crime. He knows why he is in prison: it is because he is a prophet who told the truth. He sarcastically asks for the location of the prophets who had a more positive message for the king. They said that the Babylonians would not come, but look, he points out, the armies are threatening Jerusalem. He might even be thinking specifically of a prophet like Hananiah (ch. 28), whose message has proved to be misleading, but who also had since died.

Jeremiah then asks the king not to send him back to the house of Jonathan the secretary because of its harsh conditions. Zedekiah responds positively and rather than sending Jeremiah back from where he came, he puts him in the **courtyard of the guard.** His movements will be restricted, but the conditions must have been better there. This is where he will meet his cousin Hanamel in chapter 32. He also received a ration of bread, which probably signifies that his diet had been severely restricted while he was in the house of Jonathan.

38:1–6 / In chapter 38 we begin an account of another imprisonment of the prophet (for the debate over the relationship between chapters 37 and 38, see the introductory paragraph to this unit). It begins with a listing of the individuals involved (see Additional Notes). We may presume that they are all members of a pro-Egyptian political party, one that looked to Egypt for hope against the Babylonian threat.

These men are deeply disturbed by Jeremiah's preaching. He sounds like an agent of the Babylonians, telling the people that they will survive only if they surrender. Those who resist and stay in the city will die by **sword, famine or plague,** the three scourges of a military siege (see Additional Notes at 14:2). In a word, Jeremiah is claiming that the defeat of Jerusalem by the Babylonians is something that is assured by none other than God himself.

From the perspective of these officials, Jeremiah is abetting the enemy by discouraging the troops and the population. For this crime, he should be **put to death.** They are thinking of the good of the people and Jeremiah is undermining public confidence.

They address their concerns to the king and he responds by saying, **"He is in your hands. The king can do nothing to oppose you."** It is uncertain whether this is a strategy of avoiding political responsibility or the truth. The king may want to see Jeremiah removed from the scene but would prefer others to take the lead on it. On the other hand, a city under such stress probably witnessed significant power plays between opposing political forces. It may be that the king's power has been curtailed. Later the king will be able to order the release of Jeremiah from the extremely dire circumstances he is about to be subjected to, but he has to send thirty men to see that his will is carried out. He may not be certain that these four powerful officials will simply do what he says.

But for now, he in essence allows the imprisonment of Jeremiah, though perhaps he did not anticipate the rough conditions to which these men subjected the prophet. He was lowered into a cistern (at the home of Malkijah, see Additional Notes). A cistern was a huge pit dug in the ground and typically plastered on the sides so the water would not seep out through the walls. It was to hold drinking water, and it may not have been a good sign that the water was missing from the cistern; the city may already have been running dry.

In any case, though it did not have much water, the bottom was muddy and the text describes how Jeremiah sank into the mud as he reached the bottom. Though not written for this occasion, we might imagine that Jeremiah would have found Psalm 69 particularly relevant to his situation at the time.

38:7–13 / Though Jeremiah's plight was dire, he had his advocates, and the next part of the account tells us how an official named **Ebed-Melech** interceded with the king to get him removed from the cistern and then placed under what appears to be a less life-threatening form of imprisonment.

This is our first introduction to Ebed-Melech who is called **an official in the royal palace** and a **Cushite.** The former gave him access to the king; the latter indicates that he was Ethiopian by birth or descent.

The text at this point does not present any motivation for Ebed-Melech's actions on Jeremiah's behalf, but we immediately assume that he is sympathetic toward his message. This intuition is encouraged by the divine oracle that appears in 39:15–18, where God explains why Ebed-Melech will survive the devastation by stating to him, "because you trust in me." In other words, Ebed-Melech was a true worshiper of Yahweh and must have recognized that the prophet was speaking the words of his God.

For this reason, Ebed-Melech found the king sitting in the **Benjamin Gate** (see Additional Notes on 37:13). Since a gate was a place of legal proceedings, perhaps Ebed-Melech was making a legal case to release Jeremiah. The issue was that Jeremiah's harsh imprisonment was going to be a de facto death penalty unless something happened. In Ebed-Melech's words, **these men have acted wickedly** by placing Jeremiah in the cistern.

The king responded favorably to Ebed-Melech's entreaty and ordered that thirty men be sent to the place of Jeremiah's incarceration to free him. We have already commented on the possible implications of the fact that the king felt it necessary to send thirty men to affect his will. The wicked men who imprisoned him may also be extremely powerful in the city. But in any case, Ebed-Melech and the men sent with him were able to extricate the prophet from the cistern. He was not freed, since **he remained in the courtyard of the guard.**

Though Jeremiah did not compose Psalm 30, we can recognize how relevant its words of thanksgiving would be in this situation:

> I will exalt you, O LORD,
> for you lifted me out of the depths
> and did not let my enemies gloat over me.
> O LORD my God, I called to you for help
> and you healed me.
> O LORD, you brought me up from the grave;
> you spared me from going down into the pit. (Ps. 30:1–3)

38:14–28 / The second half of chapter 38 narrates the account of another private meeting between Jeremiah and Zedekiah. In the earlier meeting Zedekiah had him brought to the palace (37:16–21), in the present story he meets the king at the third entrance to the temple. We do not know the precise significance of this location, but we can safely assume it was a very private place. As we will see, people knew they were meeting, but could not tell what they were talking about.

The king asks Jeremiah to be completely forthcoming with him (**Do not hide anything from me**), but Jeremiah is understandably cautious (**If I give you an answer, will you not kill me?**). Furthermore, Jeremiah has had a history with this king; whenever he has given him advice or counsel through divine oracles, he has ignored it (**Even if I did give you counsel, you would not listen to me**).

Zedekiah gives him his word that he will be safe (**I will neither kill you nor hand you over to those who are seeking your life**). With this assurance, Jeremiah speaks the word of the Lord directly to the king. It is no different than before (compare, for instance, vv. 17–18 with vv. 2–3), but is applied to the king as representative of the nation as a whole. In other words, if the king surrenders to Babylon, then, while they will be vassals of that great empire, the city will be spared and Zedekiah and his officials and the people will be spared. But if they resist, then they will feel the full force of Babylon's power. Jeremiah also specifically applies this message to the king (**you yourself will not escape from their hands**).

Zedekiah does not reject Jeremiah's message out of hand. But he does register fear. Interestingly, he is afraid of his people who have already gone over to the Babylonians. Apparently some people have heard Jeremiah's message or have simply read the "writing on the wall" and have defected to the Babylonian side. Zedekiah is afraid that he will be treated roughly by these people. Jeremiah assures him that they will not (**it will go well for you, and your life will be spared**).

But if Zedekiah does not act on the divine direction to surrender to Babylon then horrible things will happen to the city and its inhabitants. Now Jeremiah concentrates on the fate of the women of the palace, perhaps another attempt to appeal to Zedekiah's sense of self-preservation for himself and his family. He says that they will be brought out to the officials of the king of Babylon, and specifically "all your wives and children will be brought out to the Babylonians." While their fate is not specified, the king would know what this meant. Enemy women in the ancient Near East were raped, forced into marriages, or killed. It was not a pretty picture.

Zedekiah does not respond one way or the other on the spot. However, from the events that will soon transpire we understand that he did not follow Jeremiah's divinely-inspired advice. The next chapter will narrate the fall of Jerusalem. For the moment, he is concerned to cover his tracks with others in his court who would be extremely agitated if they knew he was talking to Jeremiah in this way. So the prophet and the king devise a cover-up story. If the officials interrogate Jeremiah about the substance of their meeting, and they do, he is to tell them that he was begging the king not to subject him to reimprisonment in **Jonathan's house** (37:15).

The chapter ends with a note that Jeremiah remained under restricted movement in the **courtyard of the guard until the day Jerusalem was captured.** That story is the subject of the next chapter.

Additional Notes §81

37:13 / The **Benjamin Gate** is mentioned also in 38:7 as well as Ezek. 48:32 and Zech. 14:10. While there have been many attempts to identify this gate with other names, what is obvious is that this gate must have allowed access to a road that went to Anathoth and thus was north of the city. The Upper Gate of Benjamin mentioned in 20:2 is a different gate leading from the temple area into the city proper.

37:15 / Jeremiah was **imprisoned in the house of Jonathan the secretary.** According to the available evidence, the ancient Near East did not know prisons like we have in the modern western world. Prisons were not for punishment (notice that the penalties in the biblical and extra-biblical legal codes do not mention prison terms), but rather as holding places for future judgment.

38:1 / Four specific individuals are named as those who plot to get Jeremiah arrested and thrown into prison. Two of them have appeared before in the book of Jeremiah. **Pashhur son of Malkijah,** not to be confused with Pashhur son of Immer (20:1), appeared in 21:1 as part of an embassy to Jeremiah. **Jehucal** (here spelled Jucal) **son of Shelemiah** was a part of the embassy sent to the prophet in 37:3. **Gedaliah son of Pashhur** occurs only here in the Bible. He is not to be confused with Gedaliah son of Ahikam son of Shaphan, who will be appointed governor of postdestruction Judah later in the book. His "father" Pashhur could conceivably be Pashhur son of Malkijah or even Pashhur son of Immer. **Shephatiah son of Mattan** is only known from this event.

38:6 / Jeremiah was placed in a cistern, which was in the courtyard of the guard, connected with a man named **Malkijah,** who is identified as **the king's son,** implying that the location must be connected to the palace (38:11). Since Zedekiah was twenty-one when he became king in 597 B.C., he must be thirty-two during the siege. He is likely too young to have a son who would have his own house. Thus, there is a debate among scholars (see Lundbom, *Jeremiah 37–52,* p. 68) on the status of this title. It is possible that he was a son of one of his royal brothers or that this was some kind of honorific title. It is unlikely that this is the Malkijah who is the patronymic of Pashhur in 38:1.

38:7 / The NIV translates *ʾis saris* as **"official,"** though some (Lundbom, *Jeremiah 37–52,* p. 70) think the phrase should be taken in its etymological sense as "eunuch man" (see also NIV footnote). It is true that eunuchs were employed in royal service, particularly as attendants of the harem. However, there is also evidence that "eunuch" was a general term for any official.

38:22 / Jeremiah anticipates that the women who will be brought out to the Babylonians will sing or recite a poem. They will mock Zedekiah for trusting deceitful men, probably thinking of officials like those listed in 38:1. As a result, Zedekiah's feet will sink in the mire, like Jeremiah's just did as he was placed in the cistern (and as we have seen in the citation of Psalm 69 sinking into the mire was a metaphor for serious trouble). The king will be left all alone.

§82 The Fates of Zedekiah, Jeremiah, and Ebed-Melech (Jer. 39:1–40:6)

This section narrates the fall of the city of Jerusalem at the hands of the Babylonians, and then focuses in on the fate of three specific people: Zedekiah, Jeremiah, and Ebed-Melech. The section concerning the latter breaks up the story of the Babylonian's treatment of the prophet. The lesson of all three vignettes is that God repays those who obey him as well as those who do not.

Much of this chapter is paralleled to Jeremiah 52:4–16 and 2 Kings 25:1–12. It is interesting to note that Jeremiah 39:4–13 is not found in the Septuagint. It seems that the Masoretic Text places these verses here to bring the prophecy of Jeremiah concerning Judah (which ends here) to a fitting climax.

39:1–10 / For years, Jeremiah has been warning Judah and its leaders that disobedience and a refusal to repent would ultimately lead to the destruction of Jerusalem and exile of its people. Chapter 39 begins with a simple report of the fall of Jerusalem (**This is how Jerusalem was taken**). Jeremiah 52 provides a longer account of the defeat of the city.

The siege began in **the ninth year of Zedekiah king of Judah, in the tenth month.** In Jeremiah 52:4, we have the additional information that it was on the tenth day of the month. Taking account of the fact that Judah used a lunar calendar, the most likely date, according to absolute chronology, for this event is January 15, 588 B.C. (though there is significant debate about the type of calendar in use in Judah at this time).

An ancient siege essentially cut a city off from its necessary supplies. All the people, including those in surrounding agricultural villages would seek refuge behind the walls of the city. While the walls of Jerusalem provided significant security, a siege would leave its inhabitants with limited food and water. While the population would weaken, the attacking army would work at trying to breach the walls. Ancient warfare strategy attests going over walls by ladders, picking out stones so the wall would collapse, and digging under the walls. The means is not specified in this case, but the text does say that it took the Babylonian army one and half years to break through the wall (**the ninth day of the fourth month of Zedekiah's eleventh year,** that is, July 18, 586 B.C.).

Once the wall was breached, that was the end of the story for the Judean cause. The text here does not even narrate the resistance, if any, that the Babylonians encountered once they entered the city. The next verse simply remarks that the leading officials of the Babylonian army who were present (see Additional Notes) **took seats in the Middle Gate.** In essence, their position in the gate indicates that they now controlled and ran the city.

The narrative then turns attention to the postdefeat actions of Zedekiah. He knew that horrible consequences were in store for him, so he fled. After all, his refusal to surrender caused the Babylonians to spend significant resources to subdue the city. He tried to escape under the cover of darkness (**at night**) through what may have been a secret passageway connected to the palace (**king's garden**), through the inner and outer walls (**between the two walls**) and out of the city. He and a contingent of surviving soldiers were heading toward the **Arabah.** Arabah means "steppe"; it is a close synonym to "wilderness" (*midbar*). Typically it refers to a desolate area to the east and southeast of Jerusalem, that is, to the Jordan River valley or to the small wadis that drain into it. It may be significant that the text specifies that he departed from his garden (a cultivated and pleasant natural environment) to the Arabah (a wild and inhospitable area). They may have been seeking refuge in the many caves in the area that have served as hiding places for refugees through the centuries, or planning on going further. We cannot know, because the Babylonians caught them in the **plains of Jericho,** some fifteen to twenty miles east of Jerusalem.

At this point, Zedekiah's worse nightmares came true. He was transported to **Nebuchadnezzar** who was at **Riblah,** in Syria (**the land of Hamath**), the staging area of all his armies in their campaigns in Syria and Palestine. His sentence was worse than death. Zedekiah first had to watch the execution of his **sons** and the **nobles of Judah.** That was the last thing he ever saw, because afterward, they gouged out Zedekiah's **eyes.** They then bound him in **chains** and deported him to Babylon. Unlike Jehoiachin who was taken to Babylon in 597 B.C. and provided a ration, we never hear of Zedekiah again, though it is a safe bet that if he ever reached Babylon, he did not live as comfortable a life as his previously exiled royal nephew.

Once Zedekiah and the other officials had been taken care of, the text turns to the description of the destruction of Jerusalem itself. The **palace** and other residences were **set on fire** and the **walls** pulled down. The walls had the most symbolic value since a city's walls provided defense against external enemies like Babylon. Under the leadership of **Nabuzaradan,** identified as **the commander of the imperial guard,** the people of Judah were then deported to Babylon. The people are identified as those who survived in the city, those who had earlier gone over to the Babylonians, and the rest of the people. The middle category, those who had gone over to the Babylonians, refers to those who saw the end in sight and had abandoned the city and surrendered to the Babylonians before the end of the siege. This move assured their survival, but not their continued presence in the land.

Even so, the text acknowledges that the land was not totally depopulated. There were some whom the Babylonians purposefully left behind (in ch. 40 we will learn of some others who continued to resist Babylonian occupation). These are identified as the **poor of the land** (see Additional Notes). They were given agricultural lands.

39:11–14 / While Zedekiah meets a horrible fate upon the fall of Jerusalem, Jeremiah is treated with grace considering the circumstances. It would stretch the truth to say he received a reward, because his life does not get easier, but in another sense, it could have been much worse. This paragraph is the first of two accounts of the Babylonian treatment of Jeremiah after the conflict. We will deal with the question of their relationship in connection with the second account in 40:1–6. The oracle illuminating the fate of Ebed-Melech in 39:15–18 separates the two accounts of Jeremiah.

Nebuchadnezzar, presumably still at the military staging area in Riblah, issues an order to **Nebuzaradan** concerning Jeremiah. How would the Babylonian king know about Jeremiah: military intelligence? We might speculate that it was through the Judeans who had earlier deserted and come over to the Babylonian side. Why would Nebuchadnezzar be positively inclined toward the prophet? We have seen time and again that Jeremiah was viewed as a collaborator by the royal and military authorities, and indeed from a human perspective he acted like one. He went around the city telling Judeans that they did not stand a chance at the hands of the Babylonians and that they should simply put their arms down and surrender. From Nebuchadnezzar's point of view, Jeremiah was a boon to his efforts. He wanted Jeremiah found and treated well.

Nebuzaradan and two other officers (**Nebushazban** mentioned here for the first time and **Nergal-Sharezeer,** the *Rab-mag* [translated **a high official**], mentioned in 39:3, see Additional Notes to that verse) then found Jeremiah in the **courtyard of the guard.** We have already seen that Jeremiah was imprisoned there at the time of the Babylonian siege (32:2; 37:20; 38:28). In essence then, they released him from prison and turned him over to **Gedaliah son of Ahikam, the son of Shaphan.** It is here for the first time that we meet Gedaliah. Earlier in the book (26:24), we saw that Jeremiah was spared death because **Ahikam son of Shaphan** interceded for him. 2 Kings 22 mentions both Ahikam (vv. 12, 14, 22) and his father, Shaphan (2 Kgs. 22:3, 8, 9, 10, etc.), as officials during the reforms of Josiah. We might presume then that their support for Josiah made them favorably disposed toward Jeremiah. They likely walked a political tightrope with Josiah's son, Jehoiakim, but had enough power to do so. In short, Gedaliah's father and grandfather were godly men who managed to retain important positions during the last few years of Judah's existence. And now their descendant Gedaliah will serve an important function. In 40:5 we will learn that Nebuchadnezzar appointed him to be governor of what is now the Babylonian province of Judah.

39:15–18 / Suddenly the topic of interest shifts from Jeremiah to Ebed-Melech. To do so, narrative time has to go back to the time Jeremiah was still imprisoned in the courtyard of the guard. The rationale for doing so is that the oracle that Jeremiah received at that time is now coming to fruition.

The oracle first tells **Ebed-Melech** that the divine word against Jerusalem, namely, the announcement of its destruction, is going to come about. But the oracle is a divine word of assurance toward Ebed-Melech, because God will see to it that he will not die in the process (**you will not fall by the sword but will escape with your life**). God is acting this way toward Ebed-Melech because he **trusts in** Yahweh.

This hearkens back to Ebed-Melech's actions as they are recorded in Jeremiah 38:7–13. Here we see that it was this man who saved Jeremiah from what would have certainly been a slow and gruesome death after he was thrown into a cistern. Ebed-Melech interceded with the king who sent a force to remove Jeremiah from the cistern and allowed him to be imprisoned under more humane circumstances. Thus, again, as with the narration of the fate of Zedekiah and Jeremiah, we learn that consequences, bad and good, come about in accordance with obedience or disobedience to the divine word.

40:1–6 / We now return to the subject of Jeremiah's fate after the fall of Jerusalem (39:11–14). However, what is the relationship between these two narratives? In the earlier account, Nebuzaradan found Jeremiah imprisoned in the courtyard of the guard and released him into the care of Gedaliah. Here Nebuzaredan finds Jeremiah in chains, about to be deported in the city of Ramah. He then gives Jeremiah a choice, come to Babylon (presumably not in chains) or stay in Judah. Before pursuing an analysis of this second story, we will address the relationship between the two.

It is possible to harmonize the two stories in the following way. Nebuzaradan, on commission from Nebuchadnezzar, finds Jeremiah in the courtyard of the guard. He releases him into the care of Gedaliah. This is the story of 39:11–14. To provide a background for the events of 40:1–6, we would need to presume that somehow in the confusion of post-war Jerusalem, soldiers, not knowing that Jeremiah was given a free pass, take him to **Ramah** (a site identified with er-Ram, about five miles north of Jerusalem, or Ramallah, about 9 miles north), which apparently was a staging area for the deportation to Babylon. Nebuzaradan finds him there and frees him a second time. This time he gives Jeremiah a choice. Jeremiah chooses to stay in Judah and is placed in the care of Gedaliah.

Of course, any such harmonization is speculative, involving a reconstruction of events. Whether this harmonization is correct or we have two separate traditions of the one release of Jeremiah, the point is that the prophet takes the opportunity to stay in Judah.

While we can only speculate why, we might consider the fact that though he looked like a collaborator, he really wasn't and had no love for Babylon. He held property in Judah (ch. 32) and, just as he knew that Jerusalem would be destroyed, he also knew that it would be restored. There are any number of reasons why Jeremiah might have stayed, even though life in the province would not be easy. As a matter of fact, as we will see as the story continues, it will be even harder than one might imagine at this stage.

It is interesting to note that this section is introduced as if a divine oracle delivered through the prophet might follow (40:1: **the word came to Jeremiah from the LORD**). The fact that Jeremiah does not speak a divine oracle in what immediately follows leads to all kinds of possible reconstructions. But the solution might be as simple as understanding that the divine word here comes to Jeremiah through Nebuzaradan (so Lundbom, *Jeremiah 37–52,* pp. 99–100), when he proclaims that it was Yahweh who decreed the destruction of Jerusalem because of the sins of Israel. Some readers are amazed that a pagan military leader would speak in such terms. However, such language is far from unprecedented. It was not at all unusual for a conquering army to attribute their success to the permission or active involvement of the conquered people's deity. Within the Bible, we can see the language used by the representatives of the Assyrian army before the walls of Jerusalem during the reign of Hezekiah (Isa. 36). While here they falsely claimed to be speaking in the name of Yahweh, we are also reminded of the fact that Josiah later died because he did not heed the word of Yahweh as it was spoken through the mouth of Neco, pharaoh of Egypt (2 Chr. 35:20–22). Outside of the Bible the same understanding may be found as illustrated by the so-called Apology of Tukulti-Ninurta, where that Assyrian king claims that Marduk, the god of Babylon, commanded him to destroy that city.

Additional Notes §82

39:3 / The text mentions some specific high-ranking Babylonian military and political officials. With the exception of Nebuzaradan they are not mentioned in the account in Jeremiah 52 or 2 Kings 24. Indeed, the reading of these names in 39:13 is difficult because there are some ambiguities, some of which are caused by the difficuly of rendering Babylonian names in Hebrew. Their titles are also of a general nature for the most part. According to the NIV rendering in 39:3 the following are found:

Nergal-Sharezer of Samgar (a province of Babylon? a title?)
Nebo-Sarsekim a chief officer
Nergal-Sharezer a high official (*Rab-mag*)

The name Nergal-Sharezer (given to two individuals in the verse) is thought to be equivalent to the name of the son-in-law of Nebuchadnezzar, a man otherwise known as Neriglissar, who would eventually be king in Babylon from 560 to 556 B.C. If so, which Nergal-Sharezer should be so identified is unclear.

However, some would divide the names and titles in a different manner. NRSV, for instance, renders the verse as having four individuals: "Nergal-sharezer, Samgar-nebo (taking into account the *maqqef* in the MT), Sarcechim the Rabsaris, Nergal-sharezer the Rab-mag."

In favor of the NIV rendering is the fact that there are three names and three titles, thus symmetry. Also, Samgar is now identified as an Akkadian official title or place name (so Lundblum, *Jeremiah 37–52,* pp. 84–5). *Rab-mag* (NIV: **high official**) is the Hebrew form of an Akkadian military title *rab-mugi.*

> Indeed, the NIV's rendition of the name as Nebo-Sarsekim has just been confirmed by the discovery of a cuneiform tablet in the British Museum (July 2007 by the Assyriologist Michael Jursa), which mentions him as the "chief eunuch of Nebuchadnezzar.

The details of this list continue to escape the modern reader. However, the gist is clear. Leading Babylonian officials are now in charge of the city.

39:10 / There is considerable scholarly debate at present about the extent of the exile. Some texts, including this one, would lead to the conclusion that the land of Judah was virtually empty after the exile took place. However, as Jeremiah 40–41 will indicate, there is a significant population still left in the land. Furthermore, when precise numbers of exiles are given (see 52:28–30), we see that they are not huge numbers. The biblical texts emphasize the horror of the devastation of the time by focusing on the exile, not on those who are left in the land. Furthermore, the ones who were deported were the ones who were in charge, the leaders of the community. It is wrong-minded to accuse the biblical text of perpetuating a fictional "myth of the empty land" (so Barstad).

40:6 / Jeremiah, having chosen to stay in Judah, goes to Gedaliah who is at **Mizpah.** Since Jerusalem was destroyed, Gedaliah's government would be located at the modest city of Mizpah. Mizpah had religious and political significance since early in history (Judg. 20:1–3; 1 Sam. 7:5–14; 10:17–24). Though scholars are not certain, many identify Mizpah with Tel en-Nasbeh, which is eight miles north of Jerusalem.

§83 The Assassination of Gedaliah (Jer. 40:7–41:15)

The narration of the immediate postdestruction period in Judah continues. While the leaders of Judah are being carted off to Babylon, the narrator stays with Jeremiah in Judah. The focus shifts momentarily from the prophet to the new Babylonian-appointed governor of the Persian province of Judah, Gedaliah (see commentary on 39:11–14), who is ruling from the town of Mizpah. The story that follows is the first part of an account of an episode that will explain why a significant postexilic group of Jewish people ends up living in Egypt. It also shows that matters can still get worse for the Jewish people and specifically for Jeremiah. G. Yates ("New Exodus and No Exodus in Jeremiah 26–45") has uncovered the use of exodus imagery in chapters 40–43 that shows that the people who stay in Palestine will experience no exodus in the future. In this way, the book suggests that the future of the people of God lie not with these people who descend into Egypt again, but with those who went into exile in Babylon (see ch. 24). It is to the latter that the oracles of salvation of chapters 30–33, some of which are couched in exodus language, are directed.

40:7–10 / In the previous chapter, we learned that Nebuchadnezzar had turned Judah into a province of his vast empire and that he had chosen a native, Gedaliah, to function as the governor. Gedaliah was the man to whom Jeremiah reported after he chose to stay in Judah rather than going to Babylon.

The first group to respond to this selection was **all the army officers and their men who were still in the open country.** These appear to be elements of the Judean army that were still on the loose. Today we might call them insurgents. They could still cause some havoc even after the Babylonian defeat of Judah, and so the Babylonians issue a kind of amnesty through their Judean governor, and they appear to accept its terms.

A group of specific army officers are then named: **Ishmael son of Nethaniah, Johanan and Jonathan the sons of Kareah, Seraiah son of Tanhumeth, the sons of Ephai the Netophathite, and Jaazaniah the son of the Maacathite.** Only the first two will play a role in the events of the episode narrated here.

In any case, Gedaliah assures these leaders and their followers that if they serve the Babylonians, they can stay in the land and farm and they will not be harmed.

40:11–12 / It is not only these remnants of the military who broker a deal to stay in the land. The text goes on to say that some of the Israelites who had scattered to nearby areas (**Moab, Ammon, Edom** [nations to the east of Judah] **and all the other countries**) also returned to place themselves under the protection of Gedaliah. They too turned to agricultural pursuits.

40:13–16 / In this paragraph we learn of an insidious plot that will undo the brokered peace. Gedaliah gets a clear warning from Johanan the son of Karah as well as other army leaders that Ishmael has a plan to assassinate him.

What were Ishmael's motives? The text does not say explicitly, but it could be connected to the fact that he was a part of the royal family and was a high ranking member of Zedekiah's army (41:1). He might have had royal pretensions. Or he may simply have hated and not trusted the Babylonians and those who would seem to him to be their puppets, including Gedaliah. In any case, the deceptive nature of his plot is what marks him as despicable.

In the first place, it was a preplanned conspiracy. Ishmael was in collusion with **Baalis, the king of Ammon.** It appears that Ammon was staunchly anti-Babylonian. In Jeremiah 27:1–7 we saw that Ammon was part of a coalition that considered rebellion against Babylon early in the reign of Zedekiah. We do not know whether Baalis was the ruler then or the rebel was the king before him, Amminadab II. This plot did not materialize and Jeremiah had stood against it. It is even conceivable that Gedaliah or his father had resisted it as a member of the earlier government (and as a family in agreement with Jeremiah's position). This may have been an act of revenge. Maybe the Ammonites were making a play on Judah. Some years later in 582 B.C. Nebuchadnezzar subjugated Ammon, perhaps for meddling with Judean politics in this way.

Johanan, one of the informants of the plot, volunteers to go and preemptively kill Ishmael. Gedaliah, who is portrayed as someone seeking harmony and thinking the best of people, does not heed the warning. He should have listened, because Johanan will prove to be correct when he worries that Ishmael will **take your life and cause all the Jews who are gathered around you to be scattered and the remnant of Judah to perish.**

41:1–3 / The time reference to the **seventh month** indicates either the seventh month after the destruction of Jerusalem or perhaps the seventh month of Gedaliah's rule (both of which would have been relatively close to each other). In the opening verse we learn that **Ishmael** is of **royal blood.** He was also one of the **king's officers.** High ranking officers were often related to the king, a tradition going back to Joab who was David's nephew.

The fatal blow came when Ishmael and ten of his men came to dine with Gedaliah. The fact that the assassination took place during a meal greatly diminishes Ishmael's reputation. While Gedaliah played the host trying to broker a deal, Ishmael slaughtered him while accepting his hospitality and without warning when Gedaliah would have had his guard down. The repetition of Gedaliah's parentage (**son of Ahikam, the son of Shaphan**) may have been a way of reminding the reader that the governor came from a line of godly men who supported the prophet. But the fact that Gedaliah is also described as **the one whom the king of Babylon had appointed as governor over the land.** Because of this brutal act, there likely will be consequences to pay.

Ishmael's murderous treachery extended even beyond Gedaliah. The text informs us that he also **killed all the Jews who were with Gedaliah at Mizpah** and the **Babylonian soldiers.**

41:4–9 / Ishmael's atrocities do not stop at this point. The day after the assassination, eighty men came through the area on their way to Jerusalem to make an offering at **the house of the Lord.** These men were coming from the north, specifically from Shechem, Shiloh, and Samaria. It is unclear who exactly these men were. All three cities were important centers in the northern kingdom. It could be that they were Judeans who had fled to the north in the light of the arrival of the Babylonian army, but it is perhaps more likely that they were northerners who worshiped the Lord and were grieving over the events that had just befallen the temple.

Did the fact that they were coming to the house of the Lord to make offerings indicate that they did not know that the temple had been destroyed? That is doubtful. The fact that they were coming with grain offerings and incense and not animal sacrifices is likely an indication that they knew that the temple had been destroyed and that they could not offer animal sacrifices. They were likely going to the site of the destroyed temple to make these offerings. And it is likely that, though their intentions may have been good, their actions would have been in one sense futile. After all, God had abandoned the temple before its destruction (Ezek. 9–11), so the site held no real theological significance at the moment.

Even so, none of this minimizes the brutality of Ishmael's actions. They came mourning; they **had shaved off their beards, torn their clothes and cut themselves.** They were distraught over these events, and Ishmael deceived them by mimicking their mournful posture (**weeping as he went**). He thus dupes them into coming to Mizpah on the ruse of meeting Gedaliah. When they come to Mizpah, he kills seventy of them and throws their bodies into a cistern, apparently the same cistern into which he had thrown the body of Gedaliah. This cistern was apparently a well-known landmark since it was identified as the one that **King Asa** (913–873 B.C.) of the southern kingdom had built during his wars with King Baasha (900–877 B.C.) of the north early in the history of the divided kingdom (see 1 Kgs. 15:9–24; 15:33–16:7, with the comment that Asa had built up Mizpah). Perhaps Asa and Baasha are also mentioned here because these worshipers were from northern cities and Ishmael was a southerner.

It is unclear why Ishmael perpetrated this act. That it was not done out of principle may be seen by the fact that he allowed ten of the men to live when they told him that they had hidden provisions (**we have wheat and barley, oil and honey, hidden in a field**). The account serves the purpose of heightening our distaste for this brutal figure and reinforcing the fact that he was further disrupting any possible start to a restoration after the judgment.

41:10 / This verse tells us that Ishmael not only killed a number of people, but he also **took captive the rest of the people who were there in Mizpah.** It is possible that this may include only the most significant citizens (probably even including Jeremiah and Baruch), but especially notable was the capture of **the king's daughters.** These women would be the daughters of King Zedekiah and were an especially important prize. This is the first time we have heard about the king's daughters. Zedekiah's sons were killed by the Babylonians upon the defeat of Judah, but apparently the daughters were not only allowed to live, but were permitted to stay in Judah.

It is possible, though only speculation, that the reason why Ishmael is taking these women to Ammon is because Baalis, who is directing Ishmael here, is interested in marrying into the family of David in order to have some kind of claim on the land. Perhaps Baalis is foolishly thinking that if he, through Ishmael, destroyed the Babylonian garrison and its Judean puppets he might be able to exert hegemony over the area. This might be the significance behind the fact that Ishmael **took them captive and set out to cross over to the Ammonites.**

41:11–14 / **Johanan the son of Kareah** had earlier tried to warn Gedaliah about the plot to assassinate him (Jer. 40:13–14). Now he sets out to rescue those whom Ishmael had kidnapped and to avenge the deaths of Gedaliah and the others. The band overtook Ishmael at **the great pool in Gibeon.** This pool had been the location of an earlier fight between the men of David and those, including Abner, who for the moment were still loyal to the house of Saul (2 Sam. 2:8–3:5). The present fight, if there was one, is not described, but may be implied by the fact that Ishmael had only **eight** men with him when he escaped (earlier he was said to have ten men with him). The text simply says that those who were kidnapped came over to Johanan. Ishmael and his remaining men **fled to the Ammonites,** whose king had sponsored their activities.

Additional Notes §83

41:1 / The fact that the events of the chapter take place in the **seventh month** is particularly significant for the episode narrated in 41:4–9. After all, a number of important religious rituals took place in the seventh month and this may give background to their pilgrimage. The Day of Atonement, for instance, was observed in the seventh month (Lev. 16), as was the Feast of Trumpets and the Feast of Tabernacles (see Num. 29).

41:4 / The eighty men who were on pilgrimage to Jerusalem **had shaved off their beards, torn their clothes and cut themselves.** On the surface of it, Deuteronomy 14:1–2 as well as Leviticus 19:28 and 21:5 seem to identify these as foreign rituals that are forbidden to the Israelites. However, in the first two passages it is prohibited in reference to "the dead." In the last passage, the practice is not specified as relating to the dead, but it is forbidden for priests.

However, even granting that this practice was not legitimate, it does not seem likely that we should understand Ishmael as a kind of Jehu figure who was killing to purify Israel from false worship. The stance of the text seems decidedly anti-Ishmael. It does not extol him, but portrays him as a wild-eyed murderer. His killing of defenseless worshipers, even if they are misguided in their practice, was a further cause for condemnation.

41:4 / The worshipers came from **Shechem, Shiloh and Samaria.** These were three cities important to early Israelite history. Shechem and Samaria were former capitals of the northern kingdom. Shiloh was the place where the tabernacle was kept during the period of the Judges (1 Sam. 1–4). We should also remember that Josiah had earlier extended his religious reform to the north (2 Kgs. 23:19–20).

41:12 / The fact that the encounter between Johanan and Ishmael took place in **Gibeon** is a bit confusing in that Gibeon is southwest of Mizpah, while Ammon, Ishmael's final destination, is southeast. We can presume that there was some kind of unknown exigency that demanded that Ishmael not go directly to Ammon.

§84 Forced to Go to Egypt (Jer. 41:16–43:13)

The remnant in Judah is now faced with a hard decision. Should they stay in Judah and perhaps face an angry Nebuchadnezzar or should they flee to Egypt?

41:16–18 / By virtue of the murder of Gedaliah and his own defeat of Ishmael, Johanan found himself as the de facto leader of the remnant of Judah. His first reaction was to take them all away from Judah and go to Egypt in order to find safe haven. The remnant is described as **the soldiers, women, children and court officials.** Johanan reasonably expected that Nebuchadnezzar would mobilize his army to punish those who had overrun his garrison and decimated his provincial government by killing Gedaliah. On the way, the Judeans stopped at a site named **Geruth Kimham,** noted only here in the Bible, where it says it was near the better known city of **Bethlehem,** about four miles south of Jerusalem. Perhaps this village was named after the person Kimham who is known from the David narrative (2 Sam. 19:37–40).

Egypt was the intended destination for refuge from Babylon. Egypt was no friend of Babylon. They probably already suspected that Nebuchadnezzar considered their nation his ultimate prize. The Judeans could hardly flee elsewhere since most of the rest of the Near East was already subjugated. And of course Ammon was not a possibility since Johanan and the others worked against the strategy of their king Baalis by interfering with the murderous plot of Ishmael.

42:1–6 / With Gedaliah dead, it appears that **Johanan,** the military leader who rescued the remnant of Judah from Ishmael, had assumed the leadership role. Also specifically mentioned is **Jezaniah son of Hoshaiah.** Some scholars (Lundbom, *Jeremiah 37–52*, p. 129) think that he is the brother of Azariah son of Hoshaiah in 43:2, while others (Fretheim, *Jeremiah*, p. 545) think there is a textual confusion and that the name should read Azariah in both places. We know nothing beyond the titles of Jezaniah/Azariah anyway.

There is also the mention of other military leaders, some of whom might be those listed in 40:8.

In any case, these leaders now appeal to God through Jeremiah for guidance about what to do next. They know they are in a very difficult position. Thanks to Ishmael's actions they know that Nebuchadnezzar will come soon to restore order in his new province, and he might not care to distinguish the culprits from those who remained loyal. That thought would lead them to flee Judah to Egypt; indeed, they were already en route (41:17). However, to leave Judah would be a dangerous proposition.

Thus, they come to Jeremiah and ask him to **pray to the LORD** for guidance. Their prayer is right and proper. It is God who should tell them **where we should go and what we should do.**

Jeremiah readily receives their request. He likely was encouraged by their earnest desire to seek the guidance of Yahweh in this matter. He promises them that he will inform them of the answer (**I will tell you everything the LORD your God will tell us where we should go and what we should do**).

The people then respond and put themselves totally at God's disposal. They promise on oath that they will do whatever God tells them to do whether they want to or not. They even invoke Yahweh as their **witness** to their promise to behave in such a way. Again, this attitude is the right one, the one that would have kept Israel from the judgment that just befell them as a nation.

42:7–18 / After a period of **ten days,** God spoke to Jeremiah. Presumably, Jeremiah had spent those ten days praying to God to provide an answer to his inquiry. The form of the divine response is not clear, but Jeremiah spells out its contents in detail.

Once he received the divine response, Jeremiah called together **Johanan** and the others who had pledged themselves to follow God's advice. There are two parts to the response, the first has to do with God's instructions and what will happen if they follow those instructions. The second has to do with the consequences of disobedience.

In many ways, the form of the response follows a typical covenant structure. God is giving the people instructions (law) backed by sanctions (rewards and punishments). The fact that the people have called on God as witness to this transaction further suggests this identification. In this light, we might remember that the destruction of Jerusalem took place because Judah had broken the law of the covenant and so received the penalty of the curses. Now the remnant of Judah will have another chance.

God instructs Johanan and company to stay in the land. They need not flee Nebuchadnezzar because God is with them. If they follow this advice they will not be destroyed but rather will be established and prosper. The consequences are tellingly spelled out using the language of Jeremiah's call (repeated a number of times in the book) found in 1:10. According to 42:10 if they stay, God promises, **I will build you up and not tear you down; I will plant you and not uproot you.**

Interestingly, God then says that his motivation for such a promise is that he is **grieved** over the disaster that he inflicted on them. Earlier in Jeremiah (i.e., 18:8, 10), this verb (*nkhm*) was used to indicate what God would do if the people repented. He announced their judgment but would relent or change his mind if they repented. We are not to think that God came to believe he made a mistake in the judgment of the exile. But we are to recognize that God loves his people so much that it hurt him to have to judge them and he is looking passionately for an opportunity to restore them. As we will see, though, the people will once again miss their opportunity to experience God's compassion.

But before hearing the response of the people to the divine instruction to stay in Palestine, Jeremiah made clear to them the consequences of disobeying. If they say, **we will go and live in Egypt,** then they will bring on themselves punishments that are similar to those listed in Deuteronomy 28 for those who break the covenant. By fleeing they think they will be avoiding war and famine (v. 14), but in reality they will find in Egypt **sword, famine and plague** (see Additional Notes on 14:12).

42:19–22 / After delivering the divine oracle, Jeremiah then follows up with some hard words of his own. His statement may imply that he already knew what decision the leaders and people had made. He addresses them as the remnant of Judah and says that they made a fatal mistake. They asked him to seek the Lord's instructions and promised to obey it no matter what. However, he says to them, **you still have not obeyed the LORD your God in all he sent me to tell you.** Thus, they will become the recipients of all the above-mentioned punishments within the land of Egypt.

43:1–3 / As anticipated in Jeremiah's report of the divine decision, **Azariah** (see comment on 42:1–6) and **Johanan,** the two named leaders, as well as all the **arrogant men** erupted with an angry rejection of Jeremiah's proposal to stay in Judah. The arrogance, of course, is a function of their putting their own opinion above that of the Lord's will.

In essence, they accuse Jeremiah of being a false prophet (**You are lying! The Lord has not sent you to say**). They also curiously accuse him of being a puppet of Baruch (**Baruch son of Neriah is inciting you**), whom they imply is a toady of the Babylonians. We know Baruch as Jeremiah's scribe (Jer. 36, see also ch. 45), but something has given these people the impression that Baruch is calling the shots. Their reaction is desperate, and since the accusation of Jeremiah as false prophet is wrong, so is their statement that he was put up to it by Baruch.

Neither do we know why the Judeans have moved from their position of complete openness to God's leading through Jeremiah to this utter rejection of the divine word. Perhaps they expected a different response or perhaps the ten-day delay had so raised their anxiety about Babylonian retribution that they cannot think straight. Whatever the reason, their oath to Jeremiah in 42:5–6 now comes back to condemn them.

43:4–7 / Johanan and the other leaders followed through on their rejection of God's will that they stay in the land, taking all who were with them, including those whom the Babylonian authorities allowed to stay in the land as well as those who had returned to Judah from the nearby nations where they had fled in the face of the Babylonian onslaught. Specifically mentioned are **the king's daughters, Jeremiah,** and **Baruch.** They took them to Egypt as far as **Tahpanhes** (see Additional Notes).

43:8–13 / The Jewish leaders had hoped to escape the punishment of the king of Babylon by fleeing to Egypt. By refusing the divine word spoken through Jeremiah they were also fleeing from God. But the sad truth was that they would escape neither.

God still speaks through Jeremiah even though they were in the pagan land of Egypt, directing the prophet in a symbolic action that will make vivid the oracles. He is to speak his prophecy after he takes **some of the large stones and bury them in clay in the brick pavement at the entrance to Pharaoh's palace in Tahpanhes.** Perhaps the Egyptians put the Judeans to manual labor on their arrival, though the advanced age of Jeremiah at this time would keep us from thinking that he was hauling large stones by himself.

No matter what the conditions were for this action, its significance is clear. Nebuchadnezzar would set up his throne on the spot marked by these stones. And he would defeat Egypt and kill and exile the people there. Just as he burned the temple in Jerusalem, so he will burn the temples of the Egyptian gods, including the one dedicated to that most important deity, the sun god.

Fretheim points out that this return to Egypt is a type of reversal of the exodus. Just as God defeated Egypt at that time; he will use Nebuchadnezzar to once again undermine it (Fretheim, *Jeremiah,* pp. 556–58). Historically there is some ambiguity over the extent of Nebuchadnezzar's involvement in Egypt. Josephus provides some evidence that he invaded in 582 B.C., and Babylonian sources suggest that he attacked the Egypt of Pharaoh Amasis in 568 B.C. Although he invaded it, he did not completely subjugate it.

Additional Notes §84

43:7 / Johanan and the other Jewish leaders forced the remnant, including the prophet, to go to Egypt. Here **Tahpanhes** is specifically mentioned (see also 2:16). This site is commonly identified with Tell Defeneh, which is a little west of Qantara in the eastern region of the Nile Delta. It is on a major route leading to Syria-Palestine. It was partially excavated by Petrie in the late nineteenth century. Abundant Greek artifacts lead to the conclusion that it was a place where Egyptians situated Greek mercenaries in the seventh and sixth centuries B.C. See J. Hoffmeier, *Israel in Egypt* (New York: Oxford, 1997), p. 190.

43:9 / Perhaps **the Pharaoh's palace in Tahpanhes** is to be identified with the large structure uncovered by archaeologists at Tell Defeneh. Though Tahpanhes was not a capital, the palace may be a center of regional government.

§85 *Idolatry and Its Consequences (Jer. 44:1–30)*

One would think that the events of the past few decades would have made the people sensitive to Jeremiah's guidance and obedient to the Lord. In Judah they had witnessed God's word through Jeremiah come to a horrible reality in the destruction of Jerusalem. But in the previous chapter we observed how they continued to be hard-hearted toward the Lord and his prophet. Against God's will they fled to Egypt. In this chapter, we will learn that matters get worse still. While in Egypt, they take up the worship of foreign deities, which earlier had brought God's judgment upon them.

44:1–6 / When the divine word comes to Jeremiah this time, Israelites were living in a variety of locations in Egypt. **Migdol** and **Tahpanhes** were in the Delta region. **Memphis** was an important capital city in central Egypt and **Upper Egypt** refers to the southern parts of that nation. It is unclear whether it was the group that came with Jeremiah that fanned out in the region or whether there were waves of Israelite refugees who had come at various points of time. In any case, this oracle is directed to all the Israelites in Egypt.

God reminds the Jewish residents of Egypt of the horrible disaster he had brought on them in Judah because of their worship of false gods (**they provoked me to anger by burning incense and by worshiping other gods**). He had warned them repeatedly to repent of this sin by sending prophets like Jeremiah and Ezekiel. But they refused to listen and obey, and so they experienced the awful judgment of God.

44:7–10 / But apostasy and idolatry were not only problems in the past. With the simple word **now** the oracle switches its attention from the past to the present. Incredibly, the people still have not learned their lesson. Though Jerusalem was in ruins and they had to flee the wrath of Nebuchadnezzar, the people of God still worshiped the deities of the land of Egypt. They burned

incense to these Egyptian gods. In this way, they provoke God to anger. God is again using his prophet to warn his people that they are running the great risk of experiencing his judgment yet again. They will be cut off and this time without a remnant. At the heart of their rebellion is their refusal to follow God's **law** and **the decrees** that God gave their ancestors. This is a reference to the Ten Commandments and the rest of the Mosaic law, which has as its fundamental requirement the worship of Yahweh only.

The rhetorical strategy of this oracle centers on the question **Why?** Why are God's people acting in such a foolish way? God surely knows why, but the question intends to get the hearer to think about what he or she is doing.

44:11–14 / God now announces the consequences for those who fled Judah to go to Egypt, the group being referred to as the remnant of Judah. They **were determined to go to Egypt to settle there** and now **God is determined to bring disaster on them.** They will die in Egypt, never to return to Judah. Only a **few fugitives** will return, but the bulk of them will die there rather than return to Judah as they would wish to eventually. In other words, only a few stragglers will return, not the entire community.

The Jewish inhabitants of Egypt never came to a complete end. However, from what we known about their history (see Additional Notes), they often experienced violent ends (**sword**) either because of pogroms or because Egypt itself, for which the Israelites often served as mercenaries, became the object of hostilities (first with Persia; later in the internecine war between the Seleucids and Ptolomies). They had hoped to avoid sword and famine by fleeing, but because of their actions, disaster will catch up with them.

44:15–19 / The people utterly reject the divine oracle delivered through Jeremiah. As a matter of fact, they believe that their hard times were not the result of neglecting the worship of Yahweh but rather ignoring the worship of the **Queen of Heaven** (see Additional Notes)!

It may be that the worship of the Queen of Heaven was a matter of individuals and families. Both men and women are involved in the cult, but the women seem to occupy a special place since they are the ones who are offering the special **cakes** to her (see Z. Zevit, *The Religions of Ancient Israel,* pp. 553–55). Though perhaps a family-based religion, it appears to have spread widely among the Jewish inhabitants of Egypt since the large assembly that comes together is said to come from **Lower** (northern) and **Upper** (southern) **Egypt.**

44:20–23 / Jeremiah now responds to the people's rejection of the divine oracle. He once again reminds them of their ignominious past. **The LORD remembered** the incense that the pre-exilic people of God burned to false deities. To remember entails more than cognition; it implies action. And as a result of God's remembering, after his longsuffering patience ran out, the land of Judah became **an object of cursing and a desolate waste.** It is because they have not obeyed the law (which includes the worship of Yahweh alone) that this has happened. They **can now see** it.

44:24–30 / After the preamble in verses 20–23, Jeremiah delivers a formal oracle against the rebellious people (**Hear the Word of the LORD. This is what the LORD Almighty, the God of Israel, says).** It is addressed to all the people, but the women are particularly mentioned because of their special role in the worship of the Queen of Heaven. In verse 25 the Lord indicates that he has heard them clearly. They have announced their intention to continue their offensive and false worship.

In the light of this explicit statement, God will now give up his attempts through the prophet to persuade them otherwise (**Go ahead then, do what you promised! Keep your vows!**). But he will now be clear with them about the consequences of his actions. He had warned them about it earlier (44:7–14), but now he takes an oath (**I swear by my great name**) that he will follow through on his threat. With the exception of a very few individuals (**those who return to the land of Judah from Egypt will be very few**), they will perish in the land where they fled and chose to worship false gods.

In addition to this long-term punishment, God also names a specific near-term sign of his displeasure. **Hophra** (also known in Herodotus as Apries; 587–570 B.C.) was the pharaoh of Egypt when these refugees from Judah arrived. They would only have been allowed in at the pleasure of his government, so we might imagine that he was considered a protector of these people. However, God's long arm will see to the end of Hophra through his enemies. Hophra was displaced by one of his generals, Amasis, who became the next pharaoh of Egypt. Three years later Hophra was killed. Hophra was the pharaoh who marched out against the Babylonians while Jerusalem was under siege (37:5). The Egyptians only temporarily distracted the Babylonians.

Chronologically speaking, this oracle is the last of Jeremiah's prophetic utterances. Nowhere in the Bible is Jeremiah's death described. Tradition records that he died in Egypt. Even though this was the last oracle Jeremiah delivered during his lifetime, chapter 45 narrates one concerning Baruch that came much earlier in his life. Chapters 46–51 contain the oracles against the nations, also coming earlier in time.

Additional Notes §85

44:1 / Because the Nile flows from south to north, the southern region is referred to as **Upper Egypt** and the northern as Lower Egypt.

44:11–14 / The postexilic Jewish community is known from extra-biblical texts like the Elephantine papyri. The Jewish community located at Elephantine was a military garrison and the inhabitants were mercenaries. The origin of this community is not known, but they were there before the Persians defeated the Egyptians around 520 B.C. Hence, they may be connected to this group that fled in the early exilic period. The most interesting texts from Elephantine derive from the decade between 420–410 B.C. It is in this period that there is correspondence between an official named Hananiah who is relaying instructions from the Great King Darius II and the Egyptian satrap Arsames to the Jewish leaders at Elephantine concerning the observance of Passover. The addressee was Jedaniah known as a religious leader of the Elephatine community. What is most interesting about this letter is that it confirms a pattern of Persian involvement in the authorization of Jewish religious practices, but precisely what was at issue here (the date, the combination of Passover and Unleavened Bread, the practice of Passover in Egypt, which might be sensitive for obvious reasons) is unclear. It is some years later, 411 or 410, that we have another letter, this time from the above-mentioned Jedaniah to Bagohi (Bagoas), the governor of Judah, with the mention also that "we have set the whole matter forth in a letter in our name to Delaiah and Shelemiah, the sons of Sanballat the governor of Samaria." This Sanballat is likely the opponent of Nehemiah mentioned in Neh. 2:10, 19, which confirms the fact that he was governor. In any case the letter appeals to these two governors for permission to rebuild the temple devoted to "Yaho" (YHWH) that had been destroyed by the Egyptian priests of Khnum with the consent of an official whose name was Vidranga. In this letter they make mention of another letter that they sent concerning the matter of rebuilding to Johanan the high priest (Neh. 12:22–23), but this letter has gone unanswered. Interestingly, the finds have also yielded a memorandum of an oral response from the Judean governor and from the son of the Samarian governor to the effect that they gave permission to rebuild the temple, though permission to offer animal sacrifices is conspicuously absent, perhaps indicating a belief that this should be done only in Jerusalem. There is a contract from the Anani archive, a collection of thirteen documents found at Elephantine that relate to a family of that name, that indicates that the temple was up and operating by 402 B.C.

In the third to second centuries B.C., the Egyptian Jewish community in Alexandria is known for having produced the Septuagint, that is, the Greek translation of the Hebrew Bible.

44:17 / The **Queen of Heaven** is a reference to a female astral deity in the pantheon of the surrounding nations. The fact that the Hebrew word **cakes** (v. 19) is an Akkadian loan word, and its use in the Gilgamesh Epic (vi, 59) in reference to offerings to Ishtar, the goddess of love, war, and sex associated with the planet Venus, suggests that there is an association between this deity and the Queen of Heaven. However, it is possible that the direct reference is to her Canaanite reflection, probably Ashtart or Asherah. Her worship in Egypt may indicate that there is an equivalent deity there. See reference to her worship in preexilic Judah in 7:28.

§86 An Oracle Concerning Baruch (Jer. 45:1–5)

Unexpectedly, the book of Jeremiah continues with a short oracle directed toward Baruch, best known from chapter 36 as the prophet's scribe and assistant. The fact that this section of the book ends with this oracle may indicate that Baruch played a significant role in the final form of the book. The oracle is favorable toward him but does not aggrandize his life or achievements. Indeed, its purpose is largely to put Baruch in his place and get him to appreciate the blessings that he does receive from the Lord.

However, according to one theory, the placement of this passage might not be unexpected. Many believe that chapter 36 and 45, in both of which Baruch plays a large role, bracket a section of the book of Jeremiah which incorporates the memoirs of Baruch who had a large hand in the final form of the book.

45:1–3 / The oracle is directed toward a specific individual, namely **Baruch son of Neriah.** This is not the only oracle delivered to an individual. We can compare the oracles to Pashhur the priest in 20:4–6 and to Ebed-Melech the Cushite in 39:15–18. Later we will see one directed to Seraiah son of Neriah in 51:59–64.

Baruch is best known as Jeremiah's assistant and scribe, functioning in that way in Jeremiah 32 when Jeremiah purchased land from his cousin Hanamel and Jeremiah 36 when Baruch copied down Jeremiah's prophecies. He was also mentioned in 43:1–3 in a context where it is clear that some people think that Baruch was influential over Jeremiah rather than vice versa. Many think that Baruch was responsible for the final form of the book of Jeremiah, preserving, arranging, and perhaps supplementing the prophet's oracles after his death.

The oracle is dated to **the fourth year of Jehoiakim,** 605 B.C., the year of the events recorded in Jeremiah 36. Indeed, it is more specifically the time after Baruch **had written on a scroll the words Jeremiah was then dictating.**

The occasion for the oracle is Baruch's complaint: **Woe to me! The LORD has added sorrow to my pain; I am worn out with groaning and find no rest.** We are not given the context for this statement, but we can imagine that it is connected to the fact that he was the assistant of a very unpopular prophet. He was the one who delivered the negative news not only to the people but also to some very powerful individuals.

Interestingly, Baruch was not the only one to complain. Jeremiah's complaints are as famous as they are powerful (see, for instance, 20:7–18). Even so, God used Jeremiah not so much to assure Baruch as to remind him of the situation and his place.

45:4–5 / God begins by reminding him of the prime directive. The language of overthrowing, building, uprooting, and planting comes from Jeremiah's call in 1:10. God then asks Baruch, the one who helped deliver this message, **Should you then seek great things for yourself?** with the implied answer "no."

The oracle implies that Baruch was hoping to get great things because of his work. But God suggests that he will not. He should be satisfied with the fact that in the midst of all the forthcoming devastation and judgment, he will escape with his life. He will survive.

§87 Oracles against the Nations (Jer. 46:1–51:63)

The next six chapters contain Jeremiah's oracles against the nations. We are reminded that Jeremiah's commission appointed him not just over Judah, but "over nations and kingdoms to uproot and tear down, to destroy and overthrow, to build and to plant" (1:10). Similar types of oracles may be found in Isaiah 13–23; Ezekiel 25–32; Amos 1–2; Nahum, and Obadiah. Up to this point, his prophecies have been directed toward Judah announcing judgment against God's people because they broke their covenant with God. The foreign nations up to this point have been pawns in God's strategy of bringing judgment. This is particularly true of Babylon, the nation God used to destroy Jerusalem. Nevertheless, by using them, God has not given them a "free pass" from accountability. Indeed, as the oracles will express, they themselves have angered God through their actions. In particular, they are full of pride and have acted unjustly and unethically. Thus, God will judge them as well. The oracles begin with one directed toward Egypt, followed by Philistia (47:1–7), Moab (48:1–47), Ammon (49:1–6), Edom (49:7–22), Damascus (49:23–27), Kedar and Hazor (49:28–33), Elam (49:34–39), and finally, and most extensively, against Babylon (50:1–51:64). As Fretheim points out (*Jeremiah,* p. 578), there is a rough (and occasionally inconsistent) geographical order to the presentation of these oracles: "The oracles begin with the westernmost nation (Egypt), move to those in the near vicinity of Israel (Philistia, Moab, Ammon, Edom), and finally to those toward the east (Damascus, Arabia, Elam, Babylon)."

§88 Oracles against Egypt (Jer. 46:1–28)

Egypt played a significant role leading up to the destruction of Jerusalem and then afterward as well. According to ancient Near Eastern sources as well as the Bible, the Egyptians tried to stop Babylon from completely defeating the Assyrians in 609 B.C. As they proceeded up the coast to engage the Babylonians in the battle of Carchemish, they were attacked by the Judeans under the leadership of King Josiah, who was a godly king. They defeated and killed Josiah. Then after their defeat at the hands of the Babylonians, they manipulated the throne of Judah, placing the pro-Egyptian Jehoiakim on it. The book of Jeremiah shows that this king was no friend to the true God. He led Judah further astray.

Even after Jehoiakim, the kings of Judah would often place their confidence in Egypt in order to save them from the Babylonians. It was this false trust that likely led Jehoiakim and Zedekiah to revolt against Babylon, acts that led to their death. This hope was ephemeral, however. Even on the occasion when an Egyptian threat turned the Babylonian army away from the walls of Jerusalem (Jer. 37:11), it was only a temporary respite.

After the fall of Jerusalem, many Israelites fled to Egypt for refuge. Jeremiah considered this a lack of trust in the power of the true God (41:16–43:13).

Following a superscription that introduces the oracles against the foreign nations as a whole (46:1), the chapter contains three oracles against Egypt (vv. 1–12, vv. 13–24, and vv. 25–26), plus an oracle of encouragement directed to Judah (vv. 27–29). All but the third oracle is in poetic format.

46:1–12 / The first oracle is preceded by a superscription that introduces the whole section of oracles against the foreign nations that extends through chapter 51 (v. 1: **This is the word of the LORD that came to Jeremiah the prophet concerning the nations**). The first set of these oracles is against Egypt and is introduced at the beginning of verse 2 by the simple prepositional phrase, **Concerning Egypt.**

The second verse continues by giving a precise setting for the first oracle against Egypt as **the fourth year of Jehoiakim son of Josiah king of Judah.** The year is 605 B.C., and the reference to the battle of Carchemish on the Euphrates River is confirmed by its mention in the Babylonian Chronicle. However, the title **king** is granted to **Nebuchadnezzar** in hindsight because he did not actually become king until some months after this battle.

The form of verses 3–12 is that of an event-vision that anticipates a future event. If that is the correct interpretation, then the introduction in verse 2 would have been added after the event. An event-vision describes a future event as if it is unfolding before the prophet's eyes. In Nahum 2:3–10, for instance, the prophet sees the fate of the city of Nineveh as clearly as if he were there. He captures the downfall of the city with vivid descriptions of the battle and reactions to Nineveh's destruction.

The passage begins with commands that would be typical before a battle. They are to prepare their battle gear (**shields, helmets, spears, armor**) and to ready their **horses.** But in spite of their preparation they are defeated and the next thing we know the prophetic voice is reporting their retreat in defeat. It is a chaotic and fruitless retreat, however. Not even the **swift** can flee and they **stumble and fall** by the **River Euphrates,** which may provide a natural barrier to their flight. The consequences are not explicitly stated but death and complete destruction of the army is implied.

In verse 7 the oracle changes tone and describes the enormous pride of Egypt. This pride takes us back again before the battle. The **Nile** River was the pride of Egypt. All its fertility and its tremendous wealth depend on an annual flooding of the Nile. As the waters receded it left behind productive soil. All of Egypt's population lived close to the banks of the Nile, because to wander too far from it would bring them into desolate desert areas.

The nation of Egypt is here compared to the Nile in its rising out of its natural boundaries in order to cover the earth. In other words, the surging Nile is used as a metaphor of Egypt's imperialistic impulses that were operative in their attempt to fight Babylon in far away Carchemish. They want to cover the earth like the flooding Nile covers the ground.

Verse 9 then reverts to commands directed to the Egyptian army to engage in battle. **Cush, Put,** and **Lydia** were allied with the Egyptians and their people would have been an integral part of the Egyptian army (see Additional Notes).

Verse 10 now describes why Egypt's pride will be thwarted and its army unsuccessful. It is not because of the power of the Babylonian army, but rather because of God himself. **That day belongs to the LORD.** In other words, it is a day of the Lord, a day of his warring activity. He will see to it that Egypt is defeated by the Babylonians. Indeed, the death of the Egyptians on the battlefield is described using the language of the religious cult. The Lord **offers sacrifice** by their death. For a similar use of sacrifice in the context of battle, see Ezekiel 39:17–20.

Their wound is mortal; there is **no healing.** Earlier in Jeremiah, the theme of the incurable wound was applied to Judah (8:18–9:2). Here, as there, not even the precious balm of **Gilead** would help. Interestingly, in this context God's compassion for even Egypt is expressed through the epithet **Virgin Daughter of Egypt** (see Additional Notes). Even so, the downfall of her armies is certain and the result is that Egypt's overweening pride will be turned to **shame** as their warriors **fall down together.**

46:13–24 / The second Egyptian oracle concerns **the coming of Nebuchadnezzar king of Babylon to attack Egypt.** As we will see, it describes a rather decisive defeat of Egypt using the metaphor of men using axes to **chop down her forest** (v. 23). Relating this to a known event is somewhat difficult. Whether the oracle describes a past, current, or future event does not make it any easier since from our modern perspective it is past. We do know that Nebuchadnezzar and his armies had a number of military engagements with Egypt outside of the latter's borders. As crown prince he fought and defeated them in 609 and 605 B.C. There were other similar engagements, but the oracle describes an invasion of some significance into Egypt. There are some allusions in Babylonian annals and in Herodotus to an invasion in Nebuchadnezzar's thirty-seventh year, but there is little information about it. Concerning this, Lundbom (*Jeremiah 37–52,* p. 208) states "According to some Babylonian text fragments (BM 33041, 33053), Nebuchadnezzar, in his 37th year, i.e., 568 B.C., invaded Egypt in the reign of Pharaoh Amasis. It is generally agreed that Nebuchadnezzar did not conquer Egypt on this visit, but probably did invade the country as Jeremiah and Ezekiel said he would, inflicting indignities commensurate with an invasion." Lundbom also comments that there is evidence for Egyptian exiles in Babylon in the sixth century.

The oracle proper begins with Yahweh ordering that his word concerning Egypt be announced in that country, specifically in the frontier towns of **Migdol** and **Tahpanhes** (where Jeremiah and the refugees from Judah were located) as well as the capital city of **Memphis** (see 44:1).

As in the previous oracle (see 46:3–4), the announcement contains an ironic urgent command to get ready for war (**take your positions and get ready**). The command is ironic because the speaker knows full well that such preparations are going to be futile.

Verse 15 is problematic in translation and interpretation (see Additional Notes). In our understanding, the verse contains a question that mocks Egypt by imagining the flight of one of its most potent representations of deity, namely the Apis bull. This bull represented fertility and important annual rituals surrounded it. But here it is conceived as fleeing before the foreign onslaught. This verse also reveals the real reason why the bull flees and why Egypt stumbles. It is because the Lord thrust them down. The real power here is not Babylon but Yahweh.

The next verse talks about how the multitude **stumble** and **fall.** The theme of military defeat as stumbling and falling appeared earlier in the chapter (vv. 6, 11) and evokes the picture of a desperate and clumsy retreat. That these soldiers are foreign mercenaries is indicated by the fact that they are represented as saying that they will return to their **own people** and their **native lands.** Their final words ridicule their former leader, the king of Egypt. He is a loud noise, all talk and no action, full of bombast.

God then takes an oath that one will come to Egypt and lay waste to it. This one is not named in the oracle proper but is likely to be connected with Nebuchadnezzar, who is mentioned in the introduction as the one to attack Egypt (v. 13). He is described as **Tabor among the mountains** and **Carmel by the sea.** Tabor and Carmel are two of the most distinctive mountains in Israel. Tabor stands out in the midst of the plain of Megiddo. Carmel is a lushly forested mountain whose range juts out into the Mediterranean.

Verse 20 presents the metaphor of Egypt as a **beautiful heifer.** That pleasant word image is disturbed by the presence of a **gadfly.** Gadflies are small. They do not hurt or destroy the heifer, but they certainly are the source of annoyance. Perhaps this metaphor is appropriate for the historical reasons stated above, that is, while Babylon under Nebuchadnezzar did not destroy or occupy Egypt, it certainly was a source of incredible disturbance.

In verse 21 the mercenary troops who fought for Egypt are described. They are **like fattened calves** not fit for the battle; they will turn tail and run.

Yet another metaphor is presented in verse 22 where Egypt is likened to a hissing **serpent.** The serpent was an important symbol in Egypt. Indeed, the pharaoh had a representation of the coiled serpent (the uraeus) on his headdress. But though the serpent hisses, it stands no chance against the enemy that comes like a **locust** plague, or like men who cut down trees. The Daughter of Egypt (see v. 11) will be shamed as they find defeat at the hands of the people of the **north.**

46:25–26 / The third oracle directed against Egypt is in prose. It is not precisely dated, but the future defeat of Israel is associated with **Nebuchadnezzar, king of Babylon,** who ruled from 605–562 B.C. As mentioned above in regard to the oracle in verses 13–24, while there is no evidence of a massive defeat of Egypt during Nebuchadnezzar's reign, there is evidence of an invasion when significant damage was inflicted.

The oracle anticipates punishment coming **on Amon god of Thebes, on Pharaoh, on Egypt and her gods and her kings, and on those who rely on Pharaoh.** Either there is some repetition in this list (**Pharaoh/her kings**) or else the reference to kings is to officials just below Pharaoh. In any case, the punishment is said to fall first on Amon, who is arguably the most important deity in Egyptian religion (see Additional Notes) and then on Pharaoh, certainly the most important human being in Egypt. Of course, Pharaoh was also thought to be a god. Punishment is then more generally said to fall on **gods, kings,** and **those who rely on Pharaoh,** the latter referring to everyone who lives in Egypt. It may also be a specific jibe at those Judeans who fled to find refuge from judgment in Egypt. The expression is a way of saying "gods, rulers, and people." This punishment will let none escape.

The oracle makes it clear that this punishment will not be so severe that it will bring Egypt to an end. It anticipates the continuation of Egypt in the land (**Later, however, Egypt will be inhabited as in times past**). After Nebuchadnezzar, Egypt continued under its own native dynasty for a few more decades until they were defeated by the Persian king Cambyses in campaigns that lasted from 525–522 B.C. Even then, Egypt was able to revert to native rulers for a while after that.

46:27–28 / After three oracles directed toward Egypt, the chapter ends with an oracle directed toward exiled Judah that seeks to comfort and assure them (see the nearly identical statement in 30:10–11). In the midst of the judgment of the nations, the exiles that are in these countries are told that they will survive even if the country that they are in is completely devastated. God addresses the exiles by referring to them as **my servant,** a term of endearment. They are told not to fear in spite of the threats that surround them.

This oracle anticipates the period of the restoration that will begin after Persia defeats Babylon and allows for the return of the exiles to Judah. The comfort that God extends to Judah is based on his presence even while they are in exile. The declaration of this presence is stated with a phrase (**I am with you**) that indicates a continuing covenant relationship.

It is not that Judah has or will escape pain. After all they are being punished (**I will not let you go unpunished**), but there is a limit to this punishment. They will get only what they deserve and no more (**I will discipline you but only with justice**).

Additional Notes §88

46:9 / Three ethnic groups are here associated with the Egyptian army: **Cush, Put,** and **Lydia.** Genesis 10:6 lists Cush and Put as well as Mizraim (Hebrew for Egypt) as sons of Ham. The Cushites were from south of Egypt proper in what is today Ethiopia and Sudan. Put is identified by scholars as Libya to the west of Egypt. There is debate about the identity of Lydia. Most likely this reference is to the Lydians of eastern Asia Minor. The presence of this last group may account for the modern discovery of a bronze Greek shield on the battlefield of Carchemish.

46:11 / **Balm** "was probably the resin of the storax tree, obtained by incision on the bark of the tree" (*IVPBBCOT,* p. 650). It was used in the treatment of wounds. See Nahum 3:19 for the use of the incurable wound theme as directed toward Assyria.

Egypt is referred to here as the **Virgin Daughter of Egypt** (see also vv. 19 and 24). This term of endearment expresses God's concern for the other nations of the world that are thought of as his children. But its use in a context of judgment like this should probably be taken as ironic. Earlier in Jeremiah Judah is referred to as God's virgin daughter, also often in the context of judgment (17:17; 18:13; 31:4).

46:15 / The NIV's rendition of this verse differs from many others. NIV translates **Why will your warriors be laid low? They cannot stand, for the LORD will push them down.** The NRSV is representative of another approach when it translates

> Why has Apis fled?
> Why did your bull not stand?
> —because the LORD thrust him down.

The verse obviously is difficult. The NIV takes the Masoretic Text pretty much as it stands. The noun *ʾabbir* means "strong one." It can refer to humans (NIV takes it as "warriors," but there are places where it is in parallel with "stallion" [Jer. 8:16; 47:3; 50:11]) or can mean "bull" (Isa. 34:7; Ps. 22:17). The NRSV puts this word in the second colon and translates it bull as a reference to Apis. Working back, where does NRSV come up with "Apis"? The Septuagint translates it this way and this indicates that perhaps the words are not properly divided in the MT. The MT has *maddua*ᶜ *niskhaf ʾabbireka* and taking *niskhap* as a *niphal* of a verb *sakhap* and *ʾabbir* as "warrior," the NIV comes up with its translation. NRSV, taking its cue from the Greek, takes the first colon as *maddua*ᶜ *nas khaf.* The verb is *nas* from *nus* meaning "to flee," while *haf* is a reference to Apis, the divine bull that represents fertility. All in all, NRSV has the strongest textual argument and produces a text that makes a lot of sense.

46:25 / The god **Amon** of Thebes was one of the most important deities of Egypt. The city of **Thebes** was an important Egyptian city 325 miles south of Memphis. Indeed, it served as the capital of Upper Egypt since the early second millennium. Asshurbanipal the Assyrian general defeated it in 663 B.C. (mentioned in Nah. 3:8 where, like here, it was called by the Hebrew name *no*ʾ), but it was still important. In any case, the worship of Amon had combined with that of the sun disk Re, and the worship of this god of Thebes had spread through the entire kingdom.

§89 Oracle against Philistia (Jer. 47:1–7)

The second oracle against a foreign nation is directed toward Philistia. The order is likely determined by geographical considerations in that Philistia was next up the coast from Egypt. The Philistines have a long history in the Bible. We first hear about Philistines in the book of Genesis (Gen. 10:14; 21:32, 34, etc.). Many take these early references as anachronistic, which may be the case, or else they are indications of an early incursion of the Philistines into Canaan. In any case, it is true that the bulk of Philistine occupation of the coastal region of Canaan came in the twelfth century B.C. as part of the Sea People's movement. They probably originated somewhere in the Aegean and came east via Crete (Caphtor, see v. 4). After trying and failing to establish a beachhead in the Delta region of Egypt, they moved up the coast and settled in Canaan. The core of Philistia centered on their five capital cities each with their own king (Gaza, Ekron, Ashkelon, Ashdod, and Gath). They held a stubborn presence in Canaan until the time of David, who in effect removed them as a rival power in the area. Even so, the remnant of their presence was maintained until the sixth century. The devastation that is anticipated in this oracle, however, eradicates the Philistines from history.

47:1 / The prose superscription that introduces the oracle chronologically situates its delivery to the time **before Pharaoh attacked Gaza.** Unfortunately, we cannot date this event with precision. It may refer to the time after Nebuchadnezzar made an abortive attempt to invade Egypt in 601 B.C. Pharaoh Neco repulsed him at Migdol and in pursuit of the retreating Babylonian army took **Gaza** (according to Herodotus). Alternatively, this may be associated with the Egyptian move through Palestine in 609 B.C., as Neco moved to encounter the Babylonians at Carchemish (so Fretheim, *Jeremiah,* p. 589). As we will observe again, it may be that Gaza was taken more than once by Egypt in the give-and-take skirmishes between Babylon and Egypt that marked this period of time.

47:2–5 / The mention of the Egyptian defeat of **Gaza** should be taken only as a chronological indication of when the oracle was delivered. It is not part of the oracle, even though in verse 5 Gaza will again be mentioned as experiencing defeat. However, within the oracle proper the threat to Philistia and to Gaza comes not from Egypt but from the north. The metaphor of **overflowing** floodwaters from the **north** points rather to Babylon as the threat to Philistia. This likely refers to a recorded Babylonian incursion into Palestine with explicit mention of Ashkelon that took place in 604 B.C.

This flood is metaphorical. The roaring waters are really the galloping din of cavalry, the rumble of chariot wheels, and march of infantry as the Babylonians swept into Philistia. Indeed, the onslaught is so terrible that even **fathers** who would naturally help their children are paralyzed out of fear.

In the context of the destruction of Philistia the two Phoenician seaport powers of **Tyre** and **Sidon** are mentioned. These cities were further north up the coast in what is today Lebanon. Now that the Philistines are overtaken, they cannot provide further aid to their trading partners in the north. Of course, Nebuchadnezzar was also interested in capturing Sidon and Tyre. The former submitted to him before the fall of Jerusalem in 586 B.C., and the latter endured a thirteen year siege by the Babylonians from 585–573 B.C. The siege ended with the bulk of the city, excluding the island portion, captured.

Verse 4b returns the focus to Philistia with the general comment that God will destroy it (for reference to Caphtor, see the introduction to this passage). Two cities are mentioned, Gaza (see comments above that suggests that this defeat is different than the one mentioned in v. 1) and Ashkelon. Here the cites are personified. Gaza will shave their head in mourning, referring to a ritual of mourning that may also evoke the idea of Babylon shaving them as captives. And Ashkelon will be silenced. A noisy city is silenced in only one way, by killing its inhabitants.

Finally, in verse 5b the remaining Philistines are called the **remnant on the plain,** since they were located in the flat land before the rolling hills of the Shephelah and the hill country of Judah proper. The Lord asks them how long will they **cut** themselves. Such cutting is an ancient mourning practice mentioned in

1 Kings 18:28 when the Baal priests cut themselves due to the non-appearance of their god. Indeed, the Ugaritic Baal texts describe the high god El cutting himself when Baal is killed by Mot.

47:6–7 / The oracle against Philistia ends with an address to the **sword of the LORD,** which is here personified and represents God's destructive power. In the Hebrew it is unclear who is speaking to the sword. The NIV adds **you cry** but this is not found in the Hebrew (as indicated by half brackets in the NIV). This interpretation, "you cry," is the best in spite of Fretheim's suggestion (*Jeremiah*, pp. 591–2) that the Lord speaks here. In this way, he believes that the Lord is distanced from the killing to a certain extent. However, the oracle shows no interest in such distancing, for instance, in verse 4 where it says **the LORD is about to destroy the Philistines.**

The best approach is to imagine the Philistines begging the sword of the Lord to desist. But v. 7 answers their question by stating that it cannot stop as long as God has ordered it to attack.

§90 Oracle against Moab (Jer. 48:1–47)

After Egypt and Philistia, Moab is the next object of God's attention. The geographical movement is from south to north and then west to east. While Philistia is to the west of Israel, Moab is directly to the east on the eastern shores of the Dead Sea. Today, this region is occupied by the country of Jordan. It is a region typified by deep wadis and extensive plateaus.

The Bible paints the origin of the Moabites in dark colors. In Genesis 19, after the destruction of Sodom and Gomorrah and the death of Lot's wife, Lot's daughters get him drunk and have intercourse with him. The products of this act are two boys named Ammon and Moab.

Later, when Israel is freed from Egyptian bondage and travels toward the promised land, they have to pass through Moabite territory. King Balak of Moab recruits a pagan prophet named Balaam to try to stop or even destroy them (Num. 21–23). When this strategy fails, the women of Moab seduce the men to worship foreign gods (Num. 25). Only the quick actions of a priest named Phinehas saves the day. For this reason, the law of Moses forbids any Moabite or their descendants for ten generations to enter the sacred assembly (Deut. 23:3–6).

During the period of the judges, Eglon of Moab oppressed part of Israel until Ehud the judge delivered them. Conflict continued with the Moabites down through Israelite history. From the Moabite side, we have a document now known as the Moabite Stone which documents a conflict between Omri the king of Israel and king Mesha of Moab. With this long difficult history in mind, the reader can appreciate the length and intensity of the oracle against Moab.

48:1–9 / After a superscription identifying Moab as the object of the oracle and God as its originator, the prophecy begins with a **woe** oracle. Ancient Israelites would say "woe" during moments of mourning, as during a funeral (see Additional Notes on

10:19–22). However, in these prophetic oracles, the woe is stated with irony. It is a way of saying that Moab is as good as dead.

The Moabite oracle is filled with references to specific place names, some of which we know better than others. It begins with **Nebo,** a city or village that should be associated with the region of the mountain which is famous as the place Moses ascended to die before the Israelites entered the promised land. In the above mentioned Moabite Stone, Mesha describes how he took Nebo back from Israel.

Kiriathaim, with its **stronghold,** will also be humiliated by being captured. This city is mentioned in Numbers 32:37; Joshua 13:19; 1 Chronicles 6:76; Ezekiel 25:9, along with Jeremiah 48:23. This site is also mentioned in the Moabite Stone.

Because of her devastating defeat, Moab will no longer be praised. Indeed, in **Heshbon men will plot her downfall.** Heshbon was on the northern boundary of Moab with Ammon and during some period of history was a Moabite city. If it still was at this time, then the idea must be that a foreign enemy has taken it over (the Babylonians most likely) and now plan to move south against Moab. Perhaps at this point Heshbon (identified with Tell Hesban, fifty miles to the east of Jerusalem), was controlled by the Ammonites (see 49:3). **Madmen** is a Moabite city of uncertain location (see Additional Notes).

The next few verses vividly describe the mourning and devastation of other locations in Moab: Horonaim and Luhith. The call goes out for them to flee from the coming destruction.

Verse 7 points to a fault that leads to Moab's captivity. They **trust in wealth** and in their own power (**deeds**). Not only will they be taken captive but their god **Chemosh** will be taken into captivity as well. This is more than a metaphor since the idols of defeated cities were usually carted away to the foreign temple of the victor.

The destruction of Moab will be extensive, even total. Mention is made of every town. Valley and plateau will be ruined. Not only that but the call goes out to put **salt** on it. This was both a symbolic act of complete devastation as well as a method of keeping the ground from producing crops. See the similar action by Abimelech after he took the city of Shechem (Judg. 9:45).

48:10 / The oracle continues with **a curse** on those commissioned by the Lord to execute his violent judgment against Moab but who refuse to do so. We are not to think that the Babylonians and others were slow to attack their enemy, but this curse is a way of expressing God's own determination and urgency in seeing to the destruction of the Moabites.

48:11–13 / The next part of the oracle likens Moab to a jar of wine that has been left to age. The metaphor is especially appropriate since Moab was a wine producing nation (Isa. 16:8–10). Thus, Moab is a premium wine (**she tastes as she did, and her aroma is unchanged**). But soon she is to be opened and exposed to the air, **poured from one jar to another.** The implication is that this wine will be spoiled (see Additional Notes). Not only that, but once poured out of its original jar, the jar itself will be smashed. The metaphor points to the upcoming **exile** of Moab. Moab had seen its battles through the centuries, but for the first time it will face the exile of its citizens. Such a fate will lead the Moabites to be embarrassed with their chief god **Chemosh,** presumably because Chemosh was unable to preserve them from exile. Such a moment is likened to the time in Israel when they trusted in **Bethel.** Since Bethel is parallel with Chemosh, it is possible that this is a reference to a god Bethel who is attested in personal names and also referenced as a god in the late fifth century B.C. documents from Elephantine. However, it could also be a reference to the place Bethel, where Jeroboam erected a golden calf shrine (1 Kgs. 13:26–33; Amos 7:13).

48:14–17 / Verse 14 begins with a taunting rhetorical question: **How can you say, "We are warriors, men valiant in battle?"** This question, directed toward Moab implies that they were not such warriors. Perhaps the implication is that they have been "at rest from youth" (v. 11), or perhaps their lack of ability as warriors anticipates their future easy defeat.

God, after all, has declared their destruction (v. 15). The call accordingly goes out to begin mourning for her. Verse 17 ends by lamenting the breaking of the **mighty scepter,** the **glorious staff,** metonymies for the monarchy of Moab.

48:18–25 / The oracle then addresses the Moabites as the **inhabitants of the Daughter of Dibon,** an important Moabite city in the heart of Moabite territory. King Mesha of the Moabite Stone describes himself as a Dibonite, likely indicating that at least at that time (mid-ninth century B.C.) it was the capital of Moab. These people are perched high in glory, but because of the invasion they must move to parched ground. Then the attention of the oracle shifts to **Aroer,** a nearby city. Here the inhabitants are drawn to the road where refugees are from Dibon and central Moab to the west. In response to their anxious question, "What has happened?" a fleeing man and a fleeing woman announce that Moab is disgraced. To specify the disaster, they list a number of sites on the Moabite plateau (**Holon, Jahzah, Mephaath, Dibon, Nebo, Beth Diblathaim, Kiriathaim, Beth Gamul, Beth Meon, Kerioth, Bozrah**). By way of climax to this part of the oracle, it is announced that Moab's horn is broken off. The **horn** is a symbol of power. The origin of the image is a synecdoche of an animal like a bull whose horns are the source of its pride and power.

48:26–28 / The next section of the oracle continues with a common prophetic theme of judgment, drunkenness (**make her drunk**). Moab will get drunk and **wallow in her vomit** and become an object of ridicule. Behind this description may be the motif of God's cup of wrath. God's enemies drink the cup of wrath that makes them deeply intoxicated and eventually does them in. In their drunken stupor the enemies are weakened and vulnerable. For other uses of this theme, see Isaiah 19:14; 51:17; Jeremiah 25:15–38; Nahum 1:10.

From the perspective of the oracle, this humiliation of Moab is only fair in light of the fact that she has humiliated Israel. This is likely a reference to the fact that, whenever Israel was put in a vulnerable condition (as when Babylon threatened them), Moab took advantage of the situation.

For this reason judgment is coming, so they are well advised to seek refuge in the numerous caves that dot the deep ravines (like that of the Arnon) of Moab. Indeed, they should make themselves like the doves that make their nests in such caves.

48:29–39 / This section of the oracle against Moab is close to that found in Isaiah 16:6–12. Moab's **pride** was a well-known fact. Their excessive pride is emphasized in these two verses by frequent repetition of the word pride or a synonym (**conceit, arrogance, haughtiness, insolence, boasts**)

Because of its pride, the Lord weeps for **Moab,** naming specifically the men of **Kir Hareseth,** a city in the southern portion of Moab. **Jazer** is further north on the border with Ammon, and **Sibmah** is of uncertain location. Jazer weeps for itself as God weeps for Sibmah.

Moab is here likened to a grape vine, appropriate for a region with a reputation for grape production and wine making.

This vine had spread far and wide, representing the prosperity of Moab in the past. The **sea,** in the case, surely refers to the Dead Sea.

However, a destroyer, a foreign invader probably to be identified with Babylon, has ravished this vine, and now joy is gone from their fields. No longer is this region able to produce wine. The **shouts of joy** have turned into shouts of fear and suffering.

These sounds of pain extend throughout Moab, a thought expressed by naming yet more cities of Moab (**Heshbon, Elealeh, Jahaz, Zoar, Horonaim,** and **Eglath Shelishiyah**). The reference to the **waters of Nimrin** is often taken as the Wadi en-Numeirah, which, when it has water, flows into the southern portion of the Dead Sea. Of course, the fact that these waters have **dried up** is part of the devastation of the land.

God does not object to false worship in Israel only. It displeases him also in an area like Moab. Thus, this judgment will bring an end to those who engage in the worship of false deities.

God's lament for Moab is said to be like that of a **flute,** which may have been thought of as the appropriate instrument to accompany the singing of a lament. The people are then described as engaging in ritual acts of mourning because of their pain and suffering. They **shave** their heads and beards. They engage in ritual mutilation (**every hand is slashed**) and put on **sackcloth.** They mourn their own demise.

Mourning permeates the city (**on all the roofs in the public squares**). But God's mourning is ironic. After all, he is the one who created the conditions that induced it. Their suffering was his judgment upon them. He broke them **like a jar that no one wants** (see also Jer. 19:1–13; 22:28; Ps. 2:9).

This part of the oracle ends with a declaration of the destruction of Moab (**How shattered she is!**) that references its mourning (**How they wail!**) and shame (**How Moab turns her back in shame!**). One can hear the tone of awe and horror in these words.

48:40–47 / The final part of the oracle evokes the image of **an eagle spreading its wings over Moab.** The eagle is a powerful, large bird of prey. Its wing span can be over seven feet. It hunts its prey by swooping down from high in the sky and catching it with its sharp beak and talons. While the eagle image can be used in passages of deliverance (Exod. 19:4), it is often found in judgment passages like this one (see Ezek. 17:3, 7; Hos. 8:1; Jer. 49:22 [in an oracle against Edom]).

The eagle may be a particularly apt image for the destruction of countries like Moab and Edom because they were nations of fortresses and cave refuges. (The stronghold at Kerioth and its stronghold are specifically mentioned.) Moab's warriors are then described as being gripped with fear. They are like a woman, specifically **a woman in labor.** Nahum 3:12 contains a related image as it speaks of the army of Assyria facing destruction at the hands of Babylon. Obviously in times when women fight in all manner of armed forces, calling enemy troops "women" does not have the same force today as it would have when originally written, but we can still understand the point.

The reason for Moab's destruction is because they have **defied the LORD.** The rebellion may specifically be linked to false worship (v. 35), but also mischievous behavior toward God's people.

The oracle then turns to hunting images—the **pit** and the **snare**. There is no escape. The refugees from Moab will fall into a pit, and if some are able to crawl out of the pit they will be caught in a snare.

The oracle ends with its focus on **Heshbon,** already mentioned in verse 2 and an extremely important city in the region. The **fugitives** mill outside the walls (**in the shadow**) of Heshbon. They are helpless. The reason for this condition is given by way of a quote of Numbers 21:28a (Fire went out from Heshbon, a blaze from the city [Jeremiah has **midst,** though there are suggested emendations] of Sihon). By citing the passage from Numbers, Jeremiah is reminding readers of an earlier Israelite defeat of this city, though the city at that time (at the end of the wilderness wanderings) was under the control of **Sihon** the Amorite who had taken the city from the Moabites. The point remains the same. Those who resist the Lord will pay with their lives. The fire is pictured as going out from Heshbon because that city is on the northern boundary of Moab, where the attack of the Babylonian army likely started before moving south.

The fire burns the heads of the Moabites, though they are **noisy boasters** (see vv. 29–30). They will be taken into **exile** (vv. 11–13). Even so, this lengthy oracle of judgment ends with a glimmer of future hope (**yet I will restore the fortunes of Moab in days to come**).

Additional Notes §90

48:2 / Verse 2 has a soundplay based on the name of the cities. In Hebrew **Heshbon** is associated with the verb translated **will plot** (*khashebu*). **Madmen** is associated with the verb rendered **will be silenced** (*tiddommi*).

48:11 / Interestingly, it is a natural part of the fermentation process to pour wine from jar to jar. After letting the wine rest on its lees for a while to get flavor, the pouring process separates clear wine from the dregs. Even so, for the purposes of this metaphor the pouring of the wine from jar to jar actually has a negative ramification since it is connected to the exile of the nation. This interpretation differs from that of scholars like Fretheim (*Jeremiah*, p. 599) who believe that the negative statement about Moab here is that they, like the wine resting on its dregs, were complacent. But this does not seem right because the decanting and pouring are done by those who want to harm Moab.

48:41 / There are related examples in treaty curses. D. Hillers (*Treaty-Curses and the Old Testament Prophets* [Rome: Pontifical Biblical Institute, pp. 66–68]) cites as parallels wording in other ancient Near Eastern documents: "Let them change his troops into women"; "may his warriors become women" (ANET, p. 354 [the Hittite Soldier's Oath] and p. 533 [an Assyrian treaty]).

48:43 / The Hebrew for **terror** and **pit** and **snare** creates a strong alliteration (*pakhad . . . wafakhat . . . wafakh*).

§91 Oracle against Ammon (Jer. 49:1–6)

The oracles against the foreign nations have been presented in a basically south-to-north direction. Just to the north of Moab lay Ammon, to the east of the Jordan River and extending to the desert on its eastern boundary.

As with Moab (see above), the book of Genesis paints a dark picture of Ammon's origins. Moab and Ammon were the children born to Lot after he slept with his daughters (Gen. 19:30–38). Israel under Moses came into contact with the Ammonites as they journeyed toward the promised land. God told Israel not to bother the Ammonites (Deut. 2:19), but the Ammonites tried to stop the Israelites from reaching their destination. Deuteronomy 23:3–6 names them along with the Moabites as responsible for hiring Balaam in the abortive attempt to curse the Israelites.

At the time of the settlement, the tribe of Gad was given "the territory of Jazer, all the towns of Gilead, and half the Ammonite country as far as Aroer, near Rabbah" (Josh. 13:28). Internecine war plagued Ammon and Israel all throughout their common history. There are numerous examples in the Bible. The judge Jephthah had to counter Ammon's attempt to push into territory Israel claimed (Judg. 10–11). Saul fought with Nahash the Ammonite king over the city of Jabesh Gilead (1 Sam. 11). It was while Joab was leading the armies of Israel against the Ammonites that David impregnated Bathsheba (2 Sam. 10). Jehoshaphat engaged in battle against the combined forces of the Ammonites and Moabites (2 Chr. 20).

During the time of Jeremiah, Ammon had become a vassal of Babylon, helping Babylon when Jehoiakim rebelled in 597 B.C. (2 Kgs. 24:2). Later Ammon worked against the interests of Judah, wanting to take advantage of its weakened position. King Baalis was reportedly behind the successful assassination of Gedaliah, the Babylonian-appointed governor of postdestruction Judah (Jer. 40:7–41:15). Eventually, though Babylon did subjugate Ammon and brought it to an end as a separate political power (582 B.C.). It is likely the latter that this oracle anticipated. For related oracles against Ammon, see Ezekiel 25:1–7 and Zephaniah 2:8–11.

49:1–2 / After a rubric indicating that the section concerns the Ammonites, the divine oracle begins with two taunting rhetorical questions (**Has Israel no sons? Has she no heirs?**). The answer is obviously affirmative (if thought of in terms of all Israel, rather than specifically of Gad, which was exiled by Assyria and never to be heard of again). Before and after the destruction of Jerusalem there were numerous descendants of Israel around. If so, the oracle goes on to ask, why are there Ammonites who worship the god **Molech** (see Additional Notes) where Gad used to dwell? As the introduction to this section indicated, when Israel had first settled in the land it was the Gadites who were given possession of land in the Transjordan traditionally occupied by Ammonites.

Though it had been a very long time since Israelites dwelt in that part of the world, the Lord announces that the Ammonites will come under attack again. It looks to the day when its capital **Rabbah** will come under attack and be destroyed. Here it is specifically Israel who drives them out of the land.

49:3–5 / The oracle personifies the city of **Heshbon** and calls on it to wail because of the destruction of a city named **Ai.** Heshbon was mentioned in the Moabite oracle (48:2, 45). It was right on the boundary between Moab and Ammon and perhaps had a history of belonging to each in turn, but it is traditionally an Ammonite city. Its appearance in the Moabite oracle perhaps should be explained by the fact that it was a staging area for the armies that destroyed Moab. As for Ai, it cannot be identified with the Ai of Joshua 7–8. There must have been another city of that name near Heshbon, though it is not otherwise known. Ai itself means "dump," and it may be ironical that this city is said to be destroyed.

Rabbah is mentioned again, here personified. It too is encouraged to mourn. The god **Molech** will go into exile. This expression reflects the practice of a victorious army that steals the statues of the defeated's gods and places them in their own temple. Not only will the god be taken away, but so will the **priests and officials.**

Verse 4 questions Ammon's propensity to have pride and confidence in its fruitful valleys and riches. These will not help when God himself attacks that nation.

49:6 / Yes, they will be exiled, but as with Egypt and with Moab (but not Philistia), God also declares that the Ammonites will survive (**I will restore the fortunes of the Ammonites**).

§92 Oracle against Edom (Jer. 49:7–22)

Edom's order in the foreign oracles is a slight departure from the generally south-to-north orientation that we have encountered thus far. Edom is located south of Moab in the region to the southeast of the Dead Sea. It is a region of rugged mountains and wadis, making it difficult to attack.

The Bible attributes Edomite origins to Esau, Jacob's brother, whose other name is Edom or "Red" (see Gen. 36). Notice that by the time Jacob returned from his sojourn in Paddam-Aram, Esau, having already amassed a significant fortune, was dwelling in the region of Seir (a common synonym for Edom, see Gen. 32).

It is true that Edom, like Moab and Ammon, refused Israel passage during the wilderness wanderings (Num. 20:14–21); however, it appears that Israel had some options at that time, so they found another way, avoiding violent confrontation. But there were later battles between Edom and Israel. David, for instance, is described as having taken Edom as a vassal (2 Sam. 8:14). Jehoshaphat had control over it (1 Kgs. 22:47). An Edomite monarchy rose about the time of Jehoram (2 Kgs. 8:20), and Elath, an important seaport, was taken by the Edomites during the reign of Ahaz (2 Kgs. 16:6).

At the time of the Babylonian destruction of Jerusalem, Edom had taken advantage of the situation in some way. While not precisely described, this point can be established by reference to texts like Psalm 137:7; Lamentations 4:22; Ezekiel 35:15; Obadiah 10–14.

49:7–11 / The oracle begins with a rubric identifying it as directed toward Edom, and then, as with the previous oracle against Ammon, it begins in earnest with a series of taunting rhetorical questions. These questions concern the lack of **wisdom** in Edom. Apparently Edom was known for its wisdom (see also Obad. 8). Eliphaz, the first of the three friends of Job, is said to be from **Teman,** an area sometimes thought to be synonymous with Edom or a reference to a northern region (Job 2:11), mentioned in the first of the series of rhetorical questions here. Edom's lack of wisdom likely lies in the way they have been treating Israel, or perhaps in their inability to anticipate their future trouble.

The inhabitants of another region to the southeast of the Dead Sea, **Dedan,** are told to flee and hide in **caves,** which are in abundant quantity in this region of the world. Caves often served as refuge during times of conflict. Teman and Dedan may be a way of referring to the far north and the far south of Edom's influence.

God's extensive destruction of Edom is compared to a vineyard after **grape pickers** have gone over it and a house after a thief has stolen from it. Grape pickers would do their best to take all the grapes, but usually a few lonely grapes would be left. Even **thieves** would leave behind some worthless items. But God is going to be even more complete in his ravaging of Edom. The ravaging of Edom is likened to the stripping bare of a person. Edom will be completely **bare** after God is through with it. Many will perish, but the last line hints that some will remain. Indeed, the remnant will be made up of the most vulnerable, the **orphans and widows,** who are traditionally under God's care.

49:12–13 / The oracle now switches to the well known metaphor of the **cup** of wrath (see especially 25:15–38; 48:26–28). Edom, who deserves it, must drink it and suffer the consequences. God then takes a self-oath that **Bozrah,** another important Edomite city will be cursed and destroyed (see also Lam. 4:21–22).

49:14–18 / It is hard to analyze the structure of this section. There seems to be a staccato-like series of taunts against Edom. It begins with a picture of God rallying the nations through an envoy to come together and attack Edom. There is no escape from Edom who thought itself large because of the pride of its heart, but now is **small among the nations.** In fact, Edom was not a large nation. However, its cliffs and mountains made it a relatively easy place to protect. But these defenses will be of no avail. Edomites could build a refuge high in caves in wadi walls, but even if they did this (**though you build a nest as high as the eagle's**), there is no escape from those God will raise up to bring them down. Indeed, the cities of Edom will be like **Sodom and Gomorrah,** well-known for the horror of their devastation (Gen. 19). These cities may be mentioned because, though we do not know their exact location, they were likely somewhere in the vicinity of Edom.

49:19–22 / In ancient biblical times, lions roamed Palestine. They found a natural habitat in the thickets of the Jordan river. Here God likens himself to a **lion** coming up from the **Jordan** and pursuing the Edomites as its prey. The Edomites are like **the young of the flock** of sheep. Edom has no leader who can function as a **shepherd** and stave off God the lion. Edom the pastureland will be destroyed. The cry of these mutilated sheep will be heard even at the **Red Sea,** to the south of Edom. Verses 19–21 are similar to the oracle delivered against Babylon in 50:44–46.

Verse 22 changes metaphors. It speaks of an **eagle** swooping down on Edom in a fashion similar to that found in 48:40 in reference to Moab. It also describes Edom's warriors acting like **a woman in labor,** again similar to an image used of Moab's warriors in 48:41.

Additional Notes §92

49:1 / Milkam was the main god of the Ammonites. The name is formed from the root *mlk* which in its generic noun form means "king." However, here as in many places in the Hebrew Bible, the god is called **Molech,** which uses the consonants of "king" but uses the vowels from the word *boshet* "shame."

§93 Oracle against Damascus (Jer. 49:23–27)

The next oracle in the series moves north again, this time to Damascus, an ancient city and the capital of Syria. From the time of Solomon (1 Kgs. 11:23–25) to the mid-eighth century when Assyria, under Tiglath-pileser III, absorbed Damascus, there was fairly constant fighting between Israel and Syria. Occasionally, most notably at the battle of Qarqar in 853 B.C., Israel and Syria banded together to resist early Assyrian imperialist expansion. 2 Kings 24:2 mentions that Nebuchadnezzar sent Aramean raiders against Jerusalem sometime before the siege of that city in 597 B.C. and these may have come from the Damascus region. While Damascus may have had a short period of independence following the downfall of Assyria, by 605 it would have been firmly placed within the Babylonian empire. This oracle may come from the time period before 605 B.C. and anticipates the fall to Babylon.

49:23–27 / **Hamath** and **Arpad** are two ancient cities of northern Syria that would have been associated with **Damascus.** The **bad news** that they hear is about the weakness of Damascus. Its agitation is likened to the **restless sea.** In an image used a number of times so far in these foreign oracles (see 48:41; 49:22, and also 50:43). Damascus is like a **woman in labor,** in terror and great pain.

Verse 25 presents a special problem in that it seems the first person speaker takes an empathetic view toward Damascus even calling it **the town in which I delight.** Perhaps the best solution here is to understand the verse to be a quote from a Syrian. There is never any indication elsewhere that Damascus is the object of God's special concern. Indeed, it is God who claims responsibility for the burning of that city and its fortresses.

Additional Notes §93

49:27 / Three kings of Syria are known to have borne the name **Ben-Hadad.** Ben-Hadad 1 (ca. 900–860 B.C.), Ben-Hadad II (874–853 B.C.), and Ben-Hadad III (ca. 805–778 B.C.). Since we know alternative names for the last two, it is possible that Ben-Hadad functioned as a throne name. In any case, the fortresses are associated with Ben-Hadad in this oracle not because we know a king by that name in the late-eighth or seventh centuries (though it could still be functioning as a throne name), but because it was the name associated with the ruling house.

§94 Oracles against Kedar and Hazor (Jer. 49:28–33)

The next oracle moves to a location to the east of Edom (Kedar) and south of there (Hazor). Both are the location of Arabian tribes. Kedar is well known from the Bible and extrabiblical sources. Kedar is first mentioned in Genesis as a descendant of Ishmael. They were sellers of flocks of small animals (Ezek. 27:21). They were known for their black tents (Song. 1:5). "The Kidar were among the most powerful of the northern Arabian Bedouin tribal groups in the period between the 8th and 4th centuries B.C." (*IVPBBCOT,* p. 57). For this reason, they are mentioned in Assyrian and Babylonian records as the objects of their kings' campaigns. The Babylonian Chronicle records that Nebuchadnezzar attacked the Arabs (certainly the Kedarites) in 599/598 B.C. The oracle is likely an anticipation of that attack. Hazor, not the famous city in the north of Israel, is otherwise unknown (though perhaps Josh. 15:23–25 mentions it). But in connection with Kedar it too is to be associated with a region of Arabia.

49:28–33 / The rubric introduces **Kedar** and **Hazor** as the targets of the next oracle. In this case, it also refers to an attack by **Nebuchadnezzar** of Babylon; it is with his attack in 599/598 B.C. that we should associated this oracle.

The oracle proper begins with a divine command, presumably to Nebuchadnezzar, to mobilize an army to attack Kedar. They are Arabic tribesmen and so their plunder is counted in **tents, flocks,** and **camels.**

Verse 30 is an urgent command to the defeated tribe to flee and seek refuge in caves. Then v. 31 again urges on the attackers. The fact that these groups are at ease indicates that they will be easy pickings. Being a nomadic group, they do not live in a city protected by walls (**a nation that has neither gates nor bars**). The attack will leave the region devastated and deserted. It will revert to wilderness as typified by the fact that the **jackal** will dwell there. See also Jeremiah 9:11; 10:33 as well as Psalm 44:19; Isaiah 34:13.

§95 Oracle against Elam (Jer. 49:34–39)

Elam's appearance here is a bit surprising since we do not know that it had any direct involvement with Israelite affairs during this time. Elam is the most distant of all the nations targeted by the oracles. It was located to the east of Babylon in the Zagros Mountains, south of the Medes and north of Persia. Its capital was Susa.

Elam was an ancient Iranian power, but by the seventh century B.C. was a shadow of its previous self. In the early part of that century it found itself frequently in alliance with Babylon and in conflict with Assyria, and in 640 B.C. the Assyrian king Asshurbanipal successfully sacked the capital. Even so, the Elamites were able to reassert some form of their kingdom and they survived until Cyrus the Persian absorbed Susa and its surrounding territories into his expanding kingdom in the latter half of the sixth century.

49:34 / In this introductory verse, **Elam** (see above) is named as the object of the oracle that follows. Unlike many of the other oracles, this one is dated, specifically to **early in the reign of Zedekiah king of Judah.** This would indicate a time soon after Zedekiah took the throne in 597 B.C.

49:35–39 / In the oracle against Elam, God claims responsibility for the destruction of that nation. This assertion does not preclude God's use of secondary causes, and there is some reason to think that the prophecy has a Babylonian conquest in mind. There is some evidence, though not determinative, that Nebuchadnezzar attacked Elam in 596/5 B.C. (Lundbom, *Jeremiah 37–52*, p. 362).

God says he will **break the bow of Elam,** a country known for its skilled archers (Isa. 22:6). The bow stands for Elam's military might. He then says that he will bring the **four winds** against Elam and scatter them to the four winds. This metaphor is a way of saying that God will use overwhelming force to produce a devastating result. Elam too will suffer exile, a widespread diaspora (**there will not be a nation where Elam's exiles do not go**). God even says that he will set his **throne in Elam.** This follows the practice of a victorious king who will demonstrate his sovereignty by having a portable throne set up in a prominent place in the defeated city.

Finally, as in a number of the previous oracles (46:26; 48:47; 49:6), God says that Elam will have a future (**Yet I will restore the fortunes of Elam in days to come**). History shows that Elam's future was as a one of the core provinces within the Persian empire.

§96 *Oracles against Babylon (Jer. 50:1–51:64)*

50:1 / The superscription that begins the final oracle against the nations identifies the object of this long section as Babylon. It introduces not only the last grouping of oracles but also what are by far the longest in the oracles against the nations. The prophet pulls out all the stops to articulate the destruction that was coming Babylon's way. Jeremiah understood that the Babylonians were being used by God as an instrument of his judgment against Judah and the other nations, but this fact did not exonerate them from the onus of their own evil intentions. The Babylonians did not do their bloody work motivated by the glory and will of God, but rather for their own imperialistic interests. They were oppressors of other nations to the highest magnitude.

The heart of the Babylonian empire was in southern Mesopotamia, within the present nation of Iraq. The Babylon spoken of here was the final flourish of a culture that had its origins in the early second millennium B.C. Having its roots in an earlier Amorite immigration into southern Mesopotamia (then controlled by the Sumerians), Babylon rose to prominence first under kings like the famous Hammurabi. But this final appearance of a Babylonian empire began with the revolt of Nabopolassar, a Chaldean tribal leader in 626 B.C. Nebuchadnezzar was his son and the one who extended the empire into Syro-Palestine.

Nebuchadnezzar would die in 562 B.C. with his kingdom intact. With the accession of his son, Amel-Marduk, Babylonian power began to decline. It would be Persia that would bring the kingdom of Babylon to its end in 539 B.C. It is this devastation which the oracle anticipates.

50:2–3 / The speaker, God himself, orders an unspecified addressee, perhaps the prophet, to make an announcement **among the nations.** It is also likely that the addressee is unspecified as a literary device. It is doubtful that this announcement will be made in any other fashion than to the readers of this oracle.

The content of the announcement to the nations gets right to the point: **Babylon will be captured.** The fate that Babylon has been imposing on others will now be imposed on that great empire.

The defeat of Babylon will result in the shaming of its deities. Rather than considering the possibility that these gods have allowed the defeat of Babylon as was the faithful Judean's understanding of Yahweh's relationship to the defeat of Judah, the defeat of Babylon was thought to be a sign of the impotence of the gods of Babylon. The chief god of the city of Babylon, and thus of the empire that expanded from that city as its base, was **Marduk.** Marduk, also called **Bel** ("lord"), was the god who was thought to have won the victory over Tiamat, the primordial goddess of the sea, according to the foundational myth *Enuma Elish.* The myth describes Marduk as the creator of the cosmos and the one who formed the first human beings.

The very next poetic line substitutes **images** and **idols** for Bel and Marduk, alerting us to the fact that these gods don't actually exist. They are mere false gods on which the Babylonians futilely relied. In reality, there is nothing behind the wood statues that are coated with precious metals and jewels that represent these supposed divine forces.

The divinely-appointed executioner of Babylon will come from the **north,** just as Babylon itself descended on Judah from the north. Historical retrospection allows us to identify this new tool of the divine anger as Persia. Though situated to east and southeast of Babylon, Persian forces nonetheless attacked Babylon via Opis in the north in 539 B.C. The resulting engagement brought the Babylonian empire to a definitive end. The proclamation that **no one will live in it** (Babylon) should be understood as hyperbolic or a statement that no entity of the Babylonian empire will live there. Babylon itself would became an important provincial capital of the Persian empire. The city is only archaeological ruins today.

50:4–5 / The oracle reveals that it is talking about future realities with the expression, **In those days, at that time,** a formula that points ahead to an indeterminate time. While the previous unit anticipates the destruction of Babylon, the present verses point to the repentance and restoration of the people of God. The people are called **the people of Israel and the people of Judah together.** Perhaps the intention of this reference is to present a hopeful picture of the whole people of God, though the people of Israel had been exiled in 722 B.C. never to be heard from again. It would be the people of Judah, who likely had elements from the now long-dead north with them. Their repentance is signaled by the fact that they seek the Lord **in tears.** While the tears may be the product of their plight, it probably also indicates sadness over their sin. That they were reversing the earlier course of rejecting God is indicated by the fact that they are turning their face toward **Zion,** the place where God had made his presence known to them in Jerusalem.

The return of a repentant people of God to Jerusalem is associated with the formation of a new **covenant.** It is described as an **everlasting** covenant that will **not be forgotten.** This covenant, formally called a new covenant, is announced for the first time in Jeremiah in chapter 31:31–34.

50:6–7 / These verses play on the image of the people of God as a flock of sheep. They are **lost sheep** because their **shepherds** have let them down. The leaders (kings, priests, and prophets) have not done their duty in guiding the sheep. God is the ultimate shepherd (Ps. 23), but many other places describe the leadership of God's people as his undershepherds. Moses was the model shepherd of his people (Exod. 2:15–31), but the later prophets often pointed out the failure of Israel's leadership toward the end of its independent existence (most notably Ezek. 34; though see also Jer. 10:21).

With such bad leaders, the people of God were like sheep without a shepherd. They not only got lost but they were devoured by their enemies who acted like wolves that prey on sheep. They had wandered from their **true pasture,** the Lord, where the shepherds were supposed to keep them for their safety, and they were eaten. The picture of God as the pasture of the people means that he is the source of their security and the one who supplies their needs.

50:8–10 / Following two units that address the situation of the people of God, the opening command to **flee out of Babylon** should best be understood as directed toward them. They are to be **like the goats that lead the flock,** in other words they should be at the vanguard of the exodus from Babylon. The enemy that God will bring against Babylon will be large and **skilled.** They will be successful. So, again, it is of the utmost urgency for the people of God to remove themselves from the future battlefield.

50:11–13 / As Babylon pillaged God's inheritance, Judah, they enjoyed it **like a heifer** that frolicked as it threshed grain. Once the grain was harvested it was put on a threshing floor where one method for separating the grain from the chaff was to let a heifer or ox walk on it (Job 39:12). Deuteronomy 25:4 indicates that the animal was not muzzled and so it could eat its fill while working, thus the source of its joy. Threshing was a common prophetic metaphor of judgment.

Because of this joy in the harm that it caused Judah, God will turn the Babylonian's **mother** into **a wilderness, a dry land, a desert.** By the results we judge the mother to be known as none other than the land itself. It will be desolate.

50:14–16 / Now the oracle addresses those who are attacking Babylon. It urges them to show no mercy, but to shoot all their **arrows** at the city. The oracle reads like an event-vision (see also 4:11–12; 6:1–8; 46:1–12; 50:41–43). The commands and descriptions are given as if the speaker is actually present at this future event. In verse 15, for instance, we have the description of the surrender of the city as the defensive **towers** and **walls** crumble. The **vengeance** of the Lord here is also described using an agricultural metaphor. They are to cut off the fertility and productivity of the land by bringing an end to both **sower** and reaper. Finally, everyone should return to their own land. After the Persians asserted **dominance** over the Babylonian empire, they did issue a decree right away allowing all the people the Babylonians had exiled to return to their original homeland (see Additional Notes).

50:17–20 / The first verse here returns to the sheep metaphor of verses 6–7. The bad shepherds are complicit in making Israel a **scattered flock.** Here we have a specific historical identification of those who devoured the sheep of the flock. They are, first, the **king of Assyria** responsible for the defeat of Samaria (Shalmaneser V with mop-up operations executed by his successor Sargon) in 722 B.C. The last is **Nebuchadnezzar** who destroyed Jerusalem in 586 B.C.

As a result of (**therefore,** v. 18) the violent actions of Nebuchadnezzar, which were like those of the Assyrians before him, God will punish him just as God had punished the king of Assyria. The point of the analogy is likely that God will bring the Babylonian empire to a violent close as he brought the Assyrian empire to a violent close. Ironically, Babylon was the entity that had defeated Assyria between the years 626 and 609 B.C. Babylon's end would be even more decisive when Persia attacks and defeats it in 539 B.C.

While bringing Babylon to an end, God will restore Israel/Judah to its land. The geographical references given for the restored pastureland (**Carmel, Bashan, Ephraim, Gilead**) are in the north and the Transjordan region. It is the **remnant,** those who survive the destruction of Jerusalem and the exile, that will be restored. And they will have their sins completely forgiven so that the returned remnant will start again with a blank slate.

50:21–28 / **Merathaim** and **Pekod** are parts of Babylonia (see Additional Notes). The part of the oracle against Babylon starts with a command to an unnamed army to attack and completely destroy Babylon.

Verses 22–23 comprise an event-vision, where a future event is described as if it is unfolding before one's very eyes (see 4:11–12; 6:1–8; 46:1–12; 50:14–15). First, the speaker asks the hearer to imagine the **noise** of the battle and then conceive of the destruction of Babylon, here referred to as **the hammer of the whole earth** because it had destroyed many nations up to this point in its history. The result of its destruction leaves Babylon **desolate.**

In verse 24 the Lord reveals that Babylon's destruction is ultimately his doing. He set the trap that caught Babylon unawares for their rebellion against God. Verse 25 pictures God the warrior opening up his **arsenal** and arming those who will work his violent will against Babylon.

Verses 26–27a return to a series of divine commands to Babylon's destroyer. He urges them to completely destroy them. Verse 27b turns to a **woe** oracle, which is a form of mourning associated with funerals (see Additional Notes at 10:19–22). However, in a prophetic context like this, the woe oracle is used satirically, in effect announcing that Babylon is as good as dead. In this case the woe is uttered because the long-awaited day of Babylon's punishment has arrived.

Verse 28 shifts focus to the presumably Jewish **fugitives and refugees** who have fled Babylon and now are back in **Zion,** the holy precinct in the city of Jerusalem. There they are talking about the vengeance God has taken on Babylon. This vengeance is not for the treatment of the people, but for the disdain shown to the **temple,** the place where God made his presence known in Jerusalem.

50:29–32 / Again, the Lord commands the attackers to lay siege to Babylon (**Summon archers encamp all around her**). They are to punish (**repay**) it for its sinful deeds (**as she has done**), which are a manifestation of their rebellion against the Lord. The result will be that their young men who constitute their army will fall in the streets of Babylon. They will be unable to defend that city. As with Moab before it (48:29–30) as well as with Edom (49:16), Babylon's **arrogance** is highlighted as a reason why it will fall to its enemies.

50:33–34 / As Babylon is punished, so Israel will be freed from their oppression. The unit begins by an acknowledgement of that oppression. While it is true that the exiles were not enslaved as such, they were certainly deprived of much of their ability to chart their own lives. Daniel and his three friends are good examples. Babylon certainly would not let any Judahites return to Jerusalem. But it is God, who will act as their **Redeemer**, who comes to their aid. The promise of Babylon's desolation and Israel's redemption is fulfilled when Persia, under Cyrus, defeats Babylon and allows the Israelites to return to Jerusalem.

50:35–38 / The Lord calls for the **sword** against Babylon and then proceeds down a list of aspects of the Babylonian war machine. The sword here is a metonymy that stands for war. God calls for war against Babylon and those who are in charge of that previously expanding empire (**officials, wise men, false prophets** [see Additional Notes], **warriors**). He also calls for violence directed toward the foreign fighters (**all the foreigners in her ranks**) that are either mercenaries or are forced into battle with the Babylonians. The oracle not only calls for an attack on these people, but also on other instruments of war (**horses and chariots**) as well as the wealth that fuels Babylon's wars of expansion (**her treasures**).

50:39–40 / God will turn Babylon into a wilderness. This point is made by describing how it will become the haunt of creatures of the steppe, the **desert creatures, hyenas,** and **owl** (see Additional Notes). God will not only make this land like a wilderness, but he will make it a particularly desolate wilderness, similar to what he did with Sodom and Gomorrah (see Gen. 18:16–19:28). Sodom and Gomorrah were prosperous cities decimated by God because of their sins. The use of Sodom and Gomorrah as a metaphor of judgment may also be seen in 20:6; 23:13–15; 49:18.

50:41–46 / The oracle again presents an event-vision, describing the future as if it is unfolding before the prophet's very eyes (see 4:11–12; 6:1–8; 46:1–12; 50:14–16). The first part of the oracle is virtually identical to the judgment oracle leveled toward Judah in 6:22–24.

The oracle first draws attention (**Look!**) to an army advancing from the north. The foe from the north will turn out to be none other than Persia, whose lands are to the east of Babylon, but who will attack from the north. They are numerous so they sound like the roaring sea. The sea is symbolic of the overwhelming forces of chaos. The Persians and particularly the Medes, a tribe that the Persians engulfed, were known for their calvary (**they ride on their horses**).

As he hears about them, the king of Babylon is seized with fear. Daniel 5 describes the reaction of Belshazzar, coregent of Babylon, on the eve of the Persian attack on the city. As he sees the writing on the wall (*meneʾ, meneʾ, teqel, parsin*) his reaction is shock and utter fright. He is in extreme distress, the text suggesting that he has lost control of his most basic bodily functions, undermining all his posture of composure (A. Wolters, "Untying the King's Knots: Physiology and Wordplay in Daniel 5," *JBL* 110 [1991], pp. 117–22).

Verses 44–46 are nearly an exact duplication of 49:19–21 except that Babylon is its target rather than Edom. The oracle pictures God like a lion emerging from the thickets of the Jordan into cultivated land where it will pose a danger to civilization. Babylon is the rich pastureland, and God the lion will chase its inhabitants out in a flash. It has no leader (**shepherd**) who can resist him as he directs the Persian army toward them. Many will die (**the young of the flock will be dragged away**) and the **pasture** (Babylon) will be destroyed. And the rest of the earth will tremble since a great nation like Babylon has not been able to defend itself.

51:1–5 / Though it will be a foreign nation (Persia) that will defeat Babylon (for **Leb Kamai,** see Additional Notes), the oracle understands that God is the one instigating it (**I will stir up the spirit of a destroyer**). The foreigners will be a Persian army, that itself will include Medes and other foreign contingents of nations already subjugated by this growing empire. The destruction is likened to a winnowing.

The Hebrew of verse 3a is difficult (see Additional Notes). As rendered by the NIV, it is addressed to the Babylonian army to the effect that they might as well not even try to fight back since they will be defeated. Verse 3b, however, is clearly addressed to the Persian army that they not spare the Babylonians.

Verses 4 and 5 connect the defeat of Babylon to the fact that God has not abandoned **Israel and Judah.** He has remained involved with them in spite of their sin. He will defeat Babylon in order to initiate the next phase of his redemptive activities with his people.

51:6–10 / With urgency, the oracle calls for the abandonment of Babylon before the devastation comes. This devastation is seen to be punishment for her sins. It is the Lord's work (**his vengeance**) and she is getting her just reward.

Verse 7 describes Babylon as a **gold cup in the LORD's hand.** This metaphor acknowledges that God used Babylon for his own purposes in its destruction of many nations. This cup is the cup of God's wrath (see Jer. 25). It made the nations drunk so they went mad and could not protect themselves. The cup is gold because, as it did God's work (though unwittingly), it was greatly valued. Perhaps, too, there is an ironic reference to the golden vessels that Babylon removed from the temple (Dan. 1:2; 5:3).

But now Babylon itself will fall and be broken. The motif of the **wound** that cannot be healed is a common one in Jeremiah (see 10:19; 15:18; 30:12–13) and elsewhere in the prophets (Hos. 5:13; Mic. 1:9; Nah. 3:19). Not even **balm** will help (see Jer. 8:22; 46:11).

The punishment of Babylon is vindication for God's people. They will talk about it once they return to **Zion.**

51:11–14 / This section of the oracle begins with commands shouted to the future invaders of Babylon. They are told to prepare for battle by preparing their weapons (**sharpen the arrows; take up shields**), rallying (**lift up a banner**) and positioning the army (**reinforce the guard, station the watchmen, prepare an ambush!**). Here for the first time Babylon's enemy is given a name, **the kings of the Medes** (see Additional Notes).

The divine rationale for this move against Babylon is also given. The Lord will avenge the destruction of his temple. Nebuchadnezzar the Babylonian defeated Jerusalem and destroyed the temple. Though this was part of God's own judgment of Judah, this does not excuse Babylon. God can use the wicked acts of others to accomplish his will, while still holding those who perpetrate the evil responsible. One might think of an analogy with the crucifixion of Jesus. He was executed by wicked people who just wanted to kill him, though God used their very act for his redemptive purposes. Even so, they are still responsible for their act (Acts 2:22–24).

Verses 13–14 address the inhabitants of Babylon. They are referred to as those who live by **many waters,** presumably a reference to the Euphrates and the many canals flowing from it for watering the city's agricultural fields. They are also described as extremely rich. Even with these advantages, God will cut them off. He will fill them with men **as with a swarm of locusts.** Locust swarms imply huge numbers of troops as well as their destructive power. Destructive locusts are often used as a metaphor for a destroying army (Judg. 6:5; 7:12; Jer. 46:23; Nah. 3:15–17; Rev. 9:7). The Lord himself takes an oath that this will happen and that the invaders will be successful (**they will shout in triumph over you**).

51:15–16 / This pair of verses reflects on the nature of the God who will do this destructive work. It reflects on his role as Creator. In language reminiscent of both Genesis 1 as well as Proverbs 8:22–31, it describes how he created the earth by his power and wisdom. He is also the one responsible for the incredible power and resultant fertility provided by the storm. The implication is that the destruction of Babylon will be an easy job for such a God.

51:17–19 / The true God described in the previous section is here contrasted with idols made by human beings. While God has wisdom **every man is senseless and without knowledge.** As evidence of this, the oracle goes on to describe goldsmiths and the images they produce. Images are a fraud with no power or wisdom, but the true God (**the Portion of Jacob**) has both and he has created not only the world but also the people of God.

51:20–26 / The NIV renders the tense of this unit as present (**you are my war club**), and thus is addressed to Babylon's enemy. God here is proclaiming that they are a war club in his hands and they will devastate Babylon (see Isa. 1:10). The verses go through different parts of the society of Babylon, the cumulative effect is that all of Babylon will be destroyed.

While the present tense of the verb is a possible translation of the unit, it is better to take the tense as past (you were my war club). There is no verb in verse 20a, but in verses 20b–23 it is possible to understand the form as simple perfect rather than a waw consecutive. This makes more sense (and the NJB takes this approach) since verses 24–26 clearly address Babylon and not their enemy in the second person. Therefore, this section is better understood as a reflection on the fact that God had used Babylon as his instrument of judgment in the past.

Verses 24–25 are unambiguously addressed to Babylon and God again proclaims to them that they will be destroyed out of vengeance for their past acts. They are called a **destroying moun-**

tain, not because their homeland is a mountainous region, but because they are powerful and imposing like a mountain. Because of God's actions against them, they will be a **burned-out mountain.**

At the end of this unit Babylon is likened to a building destroyed by being knocked down. In such a situation the best stones of the destroyed building were often used to rebuild, but that will not happen in this case. Not a stone of the knocked-down building called Babylon will be used to constitute a future political entity.

51:27–33 / As with 51:11–12, this part of the oracle against Babylon starts with orders issued to the army that will attack Babylon. First, they are to lift a war banner to rally around, then blow the trumpet, a signal to the army to gather together.

Three kingdoms are specifically mentioned as part of the alliance that will form to attack Babylon. They are **Ararat, Minni,** and **Ashkenaz.** These three kingdoms are to the northwest of Babylon, near Lake Van and Lake Urmia. Ararat is Urartu, a mighty kingdom, which in the 8th century was known for its battles with Sargon of Assyria. According to *IVPBBCOT,* "They were finally overwhelmed by the coalition of Medes and Scythians in a campaign in 585 that swept through their territory. Subsequently their territory was added to the Persian empire" (p. 685). Minni refers to the Mannaeans, also mentioned in contemporary texts. They too eventually were absorbed by the Persian empire. The Ashkenaz were located north of Lake Van and Lake Urmia between them and the Black Sea. They were known as fierce warriors in extra-biblical texts. Herodotus refers to them as the Scythians.

The size and destructive power of these foes are likened to a swarm of locusts (see 51:14). Verse 28 shows recognition that these other national entities will be fighting under the Median (that is, Persian) banner. The rest of this part of the oracle uses formulaic language to describe the conquest of Babylon. Their warriors no longer fight. They are exhausted. Their troops are like women (50:37; Nah. 3:13); their dwellings are on fire. The bars of her gates are broken (Nah. 3:13). Messengers come bearing news of Babylon's defeats. Bridges are taken, even the surrounding marshes are set on fire.

In verse 33 Babylon is likened to a **threshing floor.** The use of the phrase **Daughter of Babylon** to stand for the nation invites us to personify the nation and see it as a woman lying on the threshing floor. At harvest time, the grain would be placed on the floor and trampled by oxen to separate the grain from the chaff. The Daughter of Babylon is imagined in the place of the grain.

51:41–44 / Verse 34 then remembers the pain that **Nebuchadnezzar** has inflicted on Judah. He has devoured Judah making it like an **empty jar,** evoking the image of a plundered land. The second half of the same verse switches the simile and now likens the Babylonian king to a **serpent** (see Additional Notes). This serpent also has swallowed them but then spit them out. They have been used and treated with disrespect.

Such acts lead to the desire for violence against Babylon as expressed in verse 35. The inhabitants of Zion want them to experience payback for their suffering.

The desire of verse 35 leads (**therefore**) to the divine pronouncement in verses 36–44. Here God will take up Judah's cause and avenge them. Speaking of Babylon God will **dry up her sea and make her springs dry.** Literally understood, this would make their land uninhabitable. But "**sea**" also can have the symbolic value of chaos. When God comes as warrior, sources of water dry up; he subdues the chaos (Isa. 24:4; Nah. 1:4).

That Babylon's desolation is in view is explicit in verse 37, where this once prosperous, sophisticated city will be **a heap of ruins,** like an archaeological tell. It will also be a place where **jackals** move about freely, just like the wilderness (see this language in reference to Jerusalem in 9:11; 10:22, Lam. 5:18 and in reference to Hazor in Jer. 49:33).

Verses 38–39 use a simile that the Babylonians might not object to at first. They are like **young lions.** That the poet speaks of them as young may be implying immaturity, but a lion is the king of the beasts, a powerful force. God will set out a **feast** for these lions that apparently includes quite a bit of alcohol, since they will soon be drunk. This is an allusion to the cup of God's wrath, that makes people drunk and pass out, never to rise again (see Jer. 25).

Verse 40 changes the simile and now speaks of them as small animals (**lambs, sheep, goats**) being led to the slaughter. Such animals are defenseless before their slaughterers. This image of the slaughterhouse is used also at Jeremiah 11:19; 12:3.

Babylon, under the name **Sheshach** (see Jer. 25:26), will be overwhelmed, and the rest of the world will shudder to see such a great nation fall so hard. Indeed, Babylon was **the boast of the whole earth** because to this point in history no more powerful nation had existed. The sea, clearly here a symbol of the forces of chaos since the literal sea was far away, will overcome them.

Verse 44 concludes this section of the oracle with a focus on **Bel** ("lord"), a reference to the chief God of Babylon, Marduk. Yahweh the god of Judah will punish Bel. He will make him spit out what he has swallowed, including Judah itself. Babylon will not longer be a force among the nations.

51:45–48 / God then calls for his people to get out of the way of his judgment of Babylon (**Run for your lives!**) God encourages them to be strong in the light of the **rumors** that will arise as battle approaches. God says that Babylon's end and the punishment of her idols is sure. And the whole earth will celebrate its fall. Why? Because the whole earth has been the object of its violence and imperialistic impulses. Again, Babylon's end is associated with an enemy coming **out of the north.** That enemy will prove to be Persia under Cyrus the Great.

51:49–53 / The defeat of Babylon is again connected to that nation's treatment of Israel. The Babylonians have killed many, now many of them must be killed. The remnant of Judah (**you who have escaped the sword**) need to get out of the way. The exiles who are in a distant land need to **think** about Jerusalem and consider returning to it.

Verse 51 then quotes the remnant who are ashamed because foreigners have entered the holy places of the Lord's house. Indeed, they had destroyed it. God responds by saying that in the future (**days are coming**), things will be reversed. It will be Babylon's gods that will be shamed and Babylon's population that will be hurt. There is no defense against those God will send against Babylon.

51:54–58 / The last part of the lengthy oracles against Babylon starts by noting a **cry** that comes from Babylon. It is the cry of defeat as its enemies destroy the city. The responsible agent of its destruction is not the army that penetrates its walls, but the Lord who directs them toward the city. It is he who will silence their **noisy din.**

God will bring a **destroyer** against Babylon. This destroyer will turn out to be Cyrus the Persian. He indeed defeated the Babylonian army with violence at the battle of Opis. At that time Babylon's army was captured and subdued. According to the historical records, the taking of the city of Babylon itself was done with a minimum of violence. These actions brought the Babylonian empire to an end. God is a God of **retribution.** He sees that the wicked ultimately get their due reward.

God will make Babylon's **officials and wise men drunk.** The description reminds us of the picture of Belshazzar and his officials drinking and banqueting on the eve of their destruction in Daniel 5. But the drinking of which Jeremiah speaks is not drinking alcohol. Rather, they drink from the cup of God's wrath (for which see Jeremiah 25:15–38). This is a potion that will do them in (**they will sleep forever and not awake;** see also 51:39).

The final verse of the oracle announces the destruction of Babylon's **wall** and the burning of its **gates.** The Babylonians can do nothing to prevent its demise. The fact that Babylon's fall is described in this way (see 50:15) is an indication that this vision was written before the fact. We should understand this language as stereotypical to denote the fall of the city, which did happen, though, as far as we can tell from other ancient sources, not exactly the way described here (see Additional Notes on 50:15).

51:59–64 / The oracles proper ended in verse 58, but now Jeremiah gives instructions to **Seraiah, son of Neriah, the son of Mahseiah** to deliver the oracle in Babylon. This Seraiah is likely a scribe who is a brother of Baruch, who has the same genealogy according to 32:12. Seraiah was part of an official royal embassy to Babylon in 593 B.C. (Zedediah's **fourth year**). Since he shows himself to be so unsympathetic to Jeremiah throughout much of the book, it is doubtful that the king was aware of Seraiah's involvement with Jeremiah. It is also very unlikely that his oracle would have been read to Babylonians. It was likely read to the faithful among the exiles of 597 B.C. who were already in Babylon. It would have been a source of encouragement to them to think that their oppressors would ultimately get what they deserve from the Lord.

Besides orally delivering the message, Seraiah was also to perform a symbolic action that would reinforce the prophet's message. He was to take the scroll on which the oracle was written, tie it to a rock and throw it into the **Euphrates,** the great river that passed by Babylon. As the rock plummeted to the bottom of the river, Seraiah was to announce that the Babylonians themselves would have the same fate.

With these words, Jeremiah's prophecy ends. However, the book itself continues with a description of the fall of Jerusalem and the exile of its inhabitants.

Additional Notes §96

50:15 / The event-vision of the fall of Babylon here describes the crumbling of the **towers** and **walls** of the city. Indeed, most ancient sources agree that after Cyrus defeated Babylon's army led by Nabonidus at Opis, he was able to divert the waters from a river that was part of the defensive system of Babylon and enter the city without violence while the Babylonian leaders were drinking (Xenophon, Cyropaedia vii 5; Herodotus I 191; Nabonidus Chronicle [ANET, 306]).

50:16 / After the Persians defeated the Babylonians, they allowed all the people exiled by Babylon to return to their homelands. We learn this about Judah from the recording of the Cyrus Decree in 2 Chronicles 36:23 and Ezra 1:2–4. The Cyrus Cylinder, a document from the Persian government itself, states that Cyrus permitted other nations to return home and restore their temples as well.

50:21 / **Merethaim** and **Pekod** are names that refer to Babylon. The first is mentioned only here in the Bible, but is thought to be a play on the Akkadian word *marratum,* which means "salt water sea," and points to the region in the south of Babylon where the Tigris and Euphrates meet what is now called the Persian Gulf. It may also include a play on the Hebrew root *mrh* ("to rebel"). If so, it is a noun in the dual form and could mean "double rebellion." As for Pekod, it refers to an important tribe within Babylon, the Puqudu. The Hebrew root is *pqd,* which means "to punish," and thus we may have another significant word play.

50:36 / There is not a lot of evidence for the presence of **prophets** in neo-Babylonian culture. Except on rare occasions (Mari and neo-Assyria) there is not much evidence of prophecy per se. However, it is interesting that in these exceptions the prophets do play a role in the determination to go to war. It is more likely that here the oracle has in mind what we would call more precisely diviners (and the Hebrew word *bad,* used here, probably designates a diviner [see also Isa. 44:25; Hos. 11:6]), who would observe certain phenomenon (sheep livers were very popular) in order to determine whether or not the king should go to battle.

50:39 / There is some question whether the word translated **owl** (*benot yaᶜanah*) is an eagle-owl (G. R. Driver, "Birds in the Old Testament," *Palestine Exploration Quarterly* 87 [1955], pp. 1–13, also NIV) or an ostrich (NRSV). The point of the verse remains the same in either case. These are birds that dwell in ruins and desolate places. The creature is considered unclean in Leviticus 11:16. For similar use of the word in contexts of judgment, see Isaiah 13:21; 34:13; Micah 1:8.

51:1 / **Leb Kamai** is a cryptogram for Babylon. It is a form of writing called *atbash* (see also 25:25–26) where a word is represented by another word formed from a mirror image of the alphabet. Thus the first letter aleph would be replaced by the last taw; the second bet by the second to last shin. Here *l-b-q-m-y* is replaced with *k-sh-d-y-m,* which are the consonants for Chaldean, a way of referring to Babylon.

51:3 / The Hebrew text of v. 3a is very difficult here. The NIV emends the text so that the sentence is negative (emending from *ʾel* to *ʾal*). From a textual point of view, this is possible, but it does mean that it is strangely addressed to the Babylonian army. After all, v. 3b is clearly addressed to their enemies. It is possible to make a similar emendation and understand the force to be asseverative ("Let the archer string his bow, let him put on his armor").

51:11 / The **Medes** were a mountainous people who were located in the Zagros mountains to the north of Persia and to the northwest of Babylon. In the seventh century, they along with Babylon successfully overthrew the Assyrian empire. However, the Medes and the Babylonians were rivals as well as occasional allies. The Medes did attack Babylon in 539 B.C., but as a part of the Persian empire. The book of Daniel describes the ruler of Babylon after its fall to Persia as Darius the Mede (Dan. 5:30–6:28).

51:34 / The word translated **serpent** here (*tannin*) is more like a sea monster than a snake (*nakhash*). Other occurrences of this word suggest that it has mythological overtones and represents the forces of chaos (Isa. 27:1; 51:9; Ezek. 29:3; 32:2; Ps. 74:13; Job 7:12).

§97 The Fall of Jerusalem (Jer. 52:1–34)

By placing the description of the fall of Jerusalem after the oracles against the foreign nations and as last in the canonical book, the editor reminds the reader of what is of first order importance in the book. Yes, Babylon and the other foreign nations will get what they deserve, but Judah deserves its punishment as well. The description of the fall of Jerusalem also is a way of showing how Jeremiah's earlier prophetic words did come to pass. It is Jeremiah not the false prophets (see Jeremiah 28) who spoke truth.

Jeremiah 52 is very similar to 2 Kings 24:18–25:30. Indeed, this may indicate the same theological circle edited both the historical book and the prophet's words. This circle can possibly be identified as Deuteronomic in the light of the fact that many of the themes of Deuteronomy are important to Samuel-Kings as well as Jeremiah (see Introduction). The two chapters are not exactly the same and the following commentary will point out the significant differences. We might also note that 2 Chronicles 36:11–21 also has an abridged account of the fall of Jerusalem that is related to the Kings and Jeremiah passages. Jeremiah 39:1–10 also has a shortened form of this account.

52:1–3 / The account of the end of Judah and Jerusalem begins with the inauguration of **Zedekiah** as king of Judah. He became king in consequence of Nebuchadnezzar's putting down a rebellion by Jehoiakim. By the time Nebuchadnezzar got to Jerusalem, Jehoiakim was replaced by Jehoiachin, his son. Nebuchadnezzar defeated the city and took Jehoiachin into exile along with many others. The Babylonian king then put Jehoiachin's uncle Zedekiah on the throne, presumably thinking that he would be a more malleable Babylonian vassal.

He ruled for **eleven years** (597–586 B.C.). His mother was **Hamutal,** who is also mentioned as Jehoahaz' mother (2 Kgs. 23:31). Jehoiakim, along with both of them, was also a son of Josiah but he had a different mother (2 Kgs. 23:36) and of course Jehoiachin was

Jehoiakim's son, not Josiah's. Perhaps this points to a faction within the harem of Josiah, since Jehoahaz, like Josiah, was pro-Babylonian. In other words, we may have an indication why Nebuchadnezzar chose Zedekiah.

Zedekiah was just like Jehoiakim in another matter. He was **evil.** This rather general statement indicates that Zedekiah did not consistently follow Yahweh. Earlier oracles show Jeremiah's extreme displeasure with Zedekiah's policies (21:1–14; 37:1). The destruction of Jerusalem and Judah is attributed to his evil, which is simply the culmination of the evil of Judah's kings through the ages.

The text abruptly and briefly announces that **Zedekiah rebelled** against the king of Babylon. This certainly entailed the cessation of tribute payments and perhaps the expulsion of Babylonian agents in Jerusalem, but we are not told this explicitly. Nor are we told why Zedekiah rebelled. Something must have signaled to him that it was possible to succeed in such a rebellion, but we are not told what that was.

52:4–11 / In response to Zedekiah's rebellion, Nebuchadnezzar mobilized his army and marched on Jerusalem. The date for his campaign is given as **the tenth day of the tenth month** of Zedekiah's ninth year. This is January 15, 588 B.C. in our calendar. In typical fashion, Nebuchadnezzar deployed his army around the city walls of Jerusalem and laid siege to it, not allowing anyone in or out. The **siege works** would include barricades, guard posts, and the like that would effectively cut Jerusalem off from the rest of the world and its supplies. Jerusalemites would have stored as many provisions as they could before the siege, but these could * 5 and 6, the siege lasted until **the ninth day of the fourth month** of Zedekiah's eleventh year on the throne. This would be July 18, 586 B.C.; thus, the siege lasted for eighteen months. It is doubtful that Nebuchadnezzar was personally present during this long period of time. Most of it would have been quite boring work, essentially starving out the city.

According to verse 6, it was in the ninth day of the fourth month of the eleventh year that the effects of the city's **famine** became so severe that the city fell. The city wall was breached, probably because the army was so weak that it could not effectively fight. Even so, they had enough energy to run. According to verse 7 they found an opening in the Babylonian siege and managed to slip out of the city and head east toward the **Arabah,** the semiarid land directly to the east of Jerusalem. They apparently were led by none other than the king himself, because verse 8 indicates that the Babylonians overtook them in the plains near **Jericho,** just before they could cross the Jordan River. It is not clear whether or not they had a plan or a particular destination in mind.

The Babylonians were interested in Zedekiah and his family and the other officials. As for the army, it says they scattered. Among the remnants of the army would have been Ishmael who plays such an important role in the events recorded in Jeremiah 40–41.

The captives were taken to **Riblah** which was in Hamath, in what is today Syria. This site is well known from extrabiblical sources as the main staging area for the Babylonian army in Syro-Palestine. Nebuchadnezzar himself was present at this command post, and it was here that he determined the fate of Zedekiah and the others. And it was a gruesome fate. He began by having Zedekiah's sons executed in front of the defeated Judean king. He then blinded him; the last thing Zedekiah saw was the death of his sons. Nebuchadnezzar then had him bound and taken to Babylon where he was put in prison till he died. We never hear when that happened. Later in the chapter we hear about the release of Jehoiachin, who had been exiled in 597 B.C. (see comments to vv. 31–34).

52:12–23 / The narrative now moves to the destruction of the city of Jerusalem. These events are dated to **the tenth day of the fifth month** of Nebuchadnezzar's nineteenth year (August 17, 586 B.C.; see Additional Notes for the variant in 2 Kgs. 25:8). The shift in dating from Zedekiah's reign to Nebuchadnezzar's has to do with the fact that Zedekiah was no longer king.

It should be pointed out that the Babylonians had not been quick to destroy Jerusalem. They had tried to pacify the city in other ways since they began to control it in 605 B.C. They had initiated limited deportations in 605 B.C. (Daniel and his three friends) and 597 B.C. (Jehoiachin). They had put a legitimate Davidic descendant on the throne (Zedekiah), whom they thought was pro-Babylonian. Nonetheless, this city kept rebelling, so finally Nebuchadnezzar decided to destroy the city once and for all. He put one of his leading officials in charge of its demolition. **Nebuzaradan** set fire to the temple, for the Israelites the most horrifying aspect of this razing of the city (vv. 17–23 will continue this theme). But he also burned the royal palace as well as the houses of its ordinary inhabitants. The walls were also destroyed, rendering the city completely defenseless. Many people were led into exile (see vv. 24–30), but the Babylonians did leave some of the poor of the land. It would be a misunderstanding of the exile to imagine the country completely depopulated.

While verse 13 tells us that Nebuzardan burned the temple, verses 20–23 inform us that he plundered its valuable assets: the two **bronze pillars,** the **Sea** standing on **twelve bronze bulls,** the **moveable stands,** and the smaller items that were made from bronze (**pots, shovels, wick trimmers, sprinkling bowls, dishes**), silver, or gold (**basins, censers, sprinkling bowls, pots, lampstands, dishes,** and **bowls**). These would have been used in various rituals in the temple service. Some of these items may have been replacements for an earlier plundering of the temple, which Daniel 1 mentions took place during the third year of Jehoiakim (605 B.C.). For the details of some of these objects see the comments on Jer. 27:16–22.

52:24–27a / After listing the various items plundered by the Babylonians, the text now turns to the human toll that resulted from the defeat of the city, beginning in verses 9–11 with the fate of the king, his sons, and other various governmental officials.

Verses 24–27a speak of certain other priestly and political figures. **Seraiah,** the chief priest, and **Zephaniah,** his immediate subordinate are mentioned by name because of their importance. This Seraiah is not mentioned elsewhere in the book of Jeremiah. His son, Jehozadak, went to Babylon (1 Chr. 6:13–15) and his grandson was head priest during the immediate postexilic period (Hag. 1:1; Zech. 3:1; 6:11, see also comments at Jer. 51:59). Zephaniah might be the person of the same name in Jer. 21:1; 29:25–29; 35:4; 37:3. Also listed, though not by name, were **the three doorkeepers,** priests who were responsible to guard the entrances to the temple.

In terms of political figures, none are mentioned by name, but rather by position. These include **the officer in charge of the fighting men, seven royal advisors, the secretary who was chief officer in charge of conscripting the people of the land and sixty of his men.** All these people, priestly and political, who are listed in this unit were taken to Nebuchadnezzar in Riblah where they were executed.

52:27b–30 / The climactic statement concerning the aftermath of the destruction of Jerusalem has to do with the exile of the inhabitants. They are as follows:

In Nebuchanezzar's seventh year (597 B.C.): **3,023** people

In his eighteenth year (587 B.C.): **832** people

In his twenty-third year (582 B.C.): **745** people

As we look at these numbers, we might be surprised how low they are. As verse 30 informs us, these numbers add up to **4,600 people.** But we must remember that these people would be the leadership of Judah, and so their forced departure would be particularly difficult for the native population that remained behind. And many did remain behind, as we learn from Jeremiah 40–41. It is also possible that this number refers only to adult males. At least that is the way many understand the discrepancy between the number given for the 597 exiles here in Jeremiah (832) and the number given for the same period in 2 Kings 24:14 (10,000).

The exile of 582 persons likely refers to the almost certain Babylonian retaliation for the assassination of Gedaliah and the massacre of the Babylonian garrison.

52:31–34 / In spite of this devastating recounting of events, the book of Jeremiah (like the book of Kings) ends on a positive, not a negative, note. The final recorded event is neither destruction nor exile, but the release of King **Jehoiachin** from prison. This happened in the twenty-fifth day of **the twelfth month of the thirty-seventh year** of the exile (April 2, 561 B.C.). This was the first year of the reign of Nebuchadnezzar's son, **Evil-Merodach** (Amel-Marduk in Akkadian, meaning "man of Marduk"), and may well have been a goodwill gesture. Jehoiachin had been exiled in the 597 deportation.

Not only did the king release him from prison, but he also exalted him among all the kings in exile. Interestingly, we actually have a Babylonian palace ration list (ANET^3, 308) that mentions Jehoiachin as a recipient of royal largesse.

This final chapter serves two important purposes. First, it makes it clear that Jeremiah's message of judgment on Judah for its sin came to fulfillment. Second, it anticipates the fact that Jeremiah's message of hope after judgment (chs. 30–33) will come to realization.

Additional Notes §97

52:12 / A slight discrepancy occurs in the dating found here and in 2 Kgs. 25:8, where these actions are dated to the seventh rather than to the **tenth day of the nineteenth year.** As Lundbom (*Jeremiah 37–52,* p. 519) points out, the rabbis suggested that the events described here may have been spread out over many days.

Lamentations

Introduction: Lamentations

Title

Those who read this book in an English translation know it by the title Lamentations. Thus, the book's title describes its genre (see below) and conforms to other biblical books whose titles also identify a genre (whether correctly or not: Deuteronomy, Chronicles, Psalms, Proverbs, Song of Songs, Acts, Revelation).

The English title derives from the ancient versions and early interpreters. In antiquity, the book was referred to by its opening word: *ʾeka* ("how?"). The rabbis referred to the book as *qinot,* the Septuagint (Greek Old Testament) entitled the book *Threni,* and the Vulgate referred to it as *Lamenta*—all meaning "Lamentations."

Place in Canon

For English speaking readers of the Bible the book of Lamentations follows Jeremiah and precedes Ezekiel. This order follows the order found in ancient manuscripts of the Septuagint, which tended to order the biblical books in chronological order. Since the traditional view is that Jeremiah wrote Lamentations (see Author and Date), it was logical to append it to the book associated with that prophet.

Many ancient Hebrew editions of Bible place Lamentations in the third major section of the canon (the Writings [*Ketubim*]). Codex Leningradensis, the earliest complete Hebrew Bible, representing the climax of the work of the Masoretes, is such an example, placing Lamentations after Ecclesiastes and before Esther, in a section of five books (which begins with Ruth and ends with Esther), called the *Megillot* ("Scrolls"). The rabbis associated the *Megillot* with major annual festivals, and Lamentations traditionally was read on the Ninth of Ab, the commemoration of major disasters of the Jewish people.

Author and Date

The Hebrew text (MT) of Lamentations does not name an author or a date of composition. However, the tradition that the book was the work of Jeremiah is an ancient one, going back at least to the Septuagint, which adds to the beginning the following statement: "And it came to pass after Israel had gone into captivity, and Jerusalem was laid waste, that Jeremiah sat weeping and composed this lament over Jerusalem and said . . ." The Vulgate and church tradition follow the Septuagint, which also relocates the book from the Writings (specifically, the *Megillot*) to a position right after the book of Jeremiah (where it is found in English versions). Early Jewish tradition also associates Jeremiah with the book of Lamentations (*b. B. Bat.* 14b–15a). Even today, popular study Bibles intended for laypeople name Jeremiah as the author of the book.

It is not unfeasible that Jeremiah is the author of the book. Provan (*Lamentations,* 5), for instance, who himself is agnostic about authorship, indicates the following close connections between the book of Jeremiah and Lamentations: Lam. 2:14/Jer. 5:31; Lam. 2:22/Jer. 6:25; Lam. 3:14/Jer. 20:7; Lam. 3:53/Jer. 38:6; Lam. 4:17/Jer. 2:36.

On closer examination, doubt can be cast on the belief that Jeremiah wrote the book. The most powerful argument against Jeremiah authorship is that while Lamentations does name the sin of the people as the cause of the destruction of Jerusalem, the book is more passionate in its articulation of the pain of the people than its pointing fingers and casting blame. Of course, one might respond by simply saying that Jeremiah's postdestruction stance takes a different tone. However, what the book of Jeremiah does tell us about Jeremiah's attitude in the immediate exilic period shows no abatement in his belief that what God has done was not excessive, but rather expected, natural, and right (Jer. 40–44).

In the final analysis, we agree with many contemporary interpreters of Lamentations (Provan, Berlin, Dobbs-Allsopp) that it is possible, but doubtful that Jeremiah wrote the book. The book is thus anonymous.

The same level of skepticism should also be directed toward the idea that there are multiple authors of the book. Those who depart from Jeremiac authorship of the book are occasionally open to accepting multiple authorship. H. von der Hardt, who was the first to depart from the long-held tradition of Jeremaic authorship in 1712, argued, humorously enough, that the five chapters were written by Daniel, Shadrach, Meschach, Abednego, and King Jehoiachin respectively (Kaiser, 24). Although based in part on the fact that the five chapters may be read as five separate elegies, multiple authorship is an unnecessary hypothesis.

It is also true that there are multiple "voices" in the book. Besides the poet's voice, we also hear in the first two chapters from the Virgin Daughter of Judah and from the "man who has seen affliction" in the third chapter. Some interpreters want to make a distinction between these voices, suggesting that the Virgin Daughter convinces the poet to be more sympathetic to her plight or that the position of passive, expectant, hopeful suffering of the "man of affliction" contrasts with the scream and accusations of the Virgin Daughter. However, this reads more differences into the "voices" than are there. The Virgin Daughter and the "man of affliction" are poetic vehicles through which the poet speaks throughout. That is why the commentary that follows occasionally attributes to the poet thoughts that are articulated by the personifications of the first three chapters.

If we cannot be precise about authorship, can we at least name a specific occasion or time period for its composition? For many years, the answer to that question was affirmative, associating Lamentations with the destruction of Jerusalem by Babylon in 587 B.C. However, Provan (most clearly), followed by Berlin, Gerstenberger, and others, have pointed out that the language of the book does not definitively place the book in the exilic period. Nowhere are the destroyers of the city named. It is just an assumption of traditional readings that associate the enemy with the Babylonians, and Jerusalem was destroyed more than once between the 6th and 2d centuries B.C. (we have only to think of the damage done by the Seleucids in the middle 2d century B.C.) Gerstenberger is absolutely right that Lamentations is not a historical report, but rather a liturgical text that could be used for any number of catastrophes or for all of them (Psalms, *Part 2, and Lamentations,* p. 473: "Lamentations has been cast into the liturgical shape of ceremonial mourning, not into any kind of historical report"). Indeed, the fact that Lamentations is the main biblical text for the annual 9th of Ab commemoration (see Lamentations: Place in Canon) is an indication of this.

Even though one should not be dogmatic about it, the traditional view that Lamentations was written in the aftermath of the destruction of 587 B.C. seems a sound one. After all, much biblical material is written in anticipation of that disaster (Deuteronomic History; Jeremiah; Ezekiel). One other argument for this time frame, mentioned by Gerstenberger, is the reference to the Edomites in Lam. 4:21–22. We know that the Edomites harassed the Judeans at the time of the Babylonian siege of Jerusalem. The lament that is most like Lamentations, Psalm 137, mentions the Edomites and clearly names the Babylonians as the enemy (other lament psalms like Ps. 74 that may be and probably should be associated with 587 are more vague).

That said, how close the book was written to the destruction of Jerusalem remains a question. Many have pointed to the vivid language of the book to argue that the book was composed by an eyewitness, virtually while the smoke still filled the air. However, the fact that Mesopotamian city laments (see Genre and Ancient Near Eastern Background below), which are also vivid, clearly were part of the rebuilding ritual has led many to hesitate being so certain (Hallo, "Lamentations and Prayers," p. 1872). Berlin also points out that rabbinic literature pertaining to the defeat of the Jews in A.D. 70 and the Bar Kochba revolution of the 2d century A.D. came from a much later period. Her even more recent analogy has to do with Holocaust literature, which did not flourish immediately after that tragedy, but years later, yet without losing its intensity or vividness.

So much that seems obvious on a first reading of Lamentations becomes less obvious on a careful reading. Based on the fact that it is in the part of the biblical canon that focuses in many direct and indirect ways on the events of the sixth century, it is fair to ask the reader to keep that historical moment in mind as the most likely inspiration for the composition of the book. Still, one must recognize (along with Gerstenberger) that the text is liturgical and can be used for other moments of corporate suffering.

In conclusion, the traditional authorship is certainly not impossible, but it is doubtful. The traditional date of the book (coming soon after the destruction of Jerusalem) has more merit, but that, too, is not without question. Happily, these are not crucial issues for our purposes, since the text does not insist on Jeremiah being its author nor the exilic period as its date of composition. Interpretation does not depend on the answer to these questions (Provan, *Lamentations,* pp. 7–11).

Genre and Ancient Near Eastern Background

A Lament

Throughout the history of interpretation, the title (see above) given to this book has consistently recognized it as a lament. A lament is a cry uttered when life falls apart.[1] The laments of the psalms, with which Lamentations has many similarities, are typically cries to God, prayers in which the speakers describe how their life has become disoriented and often challenge God on that basis.

The poet of Lamentations speaks from the perspective of a suffering survivor of the destruction of Jerusalem, the immediate cause of the complaint that leads to the lament. Ferris (1992), correctly associates Lamentations in particular with the communal laments of the Psalms. He identifies about twenty examples of such psalms, some of which could be debated, but especially relevant are the five which give expression to the despair of the people after defeat in battle (Pss. 44, 60, 74, 79, 80 [I would add 137]). Lamentations is even similar to these psalms in terms of its lack of historical precision, which allows the text to be used in multiple settings, that is, after more than one defeat. While there are significant reasons to think that Lamentations was written after the defeat of Jerusalem in 587 B.C., it could be and has been (e.g., the Ninth of Ab observance) used in relationship to other national calamities.

The book of Lamentations has at least one notable difference from laments found in the Psalter. Most of the psalmic laments sound a note of confidence in God or praise for him. Indeed, some scholars believe this is a defining characteristic of a lament and thus prefer to use a different term for Lamentations (dirge).[2] However, the difference is not as stark as suggested. For one thing, it is true that Lamentations does express a note of hope in the middle of the book. This fact needs to be recognized in spite of the argument that that hope has been overemphasized (Linafelt in particular). Psalm 44 is similar to Lamentations in that its note of confidence is found in the middle part of the prayer (vv. 6–8), and like Lamentations, it concludes with a series of questions and challenges directed to God with the hope of rousing him to action (see the similar ending in Ps. 60).

The identification of Lamentations as a corporate lament stands in spite of the fact that the poet often speaks with the voice of an individual, whether directly in his own voice, in that of the Virgin Daughter of Zion (chs. 1–2), or in that of the "man of affliction" (ch. 3). It is only in chapters 4–5 that the poet speaks in the first person plural ("we"/"us"). As explained above as well as at various points in the commentary, these individual voices are speaking on behalf of the community, the Virgin Daughter and the "man of affliction" being personifications of the survivors of the destruction.

Thus, the book is best described as a corporate lament on the occasion of the destruction of the city. It gives expression to the pain, suffering, disappointment, and anger of the survivors of that destruction. Though not a dominant tone, it also expresses the guilt and hope of these survivors. They don't only blame God or human agents (most likely the Babylonians originally, though they are not named, as well as the Edomites, who are [4:21–22]), they also blame themselves and hope that God will rescue them. As a matter of fact, it is through a combination of complaint, confession, cajoling, perseverance, cries, and screams that they hope to provoke God into action on their behalf.

Ferris points to 1 Kings 8:33–34 as an anticipation for precisely this kind of appeal to God. The setting is Solomon's dedication of the temple, and in these verses he anticipates the disaster that the survivors of the destruction of that temple now faced: "When your people Israel have been defeated by an enemy because they have sinned against you, and when they turn back to you and confess your name, praying and making supplication to you in this temple, then hear from heaven and forgive the sin of your people Israel and bring them back to the land you gave their fathers."[3]

Ancient Near Eastern City Laments

Lamentations is best understood as a corporate lament bemoaning the destruction of a city, that is, a "city lament." As such, the book does not exist in a generic vacuum. There is a well-established genre of city laments known in particular from five compositions that derive from the period of the destruction of the Ur III dynasty (ca. 2100–2000 B.C.) at the hands of invaders from the east and the west.[4] This destruction had a catastrophic effect on the minds of those who survived it.[5] This highly developed and civilized kingdom was the result of a Sumerian renaissance after a period of Akkadian rule that may have considered itself impregnable from attack from the outside world. Ibbi-Sin, the last ruler of the dynasty (ca. 2028–2004 B.C.), actually started his reign in a relatively strong position, but soon he was under siege and was perhaps explanted by Ishbi-Irra of Mari.

In any case, the destruction of Ur, its temples, and surrounding cities worked deep into the psyche of those who witnessed it. Indeed, five compositions[6] survive that lament the fall of the city. These include:

The Lamentation over the Destruction of Ur

The Lamentation over the Destruction of Sumer and Ur[7]

The Nippur Lament

The Eridu Lament[8]

The Uruk Lament[9]

A translation of the first two lamentations is easily accessible,[10] while the other three are translated and discussed in more specialized literature.

All five texts refer to the fall of the Ur III kingdom. Their tone is one of fear and disbelief. The first two refer specifically to the fall of the capital city of Ur. The Lamentation over the Destruction of Ur, a composition of some eleven "songs" for a total of 436 lines, will serve as our example of the Sumerian genre. It begins with a list of deities from various cities of the realm who have left their temples (referred to as "their sheepfold") in anticipation of the destruction of the city. A typical example refers to Inanna:

> Inanna has abandoned their house Erech, her sheepfold (has been delivered) to the [wind]

The second song is a "bitter lament," which ends with a question, "The lament which is bitter—how long will it grieve the weeping Nanna?" Nanna is the city-god of Ur, and his wife Ningal complains in the next two songs that the chief gods of the pantheon had decreed the destruction of the city. Songs 5 and 6 describe the destruction of the land in mythological and human terms, which results in Ningal leaving the city:

> Its lady like a flying bird departed from her city;
> Ningal like a flying bird departed from her city.

The conclusion of the composition prays for the return of the deities who have acted like an enemy toward the city.

At first it was argued that the feelings were so raw and the description so realistic that the composition of these texts had to have occurred soon after the events. A closer look at the compositions show that two of them (the Nippur and Uruk laments) mention King Ishme-Dagan of Isin, so they had to have been written at least fifty years after the destruction. Today, most scholars[11] suggest that the purpose of these texts is to assuage the wrath of the gods on the occasion of the rebuilding of the temples. In Hallo's opinion, "they seek to absolve the royal rebuilder by heaping blame on the foreigners who caused the original devastation."[12] Kutscher believes that the reason why there are multiple lamentations for the same destruction is because "a new lament was composed for the restoration of each temple," and the reason why so many copies of the text survived in different cities was because "once used," they were "put into circulation in the scribal schools."[13] The conclusion that these Sumerian city laments were composed at the time of the rebuilding of the temples rather than soon after the destruction has had a significant effect on the debate concerning the date of the composition of Lamentations (see Author and Date).

While on the surface the similarities of content, tone, motifs, and themes between the book of Lamentations and these Sumerian city laments are unmistakable, the long period of time between the two has not gone unnoticed. After all, there is at least a period of thirteen centuries between them. For this reason, scholars like T. F. McDaniel have questioned whether the Sumerian texts are relevant at all for the study of the biblical book.[14] Even more recently, though, Gwaltney[15] and others have suggested that a line of continuity may be drawn between these early Sumerian texts and two Akkadian lament genres, the *balag* and the *ersemma* texts. The *balag*[16] are congregational city laments from the Old Babylonian, Neo-Assyrian, Neo-Babylonian, and Seleucid periods (ca. 18th to 2d centuries B.C.). The main difference with the earlier Sumerian lament is that these are more liturgical and less historically specific, thus actually making them closer to the type of literature we find in Lamentations.

Literary Features

The author(s) of Lamentations wrote compelling, imaginative, heartrending poetry. It is marked by all the typical features of Hebrew poetry, including tersely written cola combined into parallel lines and a striking use of imagery. In terms of imagery, one poetic strategy especially stands out: the use of personification. Chapter 1 presents the figure of the Virgin Daughter of Jerusalem, widowed and deserted, while in chapter 3 the people of God are again personified this time as a man of affliction. These and the other metaphors of the book will be unpacked in the commentary.

Perhaps the most striking literary feature of the book of Lamentations is its use of the acrostic form. Even those who read the text in English can notice an interesting symmetry in the number of verses of the chapters. Chapters 1, 2, 4, and 5 each have

22 verses, and chapter 3, which is the lone exception, has 66 verses (a multiple of 22). Those who know the basics of Hebrew know that there are 22 letters in the Hebrew alphabet, and those aware of ancient Hebrew literary conventions know that poets will occasionally use a device called an acrostic to direct and structure their poems.

In an acrostic, the first letters of the poetic lines form a meaningful pattern.[17] Some acrostics, attested in other ancient Semitic languages like Akkadian but not Hebrew, may spell the poet's name or give a message of some sort. In the Hebrew Bible, we find only one type of acrostic, namely an abecediary, that is, poetic lines that begin with successive letters of the Hebrew alphabet.

Upon closer look at the five chapters of Lamentations we can observe an asymmetrical use of the acrostic form. The first chapter has 22 long verses, each verse starting with a successive letter. The second chapter is similar to the first. As mentioned, the third chapter departs from this pattern with its 66 verses and in this case, the letters appear in groups of 3, and the verses are much shorter. For instance, in verses 1–3 each word begins with an *alef,* the first letter of the Hebrew alphabet, and for verses 4–6 each word begins with a *bet,* the second, and so on through the entirety of the alphabet. Chapter 4 returns to the pattern of the first two chapters (each verse begins with a successive letter). Most surprising, however, is chapter 5. In this final chapter, there are again 22 verses but in this case, contrary to expectation, there is no pattern to the opening letter.

Acrostics are easy to describe, but it is not so easy to understand their rationale. Is there meaning to this form?

Scholars have ascribed many motivations to the acrostic form. Some have felt it was a form that helped memorization. Others have felt it communicates wholeness or completeness. Proverbs 31:10–22 is an acrostic that extols the "virtuous woman." One can see how that poem might be taken as a complete description of such a woman. Psalm 119 is a massive acrostic, and after reading it, one does have the sense that everything has been said that could be said about the poet's love of the law.

Developing this last approach, some feel that an acrostic is also a way that a poet communicated a sense of order. Of course, Lamentations as a book communicates just the opposite: disorder, chaos, trouble, incompletion. However, such a rationale for the acrostic could conceivably be operative for Lamentations. After all, the book that begins and continues an acrostic for four chapters finally falls apart in the fifth. Nahum 1 may provide an interesting analogy. The Divine Warrior hymn that begins the book, after the superscription, begins as a fairly straightforward acrostic (though 1:2 is longer than the others), but halfway through the alphabet, the acrostic begins to falter and then falls apart. Since Gunkel,[18] there have been scholars who have tried to "fix" the acrostic. However, I have suggested that here meaning follows form. The poem is about how rivers dry up and mountains quake and fertile areas wither. Poetically, the broken acrostic mirrors that disruption. It may be that the poetic effect of the lack of an acrostic in the final chapter wants to serve the same purpose. Perhaps the extraordinary length of the third chapter and its more elaborate acrostic serves to draw our attention to the middle of the book where we find its only clear message of hope. We might also note that the book of Jeremiah, too, strikes its note of hope in the middle of the text (Jer. 30–33).

But then again maybe the poet just couldn't make the acrostic work in the final chapter. The poet could not communicate his message and retain the acrostic form. Even those of us who believe that God speaks through the authors of the Bible do not believe that they wrote perfect poetry. The point is that we are left to speculate about the function and purpose of the acrostic form.

Theological Themes

Divine Warrior and Covenant

The predominant picture of God in the book is that of a warrior. This metaphor of God's relationship to his people is particularly pervasive in chapter 2, but runs throughout the book. God has assumed a hostile stance toward his people and comes to wage war against them due to their sin.

The Divine Warrior theme runs throughout the Old Testament.[19] Typically, and normatively, God is a warrior who fights on behalf of his people. The first time Yahweh is explicitly called a warrior is in Exodus 15:3, "The LORD is a warrior; the LORD is his name." This statement appears in the context of his rescue of Israel and destruction of the Egyptian army at the Re(e)d Sea. Many of the stories of the Old Testament histories recount God coming to battle on behalf of his people. Some of the most memorable are the battle of Jericho, the defeats of the southern and northern coalitions of the Canaanites, Gideon's defeat of the Midianites, David's defeat of the Philistines, and the list goes on.

A striking example of God's work as a warrior is not a battle between Israel and another nation, but between a representative of that nation, namely David, and a pagan nation, Goliath of Philistia (1 Sam. 17). While Goliath was a professional soldier, physically mammoth, and well-armed, David stood before him as an inexperienced youth, wearing no armor, and armed with a simple slingshot. Even so, he was aware of God's presence with him as a warrior that assures his victory (1 Sam. 17:45–47).

David and Israel's confident attitude was based on the covenant, the relationship between God and Israel that was modeled on ancient Near Eastern treaties between the king of a great nation and a king of a subordinate nation. In such a treaty/covenant, the great king would impose certain requirements (law) on the subordinate. These requirements were sanctioned by a system of rewards and punishments. Deuteronomy bears a similar structure to such an ancient Near Eastern treaty since it is a renewal of the relationship established between God and Israel at Sinai. Deuteronomy 27–28 contain a series of rewards for obedience to the law, many of which are military in nature. An example is Deuteronomy 28:7: "The Lord will grant that the enemies who rise against you will be defeated before you. They will come at you from one direction but flee from you in seven."

However, on the flip side, disobedience to the covenant Lord leads to punishment, which includes military defeat. Deuteronomy 28:25 is the mirror opposite of verse 7: "The Lord will cause you to be defeated before your enemies. You will come at them from one direction but flee from them in seven." The curses for disobedience are developed even further than the rewards for obedience (perhaps anticipating what was to become reality). They include gruesome descriptions of siege and destruction.

Lamentations is a text that depicts the coming of God in response to covenant disobedience (see below). God moves against Jerusalem because of the people's sin. Indeed, Lamentations 4:10 may be compared with a specific covenant curse found in Deuteronomy 28:53–57.

Lamentations was not the first instance of what Moran called "reverse holy war,"[20] in which Israel was the object of God's warring activity. Right after the battle of Jericho, the most powerful city-state of Canaan, Israel experienced defeat at the hands of Ai, a town whose very name means "dump," because of Achan's infringement of the requirement that all war plunder be turned over to God (Josh. 7). In the early chapters of Samuel (1 Sam. 4–7) we read of the capture of the ark by the Philistines. Israel's army under the leadership of Eli's sons, Hophni and Phinehas, had trifled with the ark of the covenant; consequently, God allowed the Philistines to defeat Israel and capture the ark. Even though there are precursors to Lamentations, it is clear that the most terrifying appearance of God as a warrior against Israel took place when the Babylonians defeated Jerusalem, the event most likely behind the composition of the book. Even so, a canonical reading of the book of Lamentations shows that that horrible defeat is not the end of the story of God's involvement as a warrior on behalf of his people.

Reading Lamentations in the Light of the New Testament

Above we noted that Lamentations recognizes God as Israel's enemy. I have argued contrary to much recent opinion (Linafelt; O'Conner; Dobbs-Allsopp) that God has moved against Israel in reaction to Israel's sin as threatened in advance by the covenant curses. The note of hope in the book (Lam. 3:19–27) finds initial fulfillment in the restoration to the land following the decree of Cyrus in 539 B.C. (see Provan, Long, and Longman, pp. 286–97). Though the people return to the land, they are not politically independent. Though the temple is rebuilt, it does not have its former glory. The people are left expecting more. Even after a report of the spiritual and material progress that took place during the work of Ezra and Nehemiah in the fifth century, the final chapter of Ezra-Nehemiah pictures Nehemiah bemoaning continued problems in the covenant community.

The prophets of the exilic and postexilic periods look to the future and see the Divine Warrior. Their vision is not of God as an enemy of his people; rather, it is a vision of a future intrusion of God the Warrior to fight on behalf of his people (Dan. 7; Zech. 14; Mal. 4). The New Testament identifies Jesus as the Divine Warrior who defeats the forces of evil on the cross (Col. 2:13–15) and as the one who will come again in the future for the final battle against all human and spiritual enemies of God (Rev. 19:11–21). Jesus Christ is the Divine Warrior who fights on behalf of his people against the most powerful enemy of all, Satan.

Guilt and Pain in Lamentations

The book of Lamentations articulates the incredible pain and suffering experienced by those who survived the destruction of Jerusalem. The language is vivid and intense; the reader can almost smell the smoke from the smoldering buildings, see the bodies lining the street, and, most poignantly, hear the cries of the children. The poet is so effective that it is almost too much for the reader to bear and makes the sensitive reader ask, who is to blame for this carnage?

Recent interpreters have suggested that the traditional reading of the book, which emphasizes the sin and guilt of the people, has been misleading. Dobbs-Allsopp, O'Connor, and especially Linafelt have argued that the book points an angry finger at God.[21]

These scholars are correct to argue that the genre of lament and God's invitation to complain about suffering have been inappropriately suppressed in Christian circles. The lament psalms (i.e., 3, 77, 88) provide models for turning to God and calling on him to respond in times of suffering. Not all suffering and pain is a result of sin, not even suffering that comes from the hand of God (Genesis 37–50 [see 50:19–20], Job; John 9). A number of lament psalms contain an acknowledgement of sin, but some protest innocence and call on God to remove undeserved punishment (e.g., Ps. 26).

Furthermore, it is also true that Lamentations has a different emphasis than the Deuteronomic historians or the prophets, who squarely, consistently, and constantly describe the suffering of Jerusalem as a result of guilt and sin.

The poet of Lamentations draws God's attention to the extreme suffering of his people in order to draw empathy from him, perhaps even to suggest that the suffering has gone beyond what the sin deserves. However, the tone is not bitter and angry, but questioning. In addition, and here is where the recent interpretive innovations are clearly wrong, the book, in all its chapters, and in all of its "voices," is well aware that the final blame lies on the people and their sin.

Not even Linafelt doubts this about chapter 3. In this chapter, the poet speaks through "the man who has seen affliction." This "man," a poetic figure that represents the community of Judah, advocates a patient suffering before God (3:28–30) and a sure expectation that God will change his present angry disposition against his people to a positive one in what is the only clear statement of hope in the book (see especially 3:19–27). That the "man" understands his predicament as the result of his (the community's) sins is very clear from verse 39, "Why should any living man complain when punished for his sins?" Thus, it is not surprising that the "man" advises his hearers to repent by confessing these sins and turning toward God (vv. 40–42).

But Linafelt suggests that interpreters have obsessed on chapter 3 to the neglect of other chapters. He charges that such neglect is the result primarily of misogyny that draws interpreter's attention to a male personification rather than a female one (as in chapters 1 and 2), and also a Christian bias that finds in the "man of affliction" a type of Christ. Furthermore, traditional interpretation is drawn to chapter 3 because it, as mentioned above, does contain the only expression of hope in the book.

Linafelt is correct to suggest that it is wrong to ignore the rest of Lamentations in the interests of chapter 3, though my own reading of other commentators does not support his contention that this actually is the case. Even so, there are reasons to believe that chapter 3 is important to the message of the book. It is the center of the book, a place that often has literary importance in Hebrew literature (and that the message of hope comes in the middle of this center chapter is probably not a literary coincidence). It also draws attention to itself by its extraordinary length.

However, it is not important to argue that Lamentations 3 has extraordinary importance in the book to show that the poetic voices in Lamentations are well aware of the leading role that sin played in producing their horrible predicament. The poet states clearly that "The LORD has brought her grief because of her many sins" (1:5b) and "Jerusalem has sinned greatly and so has become unclean" (1:8a). Personified Jerusalem herself proclaims, "My sins have been bound into a yoke; by his hands they were woven together" (1:14a). As opposed to Linafelt, she exonerates God in 1:18a, "The LORD is righteous, yet I rebelled against his command."

Now it is true that the book also calls for punishment on the human agents who have brought suffering on the people. They have been wicked and thus deserve destruction, but this does not mean that the suffering of the people of Jerusalem was not deserved as again the Virgin Daughter herself states in 1:22, "Let all their wickedness come before you; deal with them as you have dealt with me because of all my sins." The prophets also anticipated the deserved punishment of those whom God used to punish his people while at the same time announcing that the people of God deserved the punishment.

The commentary that follows will explicate further the texts cited above and will also point out other relevant sections of the text. Dobbs-Allsopp, O'Connor, and Linafelt have correctly drawn our attention to the cry of pain and suffering in the book. It is a cry that comes before God in order to elicit pity from him. However, the book also has a deep and pervasive understanding that the people of God themselves have acted in a way that has led to their present suffering. It is not, after all, as if they had not been warned. The terms of the covenant were clearly spelled out as were the consequences of not obeying those terms. In this regard, it is interesting to note that neither O'Connor nor Linafelt show any awareness of the Deuteronomic background to the horrific description of women eating their children in 4:10 (see Deut. 28:56–57). Recognizing such a connection makes it clear that the poet understands that their present predicament is the result of their betrayal of the covenant.

Notes

1. Ferris (1992, p. 10) gives a more detailed definition of a communal lament as "a composition whose verbal content indicates that it was composed to be used by and/or on behalf of a community to express both complain, and sorrow and grief over some perceived calamity, physical or cultural, which had befallen or was about to befall them and to appeal to God for deliverance."

2. Indeed, Hermann Gunkel initiated the modern discussion of the genre of Lamentations by concluding that it was a "mixed genre" (*Mischgattung*), where chapters 1, 2, and 4 were dirges (funeral songs) and chapter 3 an individual lament, and chapters 5 a communal lament.

3. Ferris (1992, p. 106).

4. Among the invaders were Gutians, Elamites, and Amorites.

5. For a brief summary of the time period, see W. W. Hallo and W. K. Simpson, *The Ancient Near East*, pp. 72–87.

6. Hallo adds a sixth lament that focuses on Ekimar. See W. W. Hallo, "Lamentations and Prayers in Sumer and Akkad," p. 1872.

7. For which, see P. Michalowski, *The Lamentation over the Destruction of Sumer and Ur* (Winona Lake, Ind.: Eisenbrauns, 1989).

8. M. W. Green, "The Eridu Lament," *Journal of Cuneiform Studies* 30 (1978), pp. 127–67. "The lament describes an onslaught against the city Eridu, the destruction of the city along with its temple and cult, the anguish of Eridu's primary deities Enki and Damgalnunna, and their abandonment of their city shrine" (see p. 127).

9. M. W. Green, "The Uruk Lament," *Journal of the American Oriental Society* 104 (1984), pp. 253–79.

10. For the Lamentation over the Destruction of Ur, see *ANET*, pp. 455–63, and for the Lamentation over the Destruction of Sumer and

Ur, see *ANET*, pp. 611–19. Confusingly, *COS* 1:535–39 presents a partial translation of the former text, but refers to it as the Lamentation over the Destruction of Sumer and Ur! We will follow the nomenclature of *ANET*. Translations are taken from this source (S. N. Kramer).

11. From his brief comments, it appears that J. Klein (*COS* 1:535, "the laments were composed not long after the events they record") is an exception.

12. W. W. Hallo, "Lamentations and Prayers in Sumer and Akkad," in *Civilizations of the Ancient Near East* (4 vols. in 2; ed. J. M. Sasson; Peabody, Mass.: Hendrickson, 1995), p. 1872.

13. R. Kutscher, *Oh Angry Sea (a-ab-ba hu-luh-ha): the History of a Sumerian Congregational Lament* (New Haven: Yale University Press, 1975), p. 3.

14. T. F. McDaniel, "Alleged Sumerian Influence on Lamentations," *VT* 18 (1968), pp. 19–29.

15. W. C. Gwaltney Jr., "The Biblical Book of Lamentations in the Context of Near Eastern Lament Literature," *More Essays on the Comparative Method* (Scripture in Context 2; ed. W. W. Hallo, J. C. Moyer, and L. G. Perdue; Eisenbrauns, 1983), pp. 191–211.

16. The definitive work on the *balag* is M. E. Cohen, *The Canonical Lamentations of Ancient Mesopotamia* (2 vols.; Bethesda, Md.: CDL Press, 1988).

17. W. G. E. Watson, *Traditional Techniques in Classical Hebrew Verse* (Sheffield: Sheffield Academic, 1984), pp. 190–200.

18. H. Gunkel, "Nahum 1," *ZAW* 13 (1893), pp. 223–44.

19. For a detailed account of this theme throughout the Bible, see T. Longman III and D. Reid, *God Is a Warrior* and the bibliography therein.

20. W. L. Moran, "The End of the Unholy War and the Anti-Exodus, *Biblica* 44 (1963), pp. 333–42.

21. Dobbs-Allsopp, *Lamentations*; K. M. O'Connor, *Lamentations and the Tears of the World*; T. Linafelt, *Surviving Lamentations*.

§1 Lament for and by Jerusalem (Lam. 1:1–22)

1:1–2 / *Alef/Bet.* The poet does not name Jerusalem at the start, but simply speaks of **the city.** The name of the city does not have to be spoken; poet and readers would know the identity of the now deserted city of Jerusalem. As today there is no doubt when a New Yorker refers to "the city," so there is no secret concerning the identity of the city among Judeans. This once bustling place (a city "closely compacted together" [Ps. 122:3]) is now eerily deserted. The poet engages the readers by using an exclamation to get them to picture the scene of the deserted city in their imagination (**How deserted lies the city once so full of people**!). We feel the poet's sadness right from the start as he compares the formerly populated city to the nearly empty one now.

He goes on to compare the city with a widow in a second exclamation (**How like a widow is she . . .** !). This personification also invites the reader to contrast the city's past with its sad present. Once **great among the nations,** this city is like a widow, one bereft of a husband. A widow is now alone when she had once had companionship. She is sad when before she was happy. She who had solid social standing when her husband was alive has now been moved to the bottom rung of life. "Marriage is an image of domestic fullness in Scripture; widowhood is an image of loss and emptiness" (*DBI,* p. 946).

A second image is used that underlines the contrast between the city's past and its present. In the past, she was like a queen—honored, respected, and well cared for. Now she is a slave—despised, exploited, needy.

Verse 2 continues the metaphor of Jerusalem as a widow in mourning. Here she **weeps at night.** The nighttime setting accentuates the loneliness of the scene. The second colon of this first poetic line concretizes the image by citing the **tears** that roll down her **cheeks.**

In a fashion similar to that in Ezekiel 16 (see v. 15), the poet refers to Judah's hoped-for political allies as her **lovers.** The historical books and the prophets (Jer. 2:18, 36; 37) reveal that Judah hoped to fend off the Babylonian threat by means of powerful allies like the Egyptians, not as they should by trusting God. The metaphor of allies as lovers also evokes the metaphor of God as Judah's husband. By taking on other lovers, Judah is committing spiritual adultery against God. These lovers are no longer there. They were unable and unwilling to help Judah in her need. Some even turned against her. The third poetic line of the verse continues this idea. Here Judah's potential allies are called her **friends** rather than her lovers, but the point in the same. They are no longer her friends/allies; they are now her **enemies.**

1:3–4 / *Gimel/Dalet.* The reason Judah is desolated is because she has **gone into exile.** The exile, of course, here refers to the aftermath of the Babylonian defeat of Judah in 586 B.C. Not all citizens of Judah, but the leading citizens, are taken away from Judah and brought to Babylon, thus causing major social disruption (see Jer. 52:28–30). Babylon's final victory in 586 B.C. was preceded by earlier sieges in 605 (Dan. 1:1–2) and 597. These conditions brought **affliction and hard labor.** There was also inner turmoil as godly prophets like Jeremiah sought to sway a hostile monarchy to repent.

As a result of the exile, Judah no longer enjoys a separate existence, but rather **dwells among the nations.** The promised land had been a **resting place** for them but now their leaders live in a land not their own. She has become vulnerable to her enemies (**all who pursue her have overtaken her**).

The desolation of Judah continues to be the theme of verse 4, where the initial focus is on the roads at the time of the **appointed feasts.** The three feasts are Passover, Pentecost, and Tabernacles. At these times, all God's faithful were to travel to Zion (Jerusalem) to celebrate. The **roads to Zion** would have been packed with joyful celebrants. Indeed, most scholars believe that the "Psalms of Ascent" (Pss. 120–134) were sung during these pilgrimages. This picture contrasts vividly with the empty roads of the period after the destruction of Jerusalem and the deportation of its leading citizens.

With travelers off the road, the **gateways** into Jerusalem are also empty. The gates of a city in the ancient Near East were typically teeming with people, but because of the deportation of many and the suppression of those who remained, they are **desolate.** In particular, **maidens** and **priests** are said to be depressed and the city itself, still being personified as a woman (**she**), is said to be in **anguish.** Priests would have played a special role during the appointed (religious) feasts and women too are often associated with such joyous occasions (see Provan, *Lamentations,* p. 40, who lists Judg. 21:19–21; Jer. 31:13; Ps. 68:25).

1:5–7 / *He/Vav/Zayin.* Her unfortunate situation has come about because **her foes,** most notably Babylon, have become **her masters.** In 586, not only was Judah taken and Jerusalem significantly destroyed, but the land was incorporated into the Babylonian empire as a province. No longer was there a king in Judah. Now a Babylonian-appointed Judean governor, Gedaliah, was the local official representing the empire. The siege of Jerusalem completed, Babylon was now **at ease,** having subdued the people of God.

The second parallel line of verse 5 articulates the reason for Jerusalem's present problems. It is her **many sins.** These sins are not detailed here, but the prophet Jeremiah mentions a number including lying, kidnapping, murder, theft, and Sabbath-breaking (Jer. 7:9–11; 9:5; 17:19–27). They even offered their own children as sacrifices (Jer. 7:30–34). The people of God also offended God by forming illegitimate and ill-advised foreign military alliances, showing they trusted other nations to protect them rather than God their Divine Warrior. But worst of all was their idolatry (Jer. 10:1–16). In this way, Israel broke covenant (Jer. 11:1–17) and thus deserved the punishment that it received.

These sins have led to Jerusalem's destruction and the **exile** of many of her leading citizens. Among the exiles would be **children,** the poet focusing on them to increase the pathos of the description.

The poet then remarks that the **splendor** has departed from the **Daughter of Zion.** Zion is the mountain made sacred by the presence of the temple. "Daughter" is sometimes used with geographical terms to indicate those areas that are in some sense dependent on the named geographical location. In that case, the Daughter of Zion would be a reference to Jerusalem and its surrounding villages. Referring to Jerusalem as the Daughter of Zion also effectively communicates a kind of intimacy and concern for the place that makes its destruction all the more tragic.

The splendor (*hadar*) of the Daughter of Jerusalem speaks to its eminence and majesty (Ps. 48:1–3). However, "splendor" is a word that is often associated with God himself (Ps. 29:4; 96:16; Isa. 2:10, 19, 21). To say that splendor has departed certainly should be connected to the idea that God abandoned his temple on the eve of the destruction of Jerusalem (Ezek. 9–11).

In the midst of such a crisis one would expect the leaders of the people to take charge and provide direction. However, the poet describes them (**her princes**) like **deer** with no pasture. Such deer would wander from place to place in desperation to find food. Deer don't typically attack those who hunt them; they flee as do Judah's princes before those who pursue them.

In verse 7, the NIV does not well represent the proper syntax of the first two cola (see Additional Notes), creating a slight change of meaning. **Jerusalem,** still personified as a bereaved woman) **remembers her affliction and wandering.** The latter refers to the destruction of the city of Jerusalem and the subsequent displacement of its population. In addition, the personified city remembers her previous esteemed position before God's judgment led to her downfall (**all the treasures that were hers in days of old**). While Israel and Judah never achieved superpower status, they knew days when they had more than enough resources to enjoy the life God gave them in the land.

The second two cola of this verse reflect on the powerlessness of the people of God at the time of their fall. When the **enemy** (the Babylonians) attacked, they had no one to help them, not even Egypt, which had indicated that they would help them against the onslaught from the north. The allies they had depended on had let them down. Since they were so defenseless, their enemies simply **laughed** at them since their defeat was so easy. An obedient, godly Israel would be the occasion for God's laughter at their enemies (Ps. 2:4), but here the enemies laugh at God's people because he has abandoned them.

1:8–9 / *Khet/Tet.* Again (see 1:5) the poet points to the excessive sinfulness of God's people as the cause of their present condition. They have rendered previously holy Jerusalem **unclean.** The book of Leviticus describes the conditions that render a person unclean. Since Jerusalem continues to be personified as a woman in this passage, perhaps the reader is to think of her as menstruating or as experiencing some other type of vaginal discharge (Lev. 15:19–30). Of course, if this is right, it is metaphorical of an uncleanness caused by moral rather than ritual infractions. Her uncleanness has rendered her repulsive not only to others but even to herself (**she herself groans and turns away**).

The **filthiness** on her skirts likely refers to the menstrual blood (though for the possibility that it is the result of sexual violence, see Additional Notes). The reversal was a shock (**her fall was astounding**). The surprise of Jerusalem's defeat was not the result of having no warning. God sent many prophets (including Ezekiel and Jeremiah) to warn them. It must have been the theological presumption of the citizens of Judah that led them to think that they would never be defeated (see Jer. 7). With no one to comfort her, personified Jerusalem turns to God and pours out her heart as she expresses her pain. Her brief prayer serves to elicit some measure of sympathy on the part of the reader.

1:10 / *Yod.* The metaphor of the violated woman in 1:8–9 prepares the way for the description of the violated temple. Nothing disturbed the psyche of Judeans, especially the faithful, more than the pillaging of the temple. The temple was the place God made his presence known on earth. Even apostate Judeans felt that the temple was special; it was a sacred spot. Jeremiah (see chs. 7 and 26) castigated the sinful people of God not for neglecting the temple, but in being presumptuous about its significance. They felt that since the temple was in Jerusalem nothing would happen to that city. How wrong they were. God abandoned the temple (Ezek. 9–11) and then used the Babylonians to rob its remaining **treasures** and destroy it.

To do so, soldiers from Babylon and their vassal states (**those you had forbidden to enter your assembly**) had to enter the holy precincts. Such an act in and of itself would be considered sacrilege. Psalm 74 presents a horrifying description:

> Your foes roared in the place where you met with us;
> they set up their standards as signs.
> They behaved like men wielding axes
> to cut through a thicket of trees.
> They smashed all the carved paneling
> with their axes and hatchets.
> They burned your sanctuary to the ground;
> they defiled the dwelling place of your Name.
> They said in their hearts, "We will crush them completely!"
> They burned every place where God was worshiped in the land. (Ps. 74:4–8)

1:11 / *Kaf.* The devastation of the land left the people homeless and struggling to survive. After such an attack, **food** would have been scarce for those who survived and those who were not deported. **Treasures** mean nothing if one is starving, and the people are willing to give them up for simple bread. Earlier, personified Jerusalem appealed to God to consider her suffering (1:9), now the people (or perhaps since the prayer is in the singular [**I**] personified Jerusalem standing for the people) plaintively speak to God to pay attention to their horrid situation.

1:12 / *Lamed.* The verse opens with personified Jerusalem questioning (see Additional Notes for an alternative understanding) those **who pass by.** Those who pass by are likely thought to be those who would walk by and marvel at the frightful sight of a destroyed city. At the same time, those who walk by might be likened to those who walk by a desolated human being. A contemporary analogy might be walking by a homeless person ravaged by a hard life and living on the streets. The temptation of those passing by would be to mock (2 Chr. 7:21–22) and to exploit (Ps. 80:12; 89:41). The most telling use of the phrase comes in Jeremiah (18:16; 19:8; 22:8; 49:17; 50:13), where those who pass by a ruined city are appalled.

Speaking to those who pass by, personified Jerusalem claims to have experienced unprecedented **suffering** and even more importantly attributes the suffering to none other than God himself. God's anger is the explanation for the horrific condition of the city.

1:13 / *Mem.* Though on the human level it was the Babylonian army that destroyed Jerusalem, the poet knows that God was the ultimate actor. Babylon was a tool of God's judgment. Here God is pictured as throwing **fire** (lightning?) down from heaven to burn personified Jerusalem. Indeed, the fire is said to go to her very **bones,** as inward as one might get. The second parallelism uses the common image of a snare to describe the downfall of the city. The **net** is a hunting image and Jerusalem is the prey. Personified Jerusalem was rendered totally weak (**faint**).

1:14 / *Nun.* This verse again pinpoints the cause of God's judging actions on the sins of the people. God has taken the sins and shaped them into a **yoke** that burdens the people. They are enslaved to their sins. They are like an ox or another type of beast of burden yoked to a mill or to a cart. In this way, the poet's image is similar to that of Isaiah in 5:18: "Woe to those who draw sin along with cords of deceit, and wickedness as with cart ropes." Jeremiah dramatizes the yoke image by putting an actual one around his neck and parading around Jerusalem (however, his yoke does not represent sin, but the yoke of servitude that the Babylonian king will soon impose on the people, Jer. 27). By carrying such a heavy burden, personified Jerusalem is soon **sapped of strength.** At that point God brings them into conflict with Babylon (**those I cannot withstand**).

1:15 / *Samek.* Judah had an **army,** but its effectiveness did not depend on its size or the quality of its troops but rather on the disposition of God toward it. Israel won tremendous victories with insufficient troops and/or fighting skill (Jericho; Gideon) and they lost battles with superior strength (Ai). Thus, the fact that God has rejected Judah's warriors is all that is needed to assure defeat. Against Judah's rejected army, God raised an army (Babylonian) to defeat them. The third parallelism in the verse likens her defeat to the crushing of grapes in a **winepress** (see also Isa. 63:1–6). The image is gruesome as one pictures the blood-red juice of a crushed grape and likens it to a crushed, bleeding battlefield casualty.

1:16 / *Ayin.* Like the lamenting psalmist, personified Jerusalem punctuates her sorrowful words with overflowing **tears** (Pss. 6:6; 42:3; 56:8; 80:5; 102:9; 116:8; 119:136). The depth of her anguish is deepened by the fact that there are no comforters for her; no one to tell her that things are going to be better or that there is a positive meaning to her suffering. Indeed, God is meant to be the one who is to **comfort** and to **restore** one's soul (Ps. 23). However, God has left her to wallow in her misery. And it is not her misery alone. The enemy has turned her **children** into paupers. We are probably to think of personified Jerusalem's children as another way to describe the inhabitants of that city. Alternatively it may be a way of referring to the villages and smaller towns that were in the vicinity and thus in a economic and political relationship with Jerusalem.

1:17 / *Pe.* Here we have a one verse narrative statement that divides the two speeches (vv. 12–16 and vv. 18–22) of the woman who represents Jerusalem. **Zion** is the name given here to personified Jerusalem, pointing to the fact that the city contained the most sacred place on earth. However, Lamentations bemoans the destruction of the temple on Mount Zion and so she stretches out her hands with hope to beseech help, but again (1:16, but also vv. 2 and 21) no one, not even God, is there to **comfort her** (see also 1:21). Indeed, not only is there no comfort from God or from any human being, God has appointed Judah's **neighbors** to be hostile toward it. Of course, this means Babylon, but also the smaller states nearby. Most notably Edom (see Obadiah) harassed Judah whenever they were given the opportunity. They are hostile toward Judah because she has become **unclean** (see 1:8–9). As such, she is either ignored or pelted with stones.

1:18–19 / *Tsade/Qof.* The second extended speech of the woman Jerusalem begins with a confession and acknowledgement that God is **righteous** and that she has sinned (**rebelled**) against his command. This provides at least an implicit recognition that her suffering is deserved (contra Dobbs-Allsopp, *Lamentations,* 71). Thus, as she turns and invites the peoples to view her suffering it may be for a didactic purpose: "See what happens when one rebels against God." Her suffering is further described as the exile of her young citizens, referring to the deportation of Judeans to Babylon (beginning in 605 B.C. with Daniel and his three friends, continuing in 597 with Jehoiachin and Ezekiel among others, and then culminating with the exile of 587 B.C.).

At the time of her duress when under Babylonian siege, Jerusalem's political **allies** let her down. Aside from an abortive attempt by Egypt to move against the Babylonians (Jer. 37), there were no other attempts on the part of allies to help them. As a result, the people languished. Here **priests** and **elders,** religious and political leaders, are described as looking for food to keep themselves alive, presumably during the siege.

1:20 / *Resh.* Personified Jerusalem is in emotional torment. She calls God's attention to her state of mind, perhaps to elicit his pity and compassion. However, she realizes that she has only herself to blame. She does not blame God, but only her own rebellion. **Death** is all around her. **Outside** (literally, "in the street") and **inside** (literally, "in the house")—everywhere—there is death. Presumably she refers to inside and outside of the city. Outside is the enemy army that deals death by the sword. Inside the besieged city there is famine and disease.

Interestingly, Dobbs-Allsopp does not comment on this verse in his commentary on the book. He is so intent on building a picture of woman Jerusalem as offended by a violent God that he passes quickly or in silence over those passages where woman Jerusalem owns her own responsibility for her plight.

1:21 / *S(h)in.* Her inner turmoil has issued outer groans that are heard by people who do not come to her aid. No one comforts her (see 1:17); indeed, her groans bring shouts of joy from her enemies. This verse continues an address to God, so the second person address (**you**) refers to God and again shows awareness of that Jerusalem's destruction was ultimately the result of God's decree to judge them for their rebelliousness.

Nowhere in the book of Lamentations thus far is there any reference to **the day** God has **announced,** a time when Jerusalem's enemies will become like Jerusalem, overrun by their enemies and destroyed. This colon shows some awareness of the prophetic message in books like Isaiah and Jeremiah. God promised destruction by an enemy who would serve as the tool of his anger, but he also pointed out that this very nation would suffer their own punishment since they fought for their own glory and imperialist purposes and not for the glory of God. Such a message is found in the so-called oracles against the nations. For an example, see the oracle against Babylon in Jeremiah 50. God has used Babylon for his purposes, but now they will suffer the effects of their own rebellion even as Judah is restored.

1:22 / *Tav.* The final verse of the first poem both reaffirms Jerusalem's awareness that her sad state is her own fault (**because of all my sins**) and also calls down God's wrath on the enemies that he used to punish them. It is only fair; God's people suffered a horrible fate because of their sin, so now should their enemies.

The poem ends, though, with a restatement of woman Jerusalem's inner turmoil and the articulation of that turmoil in audible **groans.**

Additional Notes §1

1:7 / The Hebrew of this verse begins with "Jerusalem remembers" and has no preposition "in" before "days of her affliction and wandering." These two cola should thus read:

Jerusalem remembers her affliction and wandering,
    (and) all the treasures that were hers in days of old.

For the meaning of this line, see commentary.

1:8–9 / In a very subtle and psychologically sensitive discussion of the theme of the unclean woman representing Jerusalem in this passage, Dobbs-Allsopp (*Lamentations*, pp. 63–65) compares and contrasts the image with the common prophetic use of a sexually abused woman. In passages like Isaiah 47:3; Jeremiah 13:22, 26–27; Ezekiel 16:15–34; 23:1–22;

Nahum 3:1–4, the sexual violence (he takes the blood on the skirts as a indication of violence rather than menstruation) and shame directed toward the woman are acts of judgment due to sin. Here the perspective is from the point of view of those who shame the woman, pointing out her uncleanness. However, in the present passage, the perspective is from the victim. Such a perspective elicits more sympathy even though it is clear that this is a well-deserved punishment.

1:12 / The phrase translated **is it nothing to you?** is literally rendered only "not to you." Some versions think that the text is so disturbed that they leave it untranslated (NAB; NJB). Provan (*Lamentations*, p. 48) believes it should be rendered something like "is it not for you?" in the sense that this devastation has happened as an example for those who pass by.

§2 The Lord Is Like an Enemy (Lam. 2:1–22)

2:1 / *Alef.* The opening word (**How**) invites the reader to contemplate the extent of Judah's destruction. It also strikes a tone of lament over that same suffering. One can hear a note of disbelief that God would bring such a horrific judgment on his people. Indeed, it is total as expressed by the fact that the **cloud of his anger** has engulfed all of the Daughter of Zion. The expression **Daughter of Zion** is an intimate way of referring to Jerusalem by its most sacred space and then personifying it as a young woman. More than that, it denotes "a special link between Yhwh and Jerusalem like that between a father and a daughter" (Goldingay, *Old Testament Theology,* Volume 2: *Israel's Faith,* p. 195). The cloud of God is sometimes a vehicular cloud, transporting God in a way reminiscent of a war chariot (Pss. 18:7–15; 68:32–35; 104 3; Dan. 7:13; Nah. 1:3). At other times, it simply represents his presence like the cloud that filled the tabernacle (Exod. 40:34–38) or the cloud that guided Israel through the wilderness (Deut. 1:33). Here of course the cloud is associated with his judgment and therefore closest to the use of the cloud as a divine war chariot; however, it is likely that we are to think merely of a storm cloud. God has covered Daughter Zion with a storm cloud that brings his destruction on them.

God's people, here called Israel, experience the most radical of all transformations—their former heavenly **splendor** as God's chosen people has been debased (**to the earth**). According to Jeremiah 7, the people of Judah had continued sinning in spite of prophetic warnings because they felt God would not turn against Jerusalem, since the temple was there. The presence of the temple made them think that God touched earth at that site; in other words it was God's **footstool.** But God did not remember, God did not regard, this footstool, but brought destruction on it.

2:2 / *Bet.* Here the Lord is described as destroying Judah (again addressed by the intimate term **Daughter of Judah**) in cold blood (**without pity**). Nothing can stand before him, certainly not **dwellings,** but not even **strongholds.** The Lord is imagined as swallowing them, perhaps reminiscent of the Canaanite myth of the god Mot (Death) who swallows his victims. He has not only destroyed them, but he has also shamed them.

2:3 / *Gimel.* The image of a **horn** evokes a picture of a proud animal like a bull with upraised horn. But God has taken away the power and confidence of Israel; he has cut off its horn out of **anger**. For most, the **right hand** is the strong hand with which one physically protects oneself and attacks a person. God's right hand was used with power to defeat the Egyptians at the time of the Red Sea crossing (Exod. 15:6, 12). But here God withdraws his hand. He will not come to his people's aid against their enemies.

2:4 / *Dalet.* God is a warrior (see Introduction: Divine Warrior). When Israel is obedient to their covenant requirements, he fights on their behalf (Deut. 28:7; the battle of Jericho), but when Israel is disobedient, God fights his own people (Deut. 28:25; the battle of Ai). The implication of God taking the posture of the **enemy** toward his own people is that they have sinned egregiously. It is a result of his judgment against sin.

Here God is pictured as an archer shooting at his enemies, his own people. In reality, his bow is the Babylonian army, but the author of Lamentations knows that the arrows of Babylon are really shot by the Lord. God is described as wielding human weapons elsewhere in Scripture. In Joshua 5:13–15 he holds a drawn sword. In Psalm 7:12–13 he takes up sword and bow.

Beauty (**those who were pleasing to the eye**) is no protection against the Divine Warrior. His wrath is like fire consuming the tent of the **Daughter of Zion** (see 2:1).

2:5 / *He.* The poet repeats the fact that God is **like an enemy** to Israel (see previous verse) and he repeats that God has swallowed up his people (see 2:2). He has reduced Judah to **mourning and lamentation.**

2:6 / *Vav.* The NIV rendering does not provide clarity (see Additional Notes). The NLT gets it right with its translation:

> He has broken down his Temple
> as though it were merely a garden shelter.

A garden shelter is temporary and fragile and easily destroyed. The same was true of the temple before the wrath of God. The temple was destroyed by the Babylonian army in 539 B.C.

God's violent intrusion has also led to the cessation of regular worship. The appointed feasts include Passover, Booths, the Day of Atonement. The weekly and yearly Sabbaths are also not observed. His anger is not only directly toward the common person but against the elite, especially the **king and priest,** the political and religious leadership, who bore considerable responsibility for the moral and spiritual depravation of the land.

2:7 / *Zayin.* God's people had a presumptuous confidence based on the presence of the temple in the midst of Jerusalem, but the Lord cannot be boxed in against his will. Solomon's dedicatory prayer (1 Kgs. 8) asserted that God was not restricted to the temple; Jeremiah's temple sermon warned that the presence of the temple was no guarantee (Jer. 7; 26); and Ezekiel described the divine abandonment of the temple (Ezek. 9–11). The poet of Lamentations here comes to grips with the reality. God has **rejected** and **abandoned** the temple. He has turned over the palace. Rather than the shouts of festal celebration, there are the shouts of pagan conquerors in **the house of the LORD.**

2:8 / *Khet.* It was God, not the Babylonian army, that destroyed the defenses of Jerusalem. The most important part of the city's defense was its **wall.** The wall, destroyed in 587 B.C., would not be built again until the time of Nehemiah (ca. 445 B.C.). God employs a **measuring line** in anticipation of his destructive work. Typically the measuring line is used to build a structure (Isa. 44:13; Zech. 1:16; Job 38:5), but here it is used to prepare for the wall's destruction (see also 2 Kgs. 21:13; Isa. 34:11). As Provan (*Lamentations,* p. 68) points out, "demolition itself requires careful planning." Indeed, the mention of the measuring line shows great premeditation on God's part. It was not an impulsive act. The wall and its **ramparts** are personified and pictured as lamenting their own destruction.

2:9 / *Tet.* The litany of destruction continues with the **gates.** The gates were the entrance and exit of the city, but they were also the place where commerce and politics took place. As the portal of the city, it was also a potential weakness of the defenses. The collapse of the gates signified the collapse of the city. These gates were locked by means of **bars** that are here described as broken and therefore ineffective. For other passages that describe the destruction of a city by means of broken gates and bars, see Ps. 107:16; Isa. 45:2; Jer. 51:30; Nah. 3:13.

But it is not just the physical city that has been desolated. The leaders (**her king and her princes**) have been sent into exile. 2 Kings 24 and Jeremiah 52 tell the story of the capture of Zedekiah, the last king of Judah. He was taken as he tried to escape Jerusalem along with his sons. The sons were butchered before his eyes and then he was blinded. Then put in chains, he was dragged off to Babylon never to be heard of again. Another king of Judah, Jehoiachin, had been exiled during an earlier invasion (597 B.C.). While he was released from his prison around 562 B.C., he never returned to the land.

With the removal of king and princes from the land, the **law** was no longer operative in the land. While the priests were supposed to teach the law, the king was to model and to apply the law to God's people (Deut. 17:14–20). Babylonian law now reigned supreme. Surely the faithful still followed God's law, but it was not until the time of Ezra (ca. 458 B.C.) that the Mosaic law as formally instituted as the law of the land again.

Finally, the **prophets** are no longer receiving **visions.** The prophets in the period leading up to the catastrophe were a mixed bunch. On the one hand, Jeremiah, Ezekiel and others were faithful in proclaiming God's true vision of the future. The people did not listen to them, but to the countless others (see Jer. 28) who offered false words of security. For now, the poet tells the reader, God is not giving prophetic visions in Israel, though Daniel is said to receive them in Babylon and a number of the Minor Prophets are dated to the postexilic period, among them Haggai, Zechariah, Malachi.

2:10 / *Yod.* Continuing the list of groups of people (see vs. 9 and references to king, princes and prophets) we now hear of the silencing of the **elders.** The elders were tribal officials, in effect local authorities. Specifically here, the elders of Jerusalem (**the Daughter of Zion**) are in mind. Rather than providing local leadership and guidance, they are engaged in mourning rituals because of the destruction of the city at the hand of God. They **sprinkle dust on their heads and put on sackcloth.** The list ends with the **young women of Jerusalem,** perhaps mentioned after the "old men" or elders by way of contrast. The women would be the wives and daughters of fallen soldiers and may have suffered the abuses often brought on the female victims of warfare. Their bowed heads signify their depressed state.

2:11–12 / *Kaf/Lamed.* Suddenly, the discourse switches from third-person to first-person speech (**My eyes; I**). A similar shift took place in chapter 1 (see 1:9c, 11c, 12–22), where the first-person speaker was clearly personified Jerusalem. Up to this point in chapter 2, however, there has been no mention of personified Jerusalem, so the first-person speaker is likely the anonymous poet.

The poet expresses his deep remorse at the fate of the people of Jerusalem. Such deep emotion over the fate of the people is reminiscent of Jeremiah, often called "the weeping prophet" (see Jer. 9:1; 13:17; 14:17; 31:16), and it is passages like this one that led to the association of that prophet with the anonymous poet of Lamentations (see Introduction: Author and Date). However, all the godly, not just the famous prophet, who witnessed the destruction of Jerusalem would have felt deep sadness. Indeed, the idiom of one's eyes failing for abundance of tears is known from the general laments of the Psalms (69:3; 119:82, 123; see also Lam. 4:17).

The cause of the poet's distress is the destruction of the people of Jerusalem. Even more poignant is the specific mention of **children and infants** fainting in the streets of Jerusalem. In a siege, the young ones would faint with hunger. In the taking of the city, enemy troops would not differentiate children from adults in their killing rage.

Verse 12 continues the description of the fainting and dying of the children and infants. The poet draws the depressing picture of these hungry children asking their distraught parents about the lack of food and drink **(Where is the bread and wine?**). Bread and wine were the staples of diet; hence, this is a way of simply asking about the lack of all food and all drink. They not only faint, but they also die (**their lives ebb away**) in their mothers' arms.

2:13 / *Mem.* The poet takes a sympathetic stance toward the people of God. Rather than berating them for rebellion, he comforts them and shares in their anguish and sadness. However, words fail him when he tries to describe the extent of their suffering. Provan puts it well, ". . . the poet is searching for an historical analogy to Zion's downfall. If such could be found, then she might find comfort knowing that her plight was not unique, and perhaps in being aware that destruction was often not the end of the story" (*Lamentations,* p. 73).

Twice the poet refers to the inhabitants of the city of Jerusalem by the epithet **Daughter,** qualifying it the second time as virginal. Such a description again heightens the pathos of the destruction. It's not a city, but a daughter that has been horribly hurt. Indeed, the destruction of the city is finally likened to a deep **wound** in the Virgin Daughter's flesh. The wound is so deep that it rivals the **sea** itself in depth. Questions surround the possibility of the Daughter's healing. Both Micah (1:9) and Nahum (3:19) utilize the metaphor of a wound to describe judgment against a city or people, but no prophet uses it more than Jeremiah. Jeremiah 6:14 and 8:11 connect the wound that is coming to God's people with the action of false prophets (Lam. 2:14 will connect the language here with false prophets as well). Jeremiah 14:17 describes the wound as inflicting Jerusalem here depicted as a virgin daughter. Other occurrences include Jeremiah 8:22; 10:19; 15:18; 30:12, 15.

2:14 / *Nun.* The prophet continues to express compassion and sympathy toward the plight of Jerusalem by blaming false **prophets.** Indeed, as the book of Jeremiah attests, false prophets were present on the eve of the destruction of Jerusalem. In Jeremiah 28, we hear the story of the contest between Jeremiah and Hananiah, who contradicted Jeremiah's warnings of judgment with message of peace and safety. The Deuteronomic History, like Jeremiah, faulted the people for not listening to the true prophet (see 1 Kgs. 13).

But the poet here adopts a different perspective. If pressed, he would acknowledge the people's blame (1:5, 8, etc.), but he elicits the reader's sympathy for those who have been destroyed. Perhaps he is trying to elicit divine sympathy for their plight with the hope that God would restore their fortunes.

2:15–16 / *Samek/Pe.* As the psalms witness, nothing is more depressing than an enemy rejoicing over one's downfall. The psalmist beseeches God:

> Let not those gloat over me
> who are my enemies without cause;
> let not those who hate me without reason
> maliciously wink the eye. (Ps. 35:19)

The poet of Lamentations here depicts all those whose journey takes them by the destroyed Jerusalem as rejoicing in its devastation. This verse is especially sad when read in the light of 1:12, where the poet looked for sympathy from those who pass by. But rather than sympathy, they give contempt. They see the destruction and they **clap** their hands in approval (Ezek. 25:6). They **scoff,** or perhaps hiss (see also 1 Kgs. 9:8; Jer. 19:8; Zeph. 2:15) at the ruined city. Shaking one's head connotes disapproval as well as wonderment at the extent of the destruction. They remember the song of Zion that was sung, which suggested the inviolability of the city. Psalm 48:2 extols Jerusalem as the **perfection of beauty and joy of the whole earth,** but now it is an ash heap.

In verse 15 those who pass by are more precisely identified as Jerusalem's **enemies.** They contemptuously hiss (**scorn**) the city and **gnash** their teeth, a sign of hatred. They also take credit for its destruction using the language of swallowing the city, which probably derives from ancient Near Eastern mythological language (see comment on Lam. 2:2).

2:17 / *Ayin.* The horrors that have come on God's people have not come contrary to his will. Indeed, he **decreed** its destruction **long ago.** It is doubtful that the decree referred to here has to do with some abstract theological category. Rather it is best to take it as a reference to the curses of the covenant spelled out in places like Deuteronomy 27–28. God there decreed that if his people betray the covenant, he would punish them. If they had bothered to listen to the law, they would know what was in store for them.

> All these curses will come upon you. They will pursue you and overtake you until you are destroyed, because you did not obey the LORD your God and observe the commands and decrees he gave you. They will be a sign and a wonder to you and your descendants forever. Because you did not serve the LORD your God joyfully and gladly in the time of prosperity, therefore in hunger and thirst, in nakedness and dire poverty, you will serve the enemies the LORD sends against you. He will put an iron yoke on your neck until he has destroyed you. The LORD will bring a nation against you from far away, from the ends of the earth, like an eagle swooping down, a nation whose language you will not understand, a fierce-looking nation without respect for the old or pity for the young. (Deut. 28:45–50)

God had **planned** that if his people broke the covenant, he would treat them in such a way, and since they did fail God in that way, he **fulfilled his word** as explicated in the curses of the covenant.

The enemy that defeated them was Babylon. Babylon and neighboring states like Edom (see Obadiah) and Ammon gloated over Judah's downfall. The image of the exalted or raised **horn** evokes the picture of an animal like a bull, which proudly lifts its head (and so its horns) as a symbol of power. (For a contrast with Israel, see Lam. 2:3.)

2:18–19 / *Tsade/Qof.* After the destruction, **the people cry out to the Lord,** an idiom that indicates repentance. The language and behavior of the people is reminiscent of that found in the book of Judges: The people would sin, and God would turn them over to an oppressor. Their woeful situation would lead them to turn to the Lord again in repentance (they "cried out" to him). God then raised up a deliverer (a judge) who freed them, establishing a time of peace. Repentance is a prerequisite for restoration, so the poet points out that the people have begun the process. He also urges the people to intensify their mourning in hopes of catching God's attention and convincing the Lord of the sincerity of their repentance. In an interesting rhetorical move, the poet personifies the wall of Jerusalem (using the intimate epithet **Daughter of Zion**) and urges it to weep. The wall was destroyed by the Babylonians and so has reason to weep. The wall also draws the outer boundaries of the city proper and thus represents all the people. But the emphasis is not just on all the people, but also on all the time. They are to weep **day and night.**

Verse 19 continues the call to weep and specifically they are to weep all through the night, starting when the **watches of the night begin.** Their motivation is to save the lives of their children who are dying of starvation as a result of the siege and destruction of Jerusalem.

2:20–21 / *Resh/S(h)in.* In the last three verses of the poem contained in the second chapter, personified Zion again speaks. She addresses Yahweh and beseeches him to pay attention to the mournful cries of the people. She appeals to God's sense of proportion. **Whom have you ever treated like this?** She implies that God has made the people suffer above what their sin deserves. They suffer more than any other person or people. She then names four particularly egregious examples of such suffering with the hope that it will grab God's attention and induce him to relent.

The first example of what personified Zion views as God's excessive punishment involves women eating their own **offspring.** Such practice was known in situations of extreme deprivation such as a siege of a city. During a siege, supplies would be cut off from the city in an attempt to starve the city to submission. An example of such a moment may be found in 2 Kings 6 during a siege of the city of Samaria by the Aramaeans. At this time the king of Israel heard a plea from a distressed woman who described a woman who said to her, "Give up your son so we may eat him today, and tomorrow we'll eat my son." The first woman did as the second suggested, but then the next day she discovered that the latter had hidden her son.

Even though personified Zion makes just such a plea (and it appeals to our modern sensibilities), one cannot help but think that the poet would know that this consequence rose from the announced punishment for the sin of rebellion and not from God's excessively harsh judgment. After all, we read the following in the covenant curses from the book of Deuteronomy:

> Because of the suffering that your enemy will inflict on you during the siege, you will eat the fruit of the womb, the flesh of the sons and daughters the LORD your God has given you. Even the most gentle and sensitive man among you will have no compassion on his own brother or the wife he loves or his surviving children, and he will not give to one of them any of the flesh of his children that he is eating. It will be all he has left because of the suffering your enemy will inflict on you during the siege of all your cities. (Deut. 28:53–55)

The second example of excessive suffering that personified Zion presents to God is the death of priests and prophets. Perhaps this example suggested itself to her (and the poet) because **priest** and **prophet** are people who have a special relationship with God. Again, however, one wonders about the effectiveness of such an argument in the light of the frequent teaching in the preexilic prophets that it was precisely the priest and (false) prophet that led God's people astray (see, for instance, Jer. 1:17–19; 2:6–8; 4:9–10; 5:30–31; 6:13–15). Personified Zion pictures the priests and prophets killed within the temple precincts (**sanctuary of the Lord**), so the verse describes holy people killed in holy space. Even so, this does not mean that they are "good" priests and prophets (which seem to have been on low supply), but still the situation is anomalous.

The third example is the death of the **young** and **old.** Granted, verse 21 begins by commenting on the death of the old and the young. This is probably not a merism, that is, the citing of polar opposites in order to indicate totality. Rather, it refers to old and young because they are at the stages of life when one is most dependent on those who are in the prime of life.

The fourth example is the death of **young men and maidens.** These are not like the young (*naʿar*) of the previous colon. They are not youths. They are men and women at their most vital. Even they cannot escape the fate brought on by the enemy.

2:22 / *Taw.* Personified Zion describes the horror and destruction that have come to her in this climactic verse. It is against her that terrors have been summoned. As people from outlying districts flow to Jerusalem on a **feast day** (Passover, Tabernacles, etc.), so **terrors** have flooded into the city. The enemy may have done the destruction, but only because the **LORD's anger** propelled them.

Additional Notes §2

2:6 / The NIV is obscure here. Its translation of v. 6a as **he has laid waste his dwelling like a garden** makes it sound as if the consequence of laying waste God's dwelling is that it becomes a garden or that he lays waste his dwelling like a garden is laid waste. But the idea is that God destroys his own dwelling (the temple) as if it were a booth in a garden.

2:13 / The poet asks, **What can I say for you?** The verb "say" comes from *ʿwd* that has a specific legal sense. From this word comes the noun *ʿed* ("witness"). In other words, the poet struggles to find the words to provide testimony on Jerusalem's behalf.

2:14 / The poet describes the prophet's visions as **false and worthless** (*tafel*). Such a translation derives from *tafel*^{I}. There is a second *tafel*^{II} in Hebrew that means "whitewash." This is the word used concerning false prophets in Ezekiel 13:10–11. It may have that meaning here as well, or at least plays on that word. A whitewash puts a thin veneer on something that is ugly or worse. The false prophets' visions covered up deep underlying problems among the people of God.

§3 *Man of Affliction (Lam. 3:1–66)*

Chapter 3 constitutes a new and complete poem. Like the two chapters that precede it, it is marked by a complete acrostic. Unlike the previous chapters where each verse started with a successive letter of the alphabet, in chapter 3 each letter repeats at the start of three verses before going on to the next letter. Thus, there are sixty-six verses, not twenty-two verses. However, since the verses are shorter in chapter 3, the overall length of the chapters is approximately the same.

The new poem also has a new speaker. So far we have heard the voice of the poet/narrator and the voice of Zion personified as a woman. Chapter 3 begins, **I am the man who has seen affliction.** The first person speech continues through verse 39, where it shifts to first person plural. It reverts to first person singular in vv. 48–66. The identity of the "man of affliction" is not clear, at least in particulars. He could be another personification of Zion and its inhabitants. If so, then the book as a whole would contain both feminine and masculine images of the people of God, perhaps indicating that men and women both suffered in the destruction of Jerusalem. On the other hand, the "man" might be the poet/narrator, who identifies with the suffering people. In any case, whether personification or narrator, the "man" represents the suffering people and articulates their emotions.

Even though this is a separate poem, Provan (*Lamentations,* pp. 80–81) rightly points out that it was never meant to be read separately from the previous two. 3:1 begins with a reference to **his wrath** rather than "God's wrath." The antecedent is provided by "the LORD's anger" in 2:22.

3:1–3 / *alef*. The stanza begins with an autobiographical introduction of the speaker who identifies himself simply as **the man.** As argued above, the man represents the suffering people of God. The Hebrew word is *geber* and is distinctively male and can mean "strong man." If so, this strong man has been rendered powerless by none other than God. He has been the object of God's punishment (**the rod of his** [God's] **wrath**). While no reason is given immediately for God's anger and punishment, later in the poem there is an acknowledgement of sin (vv. 39, 42).

There is no doubting through this entire section that the extreme suffering of the man is the result of God's actions. It is God that has **driven** him **away,** presumably from his presence and literally from Jerusalem. The passage uses language that is reminiscent of Proverbs. In Proverbs, the **rod** is used to keep a son on the straight path that leads to life (10:13; 22:8; 23:13, 14; 29:15), but here God uses the rod to drive the man off the well-lit straight path and onto the dark path that leads to death. The well-lit path is for the wise, not for the fool: "I saw that wisdom is better than folly, just as light is better than darkness. The wise man has eyes in his head, while the fool walks in the darkness" (Eccl. 2:13–14a).

In former good days, the **hand** of God, a metaphor for his effective power in the world, was used for the man's (Israel's) benefit (Exod. 3:19–20), but now it is used to punish him (see also Ps. 32:4; Jer. 21:5). This punishment was not just a one-time act, but a continuous and seemingly perpetual change of divine attitude and behavior.

3:4–6 / *Bet.* The second stanza begins a list of particular actions that describe how God has "turned his hand" against the man introduced in verse 1. We understand this man to represent the suffering people of God. God has taken a series of actions against him. The first verse (v. 4) describes God as physically afflicting the man. First, God has made the man's **skin/flesh grow old.** The verb is *blh* and can also mean "wear out." It is used of the worn-out clothes that the Gibeonites wear when they fool Joshua into thinking that they have come from a distance (Josh. 9:4, 5). Thus, the verb in connection with the skin would indicate the kind of wear and tear that would normally come from aging, but could be induced by other means (hunger [Provan, *Lamentations,* p. 85 points out that hunger goes well with the siege metaphor to follow]), illness, or being assaulted). The pairing of skin/flesh and **bones** indicates that the man's affliction permeates his whole being, both outside and in.

The next verse (v. 5) plays with the fact that the man stands for the people who live in the city of Jerusalem. In other words, it uses verbs that are appropriate for the assault of a city. God **besieged** and **surrounded** the man. Of course, this is the action that an attacking army would (and in the case of Babylon in 586 B.C., did) take against a walled city like Jerusalem. But in keeping with the metaphor of the man, this siege is accomplished not by an army but with **bitterness** and **hardship.**

The final *bet* verse (v. 6) indicates that God consigned the man to the fate of the dead. He lives now in **darkness** like a corpse in a grave. The thought of the man in darkness continues into the next stanza.

3:7–9 / *Gimel.* In the final verse of the preceding stanza, we learned that God placed the man in darkness, like the darkness of the grave. In this stanza, the man is sealed off alive in a prison with no possibility of parole or escape. Verse 7 speaks of his being **walled in** and bound in **chains.** Verse 8 notes that the walls are so thick that his shouts and **prayers** are stifled. It is interesting that the man is imagined to be trying to pray and that God refuses to hear these prayers. God had given his people the chance to repent and pray to him to reverse the fate that was coming on them, but there is a point where such prayers are ineffective. Now God will not hear their prayers at least initially. Verse 9 continues the idea of God restricting the movement of the man and adds the picture of God making the man's **paths crooked.** The latter comes from wisdom literature, notably Proverbs. While the word for path (*netib*) is not the main one used in Proverbs, it occurs often enough (see Prov. 1:15; 3:17; 7:25; 8:2, 20) as a synonym for the main word (*derek*). In Proverbs, the straight path leads to life and the crooked path leads to death. The fact that the man must follow crooked paths may be the direct result of the obstacles described in verse 8. Compare the similar language here and throughout chapter 3 with Job 19:7–12.

3:10–12 / *Dalet*. This stanza continues the description of God's assault on the "man who has seen affliction" (v. 1). The poet uses two metaphors to picture God's violent actions against Jerusalem. The first likens God to dangerous animals that pounce on an unwary traveler. As we know from its frequent use in Proverbs, the **path** stands for life's journey. From the perspective of the man, God's actions seem cruel. Other passages recognize Jerusalem's sin as a cause of this action, but the present context does not mention it, since the purpose of the poet is to build up sympathy for the suffering nation.

The **bear** and the **lion** often appear together as harbingers (sometimes metaphorically and sometimes in reality) of destruction and death (1 Sam. 17:34, 34–37; 2 Sam. 17:8, 10; Isa. 11:7; Hos.

13:8; Amos 5:19). The passages from Hosea and Amos are particularly interesting since they, too, picture God's judgment as the mauling action of these animals:

Like a bear robbed of her cubs,
I will attack them and rip them open.
Like a lion I will devour them;
a wild animal will tear them apart. (Hos. 13:8)

In Amos, it is the Day of the Lord that is the topic when God says:

It will be as though a man fled from a lion
only to meet a bear. (5:19)

Verse 12 changes metaphors. God is no longer a mauling animal, but now an archer taking **target** practice. This language is reminiscent of the suffering of Job, who complains that God has made him a target of his arrows (Job 7:20; 16:12 [here God has made him a target for the arrows of others]).

Both metaphors (wild animals and target practice) emphasize the sufferer's helplessness. A walker has no real defense against a predatory animal and a target cannot move or fight back. This description attempts to elicit sympathy from the reader (and from God?).

3:13–15 / *He*. The fifth stanza continues the metaphor from the end of the previous one. The man charged God with using him for target practice and now he reveals that God hit a bull's eye (also similar to Job, see 16:13): he is skewered. The NIV translates *kilyah* as **heart,** though technically the word means "kidney." According to *NIDOTTE* (vol. 2, p. 656), "the kidneys are viewed as the seat of human joy/grief," thus "heart" is the English idiom that is equivalent. God has pierced the seat of his emotions, thereby unleashing them.

As the object of God's violent rage, the man is reduced to helplessness. As such, those around him ridicule (**mock**) him. The psalmist often expressed the same consternation when his bad condition aroused the ridicule of those who saw him (Pss. 22:7; 69:12; 119:51). Job too felt humiliated by the mocking of people who saw him suffer (Job 30:1, 9).

God has fed the man, but he has forced him to eat revolting food. **Gall** "(wormwood) is a bitter-tasting shrub used for medicinal purposes" (*IVPBBCOT,* p. 687). The adjective on bitter herbs tells the story there. In Psalm 69, the gall the mockers made the psalmist eat (v. 21) causes him to utter a strong curse against them (vv. 22–28). The afflicted man here does not do the same toward God. His (actually the poet's) intention is to evoke sympathy from the reader.

3:16–18 / *Vav.* The sixth stanza continues and completes the description of God's violent actions against the "man of affliction" that began at the start of the chapter. The first colon complains that God has broken his teeth with **gravel.** Most likely, the image intends the reader to picture the man of affliction eating gravel and thus breaking his teeth (indeed the rare verb *grs* [occurring elsewhere only at Ps. 119:20] may better be translated "made to grind" rather than **broken,** see NRSV). The only other use of "gravel" is found in Prov. 20:17, where wealth gained by deceitful means produces a good taste at first, but ultimately is like eating gravel. The next colon pictures God trampling (the verb [*kps*] is a hapax) the man **in the dust,** not only painful but also humiliating.

The next poetic parallelism (v. 16) again (see v. 14) expresses the reflections of the man to the horrific events of his life. **Peace** is gone as well as **prosperity.** As we have earlier observed in the introduction to chapter 3, the man represents the people of Judah and the suffering they have experienced at the hand of God's judgment.

The NIV renders the first colon of v. 18 **So I say, "My splendor is gone."** There is a debate over the exact translation of the word "splendor," a better rendition is "everlastingness." That is, Judah, because of its sins, has forfeited the longlasting affection that God has demonstrated toward his people. Thus, their **hope** of a good relationship with God and the concomitant prosperity were also gone.

3:19–21 / *Zayin.* The seventh stanza continues the lament, but in the last parallel line begins a shift toward hope. While in verse 17 the man stated that he had "forgotten" his prosperity, he now states that he "remembers" his affliction. After all, he began by proclaiming that he is a man who has experienced **affliction** (3:1). Prosperity is long past; affliction is now his daily course. It is an affliction characterized by **wandering.** To be uprooted is negative under any circumstances; here it is reminiscent of exile and homelessness caused by the Babylonian destruction of homes in Jerusalem. His experience is all bitterness and **gall** (for gall, see comment on v. 15).

Such thoughts lead to depression (**my soul is downcast within me**). The language is reminiscent of Pss. 42–43 (see 42:5, 11; 43:5). These psalms (probably an original unity as indicated by the repeated refrain and lack of title on 43) bemoan separation from the presence of God and likely separation from Jerusalem.

Even so, the final line in this stanza moves to **hope.** While denying a sense of hope in verse 18, the man now expresses the birth of hope. It is based on something that he has called to mind (**this**). The next three-verse stanza will explicate what "this" is.

3:22–24 / *Het*. The eighth stanza is the most optimistic of the entire poem. Indeed, it is the most optimistic of the entire book. The fact that it is found in the middle indicates that while hope is present, it is neither the beginning nor the final thought. The pain is still too fresh and the end is not yet in sight. Even so, this stanza, though brief, indicates that the poet is has not completely abandoned himself to hopelessness.

The first line (v. 22) initially strikes one as odd. After all, the poet has repeatedly expressed the sentiment that his/their suffering is deep and pervasive. The destruction is nearly total. But here the poet acknowledges that though he and those he speaks of are deeply afflicted, they are still there. They are not completely **consumed**, and he attributes this to God's grace as expressed in his *khesed* (covenantal **love**) and his *rekhem* (**compassion**). Psalm 77 is the poem of a desperate person who attributes his suffering to God. He accuses God of betraying his *khesed* and *rekhem* in verses 8–9. The poet in Lamentations sees the fact that anyone survived the debacle as evidence of God's love and compassion.

Not only do God's love and compassion not wear out, grow weak, or vanish over time, they are **new** every morning. That is, they are renewed as vital as ever before. In addition, verse 23 introduces yet a third quality of God's covenantal love toward his people, his **faithfulness** (*ʾemuna*). This word refers to God's persistence in his relationship with his people. God is often praised as displaying faithfulness in the Psalms (33:4; 92:2 [3]; 143:1).

Because of God's love, compassion, and faithfulness, the poet, on behalf of the community, expresses his willingness to **wait for him.** Now things are bad, but God will make them good again. The metaphor of **portion** comes from land distribution. Joshua 19:9 refers to the land allotted to the tribes as their portion and associates the word with the word "inheritance" (*nahala*). The Levites had God as their special portion (Deut. 10:9), since they did not receive land, and now the man of affliction on behalf of the community lays claim to the same type of relationship.

3:25–27 / *Tet.* All three verses not only begin with the same letter of the Hebrew alphabet (*tet*), but the very same word *tob,* "good." The poet presents three things that are good for those who are faithful to him.

The first **good** stated comes from the Lord. The Lord is good to those who **put their hope in him.** The poet, speaking in the persona of the "man of affliction," has already stated that he has hope (v. 21, though the previous verse had stated that his hope was gone). According to the second colon of this verse, the one who has hope actively pursues God. The natural tendency of one who suffers at the hand of God is to try to run away, but the better course, as spelled out by verse 25, is rather to seek God. To seek God means to communicate with him, to come into his presence, and to get his help. In the light of the sin that has brought on the punishment, it likely means that they confess and repent of wrongdoing (see vv. 40–42). The Lord will be good to such people. God's goodness would begin by withdrawing from the punishment that he was presently directing at his people. He would restore them and bring them prosperity rather than pain.

The second and third lines in this stanza state what good things God's people can do. The first involves **quiet** (patient?) **waiting** for the salvation of God. This statement needs to be read in the context of Lamentations, which are words directed toward God with the hope of eliciting relief from his punishment. The poet is not silent, but neither is the poet angry and fuming toward God. He raises challenges toward God's continued affliction, but he does not question the fundamental justice of it. In other words, he acknowledges that it is punishment for their sin. However, he believes that enough is enough. He will go on to argue that the enemies that God used have overstepped their bounds and now deserve God's punishment (see vv. 52–66).

The final good of the stanza states that **it is good to bear the yoke when one is young.** The yoke here is the yoke of God's discipline. As a yoke channels the energies of animals, so God's yoke of discipline curbs the wayward actions of his people. The implication of the statement seems to be that if one experiences God's chastisement when young, then later in life the person will walk the straight and godly path. The mention of the yoke is reminiscent of Jeremiah 27 and 28. There the prophet is described as wearing a yoke and declaring God's charge that his people submit themselves to Nebuchadnezzar's rule. In other words, Nebuchadnezzar was God's instrument of discipline and the people should accept that and learn. If they did, then they would be able to stay in the land. However, if they did not, then God would bring "sword, famine and plague" (Jer. 27:13) on them, which is exactly what happened. The people chose to listen to false prophets of peace like Hananiah rather than to Jeremiah. Accordingly, they suffered a fate worse than the wooden yoke of discipline that Jeremiah wore.

3:28–30 / *Yod.* The tenth stanza continues to describe a proper attitude toward the suffering induced by God's judgment. It expands on the idea of "quiet waiting" advocated in the previous stanza. It calls on the sufferer to **sit alone in silence.** In the book of Job, Job sits in silence for the first seven days (Job 2:13). Conflict with his friends and ultimately with God begins when he utters his lament directed not toward God but toward the three friends (ch. 3). The poet assumes the position that Job ultimately came to, silently sitting in the presence of God ("I put my hand over my mouth" [40:4]). The difference of course between Job and the suffering of Lamentations is that the suffering of the former did not result from sin, whereas the suffering of the exilic generation did, as acknowledged by the poet himself (3:42 and passim).

The second poetic line of the stanza (v. 29) advises burying one's **face in the dust.** This is different than being trampled in the dust (v. 16). It involves a voluntary abasement, signifying repentance. Though not literally putting his face into the dust, Job assumes an analogous attitude when he says, "Therefore, I despise myself and repent in dust and ashes" (Job 42:6). Such an attitude and behavior moves the "man of affliction"/poet toward hope of restoration.

In the third line of the stanza (v. 30) the poet even encourages an acceptance of the abuse that comes toward him (**let him offer his cheek to the one who would strike him**). Such an attitude acknowledges the justice of the suffering.

3:31–33 / *Kaf.* The poet creates the *kaf* stanza by beginning all three verses with the particle *ki*. The NIV translates the first and the last as **for,** and the middle verse with the concessive, **though.** In this way, the stanza gives the motivation for why the sufferer, described in the previous stanzas, should passively accept the pain and quietly wait for future divine deliverance.

Verse 31 asserts that God's punishment is not eternal. It has a terminus. This poem does not state why, but elsewhere in Scripture one detects a divine strategy for the punishment of God's people. Psalm 30 is a case in point. God had blessed the psalmist with prosperity (Ps. 30:7b, "you made my mountain stand firm"), but rather than respond with faith, the psalmist became presumptuous (Ps. 30:7a, "When I felt secure, I said, 'I will never be shaken'"). God then abandoned the psalmist (Ps. 30:7c-d, "but when you hid your face, I was dismayed"). Indeed, the psalmist suffered with sickness and nearly died until he "cried for mercy" (Ps. 30:8). As a result, God's punishments came to an end and he turned the psalmist's "wailing into dancing" (Ps. 30:11a). The poet of Lamentations expects the same divine turn from wailing to dancing in his future as well.

The next verse (v. 32) shares the poet's expectation that grief will turn to **compassion** (*rekhem*). This expectation is built on his **unfailing love** (*khesed*). The latter is the same word translated "great love" in the pivotal verse 22. Notice that there too compassion is linked to love.

Verse 33 at first is surprising. What does it mean to say that God **does not willingly bring affliction or grief to the children of men?** Who is forcing him? Indeed, the description of God as a warrior attacking the city of Jerusalem shows that he was not hesitant but approached the task with a certain relish (Lam. 2:1–12). But there is an important sense in which this statement is true. The same phenomenon is found in Isaiah where, after many devastating oracles, the prophet announces that God's wrathful judgment constitutes his "strange" work (see Is. 28:21). That is, God's violent judgment is not the typical, normal, hoped-for relationship with the covenant people. The poet finds in this realization further hope that compassion will follow grief.

3:34–36 / *Lamed*. This stanza is created by three *lamed*s prefixed to verbs (forming infinitives) that describe the present experience of the people of God. They are **prisoners** (of the Babylonians) and are being **crushed** underfoot. They are powerless before their captors. They have no **rights** as the subject of an occupying empire. God had granted people rights, but they are now being denied by those who reject Yahweh.

Thus, the present experience of God's people is a life without **justice** at the hands of oppressive human occupiers. However, the final colon (**would not the Lord see such things?**) is a rhetorical question that demands a positive answer. Their present situation is not outside of the purview of the people; it is not outside of the control of their God.

3:37–39 / *Mem*. The poet poses two questions that further reveal his awareness that God is behind their suffering, and a third question that brings his readers up short when they complain about their suffering.

Verse 37 points out that no one is beyond the effective control of the Lord. They can do nothing unless God allows it. A similar dynamic may be seen in Daniel 1:1–2. From a human perspective it looked like Nebuchadnezzar has simply cowed Jerusalem into submission. However, the narrator pulls back the curtains and tells the reader, "the Lord delivered Jehoiakim king of Judah into his hand." Nebuchadnezzar could not have spoken it or had it happen if the Lord had not decreed it. The same is the case for the present condition of the people of God at the time the book of Lamentations was written.

The next verse (v. 38) asserts that good and bad things come from God. He decrees all things. After his second test, Job came to the same conclusion: "Shall we accept good from God, and not trouble?" (Job 2:10a), and with this response Job passed the second test posed by God to his piety ("In all this, Job did not sin" [Job 2:10b]).

All of this leads to the conclusion that people should not complain if they are being punished for their **sin.** If an innocent sufferer like Job was not supposed to and did not complain, how much less the exile generation whose plight was caused by their sins and the sins of their forefathers?

3:40–42 / *Nun*. The thirteenth stanza begins with the language of introspection. The poet calls on the community to **examine** their **ways** and **test them.** The way (*derek*) is a well-known metaphor from wisdom literature to represent life's journey. There are two ways, according to the pervasive teaching of Proverbs, the godly, wise, straight path and the ungodly, foolish, crooked path. The first way ends in life, the second in death. In order to improve its relationship with God, the community must comes to terms with the way they have chosen to go.

Of course, according to Jeremiah 17:9–10, since the heart is callous, it is only God who can do this with precise accuracy:

> The heart is deceitful above all things
>   and beyond cure.
>   Who can understand it?

> "I the LORD search the heart
> and examine the mind,
> to reward a man according to his conduct,
> according to what his deeds deserve."

Thus, the psalmist calls on God to examine his heart:

> Search me, O God, and know my heart;
> test me and know my anxious thoughts.
> See if there is any offensive way in me,
> and lead me in the way everlasting. (Ps. 139:23–24)

Nonetheless, it is important for the devastated community of Judah to inspect their lives as well, and take the next step and repent (**let us return to the LORD**). Such a suggestion of course implies that they have previously moved away from the Lord.

Verses 41–42 suggest words and actions to articulate the repentance. They are to assume the attitude of prayer (**lift up our hearts and our hands to God in heaven**). They are to acknowledge their wayward behavior (**We have sinned and rebelled**). However, the final thought of the stanza remarks that, even though they have repented, God has not yet seen fit to forgive them. His actions, as described in the next stanzas reveal his continuing wrath against them.

3:43–45 / *Samek*. The previous stanza has suggested community confession and repentance, but the suggestion has evoked memories of the fact that God has not yet seen fit to forgive and restore. Now and in the next few stanzas the poet dwells on God's hard judgment. The strategy is to convince God that perhaps he has gone a bit too far in his treatment of his people with the hope that his anger will subside.

Thus, though he earlier asserted that God "does not willingly bring affliction or grief to the children of men" (3:33), he now pictures him as pursuing his wrathful task with a passionate zeal. God has **pursued** them and **slain without pity.**

Not only that, but he has recused himself from their prayers (v. 44). He acts as though he does not hear their prayers of confession. The **cloud** is often associated with God in the Old Testament. It represents his presence (Exod. 40:34–38) and it also stands for the divine war chariot that he rides into battle (Ps. 18:7–19; 68: 4; 104:1–4). However, here the cloud is something that he uses as a barrier between himself and his people.

Worse still, God has made them **scum and refuse** among the nations. God's judgment has brought a tremendous reversal. With

God's blessing Jerusalem was a shining city (Ps. 48). Again, the strategy is to shock God with the idea that his people are so demeaned in the presence of the nations in hopes that he would restore them again to their previous exalted position.

3:46–48 / *Pe,* the sixteenth letter (see Additional Notes) of the Hebrew alphabet. The first two verses develop the idea expressed in 3:45 that they have become the "scum and refuse" among the nations. The nations have **opened their mouths wide** against them as in 2:16. They speak harmful words against them. The poet then sums up what has happened to them (**terror and pitfalls, ruin and destruction**) and registers his deep grief, especially as he considers the **women.** Women were noncombatants at this time, and most of them were not decision makers. Thus, they suffered a horrible fate in such situations (rape and death) and had no control.

3:49–51 / *Ayin,* the seventeenth letter (see Additional Notes for 3:46–48) of the Hebrew alphabet. The stanza expands the description of the grief of the poet, speaking in the persona of the "man of affliction." His grief is limitless; his tears do not stop. Verse 50 suggests that the poet desires that his tears will cause the Lord to pay attention with the implicit hope that that will cause him to change course in his attitudes and actions toward the city. God is in heaven and has covered himself "with a cloud so that no prayer can get through" (v. 44), but perhaps he will be moved by tears of grief. The poet has already frequently tried to get the Lord to look on their piteous state (1:9, 11, 20; 2:20; see Provan, *Lamentations,* p. 103).

But he is not forcing the tears by any means. All he has to do is look around (**what I see**) to elicit sadness (see Additional Notes). In a classic "A, what's more B" parallelism, the second colon of v. 50 speaks specifically of what in particular evokes sadness, the fate of the female population of the city. **Women** are particularly vulnerable at times like this. Men make the decision to go to battle and women lose their husbands and sons, while they themselves are subject to all kinds of abuse at the hands of the victors.

3:52–54 / *Tsade.* The "man" now turns his attention to the enemies who afflict him. He has earlier numerous times acknowledged that his (representing the city's) suffering was the result of sin and God's judgment (1:5, 8–9, 12, 14 and many more passages). Even so, the poet is able to differentiate God from the enemy that God used to bring judgment upon him so that he can complain to God about the enemy, as he does in this section of the poem. Interestingly, in the prophets God does castigate and announce judgment on the foreign nations he uses to bring punishment on his people (i.e., Isa. 10:5–19; 34; Jer. 50–51).

The description of the enemy's evil actions reminds the reader of language of the psalms. The fact that the enemy has no reason (**without cause**) to hurt the people of God makes their actions all the more reprehensible (see Pss. 7:4; 35:7, 19; 69:4; 109:3; 119:78, 86, 161; Prov. 24:28). Indeed, they are sneaky in their attack on the people of God; they hunt them like a fowler hunts birds (see Prov. 6:5; 7:23). Only God can help someone escape from the fowler's snare (Pss. 91:3; 124:7).

Verse 52 changes the metaphor, describing the way that the enemy tries to ensnare the people of God. Now the trap is a **pit** into which the people of God have fallen and they are thus the easy target of **stones** that are thrown at them. Again in the book of Psalms the pit often was a metaphor for trouble, at times even suggesting the grave or the underworld (Pss. 7:15; 9:15; 28:1; 30:3, 9, 35:78–8; 40:2; 57:6; Prov. 1:12; 22:14; 23:27; 26:27).

Verse 53 presents one more metaphor of the trouble the "man" has encountered. These are the **waters** that threaten to overwhelm him. These waters are the waters of chaos and may even be connected to the idea of the ritual of "ordeal." When someone was suspected of malfeasance, but with insufficient evidence, the judges or elders took the person to the river and threw them in. If the water overwhelmed the person, she or he was judged both guilty and punished with that one act. Ps. 69:1–2 is a comparable passage:

> Save me, O God,
> for the waters have come up to my neck.
> I sink in the miry depths,
> where there is no foothold.
> I have come into the deep waters;
> the floods engulf me.

3:55–57 / *Qof.* The NIV (see also NRSV) renders the verbs in this stanza and through verse 63 as past actions. Provan (*Lamentations,* p. 105, citing D. Michel, *Tempora und Satzstellung in den Psalmen* [AET 1; Bonn, 1961], pp. 79–81; see also Dobbs-Allsopp, *Lamentations,* p. 126) argues that the verbs in verses 55–66 should be taken as imperatives throughout and suggests "in the midst of his current distress in the pit, the speaker cries out for God's help." Beside the arguments Provan provides, it seems that such an interpretation fits better with the context, where it is said that God has not listened to the people's prayers (see vv. 43–45). Sticking with the NIV translation, but taking the verbs as imperatives rather than past tense, results in the following:

> I call on your name, O LORD,
> from the depths of the pit.
> Hear my plea: "Do not close your ears
> to my cry for relief."
> Come near when I call you,
> and say, "Do not fear."

In the previous stanza (vv. 52–54), the poet describes his plight as being thrown into a **pit** (v. 53) and now in the present stanza he turns to God from the pit. Again, the language is reminiscent of the psalms. In Psalm 30, for instance, the psalmist understands his condition as being placed in the pit with his enemies gloating over him. But he calls on the Lord who saves him from the pit. Indeed, Psalm 30 is a thanksgiving psalm, and this portion of Lamentations reads surprisingly like a thanksgiving. He not only records his pitiful cry from the pit ("Do not close your ears to my cry for relief"), but he also beseeches God to come near him at his cry with the reassuring words that he should not fear.

3:58–60 / *Resh.* See the previous stanza for information about the correct rendition of the verbs in this section. The passage is best translated:

> O Lord, take up my case;
> redeem my life.
> See, O LORD, the wrong done to me.
> Uphold my cause!
> See the depth of their vengeance,
> all their plots against me.

The poet has called on God's name to rescue him from the harsh treatment of the enemy and requests that God respond to him. Verses 58–60 are a development of verse 57. He asks that God take up his **case.** This legal language is found in the prophets to describe God as a prosecuting attorney, charging his people with breaking the covenantal law and thus making them subject to the curses of the covenant (i.e., Jer. 2:9; Mic. 6:1–2). But here the poet wants God to take the side of his people who are represented by "the man of affliction." The enemy has treated him as if he is guilty, but God should become not his prosecuting attorney but his defense lawyer, and save (**redeemed;** should be imperative, "redeem") his life. The poet is particularly concerned that God see the enemy's bad treatment of God's people. On that basis, he again appeals to God to come to his side (**Uphold my cause!**).

3:61–63 / *S(h)in.* See comment at verses 55–57 for information about the correct rendition of the verbs in this section. The passage is best translated:

> O Lord, hear their insults,
> all their plots against me—
> what my enemies whisper and mutter
> against me all day long.
> Look at them! Sitting or standing,
> they mock me in their songs.

Again, the poet appeals to God to come to his aid based on the horrible treatment he receives from the enemy. He hopes to garner God's sympathy and thus to change his attitude toward his people. The language here evokes the psalms of lament. In Psalm 69, the psalmist calls on God for help and describes his difficult situation in order to elicit God's sympathy in terms similar to the present passage:

> For I endure scorn for your sake,
> and shame covers my face.
> I am a stranger to my brothers,
> an alien to my own mother's sons;
> For zeal for your house consumes me,
> and the insults of those who insult you fall on me.
> When I weep and fast,
> I endure scorn;
> when I put on sackcloth,
> people make sport of me.
> Those who sit at the gate mock me,
> and I am the song of drunkards. (Ps. 69:7–12)

Job too complains that he has become the subject of the musical mockery of the sons of people who were beneath him (Job 30:9). The poet of Lamentations thus joins a mournful group of people who are the persistent subject of an enemy's ridicule. In the Lamentations passage this ridicule is constant as signaled by the merism **sitting or standing,** that is, all the time.

3:64–66 / *Tav.* The poet's lament ends as a number of psalmic laments end—with an imprecation directed toward the enemy. These imprecations arise from a sense of justice. They have acted wickedly and have so far gotten away with it, so the poet calls God's attention to the inequity and he calls on God to rectify the situation. Modern sensibilities struggle with imprecations because they seem so self-centeredly vengeful, but then most commentators who so hesitate are typically themselves not subject to the type of exploitative behavior that elicits such a response.

The poet calls on God to put a **veil over their hearts,** an image not found elsewhere in Scripture (the word translated "veil" is difficult and subject to debate). The heart is a way of referring to a person's inner life, perhaps with an emphasis on cognitive ability. Thus, to veil one's heart is to confuse them, to make it hard for them to make a proper decision. In this way, the enemy will be weakened and vulnerable and subject to the destruction that the poet requests in the final verse of the chapter.

Additional Notes §3

3:17 / NIV takes the verb as a third person feminine with "my soul" (*nafshi*) as the subject and then treats "my soul" as indicating first person speech. However, it is more likely that the verb is second person with God as the understood subject, producing the following more dramatic translation: "You have rejected my soul from peace."

3:18 / NIV renders *nitskhi* as "my splendor." Earlier in Lamentations, NIV renders two other words as splendor as well. In 1:6 the splendor that has departed is *hadar,* and in 2:1 it is *tif᾿eret.* While *netsakh* could be rendered something like "splendor" or "glory," other options are available and are more likely since the other two words are used to cover the semantic range of "splendor." Specifically, *netsakh* could mean "lastingness." It has this meaning in the expression *lenetsakh netsakhim* ("forever and ever," Isa. 34:10) as well as in a number of other contexts (see *NIDOTTE,* vol. 3, pp. 139–40).

3:41 / The Hebrew of the first colon (*nissa᾿ lebabenu ᾿el-kappayim*) could be rendered with NIV (**Let us lift up our hearts and our hands**) or "Let us lift up our hearts in our hands." Either translation gets the point across well, though the latter one is certainly more vivid and dramatic.

3:46–49 / Typically, *pe* is the sixteenth letter and follows *ayin,* the fifteenth letter, in the Hebrew alphabet, but in this acrostic the order is reversed.

3:51 / Literally, colon A says "My eyes inflict pain on my soul." This expression could mean that he is crying so much and so hard that it hurts or, as NIV takes it, that what he sees with his eyes emotionally damages him.

§4 The Luster Has Faded for the People of God (Lam. 4:1–22)

The fourth poem of the book is also an acrostic, but of a different structure than the previous three chapters. Each verse starts with a successive letter of the Hebrew alphabet, and in this way is similar to chapters 1 and 2. But a simple comparison of the verses in English or Hebrew shows that the verse-stanzas thus formed are much shorter (comprising two rather than three bicola per verse). Thus, this chapter is about a third shorter than chapters 1 and 2 and considerably shorter than chapter 3 which has sixty-six verses each of which is a bicolon.

Two voices are heard in chapter 4. The narrator speaks in verses 1–16, while we hear the community's voice (us/our) in the remainder of the chapter. Dobbs-Allsopp (*Lamentations,* p. 129) comments that there is a "diminution of emotion and feeling" in the chapter. One can detect a kind of sad, exhausted awe at the extent and intensity of the damage to property and especially people. In the first few verses, contrast is drawn between the glory of the past and the shame of the present. Provan (*Lamentations,* p. 110) has pointed out how often "streets" (*husot*) occurs in the chapter (vv. 1, 5, 8, 14, 18 [though here we have *rehob*]). The streets that were once the locus of public community life now display the devastation of the city.

4:1–2 / *Alef /Bet.* The opening lines contrast the glory of the past with the present sad condition of the city and its people. The chapter opens by comparing city and people to precious metal (**gold**) and gems. In the past, city and people were like the highest quality gold (**fine gold**) but now it no longer shines, but rather is **dull.** God does not become tarnished really (Hillers, *Lamentations,* pp. 78–9), making this description all the more remarkable. It's equally a surprise that a people so blessed with an intimate relationship with the Lord could be so spiritually tarnished.

The gems are no ordinary gems but **sacred gems** like the ones that adorned the ephod and the breastpiece (Exod. 25:7; 35:9, 27; 39:2–7, 8–21). After all, the city was sacred due to the presence of the temple, but now the temple was destroyed and the priests were scattered. Verse 2 associates the **sons of Zion** (inhabitants of Jerusalem) with gold (**once worth their weight in gold**). Now they are not precious metal, they are common clay. They are pots of clay in the **potter's hands.** In this context, the potter is probably their oppressors, who can do with them what they want just like a potter can shape the clay into any form.

4:3–4 / *Gimel/Dalet.* Verse 3 describes the heartlessness of God's people, a topic that will be developed later in the poem as well (see vv. 4, 10). It uses an animal image to draw its point. A **jackal** (see Additional Notes) was a detested and feared animal. It was associated with desolate areas, a predator of small animals and consumer of carcasses. Most of the animal's other appearances in Scripture associate it with God's anger and judgment (Ps. 44:19; Isa. 13:22; 35:7; Jer. 9:11). But even such reprehensible animals provide nourishment for their offspring. God's people are worse than jackals; they are more like ostriches. The only other occurrence of the term here translated **ostrich** is found in Job 39:13 at the head of a section describing the traits of that animal. Yahweh is instructing Job in his sovereignty and wisdom and explains how he endows and withholds certain abilities from various animals. While he has given the ostrich speed (39:18), he has deprived her of wisdom and good sense. Interestingly the latter is illustrated by her callous attitude toward her young:

> She lays her eggs on the ground
> and lets them warm in the sand,
> unmindful that a foot may crush them,
> that some wild animal may trample them.
> She treats her young harshly, as if they were not hers;
> she cares not that her labor was in vain. . . . (39:14–16)

Verse 4 then describes the sorry plight of the babies and children of God's people who have experienced the devastating effects of the siege and capture of Jerusalem. They are thirsty and hungry, but no one, not even their own parents apparently (see also 4:10) will give them food or water. Of course supplies would be short or perhaps even non-existent, but the implication is that whatever is available is withheld from children and saved for the adults.

4:5 / *He.* Like verses 1–2, verse 5 recounts former glories and present deprivation. The contrast elicits pathos for the speaker. In the former good days, they ate **delicacies.** Proverbs describes delicacies as the food of royals and rich people (Prov. 23:3, 6). The latter had had the best, but now they are in a horrible situation—**destitute in the streets.** That they are in the streets is a theme in the chapter (see also vv. 1, 8, 14, 18). Destitution implies that worse than having no delicacies, they have no, or minimal, food. They have moved from riches to poverty.

The second colon of the verse provides another contrast between former glory and present gloom. Before, they were **nurtured in purple.** Only the richest people could afford the clothes dyed with purple. Indeed, it was often the exclusive property of royalty. But now they sit on an **ash heap.** The people of God are thus like Job who moves from great prosperity to sit on an ash heap (Job 2:8). Both are reversals of Hannah, who, citing Psalm 113, says:

> He raises the poor from the dust
>   and lifts the needy from the ash heap;
> He seats them with princes
>   and has them inherit a throne of honor.
>   (1 Sam. 2:8, see Ps. 113:7)

4:6 / *Vav.* **Sodom** was notorious for its sin and for its punishment (see Additional Notes for possibility that the first bicolon is speaking of Sodom's sin and not punishment). The story of Sodom and its associated city, Gomorrah, is found in Genesis 19. Scripture often cites it as an example of a horrific fate (Deut. 29:23; 32:32; Isa. 1:9–10; 3:9; 13:19; Jer. 23:14; 49:18; 50:40; Ezek. 16:46–56; Amos 4:11; Zeph. 2:9; also Matt. 10:15; 11:23–24; Luke 10:12; 17:29; Rom. 9:29; 2 Pet. 2:6; Jude 7; Rev. 11:8). Even if Sodom's sin is not explicitly mentioned, the implication of the fact that Jerusalem's punishment was worse is that its sin exceeded that of Sodom as well. Another contrast may be between the quick destruction of Sodom and the slow downfall of Jerusalem.

4:7–8 / *Zayin/Het.* The *nezirim* are the subject of both these verses. NIV may well be right to take this word as a reference to **princes,** connected to *nezer* ("crown"). But it is also possible that it is related to the word for Nazirite. In any case, whatever group is meant, former glory (v. 7) gives way to present destitution (v. 8).

Verse 7 describes the princes as healthy, strong, and good looking. The first bicolon describes them as **white** and compares them favorably in their whiteness to **snow** and **milk.** Nowhere else is a white complexion complimented as physically attractive (except in regard to the whites of the eye, Song 5:12). Indeed, the very next bicolon will talk about their body as **ruddy** as **rubies,** not white but reddish. Perhaps then the first colon is commenting not so much on their physical appearance as on their former purity. The idiom "white as snow" is elsewhere associated with a purified life (Ps. 51:7; 1:18). Thus, verse 7 proclaims the previous innocence of the princes as well as their physical beauty. The latter is described in relationship to precious jewels, rubies and sapphires, reminiscent of the description of male beauty in Song of Songs 5:10–16 (see Longman, *Song of Songs,* pp. 170–76).

The former whiteness of the princes is contrasted with their blackness. They are **blacker than soot.** If we are correct above that whiteness has to do with character and not physical beauty, then the same is true here and blackness symbolizes their wickedness (in the way that today we refer to someone having a "black heart"). The second colon of v. 8 then contrasts with the second colon of v. 7 both of which do talk about physical appearance. Here their skin is horrible, showing the signs of the deprivation of food and water and perhaps the appearance of disease.

4:9 / *Tet.* The form of the first parallelism of the verse is a better-than parallelism, which gives relative values. In a siege like that which the Babylonians levied against Jerusalem, death came in many forms. In such a situation, some types of death were better than others. It is a sorry state, though, when death by a **sword** is considered a mercy. **Famine,** however, is a slow type of death that prolongs suffering. Famine, of course, would come on a besieged city because the crops that sustained the population came from the surrounding fields, which would have been seized by the attackers. The second parallelism describes the reasons for the famine (**lack of food from the field**) and the torture it brought (**racked with hunger, they waste away**). Jeremiah had warned Judah that it would fall to sword and famine, frequently adding a third threat, plague (Jer. 11:22; 14:12–18; 16:4, etc.).

4:10 / *Yod.* A siege radically and perversely inverts normal human relationships. Nothing is stronger than the love of a mother for her child. A mother nurtures and protects her child. During the siege of Jerusalem, however, mothers (**compassionate women**) cooked and ate their own children. It is not clear whether the children were dead or alive when cooked; either way, the picture is revolting and horrible.

Deuteronomy warned that Israel's rebellion would lead to such a consequence. In the context of the curses of the covenant, we read:

> The most gentle and sensitive woman among you—so sensitive and gentle that she would not venture to touch the ground with her foot—will begrudge the husband she loves and her own son or daughter the afterbirth from her womb and the children she bears. For she intends to eat them secretly during the siege and in the distress that your enemy will inflict on you in your cities. (Deut. 28:56–57)

4:11 / *Kaf.* The destruction of Jerusalem and all of its attendant horrors as described in this book are the results of God's great **anger.** Eventually the siege was successful, the Babylonians breached the walls of the city and set the city on fire. The fire even reached **Zion,** the location of the temple, which was destroyed. Psalm 74 is best interpreted as referring to this event:

> Your foes roared in the place where you met with us;
> they set up their standards as signs.
> They behaved like men wielding axes
> to cut through a thicket of trees.
> They smashed all the carved paneling
> with their axes and hatchets.
> They burned your sanctuary to the ground;
> they defiled the dwelling place of your Name. (Ps. 74:4–7)

Though it was the most devastating loss, the temple was not the only thing destroyed; indeed the whole town was destroyed. The mention of Zion, while focusing on the temple area, is a way of referring to the entire city. To say that its **foundations** are destroyed is to say that it was deeply, not superficially destroyed.

4:12 / *Lamed.* The defeat of Jerusalem was astounding, according to the poet, not just to its inhabitants, but to the **kings of the earth** and the **world's people.** Of course, such a statement is not the result of a poll, and in actuality it is doubtful that Nebuchadnezzar has significant doubt concerning the ultimate outcome of the siege. However, Jerusalem had resisted sieges in the past, thanks to Yahweh's intervention. Most notable was the time that Sennacherib of Assyria had to withdraw from the walls of Jerusalem in 701 B.C. during the reign of King Hezekiah (2 Kgs. 18:17–19:37; 2 Chr. 32:1–23; Isa. 36–37). While the psalms do express the inviolability of Jerusalem, that belief was connected to the benevolent presence of God (Ps. 48:1–5).

4:13–16 / *Mem/Nun/Samek/Pe.* Though unexpected and shocking, the devastation of seemingly impregnable Jerusalem (see v. 12) was the result of the sin of its religious leaders. The **prophets** and the **priests** let the people down. Jeremiah spoke often about the sins of priests and prophets (a selection of relevant passages include Jer. 1:17–19; 2:7–8, 26; 4:9; 5:30–31; 8:1–2, 10–11; 13:12–14; 23:9–12). The specific accusation here is that they shed **the blood of the righteous.** Again, Jeremiah attests to the violence that priests and prophets perpetrated against him. It could be that priests and prophets literally and directly saw to the death of righteous people who resisted their ways. However, it may also refer to the fact that their sinful policies and their lack of positive guidance toward repentance and restoration of the relationship with God resulted in the fall to Babylon. If so, then they are being associated with the deaths brought about by the Babylonian siege and capture of Jerusalem.

Not only do the priests share in the corporate punishment of Jerusalem, but they are in particularly bad condition after the fall of Jerusalem. Verses 14–15 describe them as ritually **unclean.** They have moved from their previously powerful position to that of the homeless and disabled (**blind**). They are rendered unclean by the **blood** on their **garments.** Murder rendered someone guilty of sin, but not ritually unclean. However, the poet is using the language of ritual purity in order to describe the perversity of their actions. Blood from wounds did not make a person unclean. It was only blood connected to a woman's reproductive cycle, menses and the blood associated with childbirth that made a person unclean (Lev. 15). The priests are described as if they were people who have been defiled by contact with menstrual blood. Thus, as they wander about the streets, people greet them with cries to get away. They do not want to be contaminated by contact with such unclean people. And it is not only Judeans who want to avoid contact with them, even the nations will not tolerate their presence. How bad is it when the unclean Gentiles cannot stand to be in the presence of these wayward priests and prophets!

The priests and prophets have fallen out of favor with God, who has scattered them. The last colon of verse 16 also adds another group, the elders, to the list of infamy. While Jeremiah does not speak negatively of their role, the fact that the elders were community leaders and did not circumvent the apostasy of the time shows that they too are culpable.

4:17 / *Ayin.* In verses 17–22 the narrator speaks on behalf of the community (first person plural), whereas in the previous verses of this poem, the poet has described the community in the third person. The change of reference indicates that the poet now identifies with the suffering community.

In songs of lament, the psalmists note the failure of their **eyes** as they look for help from God in the midst of their distress (Pss. 69:3; 119:82, 123; see also Lam. 2:11). Alternatively, the psalmists speak of their eyes failing because of the abundance of their tears (Ps. 6:7). In the present passage, the eyes of the community have worn out from looking for help from another nation. Though not named, the historical books and Jeremiah indicate that Egypt filled this role (see Additional Notes). Judah expected Egypt to come save them (Jer. 2:18, 36), a help that never materialized. One pictures Israelite soldiers in the city towers with the Babylonian army besieging the walls. They know their fate is sealed unless they get help from abroad. They look in the distance in the **vain** hope that Egypt will show up. Though once there was a rumor of their coming (Jer. 37), nothing ever came of their hope for help.

4:18–19 / *Tsade/Qof.* Though their purported allies, the Egyptians, never came to help, those who pursued them, the Babylonians and their allies, were right on their **steps.** The result was that they could not so much as walk **in the streets** of Jerusalem. Previously it has been said that the people struggled in the streets; now they are even denied peace in the streets. They were doomed. Verse 19 then envisions the people trying to escape their pursuing enemy by leaving the city and going over **mountains** and **desert.** But their flight is in vain because their enemies pursue them in these areas and catch them.

4:20 / *Resh.* The pursuers even entrapped the **LORD's anointed,** that is, the consecrated king. The importance of the office of king for the people is captured well by the phrase, **our very life breath,** which indicates that the king played a life and death role for the people. If one reads this verse in the light of Psalm 2, one can understand the surprise the king's capture might evoke. The first stanza exposes the vanity of the nations trying to resist "the LORD" and "his Anointed One" (Ps. 2:2). The final stanza (vv. 10–12) admonishes the kings of the nations to submit to the anointed king, here designated God's son, "lest he be angry and you be destroyed in your way." The second part of the Lam. 4:20 also seems to build on this expectation in saying that Judah's life among the nations would be under the king's shadow. The **shadow** is a metaphor for protection and rest.

However, reading 4:20 in the light of the historical record at the end of 2 Kings or in the light of Jeremiah's interaction with the last kings of Judah, particularly Jehoiakim and Zedekiah, paints a different picture. These kings, though descendants of David and properly anointed, did not follow the Lord or act in the best interests of their people. The reference to the anointed being **caught in their traps** may specifically refer to Zedekiah's capture and ill-treatment at the conclusion of the Babylonian siege of Jerusalem (2 Kgs. 25:5–7).

4:21–22 / *S(h)in/Tav.* Jerusalem's downfall is good news to the land of **Edom,** also associated with the **land of Uz.** Uz as a geographical location is named also in Job 1:1 and Jer. 25:20. A man whose name is Uz is found in a genealogy of Edom (Gen. 36:28 and 1 Chr. 1:42). It is likely, but not absolutely certain, that Uz is another name or a location within the area known as Edom. In any case, there is no doubt over the fact that Edom rejoiced at Jerusalem's fall because that created at least temporary room for its own territorial expansion. At the time of the Babylonian destruction of Jerusalem, Edom had taken advantage of the situation in some way. While not precisely described, this point can be established by reference to texts like Psalm 137:7; Lamentations 4:22; Ezekiel 35:15; Obadiah 10–14.

The theme of the **cup** is one frequently encountered in Jeremiah (see 13:12–14; 25:15–38; 48:26–28). Deserving special mention is Jeremiah 49:12–13, in the context of an oracle against Edom:

> This is what the LORD says: "If those who do not deserve to drink the cup must drink it, why should you go unpunished? You will not go unpunished, but must drink it. I swear by myself," declares the LORD, "that Bozrah will become a ruin and an object of horror, of reproach and of cursing; and all its towns will be in ruins forever."

The cup of God's wrath is filled with an intoxicant that makes the drinker pass out of consciousness. Others take advantage of the situation. In this case, unconscious Edom will pass out and then get **stripped naked.** The cup, in a word, is symbolic of God's judgment against a people. Edom thinks that Jerusalem's fall is to their advantage, but what they do not know is that their fall is not far behind.

Verse 22 shows that a reversal is in order. Yes, Zion, representing Jerusalem, has been punished, but the **exile** will end. As for Edom, its punishment is in the future.

Additional Notes §4

4:3 / In Hebrew, the plural for jackal (*tan/tannin*) is similar to a word with the meaning "sea monster." Accordingly, the REB renders the first part of the verse: "Even the whales uncover the teat and suckle their young." Since sea monsters were thought to represent the forces of chaos and evil in Scripture, the practical effect of the translation is not that different from the traditional understanding, which is accepted by the vast majority of translations and is almost certainly correct.

4:6 / NIV translates the first bicolon: **The punishment** (*ʿawon*) **of my people is greater than that of Sodom.** The Hebrew *ʿawon* more often means "guilt." In the second colon, NIV leaves untranslated *hattaʾt,* which can be rendered "sin" or "punishment for sin." The NIV (along with NRSV and other translations) may be correct to take it as punishment; certainly the second bicolon refers to punishment. But it could be that the first bicolon states that the sin of Jerusalem exceeded that of Jerusalem (so NLT, NJB, and JPS).

4:17 / Provan does not agree with the position taken here (and the majority of scholars) that the **nation that could not save us** is Egypt. He argues that the reference is to Edom, the only nation that is mentioned in the poem (see vv. 21–22), and that the phrase ought to be translated "the nations that would not save us" indicating unwillingness not inability (*Lamentations,* p. 121). However, due to their strained relationship and their relative weakness over against the superpowers Egypt and Babylon, it would not even have crossed the minds of the Judeans that Edom could or would have provided salvation.

§5 *A Final Lament and Appeal (Lam. 5:1–22)*

Lamentation ends with a prayer asking God to remember the suffering of God's city, Jerusalem, and his people. The prayer is one of the community as indicated by the consistent use of the first person plural pronoun. After the invocation in verse 1, the prayer continues with a long description of the suffering of a once proud and glorious place (vv. 2–18). It ends with a series of "why" questions (vv. 19–22), similar to the laments of the psalms (see Pss. 10:1, 13; 22:1; 42:5, etc., and also Job's lament in Job 3:11–26). It is significant that the book concludes not with resolution, but with an eye to the future. The lament calls on God to act to restore them.

Stylistically, chapter 5 is the only chapter that is not a true acrostic. Interestingly, though, the poet has preserved an acrostic-like style by having 22 verses. This mimicking of an acrostic serves the purpose of keeping a kind of artificial symmetry between the five chapters. Gerstenberger (*Psalms, Part 2, and Lamentations,* p. 501) calls this an alphabetizing style and cites Psalm 33 (one could add Proverbs 2). He is also correct to reject Bergler's strained attempt at reading a sentence from the consonants that begins each verse (see Bergler). However, chapter 5 is also considerably shorter than all the previous chapters since each of its 22 verses are composed of a single poetic bicolon. Chapter 3 also has only one bicolon per verse, but that chapter contains 66 verses. Verses in chapters 1, 2, and 5 all have multiple bicola.

The effect of the loss of the true acrostic form as well as the radical brevity of the final chapter may be a way of achieving closure without resolution in the poem. The lack of the abecediary may signal the fragmentation that exists in Judean society still. The brevity may point to the fact that the poet has run out of words. For a similar effect to the latter, note the shortening of the three friends speeches in the third cycle of the Job disputation (chs. 22–27).

5:1 / The final poem, a lament prayer, begins with an invocation to God to pay attention to them and, in particular, to recognize the **disgrace** that will be recounted in the verses that follow, though the community presently endures. Of course, already implicit in the very concept of remembrance in Scripture is the hope that God won't simply see the suffering, but will act. That hope will become explicit later in the poem. To **remember** is to act.

5:2 / The first item that God should remember is the defeat and occupation of the promised land. Without naming names the poet refers to the defeat of Jerusalem at the hands of the Babylonians who then exiled many of the leading citizens and set up an occupying force to manage the rest in the interests of their expanding empire. By referring to the land as **our inheritance** the poet reminds God that he gave it to them. He brought them out of Egypt and brought them in and gave them the land of Canaan. It thus became their **homes.** But now **aliens** (mainly the Babylonians) occupy their homes. The use of the passive (**have been turned over**) implicitly accuses God of this situation.

5:3–5 / The consequences of war with the Babylonians have left the Judeans decimated. The loss of parents has meant an increase in **orphans.** Some have lost their father leaving the children **fatherless,** and their mothers have become **widows.** Provan (*Lamentations,* p. 126) may be right to point out that the text says that the mothers have become **like** widows. He argues that the asseverative makes no sense here (they have indeed become widows), though he overstates his case. But his point is that they have not actually become widows by the death of their husbands; they have become like widows in that their husbands have been deported to Babylon. In actuality probably both scenarios happened.

Before the siege and conquest the staples of life were free—**water** to drink and **wood** with which to cook and provide warmth in the cold. Once the siege began there was limited water, only that which was stored within the riverless city of Jerusalem. Wood was on the hills surrounding the city, but not much could be found in the city walls. **Those who pursue** them are the Babylonians and others like the Edomites who take advantage of their weakened condition, making the weary even more tired and discouraged.

5:6 / In their dire straights, the Judeans submitted to foreign powers like **Egypt** and **Assyria.** They had hoped to mitigate the problem with the Babylonians by aligning with one of the other world powers. Such a political move would bring with it obligations to the nation who would serve as their protector. Isaiah (e.g., 28:1–33:34), Jeremiah (e.g., 2:35), and the other prophets condemned the people of God for putting their trust in other nations. The proper attitude was to trust God, not Egypt, Assyria, or any other human power to save them. After all, God was a warrior who demonstrated beginning with the Red Sea crossing his ability to defend his people over evil human kingdoms.

It is well documented that Judah under Jehoiakim and Zedekiah pursued a relationship with Egypt to rescue it from Babylon. Egypt constantly let Judah down. The reference to Assyria is more problematic. Assyria had been completely destroyed in 609 B.C. when an Egyptian force led by Pharaoh Neco was unable to bolster the remnants of the Assyrians during the battle of Carchemish. At that time, Judah was ruled by Josiah who actually lost his life when he ambushed Neco at Megiddo in an attempt to prevent him from getting to the battlefield.

The verse does not appear to be talking about conditions contemporary with the fall of Jerusalem or its aftermath. Rather, it mentions two superpowers that Judah had had recourse to in the past. Similar, though more temporarily precise, is Jeremiah's rebuke to Judah, "You will be disappointed by Egypt as you were by Assyria" (2:36b).

5:7 / While the present contains nothing like a confession, there is an acknowledgement that sin is the reason for the present tragic situation in Judah. The sin, though, is connected to their ancestors (**our fathers sinned**) rather than themselves. The fathers sinned and the present generation is punished for their sins. The praying community is pointing this out to God perhaps to distance themselves from the sin and elicit divine compassion for their sorry state.

5:8–9 / Society has completely broken down so that **slaves** have assumed an oppressive leadership over the rest of the community. The wisdom literature worried about such a "world upside down." Qohelet said, "There is an evil that I have observed under the sun, an error indeed that originates from the ruler. The fool is placed in important positions, while the rich sit in low places. I observed slaves on horses and nobles walking on foot like slaves" (Eccl. 10:5–7; see also Prov. 19:10; 30:21–22). Indeed, an apocalyptic text like Isaiah 24:2 shares a similar sentiment. In our present text, slaves not only rule; they cannot be dislodged.

A further indication of the breakdown of society is the fact that people take their lives into their hands in order to get food (**we get our bread at the risk of our lives**). Perhaps the reference is to farming which takes place outside the city walls. Dangerous elements frequently lurked in the outlying regions (**the desert**). They threatened settled areas, but a strong city provided the security for people to work in its vicinity. With the destruction of the city government, all bets are off and these nomadic elements could prey on those who go out to work the fields. The city's ruined walls no longer keep them out.

5:10 / The fall of the city has affected the health of the people as well. Hygiene and sanitation would not function as usual; disease could spread. Thus, the people grow feverish. A lack of food is specifically named as a cause of the bad condition of the people (**feverish from hunger**).

5:11–14 / The next four verses describe the sad situation of specific groups of people. The first group are **women** (v. 11). War and its aftermath are bad times for women. Rape is a horrible fate for women left defenseless by the death or imprisonment of husbands, fathers, and brothers. Verse 11a mentions that women have been violated and then verse 11b intensifies the thought by speaking of **virgins.** There is also an expansion in that verse 11a describes horrors in Jerusalem (**Zion**), while verse 11b expands to include all the **towns of Judah.** Verse 12 changes focus to the community leaders (**princes/elders**). Those to whom great respect was owed are shown none, even being physically tortured and shamed (**hung up by their hands**). Some wrongly take this as a reference to crucifixion or impalement (Dobbs-Allsopp, *Lamentations,* p. 126).

For lack of animals and adults, **Young men** (*bakhurim*) and **boys** (*neʿarim*) were forced to engage in the menial and grueling tasks of grinding (**at the millstones**) and carrying **wood.** The type of grinding envisioned here is likely not the type done in individual households (hand grinding), which was done by servants in well-to-do households and by women in lower class houses (Eccl. 12:3). Since the context implies hard work, the grinding was probably the large scale grinding where animals like oxen moved the large upper stone. During and in the aftermath of the siege, the animals would have been used for food. Since all heating and cooking depended on wood, large amounts would have been required. Again, such wood was probably brought into the city by ox-drawn carts before. We have already heard about the high price of wood (5:4).

Elders and **young men** (again *bahurim*) are the last pair, in this case because they are at polar extremes. The place for elders was the gate, where they sat in order to make important community decisions. Without the elders at the gate, the city would fall into anarchy. Their absence from the gate may imply that they are dead or exiled, but for whatever reason, the business of city government was not being accomplished. The mention of the young men not making music refers to those whose time of life allows the leisure and enjoyment to bring and experience pleasure in life. While the elders represent the mature and perhaps outgoing generation, so the young men represent the hope of the next generation.

5:15 / Perhaps it was the reference to music making in the previous verse that gives rise to the next thought. Because of their suffering, the **joy** of life is gone. **Dancing,** a bodily expression of joy, is also gone, replaced by **mourning.** Combining the reference to music in verse 14 and the disappearance of joy in verse 15 reminds one of the sentiment expressed in Ps. 137:1–4.

Lamentations reminds us that it was also difficult, if not impossible, for the faithful to sing joyful songs in the city that had just been destroyed. The psalms also remind us that God was able to reverse this and bring joy out of suffering (see especially Ps. 126, which is a postexilic psalm).

5:16 / Zion had been enthroned among the nations because of God's blessing upon it. It was king. But because of its sin, its royal status has been removed. In another more literal sense, the **crown** has also fallen from the head of God's people. With the Babylonian defeat of Judah, the last king of Judah, Zedekiah, was deposed, and not replaced.

5:17–18 / The poet's description of the suffering of God's people and the devastation of Jerusalem comes to an end in these verses. Because of all the things described in the previous verses (**because of this**), they are deeply depressed and discouraged (**our hearts are faint**). Excessive crying causes **eyes** to dim (literally their eyes "grow dark" [from *khshk*], see Ps. 69:23 [24]). Their depression and weeping is the result of the devastated condition of Jerusalem (Mount Zion is its most holy and important place due to its being the former location of the temple). **Jackals** are animals of abandoned areas; their presence in Jerusalem indicates that it is dying as a city (see also Jer. 9:11; 10:22).

5:19–22 / As noted in the introduction to this chapter, the poem ends with a series of "**why**" questions, similar to the petitions found in the laments of the psalms. If taken at face value, as one should, the poem was written before the restoration, not at the time of the rebuilding of the temple (see Introduction: Genre and Ancient Near Eastern Background). But before the poet turns to question God, he begins with an affirmation of God's kingship and therefore sovereignty. He does not question God's ultimate right to punish them, but prods God to consider whether such an attitude is really the way God wants to go. The last verse of the book even raises the possibility that God has decided to utterly reject Judah because his anger is so great, but the poet hopes against that possibility as he asks God to restore them to the kind of relationship they had in the past (**days of old**). Of course, the immediate past was a time of rebellion, indeed so was much of the past relationship between God and his people. It is possible that an ideal past is in mind. Another possibility is that the poet has in mind the past when God was simply not punishing them.

While the book of Lamentations ends with a question mark, modern readers have the advantage of reading the book from a future standpoint. We know that God did not utterly reject his people. In 539 B.C. he allowed them to return to the land and some chose to do so. The stories of Sheshbazzar and Zerubbabel (Ezra 1–6) and Ezra and Nehemiah (Ezra 7–Nehemiah 13) attest to God's continuing involvement with his people. For Christian readers, this is just the beginning of the biblical story of restoration.

Additional Notes §5

5:2 / The tragic irony of the verse is more deeply understood by contrasting the idea of **inheritance** with that of **aliens.** In connection with another context (Mic. 7:14), Waltke defines "inheritance" as "an inalienable, and therefore permanent, possession that falls to an individual or group either through its awarding in the transmission as an inheritance or through its expropriation from the preceding owner" (Waltke, *Micah*, p. 440).

For Further Reading

General

Allen, L. *Joel, Obadiah, Jonah, and Micah.* New International Commentary on the Old Testament. Grand Rapids: Eerdmans, 1976.

Childs, B. S. *Introduction to the Old Testament as Scripture.* Philadelphia: Fortress, 1979.

Eissfeldt, O. *The Old Testament: An Introduction.* Translated by Peter R. Ackroyd. Oxford: Blackwell, 1965.

Goldingay, J. *Old Testament Theology.* 2 vols. Downers Grove, Ill.: Inter-Varsity, 2003.

Gunkel, H. "Nahum 1." *Zeitschrift für die alttestamentliche Wissenschaft* 13 (1893), pp. 223–44.

Hallo, W. W., ed. *The Context of Scripture.* 3 vols. Leiden: E. J. Brill, 1997–2003.

Hallo, W. W. and W. K. Simpson. *The Ancient Near East: A History.* 2d edition. Harcourt Brace, 1998.

Hess, R. *An Introduction to Approaches to the Study of Israelite Religion.* Grand Rapids: Baker, forthcoming.

Kaiser, W. C. *The Messiah in the Old Testament.* Grand Rapids: Zondervan, 1995.

Kitchen, K. A. *The Reliability of the Old Testament.* Grand Rapids: Eerdmans, 2003.

Longman, T., III. *Ecclesiastes.* New International Commentary on the Old Testament. Grand Rapids: Eerdmans, 1998.

———. *Immanuel in our Place.* Phillipsburgh, N.J.: P&R, 2001.

———. *Proverbs.* Grand Rapids: Baker, 2006.

———. *Song of Songs.* Grand Rapids: Eerdmans, 2001.

Longman, T., III, and R. B. Dillard. *An Introduction to the Old Testament.* 2d ed. Grand Rapids: Zondervan, 2006.

Longman, T. and D. Reid. *God Is a Warrior.* Grand Rapids: Zondervan, 1995.

McComiskey, T. *The Covenants of Promise: A Theology of the Old Testament Covenants.* Grand Rapids: Baker, 1985.

Moran, W. L. "The End of the Unholy War and the Anti-Exodus." *Biblica* 44 (1963), pp. 333–42.

Provan, I. W., V. P. Long, and T. Longman III. *A Biblical History of Israel.* Louisville, Ky.: Westminster John Knox, 2003.

Ryken, L., J. C. Wilhoit, and T. Longman III. *Dictionary of Biblical Imagery.* Downers Grove, Ill.: InterVarsity, 1998.

Tsumira, D. T. *1 Samuel.* New International Commentary on the Old Testament. Grand Rapids: Eerdmans, 2007.
Waltke, B. *Micah.* Grand Rapids: Eerdmans, 2006.
Watson, W. G. E. *Traditional Techniques in Classical Hebrew Verse.* Journal for the Study of the Old Testament: Supplement Series. Sheffield: Sheffield Academic, 1984.
Wolters, A. "Untying the King's Knots: Physiology and Wordplay in Daniel 5." *Journal of Biblical Literature* 110 (1991), pp. 117–22.
Zevit, Z. *The Religions of Ancient Israel: A Synthesis of Parallactic Approaches.* New York: Continuum, 2001.

Commentaries on Jeremiah

Bright, J. *Jeremiah.* Anchor Bible. Garden City, N.Y.: Doubleday, 1962.
Brueggemann, W. *A Commentary on Jeremiah: Exile and Homecoming.* Grand Rapids: Eerdmans, 1998.
Carroll, R. P. *The Book of Jeremiah.* Old Testament Library. Philadelphia: Westminster, 1986.
Craigie, P., P. Kelley, and J. Drinkard. *Jeremiah 1–25.* Word Biblical Commentary; Dallas: Word, 1991.
Dearman, J. A. *Jeremiah/Lamentations.* NIV Application Commentary. Grand Rapids: Zondervan, 2002.
Duhm, B. *Das Buch Jeremia.* Kurzer Hand-Commentar zum Alten Testament 2. Tubingen: J. C. B. Mohr, 1901.
Fretheim, T. E. *Jeremiah.* Macon, Ga.: Smyth and Helwys, 2002.
Holladay, W. L. *Jeremiah,* 2 vols. Hermeneia. Fortress, 1986, 1989.
Lundbom, J. R. *Jeremiah,* 3 vols. Anchor Bible. Garden City, N.Y.: Doubleday, 1999, 2004, 2004.
McKane, W. A. *Critical and Exegetical Commentary on Jeremiah,* 2 vols. International Critical Commentary. T&T Clark, 1986, 1996.
Thompson, J. A. *The Book of Jeremiah.* New International Commentary on the Old Testament. Grand Rapids: Eerdmans, 1979.

Other Studies on Jeremiah

Barstad, H. M. *The Myth of the Empty Land: A Study in the History and Archaeology of Judah during the "Exilic" Period.* Oslo: Scandanavian University Press, 1996.
Boda, M. "From Complaint to Contrition: Peering through the Liturgical Window of Jer 14,1–15,4." *Zeitschrift für die alttestamentliche Wissenschaft* 113 (2001), pp. 186–97.
Brown, M. L. *Israel's Divine Healer.* Grand Rapids: Zondervan, 1995.
Chavel, A. "'Let My People Go!' Emancipation, Revelation, and Scribal Activity in Jeremiah 34:8–14," *Journal for the Study of the Old Testament* 76 (1997), pp. 71–95.
Childs, B. S. "The Enemy from the North and the Chaos Tradition," *Journal of Biblical Literature* 78 (1959), pp. 151–61.

Clines, D. J. A. and D. M. Gunn. "Form, Occasion, and Redaction in Jeremiah 20." *Zeitschrift für die alttestamentliche Wissenschaft* 88 (1976), pp. 20–27.

———. " 'You Tried to Persuade Me' and 'Violence! Outrage!' in Jeremiah xx 7–8." *Vetus Testamentum* (1978), pp. 20–27.

Dearman, J. A. "My Servants the Scribes: Composition and Context in Jeremiah 36." *Journal of Biblical Literature* 109 (1990), pp. 403–21.

DeRoche, M. "Jeremiah 2:2–3 and Israel's Love for God during the Wilderness Wanderings." *Catholic Biblical Quarterly* 45 (1983), pp. 364–87.

Driver, G. R. "Birds in the Old Testament." *Palestine Exploration Quarterly* 87 (1955), pp. 1–13.

Dubbink, J. "Jeremiah: Hero of Faith or Defeatist? Concerning the Place and Function of Jeremiah 20:14–18." *Journal for the Study of the Old Testament* 86 (1999), pp. 67–84.

Floyd, M. H. "Prophetic Complaints about the Fulfillment of Oracles in Habakkuk 1:2–17 and Jeremiah 15:10–18." *Journal of Biblical Literature* 110 (1991), pp. 397–418.

Fox, M. V. "Jeremiah 2:2 and the Desert Ideal." *Catholic Biblical Quarterly* 35 (1973), pp. 441–50.

Hoffman, Y. "'Isn't the Bride Too Beautiful?' The Case of Jeremiah 6:16–21." *Journal for the Study of the Old Testament* 64 (1994), pp. 103–20.

Janzen, J. G. *Studies in the Text of Jeremiah.* Cambridge, Mass.: Harvard University Press, 1973.

Lalleman-de Winkel, L. *Jeremiah in Prophetic Tradition: An Examination of the Book of Jeremiah in the Light of Israel's Prophetic Traditions.* Leuven: Peeters, 2000.

Lemke, W. E. "The Near and the Distant God: A Study of Jer 23:23–24 in its Biblical Theological Context." *Journal of Biblical Literature* 100 (1981), pp. 541–55.

Lewin, E. D. "Arguing for Authority. A Rhetorical Study of Jeremiah 1.14–19 and 20.7–18." *Journal for the Study of the Old Testament* 32 (1985), pp. 105–19.

Lundbom, J. "The Double Curse in Jeremiah 20:14–18." *Journal of Biblical Literature* 104 (1985), pp. 589–600.

———. "Text, Composition, and Historical Reconstruction in Jeremiah." *The Biblical Historian* 2 (2005), pp. 1–11.

McConville, J. G. *Judgment and Promise: An Interpretation of the Book of Jeremiah.* Winona Lake, Ind.: Eisenbrauns, 1993.

Mowinckel, S. *Zur Komposition des Buches Jeremia.* Kristiania: Jacob Dybwad, 1914.

———. *Prophecy and Tradition.* Oslo: Jacob Dybwad, 1946.

Nadelman, Y. "The Identification of Anathoth and the Soundings at Khirbet Der es-Sidd." *Israel Exploration Journal* 44 (1994), pp. 62–74

O'Connor, K. M. "'Do not Trim a Word': The Contributions of Chapter 26 to the Book of Jeremiah." *Catholic Biblical Quarterly* 51 (1989), pp. 617–30.

O'Day, G. R. "Jeremiah 9:22–23 and 1 Corinthians 1:26–31: A Study in Intertextuality." *Journal of Biblical Literature* 109 (1990), pp. 259–67.

Olson, D. C. "Jeremiah 4.5–31 and Apocalyptic Myth." *Journal for the Study of the Old Testament* 73 (1997), pp. 81–107.

Oppenheim, A. L. *Ancient Mesopotamia.* Chicago: University of Chicago Press, 1964.

Perdue, L. G. and B. W. Kovacs. *A Prophet to the Nations: Essays in Jeremiah Studies.* Winona Lake, Ind.: Eisenbrauns, 1984.

Rata, T. *The Covenant Motif in Jeremiah's Book of Comfort: Textual and Intertextual Studies of Jeremiah 30–33.* Forthcoming.

Robertson, O. P. *The Christ of the Covenants.* Phillipsburg, N.J.: P&R Publishing, 1981.

Rowley, H. H. "The Early Prophecies of Jeremiah and their Setting." *Bulletin of the John Rylands University Library of Manchester* 45 (1962–1963), pp. 198–234.

Schmitt, J. J. "The Virgin of Israel: Referent and use of the Phrase in Amos and Jeremiah." *Catholic Biblical Quarterly* 53 (1991), pp. 365–87.

Steiner, R. C. "Incomplete Circumcision in Egypt and Edom: Jeremiah (9:24–25) in the Light of Josephus and Jonckheere." *Journal of Biblical Literature* 118 (1999), pp. 497–526.

Stienstra, N. *YHWH Is the Husband of His People.* Kampen, Netherlands: Pharos, 1993.

Toorn, K. van der. "Did Jeremiah See Aaron's Staff?" *Journal for the Study of the Old Testament* 43 (1989), pp. 83–94.

Tov, I. "Some Aspects of the Textual and Literary History of the Book of Jeremiah." Pages 145–67 in *The Septuagint Translation of Jeremiah and Baruch.* Edited by P. Bogaert; Cambridge, Mass.: Harvard University Press, 1981.

———. "Jeremiah." Pages 145–207 in *Qumran Cave 4.* X: the Prophets. Edited by E. Ulrich, et al. Discoveries in the Judean Desert 15. Oxford: Clarendon Press, 1997.

Wilson, G. H. "The Prayer of Daniel 9: Reflection on Jeremiah 29." *Journal for the Study of the Old Testament* 48 (1990), pp. 91–9.

Yates, G. "New Exodus and No Exodus in Jeremiah 26–45: Promise and Warning to the Exiles in Babylon." *Tyndale Bulletin* 57 (2006), pp. 1–22.

Commentaries on Lamentations

Berlin, A. *Lamentations.* Old Testament Library. Louisville, Ky.: Westminster John Knox, 2002.

Dobbs-Allsopp, F. W. *Lamentations.* Interpretation. Louisville, Ky.: Westminster John Knox, 2002.

Gerstenberger, E. S. *Psalms, Part 2, and Lamentations.* Forms of the Old Testament Literature. Grand Rapids: Eerdmans, 2001.

Provan, I. *Lamentations.* New Century Bible. Grand Rapids: Eerdmans, 1991.

Other Studies on Lamentations

Bergler, S. "Threni 5, nur ein alphabetisierendes Lied?" *Vetus Testamentum* 27 (1977), pp. 304–20.

Cohen, M. E. *The Canonical Lamentations of Ancient Mesopotamia*. 2 vols. Potomoc, Md.: CDL Press, 1988.

Dobbs-Allsopp, F. W. *Weep O Daughter of Zion: A Study of the City-Lament Genre in the Hebrew Bible*. Rome: Pontifical Biblical Institute, 1993.

Ferris, P. W. *The Genre of the Communal Lament in the Bible and the Ancient Near East*. Atlanta: Scholars Press, 1992.

Green, M. W. "The Eridu Lament." *Journal of Cuneiform Studies* 30 (1978), pp. 127–67.

———. "The Uruk Lament." *Journal of the American Oriental Society* 104 (1984), pp. 253–79.

Gwaltney, W. C. "The Biblical Book of Lamentations in the Context of Near Eastern Literature." Pages 191–211 in *More Essays on the Comparative Method*. Scripture in Context 2. Edited by W. W. Hallo, J. C. Moyer, and L. G. Perdue. Winona Lake, Ind.: Eisenbrauns, 1982.

Hallo, W. W. "Lamentations and Prayers in Sumer and Akkad." Pages 1871–81 in *Civilizations of the Ancient Near East*. Edited by J. Sasson. 4 vols. New York: Charles Scribner's Sons, 1995. Repr. Peabody, Mass.: Hendrickson, 2000.

Kaiser, Jr., W. C. *A Biblical Approach to Personal Suffering*. Moody, 1982.

Kutscher, R. *Oh Angry Sea (a-ab-ba hu-luh-ha): The History of a Sumerian Congregational Lament*. New Haven: Yale University Press, 1975.

Linafelt, T. *Surviving Lamentations: Catastrophe, Lament, and Protest in the Afterlife of a Biblical Book*. Chicago: The University of Chicago Press, 2000.

McDaniel, T. F. "The Alleged Sumerian Influence upon Lamentations." *Vetus Testamentum* 18 (1968), pp. 198–209.

Michalowski, P. The *Lamentation over the Destruction of Sumer and Ur*. Winona Lake, Ind.: Eisenbrauns, 1989.

O'Connor, K. M. *Lamentations and the Tears of the World*. Maryknoll, N.Y.: Orbis, 2002.

Subject Index

Scripture Index

Old Testament

NEW TESTAMENT